DATE DUE

			PRINTED IN U.S.A.

SOMETHING ABOUT THE AUTHOR

ISSN 0276-816X

something
ABOUT THE
AUTHOR

**Facts and Pictures about Authors
and Illustrators of Books for Young People**

EDITED BY
ANNE COMMIRE

VOLUME 63

 **Gale Research Inc.** · *DETROIT* · *NEW YORK* · *LONDON*

Managing Editor: Anne Commire

Editors: Agnes Garrett, Helga P. McCue

Associate Editors: Elisa Ann Ferraro, Eunice L. Petrini

Assistant Editors: Marc Caplan, Marja T. Hiltunen, Linda Shedd

Sketchwriters: Kim Burdick, Yvette Burnham, Catherine Coray, Cathy Courtney,
Marguerite Feitlowitz, Mimi H. Hutson, Deborah Klezmer

Researcher: Catherine Ruello

Editorial Assistants: Joanne J. Ferraro, June Lee, Susan Pfanner

Production Manager: Mary Beth Trimper

External Production Assistant: Shanna Philpott

Production Supervisor: Laura Bryant

Internal Production Associate: Louise Gagné

Internal Production Assistant: Yolanda Y. Latham

Art Director: Arthur Chartow

Keyliner: C. J. Jonik

Special acknowledgment is due to the members of the *Something about the Author Autobiography Series* staff
who assisted in the preparation of this volume.

The paper used in this publication meets the minimum requirements
of American National Standard for Information Sciences—Permanence
Paper for Printed Library Materials, ANSI Z39.48-1984. ∞™

Library of Congress Catalog Card Number 72-27107

ISBN 0-8103-2273-0
ISSN 0276-816X

Printed in the United States

Published simultaneously in the United Kingdom
by Gale Research International Limited
(An affiliated company of Gale Research Inc.)

Contents

Introduction   ix

Acknowledgments   xv

Illustrations Index   203

Author Index   219

T

V

W

Introduction

As the only annually published ongoing reference series that deals with the lives and works of authors and illustrators of children's books, *Something about the Author (SATA)* is a unique source of information. The *SATA* series includes not only well-known authors and illustrators whose books are most widely read, but also those less prominent people whose works are just coming to be recognized. *SATA* is often the only readily available information source for less well-known writers or artists. You'll find *SATA* informative and entertaining whether you are:

> —a student in junior high school (or perhaps one to two grades higher or lower) who needs information for a book report or some other assignment for an English class;

> —a children's librarian who is searching for the answer to yet another question from a young reader or collecting background material to use for a story hour;

> —an English teacher who is drawing up an assignment for your students or gathering information for a book talk;

> —a student in a college of education or library science who is studying children's literature and reference sources in the field;

> —a parent who is looking for a new way to interest your child in reading something more than the school curriculum prescribes;

> —an adult who enjoys children's literature for its own sake, knowing that a good children's book has no age limits.

Scope

In *SATA* you will find detailed information about authors and illustrators who span the full time range of children's literature, from early figures like John Newbery and L. Frank Baum to contemporary figures like Judy Blume and Richard Peck. Authors in the series represent primarily English-speaking countries, particularly the United States, Canada, and the United Kingdom. Also included, however, are authors from around the world whose works are available in English translation, for example: from France, Jean and Laurent De Brunhoff; from Italy, Emanuele Luzzati; from the Netherlands, Jaap ter Haar; from Germany, James Krüss; from Norway, Babbis Friis-Baastad; from Japan, Toshiko Kanzawa; from the Soviet Union, Kornei Chukovsky; from Switzerland, Alois Carigiet, to name only a few. Also appearing in *SATA* are Newbery medalists from Hendrik Van Loon (1922) to Lois Lowry (1990). The writings represented in *SATA* include those created intentionally for children and young adults as well as those written for a general audience and known to interest younger readers. These writings cover the spectrum from picture books, humor, folk and fairy tales, animal stories, mystery and adventure, science fiction and fantasy, historical fiction, poetry and nonsense verse, to drama, biography, and nonfiction.

Information Features

In *SATA* you will find full-length entries that are being presented in the series for the first time. This volume, for example, marks the first full-length appearance of Donna W. Guthrie, Burne Hogarth, Aldous Huxley, Barbro Lindgren, Louis Sachar, and Betty Ren Wright.

Obituaries have been included in *SATA* since Volume 20. An Obituary is intended not only as a death notice but also as a concise view of a person's life and work. Obituaries may appear for persons who have entries in earlier *SATA* volumes, as well as for people who have not yet appeared in the series. In this volume Obituaries mark the recent deaths of James Gilmore Backus, Lorenz Graham, Philip Sterling, and George Selden Thompson.

Revised Entries

Since Volume 25, each *SATA* volume also includes newly revised and updated entries for a selection of *SATA* listees (usually four to six) who remain of interest to today's readers and who have been active enough to require extensive revision of their earlier biographies. For example, when Beverly Cleary first appeared in *SATA* Volume 2, she was the author of twenty-one books for children and young adults and the recipient of numerous awards. By the time her updated sketch appeared in Volume 43 (a span of fifteen years), this creator of the indefatigable Ramona Quimby and other memorable characters had produced a dozen new titles and garnered nearly fifty additional awards, including the 1984 Newbery Medal.

The entry for a given biographee may be revised as often as there is substantial new information to provide. In this volume, look for revised entries on C. S. Adler, Carol Carrick, Donald Carrick, Paula Danziger, and John Steptoe.

Illustrations

While the textual information in *SATA* is its primary reason for existing, photographs and illustrations not only enliven the text but are an integral part of the information that *SATA* provides. Illustrations and text are wedded in such a special way in children's literature that artists and their works naturally occupy a prominent place among *SATA*'s listees. The illustrators that you'll find in the series include such past masters of children's book illustration as Randolph Caldecott, Walter Crane, Arthur Rackham, and Ernest H. Shepard, as well as such noted contemporary artists as Maurice Sendak, Edward Gorey, Tomie de Paola, and Margot Zemach. There are Caldecott medalists from Dorothy Lathrop (the first recipient in 1938) to Ed Young (the latest winner in 1990); cartoonists like Charles Schulz ("Peanuts"), Walt Kelly ("Pogo"), Hank Ketcham ("Dennis the Menace"), and Georges Rémi ("Tintin"); photographers like Jill Krementz, Tana Hoban, Bruce McMillan, and Bruce Curtis; and filmmakers like Walt Disney, Alfred Hitchcock, and Steven Spielberg.

In more than a dozen years of recording the metamorphosis of children's literature from the printed page to other media, *SATA* has become something of a repository of photographs that are unique in themselves and exist nowhere else as a group, particularly many of the classics of motion picture and stage history and photographs that have been specially loaned to us from private collections.

Index Policy

In response to suggestions from librarians, *SATA* indexes no longer appear in each volume but are included in each alternate (odd-numbered) volume of the series, beginning with Volume 57.

SATA continues to include two indexes that cumulate with each alternate volume: the **Illustrations Index,** arranged by the name of the illustrator, gives the number of the volume and page where the illustrator's work appears in the current volume as well as all preceding volumes in the series; the **Author Index** gives the number of the volume in which a person's Biographical Sketch, Brief Entry, or Obituary appears in the current volume as well as all preceding volumes in the series.

These indexes also include references to authors and illustrators who appear in *Yesterday's Authors of Books for Children* (described in detail below). Beginning with Volume 36, the *SATA* Author Index provides cross-references to authors who are included in Gale's *Children's Literature Review*. Starting with Volume 42, you will also find cross-references to authors who are included in the *Something about the Author Autobiography Series* (described in detail below).

What a *SATA* Entry Provides

Whether you're already familiar with the *SATA* series or just getting acquainted, you will want to be aware of the kind of information that an entry provides. In every *SATA* entry the editors attempt to give as complete a picture of the person's life and work as possible. In some cases that full range of information may simply be unavailable, or a biographee may choose not to reveal complete personal details. The information that the editors attempt to provide in every entry is arranged in the following categories:

1. The "head" of the entry gives

    —the most complete form of the name,
    —any part of the name not commonly used, included in parentheses,
    —birth and death dates, if known; a (?) indicates a discrepancy in published sources,
    —pseudonyms or name variants under which the person has had books published or is publicly known, in parentheses in the second line.

2. "Personal" section gives

    —date and place of birth and death,
    —parents' names and occupations,
    —name of spouse, date of marriage, and names of children,
    —educational institutions attended, degrees received, and dates,
    —religious and political affiliations,
    —agent's name and address,
    —home and/or office address.

3. "Career" section gives

    —name of employer, position, and dates for each career post,
    —military service,
    —memberships,
    —awards and honors.

4. "Writings" section gives

    —title, first publisher and date of publication, and illustration information for each book written; revised editions and other significant editions for books with particularly long publishing histories; genre, when known.

5. "Adaptations" section gives

    —title, major performers, producer, and date of all known reworkings of an author's material in another medium, like movies, filmstrips, television, recordings, plays, etc.

6. "Sidelights" section gives

    —commentary on the life or work of the biographee either directly from the person (and often written specifically for the *SATA* entry), or gathered from biographies, diaries, letters, interviews, or other published sources.

7. "For More Information See" section gives

    —books, feature articles, films, plays, and reviews in which the biographee's life or work has been treated.

How a *SATA* Entry Is Compiled

A *SATA* entry progresses through a series of steps. If the biographee is living, the *SATA* editors try to secure information directly from him or her through a questionnaire. From the information that the biographee supplies, the editors prepare an entry, filling in any essential missing details with research. The author or illustrator is then sent a copy of the entry to check for accuracy and completeness.

If the biographee is deceased or cannot be reached by questionnaire, the *SATA* editors examine a wide variety of published sources to gather information for an entry. Biographical sources are searched with the aid of Gale's *Biography and Genealogy Master Index*. Bibliographic sources like the *National Union Catalog*, the *Cumulative Book Index*, *American Book Publishing Record*, and the *British Museum Catalogue* are consulted, as are book reviews, feature articles, published interviews, and material sometimes obtained from the biographee's family, publishers, agent, or other associates.

For each entry presented in *SATA*, the editors also attempt to locate a photograph of the biographee as well as representative illustrations from his or her books. After surveying the available books which the biographee has written and/or illustrated, and then making a selection of appropriate photographs and illustrations, the editors request permission of the current copyright holders to reprint the material. In the case of older books for which the copyright may have passed through several hands, even locating the current copyright holder is often a long and involved process.

We invite you to examine the entire *SATA* series, starting with this volume. Described below are some of the people in Volume 63 that you may find particularly interesting.

Highlights of This Volume

CAROL CARRICK......collaborated on thirty-six books with her illustrator husband, Donald. Both were trained in art and met while working on magazine advertising. Carol, who spent her childhood in Queens, remembers nostalgically: "My husband and I grew up in the same kind of suburban neighborhood surrounded by woods, vacant lots, and trees. We both enjoyed the kind of life that doesn't exist much any more. I lived near a pond, and would bring tadpoles home and try to feed them. Today there are wonderful 'how to' books that instruct, but in those days I didn't know; I fed them bread and they all died....Those early disappointments caused me a lot of grief, and prompted me to make my nature books as accurate as possible. Later, my children would have similar experiences, and I used some of them as the basis for books. *The Empty Squirrel,* for example, concerns a boy who nurses a fish back to health because his mother didn't want to cook it. That really happened to us."

PAULA DANZIGER......was inspired to begin her first book after being injured in a serious car accident. "I lost the ability to read....I could write backwards—a perfect mirror image of normal writing. I had recurring nightmares...and functioned with a great deal of difficulty. My feelings of helplessness and terror dredged up a lot of material from my childhood....I wrote [*The Cat Ate My Gymsuit*] in therapy, bringing newly-drafted pages to many appointments." Since that time, Danziger's writing has been dedicated exclusively to young adult literature. "I get so tired of the question, 'So when are you going to do your adult book?' As though I've just been practicing all these years to become 'good enough' to write for grown-ups....There is a widespread misconception that it is easier to write for young people than for adults. It is not....Children are arguably the most important members of society—they are the future." Danziger has yet to fulfill her second ambition "to be a stand-up comic. But I have trick knees and can't stay up too late."

BARBRO LINDGREN......is best known in America for her "Wild Baby" series, several of which were translated by Jack Prelutsky. After the publication of her first books she visited school children. "I then noticed that what I thought was important when I grew up was, in fact, just as important now. We talked about life and death, sorrow,...birth, sex and being different—such things as I would have liked to have read [about] as a child. So I went home and wrote about my experiences: about all those difficult things in life." Born in Sweden, Lindgren recalls a childhood of "happiness, sadness, and anxiety." She was afraid of the dark, afraid of school, afraid of death, yet she saw life as an adventure, and was eager to learn. "I wanted to be famous at any price—to be a child genius on the front page of the newspapers was my grandest dream."

IONA OPIE......began writing after her marriage to Peter Opie. The couple collaborated on a book about the origins of nursery rhymes, a dictionary and a book about childhood games. Iona spent twelve years visiting playgrounds every week for research. Together the Opies collected over 20,000 volumes of children's books and amassed a huge toy collection which included "...joke drinking glasses, disguises, tops from the eighteenth century, marbles with threads of twisted glass inside. We have the earliest form of dominoes....We've got knucklebones made from sheep or goats like those used by the ancient Greeks. We've got yo-yos from the 1850s....We've got everything." Since Peter Opie's death in 1982, Iona has continued researching and writing, and has started a new collection of pairs of things.

LOUIS SACHAR......grew up on both coasts—New York and California. After the sudden death of his father, Sachar returned home from college for a brief stint as a Fuller Brush Man. But his love of books and of writing beckoned him back to school. He signed up for a three-credit "teacher's aid" course, which turned out to become "the most important class I took during my college career....I played games with the kids who all called me 'Louis, the Yard Teacher.'" *Sideways Stories from Wayside School,* his first book, was stimulated by that experience. Sachar continued his education at University of California law school, but only pursued the practice of law on a part-time basis to make room for his first love—children's books.

After several other publications he wrote the sequel *Sideways Arithmetic from Wayside School* to his first book. "Having enjoyed math so much when I was in grade school, I wanted *Sideways Arithmetic* to help kids discover that math could be fun."

JOHN STEPTOE......grew up in the Bedford-Stuyvesant section of Brooklyn, and wrote and illustrated his first book at the age of sixteen. *Stevie* "is not directed at white children. I wanted it to be something black children could read without translating the language, something real which would relate to what a black child would know." Steptoe's goal was to assure black children visibility in contemporary children's literature. "There were so many things that weren't addressed for me as a child in books; there were so many things that weren't addressed and weren't dealt with for me as a black child in books. And I wanted to see those things. And I want to see them now....Something about me and my experience, or the experience of a Latino child, an Oriental child....You don't want to be deprived of the world that you live in; you want to know about where you are and how it relates to other people....And you want to be decent."

These are only a few of the authors and illustrators that you'll find in this volume. We hope you find all the entries in *SATA* both interesting and useful.

Yesterday's Authors of Books for Children

In a two-volume companion set to *SATA, Yesterday's Authors of Books for Children (YABC)* focuses on early authors and illustrators, from the beginnings of children's literature through 1960, whose books are still being read by children today. Here you will find "old favorites" like Hans Christian Andersen, J. M. Barrie, Kenneth Grahame, Betty MacDonald, A. A. Milne, Beatrix Potter, Samuel Clemens, Kate Greenaway, Rudyard Kipling, Robert Louis Stevenson, and many more.

Similar in format to *SATA, YABC* features bio-bibliographical entries that are divided into information categories such as Personal, Career, Writings, and Sidelights. The entries are further enhanced by book illustrations, author photos, movie stills, and many rare old photographs.

In Volume 2 you will find cumulative indexes to the authors and to the illustrations that appear in *YABC*. These listings can also be located in the *SATA* cumulative indexes.

By exploring both volumes of *YABC,* you will discover a special group of more than seventy authors and illustrators who represent some of the best in children's literature—individuals whose timeless works continue to delight children and adults of all ages. Other authors and illustrators from early children's literature are listed in *SATA,* starting with Volume 15.

Something about the Author Autobiography Series

You can complement the information in *SATA* with the *Something about the Author Autobiography Series (SAAS),* which provides autobiographical essays written by important current authors and illustrators of books for children and young adults. In every volume of *SAAS* you will find about twenty specially commissioned autobiographies, each accompanied by a selection of personal photographs supplied by the authors. The wide range of contemporary writers and artists who describe their lives and interests in the *Autobiography Series* includes Joan Aiken, Betsy Byars, Leonard Everett Fisher, Milton Meltzer, Maia Wojciechowska, and Jane Yolen, among others. Though the information presented in the autobiographies is as varied and unique as the authors, you can learn about the people and events that influenced these writers' early lives, how they began their careers, what problems they faced in becoming established in their professions, what prompted them to write or illustrate particular books, what they now find most challenging or rewarding in their lives, and what advice they may have for young people interested in following in their footsteps, among many other subjects.

Autobiographies included in the *SATA Autobiography Series* can be located through both the *SATA* cumulative index and the *SAAS* cumulative index, which lists not only the authors' names but also the subjects mentioned in their essays, such as titles of works and geographical and personal names.

The *SATA Autobiography Series* gives you the opportunity to view "close up" some of the fascinating people who are included in the *SATA* parent series. The combined *SATA* series makes available to you an unequaled range of comprehensive and in-depth information about the authors and illustrators of young people's literature.

Please write and tell us if we can make *SATA* even more helpful to you.

Acknowledgments

Grateful acknowledgment is made to the following publishers, authors, and artists for their kind permission to reproduce copyrighted material.

ANDERSEN PRESS. Illustration by Susan Varley from *The Long, Blue Blazer* by Jeanne Willis. Text copyright © 1987 by Jeanne Willis. Illustrations copyright © 1987 by Susan Varley./ Illustration by Susan Varley from *After Dark* by Louis Baum. Text copyright © 1984 by Louis Baum. Illustrations copyright © 1984 by Susan Varley. Both reprinted by permission of Andersen Press.

ATHENEUM PUBLISHERS. Jacket illustration by Deborah Chabrian from *Like Seabirds Flying Home* by Marguerite Murray. Text copyright © 1988 by Marguerite Murray. Jacket illustration copyright © 1988 by Deborah Chabrian. Reprinted by permission of Atheneum Publishers.

AVON BOOKS. Cover illustration from *Some Other Summer* by C. S. Adler. Copyright © 1982 by C. S. Adler./ Cover illustration from *Silver Coach* by C. S. Adler. Copyright © 1979, 1988 by Carole S. Adler./ Illustration by Julie Brinckloe from *Sideways Stories from Wayside School* by Louis Sachar. Text copyright © 1978 by Louis Sachar. Illustration copyright © 1985 by Avon Books./ Cover illustration by Sergio from *Johnny's in the Basement* by Louis Sachar. Copyright © 1981 by Louis Sachar. All reprinted by permission of Avon Books.

BRADBURY PRESS. Cover illustration by Ann Iosa from *My Camp Diary* by Suzanne Weyn. Copyright © by Parachute Press, Inc. Reprinted by permission of Bradbury Press.

CARROLL & GRAF PUBLISHERS, INC. Sidelight excerpts from *Aldous Huxley, a Biography* by Sybille Bedford. Copyright © 1973, 1974 by Sybille Bedford. Reprinted by permission of Carroll & Graf Publishers, Inc.

CHARIOT BOOKS. Cover illustration by Joe VanSeveren from *The Secret of the Spanish Treasure* by Jan Washburn. Copyright © 1980 by David C. Cook Publishing Co. Reprinted by permission of Chariot Books.

CHIVER PRESS. Cover illustration from *The Village by the Sea: An Indian Family Story* by Anita Desai. Copyright © 1982 by Anita Desai. Reprinted by permission of Chiver Press.

CRABTREE PUBLISHING CO. Illustration by Glen Loates from *Animal Babies* by Bobbie Kalman. Copyright © 1987 by Crabtree Publishing Co. Copyright © 1987 by MGL Fine Art Limited. Reprinted by permission of Crabtree Publishing Co.

DELACORTE PRESS. Jacket illustration by Joe Csatari from *Everyone Else's Parents Said Yes* by Paula Danziger. Copyright © 1989 by Paula Danziger. Jacket illustration copyright © 1989 by Joe Csatari./ Jacket illustration by Joe Csatari from *This Place Has No Atmosphere* by Paula Danziger. Copyright © 1986 by Paula Danziger. Jacket illustration copyright © 1986 by Joe Csatari./ Jacket illustration by Richard Lauter from *The Divorce Express* by Paula Danziger. Copyright © 1982 by Paula Danziger. Jacket illustration copyright © 1982 by Richard Lauter./ Jacket illustration by Bob Travers from *Too Much T. J.* by Jacqueline Shannon. Copyright © 1986 by Jacqueline Shannon. Jacket copyright © 1986 by Bob Travers./ Illustration by John Steptoe from *Mother Crocodile* by Dirago Diop. Copyright © 1961 by Presence Africaine. Illustrations copyright © 1981 by John Steptoe. All reprinted by permission of Delacorte Press.

DELL PUBLISHING CO., INC. Cover illustration from *Remember Me to Harold Square* by Paula Danziger. Copyright © 1987 by Paula Danziger./ Cover illustration from *The Cat Ate My Gymsuit* by Paula Danziger. Copyright © 1974 by Paula Danziger./ Cover illustration by Robert Chronister from *This Place Has No Atmosphere* by Paula Danziger. Copyright © 1986 by Paula Danziger./ Cover illustration by Hooks from *It's an Aardvark-Eat-Turtle World* by Paula Danziger. Copyright © 1985 by Paula Danziger./ Cover illustration from *Can You Sue Your Parents for Malpractice?* by Paula Danziger. Copyright © 1979 by Paula Danziger./ Cover illustration from *Making It on Our Own* by Fran Lantz. Copyright © 1986 by Francess Lin Lantz. All reprinted by permission of Dell Publishing Co., Inc.

DESIGN ENTERPRISES OF SAN FRANCISCO. Illustration by You-shan Tang from *Pie-Biter* by Ruthanne Lum McCunn. Copyright © 1983 by Ruthanne Lum McCunn. Reprinted by permission of Design Enterprises of San Francisco.

DIAL BOOKS FOR YOUNG READERS. Illustration by Amelie Glienke from *My Friend the Vampire* by Angela Sommer-Bodenburg. Translated by Sarah Gibson. Translation copyright © 1982 by Anderson Press Ltd. Reprinted by permission of Dial Books for Young Readers.

DOUBLEDAY & CO., INC. Sidelight excerpts and illustrations from *A Soldier Reports* by William C. Westmoreland. Copyright © 1976 by William C. Westmoreland. All reprinted by permission of Doubleday & Co., Inc.

FABER & FABER LTD. Cover illustration by Graham Percy and cover design by Pentagram from *The Faber Book of Children's Verse,* compiled by Janet Adam Smith. Reprinted by permission of Faber & Faber Ltd.

GRANADA PUBLISHING LTD. Cover illustration by Jose A. Velasquez from *Beyond the Mexique Bay* by Aldous Huxley. Copyright 1934 by Mrs. Laura Huxley. Reprinted by permission of Granada Publishing Ltd.

HARCOURT BRACE JOVANOVICH, INC. Jacket photograph by Joanne Van Os from *To Fight the Wild: A Modern Day Robinson Crusoe's True Story of Survival in the Australian Bush* by Rod Ansell and Rachel Percy. Copyright © 1980, 1986 by Rod Ansell and Rachel Percy. Jacket front copyright by Rachel Percy./ Jacket illustration by Les Morrill from *Just Like Everybody Else* by Lillian Rosen. Copyright © 1981 by Lillian D. Rosen. Both reprinted by permission of Harcourt Brace Jovanovich, Inc.

HARPER & ROW, PUBLISHERS, INC. Sidelight excerpts from *Letters of Aldous Huxley,* edited by Grover Smith. Copyright © 1969 by Laura Huxley. Preface, Chronology Notes, and Compilation copyright © 1969 by Grover Smith./ Sidelight excerpts from *Brave New World Revisited* by Aldous Huxley. Copyright © 1958 by Aldous Huxley./ Jacket illustration by E. McKnight Kauffer from *Brave New World* by Aldous Huxley. Copyright 1932, 1946 by Aldous Huxley./ Jacket photograph by Inge Aicher-Scholl from *The Short Life of Sophie Scholl* by Herman Vinke. Translated from the German by Hedwig Pachter. Text copyright © 1980 by Otto Maier Verlag Ravensburg. Translation copyright © 1984 by Harper & Row, Publishers, Inc. Jacket photograph copyright © 1980 by Inge Aicher-Scholl./ Illustration by Ed Young from *Bicycle Rider* by Mary Scioscia. Text copyright © 1983 by Mary Hershey Scioscia. Illustrations copyright © 1983 by Ed Young./ Illustration by John Steptoe from *Stevie* by John Steptoe. Copyright © 1969 by John L. Steptoe. All reprinted by permission of Harper & Row, Publishers, Inc.

HOLIDAY HOUSE, INC. Jacket illustration by Stephen Mancusi from *Christina's Ghost* by Betty Ren Wright. Copyright © 1985 by Betty Ren Wright./ Jacket illustration by Stephen Mancusi from *The Dollhouse Murders* by Betty Ren Wright. Copyright © 1983 by Betty Ren Wright. Both reprinted by permission of Holiday House, Inc.

HENRY HOLT & CO. Jacket design and illustration by Richard Mantel from *Night Ferry to Death* by Patricia Moyes. Copyright © 1985 by Patricia Moyes./ Illustration from *Build a Better Mousetrap: An Anti-Coloring Book* by Susan Striker. Copyright © 1983 by Susan Glaser Striker. Both reprinted by permission of Henry Holt & Co.

HOUGHTON MIFFLIN CO. Jacket illustration by Troy Howell from *The Cat That Was Left Behind* by C. S. Adler. Copyright © 1981 by C. S. Adler. Jacket illustration copyright © 1981 by Troy Howell./ Jacket illustration by Diane de Groat from *Always and Forever Friends* by C. S. Adler. Text copyright © 1988 by C. S. Adler. Jacket illustration © 1988 by Diane de Groat./ Jacket illustration by Ted Lewin from *Life. Is. Not. Fair.* by Gary W. Bargar. Copyright © 1984 by Gary W. Bargar. Jacket illustration copyright © 1984 by Ted Lewin./ Illustration by Donald Carrick from *The Elephant in the Dark* by Carol Carrick. Text copyright © 1988 by Carol Carrick. Illustrations copyright © 1988 by Donald Carrick./ Illustration by Donald Carrick from *Lost in the Storm* by Carol Carrick. Copyright © 1974 by Carol and Donald Carrick./ Illustration by Donald Carrick from *Patrick's Dinosaurs* by Carol Carrick. Text copyright © 1983 by Carol Carrick. Illustrations copyright © 1983 by Donald Carrick./ Illustration by Donald Carrick from *What Happened to Patrick's Dinosaurs?* by Carol Carrick. Text copyright © 1986 by Carol Carrick. Illustrations copyright © 1986 by Donald Carrick./ Illustration by Rosekrans Hoffman from *The Truth about the Moon* by Clayton Bess. Text copyright © 1983 by Robert Locke. Illustrations copyright © 1983 by Rosekrans Hoffman./ Jacket illustration by Darryl Zudeck from *Tracks* by Clayton Bess.

Copyright © 1986 by Robert Locke. Jacket illustration © 1986 by Darryl Zudeck./ Illustration by Suzanna Klein by *Womenfolk and Fairy Tales,* edited by Rosemary Minard. All reprinted by permission of Houghton Mifflin Co.

ALFRED A. KNOPF, INC. Photograph by Susan Kuklin and Herbert S. Terrace from *The Story of NIM: The Chimp Who Learned Language* by Anna Michel. Introduction by Herbert S. Terrace. Text copyright © 1980 by Anna Michel. Introduction copyright © 1980 by Herbert S. Terrace. Photographs copyright © 1979, 1980 by Herbert S. Terrace./ Jacket illustration by Alexander Strogart from *The Boy Who Lost His Face* by Louis Sachar. Copyright © 1989 by Louis Sachar. Jacket illustration copyright © 1989 by Alexander Strogart. All reprinted by permission of Alfred A. Knopf, Inc.

J. B. LIPPINCOTT. Illustration by Nurit Karlin from *The Tooth Witch* by Nurit Karlin. Copyright © 1985 by Nurit Karlin./ Illustrations by Eric Velasquez from *Journey to Jo'burg: A South African Story* by Beverley Naidoo. Copyright © 1985 by Beverley Naidoo and British Defence and Aid Fund for Southern Africa./ Illustration by John Steptoe from *Daddy Is a Monster...Sometimes* by John Steptoe. Copyright © 1980 by John Steptoe. All reprinted by permission of J. B. Lippincott.

MACMILLAN, INC. Jacket illustration by Mike Wimmer from *Split Sisters* by C. S. Adler. Copyright © 1986 by C. S. Adler and Macmillan Publishing Co. Jacket illustration copyright © 1985 by Mike Wimmer./ Ilustration by Donald Carrick from *Secrets of a Small Brother* by Richard J. Margolis. Text copyright © 1984 by Richard J. Margolis. Illustrations copyright © 1984 by Donald Carrick./ Illustration by Reg Cartwright from *My Dog* by Judy Taylor. Text copyright © 1987 by Judy Taylor. Illustrations copyright © 1987 by Reg Cartwright. All reprinted by permission of Macmillan, Inc.

WILLIAM MORROW & CO., INC. Illustration by Donald Carrick from *Doctor Change* by Joanna Cole. Text copyright © 1986 by Joanna Cole. Illustrations copyright © 1986 by Donald Carrick./ Photograph by Susan Kuklin from *Thinking Big: The Story of a Young Dwarf* by Susan Kuklin. Copyright © 1986 by Susan Kuklin./ Illustration by Eva Eriksson from *Sam's Wagon* by Barbro Lindgren. Text copyright © 1986 by Barbro Lindgren. Illustrations copyright © 1986 by Eva Eriksson./ Illustration by Eva Eriksson from *The Wild Baby* by Barbro Lindgren. Adapted from the Swedish by Jack Prelutsky. Swedish text copyright © 1980 by Barbro Lindgren. English text copyright © 1981 by Jack Prelutsky. Illustrations copyright © 1980 by Eva Eriksson./ Illustration by Eva Eriksson from *Sam's Teddy Bear* by Barbro Lindgren. Swedish text copyright © 1981 by Barbro Lindgren. English translation copyright © 1982 by William Morrow & Co., Inc. Illustrations copyright © 1981 by Eva Eriksson./ Illustration by Eva Eriksson from *Sam's Bath* by Barbro Lindgren. Swedish text copyright © 1982 by Barbro Lindgren. English translation copyright © 1983 by William Morrow & Co., Inc. Illustrations copyright © 1982 by Eva Eriksson./ Illustration by John Steptoe from *The Story of Jumping Mouse,* retold by John Steptoe. Copyright © 1984 by John Steptoe./ Illustration by John Steptoe from *Baby Says* by John Steptoe. Copyright © 1988 by John Steptoe./ Illustration by John Steptoe from *Mufaro's Beautiful Daughters: An African Tale* by John Steptoe. Copyright © 1987 by John Steptoe./ Illustration by John Steptoe from *Jeffrey Bear Cleans Up His Act* by John Steptoe. Copyright © 1983 by John Steptoe./ Illustration by Susan Varley from *The Monster Bed* by Jeanne Willis. Text copyright © 1986 by Jeanne Willis. Illustrations copyright © 1986 by Susan Varley. All reprinted by permission of William Morrow & Co., Inc.

NC PRESS. Illustration by Mark Thurman from *Douglas the Elephant and Albert Alligator: Some Sumo* by Mark Thurman. Reprinted by permission of NC Press.

OXFORD UNIVERSITY PRESS. Illustration by Judith Crabtree from *The Sparrow's Story at the King's Command* by Judith Crabtree. Copyright © 1983 by Judith Crabtree./ Jacket illustration from *The Oxford Book of Children's Verse,* compiled and edited by Iona and Peter Opie./ Jacket illustration from *The Oxford Book of Narrative Verse,* compiled and edited by Iona and Peter Opie./ Illustrations from *Children's Games in Street and Playground* by Iona and Peter Opie. Copyright © 1969 by Iona and Peter Opie./ Illustration from *The Oxford Nursery Rhyme Book,* compiled by Iona and Peter Opie. Copyright 1955 by Iona and Peter Opie./ Jacket illustration by Adam Buck from *The Oxford Dictionary of Nursery Rhymes,* edited by Iona and Peter Opie. All reprinted by permission of Oxford University Press.

PARNASSUS IMPRINTS. Jacket design by Ruth Robbins and photograph by Clayton Bess from *Story for a Black Night* by Clayton Bess. Copyright © 1982 by Robert H. Locke. Photographs copyright © 1982 by Clayton Bess. Reprinted by permission of Parnassus Imprints.

PAVILION BOOKS LTD. Photograph by Angelo Hornak and illustration from *The Treasures of Childhood: Books, Toys and Games from the Opie Collection* by Iona and Robert Opie and Brian Alderson. Introduction and books section text copyright © 1989 by Brian Alderson. Toys section text copyright © 1989 by Iona and Robert Opie. Collection copyright © 1989 by The Bodleian Library. Toys and Games collection copyright © 1989 by Iona Opie. Both reprinted by permission of Pavilion Books Ltd.

PENGUIN USA. Sidelight excerpts by Alice Hegan Rice from *The Inky Way* by Alice Hegan Rice./ Illustration by Bob Graham from *Crusher Is Coming!* by Bob Graham. Copyright © 1987 by Blackbird Design. Both reprinted by permission of Penguin USA.

THE PUTNAM PUBLISHING GROUP, INC. Illustration by Peter Cross from *Dudley Bakes a Cake* by Judy Taylor. Text copyright © 1988 by Judy Taylor. Illustrations copyright © 1988 by Peter Cross./ Cover illustration from *Good-bye Pink Pig* by C. S. Adler. Copyright © 1985 by C. S. Adler./ Illustrations by Peter Cross from *Dudley in a Jam* by Judy Taylor. Text copyright © 1986 by Judy Taylor. Illustrations copyright © 1986 by Peter Cross./ Photograph by Susan Kuklin from *Mine for a Year* by Susan Kuklin. Copyright © 1984 by Susan Kuklin./ Jacket illustration by Leslie Morrill from *Super Sleuth: Twelve Solve-It-Yourself Mysteries* by Jackie Vivelo. Copyright © 1985 by Jackie J. Vivelo. All reprinted by permission of The Putnam Publishing Group, Inc.

RANDOM HOUSE, INC. Cover illustration from *Black Odyssey: The Afro-American Ordeal in Slavery* by Nathan Irvin Huggins. Copyright © 1977 by Nathan Irvin Huggins. Reprinted by permission of Random House, Inc.

THE ROSEN PUBLISHING GROUP. Photograph from *Your Future in Aviation: In the Air* by Kimball J. Scribner. Copyright © 1979 by Kimball J. Scribner. Reprinted by permission of The Rosen Publishing Group.

SCARECROW PRESS, INC. Sidelight excerpts from an article "Black Perspective in Books for Children," by Judith Thompson and Gloria Woodard in *The Black American in Books for Children: Readings in Racism,* edited by Donnarae MacCann and Gloria Woodard. Copyright © 1972 by Scarecrow Press, Inc. Reprinted by permission of Scarecrow Press, Inc.

SIMON & SCHUSTER, INC. Cover illustration by Loren H. Blackburn from *The Luftwaffe in World War II: The Rise and Decline of the German Air Force* by Richard L. Blanco. Copyright © 1987 by Richard L. Blanco./ Cover photograph by Peter Riding and cover design by Joel Avirom from *No Bad Dogs: The Woodhouse Way* by Barbara Woodhouse. Copyright © 1978, 1982 by Barbara Woodhouse. Both reprinted by permission of Simon & Schuster, Inc.

STANDARD PUBLISHING. Cover illustration from *Another Jennifer* by Jane Sorenson. Copyright © 1986 by Standard Publishing. Reprinted by permission of Standard Publishing.

VESTA PUBLICATIONS LTD. Cover illustration by Bob Eadie from *Simon and the Snow King* by Stephen Gill. Copyright © 1981 by Vesta Publications Ltd. Reprinted by permission of Vesta Publications Ltd.

VIKING PENGUIN INC. Illustration by John Steptoe from *My Special Best Words* by John Steptoe. Copyright © 1974 by John Steptoe. Reprinted by permission of Viking Penguin Inc.

WALKER BOOKS LTD. Illustration by Reg Cartwright from *My Cat* by Judy Taylor. Text copyright © 1987 by Judy Taylor. Illustrations copyright © 1987 by Reg Cartwright./ Illustration by Shirley Hughes from *Tail Feathers from Mother Goose: The Opie Rhyme Book* by Iona Opie. Text copyright © 1988 by Iona Opie. Illustrations copyright © 1988 by Shirley Hughes./ Illustration by Anne Dalton from *Tail Feathers from Mother Goose: The Opie Rhyme Book* by Iona Opie. Text copyright © 1988 by Iona Opie. Illustrations copyright © 1988 by Anne Dalton. All reprinted by permission of Walker Books Ltd.

FREDERICK WARNE. Illustration from *Beatrix Potter: Artist, Storyteller, and Countrywoman* by Judy Taylor. Copyright © 1986 by Judy Taylor. Reprinted by permission of Frederick Warne.

WATSON-GUPTILL PUBLICATIONS. Sidelight excerpts by Walter James Miller from the Introduction to *Jungle Tales of Tarzan* by Burne Hogarth./ Illustrations by Burne Hogarth from *Tarzan of the Apes: Book One* by Burne Hogarth. Original text by Edgar Rice Burroughs. Adapted by Robert M. Hodes. Introduction by Maurice Horn. Copyright © 1972 by Edgar Rice

Burroughs, Inc./ Illustrations by Burne Hogarth from *Dynamic Light and Shade* by Burne Hogarth. Copyright © 1981 by Burne Hogarth./ Illustrations by Burne Hogarth from *Jungle Tales of Tarzan,* adapted by Burne Hogarth and Robert M. Hodes. Original text by Edgar Rice Burroughs. Copyright © 1976 by Edgar Rice Burroughs, Inc. All reprinted by permission of Watson-Guptill Publications.

FRANKLIN WATTS, INC. Jacket illustration by Toby Gowing and jacket design by Sylvia Frezzolini from *Julia's Mending* by Kathy Lynn Emerson. Copyright © 1987 by Kathy Lynn Emerson and Orchard Books. Reprinted by permission of Franklin Watts, Inc.

Sidelight excerpts from *Aldous Huxley* by Sybille Bedford. Copyright © 1973, 1974 by Sybille Bedford. Reprinted by permission of Sybille Bedford./ Photograph by UPI/Bettmann Newsphotos in *Women in Politics* by Sharon Whitney and Tom Raynor. Copyright © 1986 by Sharon Whitney and Tom Raynor. Reprinted by permission of Bettmann Newsphotos./ Illustration from *Censoring Reality: An Examination of Books on South Africa* by Beverley Naidoo. Reprinted by permission of British Defence and Aid Fund for Southern Africa./ Sidelight excerpts from *Censoring Reality* by Beverley Naidoo. Reprinted by permission of British Defence and Aid Fund for Southern Africa./ Sidelight excerpts from an article "Introducing: Mark Thurman," by Emily Hearn, December, 1982 in *CANSCAIP News.* Reprinted by permission of *CANSCAIP News.*/ Sidelight excerpts from an article "Mufaro's Beautiful Daughters," by John Steptoe, January/February, 1988 in *The Horn Book Magazine.* Reprinted by permission of The Horn Book, Inc.

Sidelight excerpts from an article by Jacques Michel, March 11, 1966 in *Le Monde.* Reprinted by permission of *Le Monde.*/ Cover illustration by Jo Manning from *Going the Distance* by Raymond Souster. Copyright © 1983 by Raymond Souster. Reprinted by permission of Jo Manning./ Cover illustration "Sleeping Woman" by Janet Moore from *Asking for More* by Raymond Souster. Copyright © 1988 by Raymond Souster. Reprinted by permission of Janet Moore./ Sidelight excerpts from an article "Mark Thurman: You Bug Me," 1985-1986 in *Our Choice/Your Choice.* Reprinted by permission of *Our Choice/Your Choice.*/ Sidelight excerpts from an article by Mark Thurman, October, 1985 in *Quill & Quire.* Reprinted by permission of *Quill & Quire.*/ Sidelight excerpts from an article "The Life and Death of Little Jo," February 26, 1944 in *Saturday Review of Literature.* Reprinted by permission of *Saturday Review of Literature.*

Sidelight excerpts from an article "The Story behind Journey to Jo' burg," by Beverley Naidoo, May, 1987 in *School Library Journal.* Copyright © 1987 by Reed Publishing Co. Reprinted by permission of Reed Publishing Co./ Sidelight excerpts from an article "Chinese Americans: A Personal View," by Ruthanne Lum McCunn, June/July, 1988 in *School Library Journal.* Copyright © 1990 by Reed Publishing. Reprinted by permission of Reed Publishing Co./ Illustration by John Steptoe from *OUTside INside: Poems* by Arnold Adoff. Text copyright © 1981 by Arnold Adoff. Illustrations copyright © 1981 by John Steptoe. Reprinted by permission of The Estate of John Steptoe./ Sidelight excerpts from an article "Writing for Children: Where Does It Come from and How Is It Different from Writing for Adults?" by John Steptoe, September, 1988 in *Pen Newsletter.* Reprinted by permission of The Estate of John Steptoe./ Sidelight excerpts from *The Life and Death of Little Jo* by Robert Bright. Reprinted by permission of The University of New Mexico Press.

PHOTOGRAPH CREDITS

C. S. Adler: Pamela Mendelsohn; Karen Barbour: David Scheff; Paula Danziger: Bob Newey; Bob Graham: Copyright © by John Vigurs (Walker Books); Aldous Huxley: Douglas Glass; Julia Killingback: Cedric Barker; Susan Kuklin: Bailey H. Kuklin; Beverley Naidoo: Kitchenham Ltd.; Angela Sommer-Bodenburg: Copyright © by Gertraud Middelhauve (Verlag, Koeln); Raymond Souster: B. M. Litteljohn; John Steptoe: Loretta J. Farmer; John Steptoe (with children): Bobby Shepard; Sharon Whitney: Copyright © 1988 by Stefani Photography; Barbara Woodhouse: Jonathan Trackman.

SOMETHING ABOUT THE AUTHOR

ADAM SMITH, Janet (Buchanan) 1905-

PERSONAL: Born December 9, 1905, in Glasgow, Scotland; daughter of Sir George (a minister and university principal) and Lady Lilian (Buchanan) Adam Smith; married Michael Roberts (a poet), June 22, 1935 (died, 1948); married John Dudley Carleton (a headmaster), August 5, 1965 (died, 1974); children: (first marriage) Andrew, Henrietta Roberts Dombey, Adam, John. *Education:* Somerville College, Oxford, B.A., 1927. *Politics:* "Floating voter." *Religion:* Church of Scotland. *Home:* 57 Lansdowne Rd., London W11 2LG, England.

CAREER: Author and journalist. British Broadcasting Corp., London, England, 1928-35; *Listener,* London, subeditor, 1928-30, assistant editor, 1930-35; *New Statesman,* London, assistant literary editor, 1949-52, literary editor, 1952-60; free-lance writer and broadcaster, 1960—. Trustee, National Library of Scotland, 1950-85; Virginia Gildersleeve visiting professor, Barnard College, 1961, 1964; president, Royal Literary Fund, 1976-84. *Member:* Ladies' Alpine Club (president, 1962-65), Alpine Club (vice-president, 1978-80). *Awards, honors:* LL.D. from Aberdeen University, 1962.

WRITINGS:

R. L. Stevenson (biography), Folcroft, 1937, reissued, Norwood Editions, 1978.
Life among the Scots (nonfiction), Collins, 1946.
Children's Illustrated Books, Collins, 1948.
Mountain Holidays (reminiscences), Dent, 1946.
John Buchan: A Biography, Hart-Davis, 1965, Little, Brown, 1966.
John Buchan and His World (biography), Scribner, 1979.

EDITOR

Poems of To-morrow: An Anthology of Contemporary Verse, Chatto & Windus, 1935.
(And author of introduction) *Henry James and Robert Louis Stevenson: A Record of Friendship and Criticism* (correspondence), Hart-Davis, 1948, reissued, Hyperion Press, 1980.
Robert Louis Stevenson, *Collected Poems,* Hart-Davis, 1950, 2nd edition, Viking, 1971.
Michael Roberts, *The Estate of Man,* Faber, 1951.
The Faber Book of Children's Verse (juvenile), Faber, 1953, revised edition published as *The Looking Glass Book of Verse* (illustrated by Consuelo Joerns), Looking Glass Library, 1959.
(And author of introduction) M. Roberts, *Collected Poems,* Faber, 1958.
The Living Stream: An Anthology of Twentieth-Century Verse, Faber, 1969.
(Editor of supplement) M. Roberts, editor, *The Faber Book of Comic Verse,* revised edition, Faber, 1974 (Adam Smith was not associated with earlier edition).

TRANSLATOR

Roger Frison-Roche, *First on the Rope,* Methuen, 1949.
(With Nea Morin) Maurice Herzog, *Annapurna: Conquest of the First 8000-Metre Peak (26,493 Feet),* J. Cape, 1952.
(With N. Morin) R. Frison-Roche, *The Last Crevasse,* Methuen, 1952.
(With N. Morin) Bernard Pierre, *A Mountain Called Nun-Kun,* Hodder & Stoughton, 1955.
(With N. Morin) Giusto Gervasutti, *Gervasutti's Climbs,* Hart-Davis, 1957.

Contributor to literary journals and periodicals, including *Times Literary Supplement* and *New York Review of Books.*

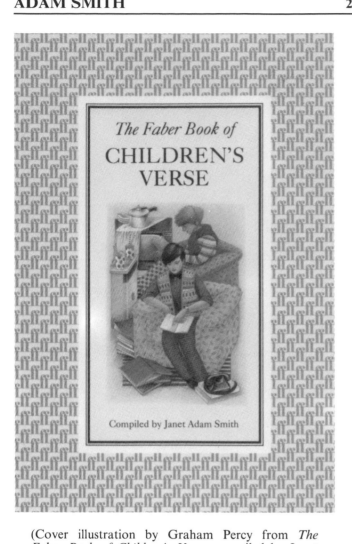

FOR MORE INFORMATION SEE:

Times Literary Supplement, November 27, 1953.
New York Herald Tribune Book Review, November 14, 1954.

ADAMSON, George 1906-1989

OBITUARY NOTICE: Born in 1906 in India; died from gunshot, August 20, 1989, in Kenya; buried in Kora, Kenya. Game warden, wildlife conservationist, safari hunter, and author. Adamson was famous for his conservationist efforts with lions in the Kora National Reserve of Kenya. He first came to the African country in 1924. After working at various occupations, including a professional safari hunter, he became an assistant game warden in 1938. Adamson began raising lion cubs in the 1950s, teaching them how to survive in the wild before releasing them. His work became known when his wife, Joy, wrote *Born Free,* the story of the first lion cub freed by Adamson. By the end of his career, Adamson had saved twenty-three lions from life in captivity. He was killed while investigating an assault on some of his assistants by trespassing nomads who shot him as he approached them in his car. Adamson authored two books, *Bwana Game* and an autobiography, *My Pride and Joy.*

FOR MORE INFORMATION SEE:

People Weekly, November 22, 1982 (pg. 161).
Smithsonian, July, 1983 (pg. 102ff).

OBITUARIES

Chicago Tribune, August 22, 1989.
Los Angeles Times, August 22, 1989.
New York Times, August 22, 1989.
Times (London), August 22, 1989.
Washington Post, August 22, 1989.
Contemporary Authors, Volume 129, Gale, 1990.

ADLER, C(arole) S(chwerdtfeger) 1932-

PERSONAL: Born February 23, 1932, in Long Island, N.Y.; daughter of Oscar Edward (a car mechanic and chief petty officer in the Naval Reserve) and Clarice (an office manager; maiden name, Landsberg) Schwerdtfeger; married Arnold R. Adler (an engineer), June, 1952; children: Steven and Clifford (twins), Kenneth. *Education:* Hunter College (now Hunter College of the City University of New York), B.A. (cum laude), 1953; Russell Sage College, M.S., 1967. *Home:* 1350 Ruffner Rd., Schenectady, N.Y. 12309.

CAREER: Worthington Corp., Harrison, N.J., advertising assistant, 1952-54; Niskayuna Middle Schools, Niskayuna, N.Y., English teacher, 1968-77; writer, 1977—. Volunteer worker in child abuse and protection program at local children's shelter, and as tutor of foster children. *Member:* Society of Children's Book Writers, Author's Guild, Phi Beta Kappa.

AWARDS, HONORS: Golden Kite Award for Fiction from the Society of Children's Book Writers, Children's Choice from the International Reading Association and the Children's Book Council, and selected one of Child Study Association of America's Children's Books of the Year, all 1979, and William Allen White Children's Book Award, 1982, all

(Cover illustration by Graham Percy from *The Faber Book of Children's Verse,* compiled by Janet Adam Smith.)

SIDELIGHTS: "From the age of four I devoured books. My parents and my teachers both believed in learning poems by heart—so I built up a store of poems in my mind which in my old age are a great comfort, especially on sleepless nights. I have memorised many poems since childhood, but I think those committed to memory before, say eighteen, stay in the mind much longer. My life would have been far poorer if I had not loved poetry."

In addition to writing several well-received biographies, including two on prolific author John Buchan, Janet Adam Smith has edited a number of books for both children and adults. In *The Faber Book of Children's Verse* she has compiled a potpourri of poems described by a reviewer for *Times Literary Supplement* as "... a generous variety of period, mood, and subject." The same critic noted: "It can be verse that children appreciate, whether in part or fully; some of it written perhaps in a childish mood, some of it in the high heroic vein that fires the adolescent, and some in the enchantment of a spirit drenched in wonder...." *New York Herald Tribune Book Review*'s L. S. Bechtel observed that any child who is "... equipped with the background Miss Adam Smith offers in this wide range from English lyric poetry ... will indeed be ready to continue the pursuit of poetry with pleasure."

HOBBIES AND OTHER INTERESTS: Mountain walking.

C. S. ADLER

for *The Magic of the Glits; The Shell Lady's Daughter* was selected one of American Library Association's Best Young Adult Books of the Year, 1983; Child Study Children's Book Award from the Child Study Children's Book Committee at Bank St. College of Education (N.Y.), 1985, for *With Westie and the Tin Man.*

WRITINGS:

The Magic of the Glits (illustrated by Ati Forberg), Macmillan, 1979.
The Silver Coach (Junior Literary Guild selection), Coward, 1979.
In Our House Scott Is My Brother, Macmillan, 1980.
Shelter on Blue Barns Road, Macmillan, 1981.
The Cat That Was Left Behind (Junior Literary Guild selection), Clarion Books, 1981.
Down by the River, Coward, 1981.
Footsteps on the Stairs, Delacorte, 1982.
Some Other Summer, Macmillan, 1982.
The Evidence That Wasn't There, Clarion Books, 1982.
The Once in a While Hero, Coward, 1982.
Binding Ties, Delacorte, 1983.
Get Lost, Little Brother, Clarion Books, 1983.
Roadside Valentine, Macmillan, 1983.
The Shell Lady's Daughter, Coward, 1983.
Fly Free, Coward, 1984.
Good-bye, Pink Pig, Putnam, 1985.
Shadows on Little Reef Bay, Clarion Books, 1985.
With Westie and the Tin Man (Junior Literary Guild selection), Macmillan, 1985.
Split Sisters (illustrated by Mike Wimmer), Macmillan, 1986.
Kiss the Clown, Clarion Books, 1986.
If You Need Me, Macmillan, 1987.

Carly's Buck (Junior Literary Guild selection), Clarion Books, 1987.
Eddie's Blue-Winged Dragon, Putnam, 1988.
Always and Forever Friends, Clarion Books, 1988.
One Sister Too Many: A Sequel to Split Sisters, Macmillan, 1989.
The Lump in the Middle, Clarion Books, 1989.
Ghost Brother, Clarion Books, 1990.
Help, Pink Pig! (sequel to *Good-bye, Pink Pig*), Putnam, 1990.

Contributor of articles and stories to periodicals, including *American Girl, Co-Ed,* and *Ingenue.*

ADAPTATIONS:

"Get Lost, Little Brother" (cassette), Talking Books, 1983.

SIDELIGHTS: Born in Rockaway Beach, Long Island, C. S. Adler has lived all over New York City. "I had a restless father, so we moved every couple of years; I saw all the boroughs. New York City was filled with empty lots I used to explore. I was fascinated with the interesting weeds, bugs, wee beasties and flowers like honeysuckle, roses, and morning glory. And there was the zoo and the park. Manhattan's park at Riverside Drive was a teenage hangout and a great place to sunbathe.

"An only child, my family consisted of my mother, father, grandmother, and an aunt. My father was a chief petty officer in the Naval Reserve and a car mechanic; my mother was an office manager; and my grandmother was in charge of me. I roamed around a lot on my own and usually had friends to roam with. New York City in those days was pretty safe, so

(Cover illustration from *Good-bye, Pink Pig* by C. S. Adler.)

Yesterday's fears evaporated along with the morning dew. (From *The Silver Coach* by C. S. Adler.)

when I got to be ten or eleven, I used the subways to prowl museums and parks. The city offered many options; it was a good place for a poor kid to grow up. We didn't have a lot of money, but you didn't need a lot of money when I was young.

"Moving around so much was probably good experience for becoming a children's author, because one of the most traumatic things in a child's life is moving and being new in a new school. I was a very shy child who didn't make friends easily, yet friends were very important. So it was difficult. That experience made me sympathetic to that particular aspect of a child's problems."[1]

Adler's father left the family when she was twelve. "That was another experience that made me comfortable writing about divorce and separation.

"I was very close to my mother. She was understanding, liberal, and tolerant of all people. She taught me to treat everybody as an individual, evaluating a person on his character rather than anything else. All those good values have stuck with me, I think. My mother had the advantage of being a working mother. My grandmother took the brunt of the nagging business of child raising. I never stopped being close to my mother. I also was, and am, very close to my aunt.

"My mother and aunt encouraged me to think well of myself. They also pointed out my negative aspects—reminding me that I wasn't perfect—but basically, I knew they loved me

and thought I was wonderful. Having someone who thinks that is just what you need when you're a child.

"As a youngster, I was boring. Reading and writing were the only things that interested me. I was an omnivorous reader. I went to libraries and read just about everything I could get my hands on: adult books, fairy tales, the Alcott books—anything that was there. I'd get excited about one book and two weeks later, I'd be excited about another.

"I remember reading about the Nazi concentration camps in the newspaper. Although I was brought up with no religion, I empathized tremendously. I am half Jewish and half Lutheran. I identified strongly with the Jewish half during that period.

"The writing came almost immediately after I'd learned to read. By age seven, I'd begun writing stories for myself. I remember writing a book about a boy in China. I had no idea what China or Chinese boys were like, but it seemed exotic. I'd write little stories and put them together with cardboard covers and rubber bands to make them look like a book. Every once in awhile, I would con a friend into listening to one. I never showed them to teachers. It was just something I liked to do for fun. Even if nobody had published my books, I'd still be writing. Some people talk a lot; I write a lot."[1] At thirteen, Adler sent her first story to a professional magazine. "Thereafter, I got the proverbial drawer full of rejection slips."[1]

Other than reading, writing, nature, and people, not much else interested her. "I wasn't much of an athlete. As a matter of fact I had asthma and a heart condition. So I had sort of a restricted youth, first by my family, and then because I had to stay out of gym classes. My family thought I was delicate. I imagined that I had no physical ability. As it turns out, I have plenty; I'm as strong as a horse. (My husband calls me a middle-aged jock.)

"As a student, I was a well-behaved, dutiful child who sat quietly, listened, did her homework, and got good marks—the kind of student teachers like. I always managed a friend or two, but I never felt popular. After my father left, we stayed put in Manhattan. I went to Hunter High School which was a very stimulating school, very challenging. I had a number of friends and those were good years.

"I met my husband, Arnold, when I was sixteen by crashing one of the dances at City College where he was a veteran who'd returned to school. I was a New York girl, a sophisticated dresser, and very tall, so I looked about twenty. We dated, but I never told him how old I was. I did tell him I went to Hunter, but he thought I meant Hunter College. My mother liked him as soon as she met him; she thought he was charming. Besides, she trusted my judgment."[1]

Legitimizing the misunderstanding, Adler attended Hunter College. "I always wanted to be a writer, but my mother informed me that I shouldn't just take English and psychology courses because I'd probably have to earn a living. So I nearly lost my Phi Beta Kappa key by taking typing and stenography, at which I was terrible. Unfortunately, I was most interested in getting home, speaking to Arnold over the phone, going out weekends, and getting my degree so that he would marry me. I raced through college, and finished in three years.

"I can't say that there were any particularly influential professors for me. Actually, Arnold was much more influential because he was a great deal older. An engineer, he was also interested in literature. At sixteen, he had me reading the *Partisan Review*. I would say that he helped develop my cultural interests."[1]

Completing course work at Hunter in 1952, Adler married at twenty. "My husband worked for General Electric, so for the first nine years of our married life, we moved every two or three years. I got used to that; it didn't bother me. We lived in Cincinnati, Ohio and parts of New York State and New Jersey. We finally settled in Schenectady, where we've lived for twenty-five years. I love having a sense of belonging and having people know who I am. If I go to the theater, I say hello to a dozen different people. That's exciting for someone who comes from New York City.

"I had never had much interest in children before I married, although I knew I wanted them. Everyone in my generation did. Once I had them, three sons—two were twins, I fell madly in love with them and became a very happy home-

(Jacket art by Diane de Groat from *Always and Forever Friends* by C. S. Adler.)

For two mornings in a row he had seen the cat.
(Jacket illustration by Troy Howell from *The Cat That Was Left Behind* by C. S. Adler.)

maker. I emulated my mother as well as I could because I admired her tremendously. I tried to be as loving, understanding, open-minded, and encouraging of independence as she was. I had no desire to go out and work. I wanted to stay home with the children, so I continued writing and getting rejection slips. But my main interest in life was raising the kids until they were all in school.

"By then, I had figured that I was never going to make it as a writer and began to think in terms of a more sensible career. I went back to get my master's degree and began teaching, an alternative that allowed me to stay home summers with the children."[1]

Adler taught sixth- and eighth-grade English for nearly ten years. "The experiences I had teaching were what made me a writer, and that's the age I write about. I was fascinated by my students; I thought they were the most interesting people around. Teenagers are up front with their problems and emotions. You have to know adults a long time before you know what they are about. Many of us wear facades—children don't. Watching them, I empathized and got into emotional relationships with them, all very useful in my writing as it turned out. Many of the kids I taught appear in my books, not their particular problems or lives—I don't do that—but their personalities.

"The discipline, however, was very difficult. Eighth-graders are not easy to deal with in groups of thirty, and the amount of paper work was gigantic. I was working seventy hours a week, taking 150 papers home a night. It became too much. I decided that if I was ever going to be a writer, it was then."[1]

Her first book, *The Magic of the Glits*, was published in 1979. "My husband and I were in Wellfleet, Cape Cod. He was surf-casting and I was up in the dunes doing what I do, which is writing to entertain myself. I wrote a fifty-page story about fairies and the ocean. The boy, Jeremy, was based on a boy I had once had in class. When I got home, I developed the story and sent it out. It didn't sell right away. It got rejected and had to be rewritten, but eventually it sold. That was a marvelous, marvelous day. I invited everyone over and we had wine and cheese to celebrate.

"Ever since that first book, I've sold most everything I've written. I've been able to indulge my passion, producing more than two books a year."[1]

Besides *The Magic of the Glits*, several of Adler's books have contained some element of magic. "*The Silver Coach*, my second book, was suggested by an anniversary gift given by my son, Steven, to my husband and me, a silver filigree coach the size of a fist with doors that open and wheels that turn, so charming it seemed to demand to be put into a book."[2]

"About a quarter to a third of my books have some magical influence. Don't ask me where it comes from. Not only was I *not* interested in magic, I'm *still* not interested in it. I have absolutely no idea why I have it in my books."[1]

But "family is a common theme. Divorce is not. If you look at the thirty books that I have now written, only about a third of them have anything to do with divorce or separated parents. That's a fair match to what is true in society today.

"Writing about families very different from mine is more interesting than writing about my own. In fact, I'm least successful when writing about someone most like my own relatives or myself. I try not to duplicate my own life in my books. The fun of being an author is projecting yourself into other people's lives. That is particularly enjoyable when the person is very different from you. I'm not a very funny person, but I love getting into the character of a funny girl. I find other people fascinating.

"My interests are basically personal: emotional problems and family relationships. Those things fascinate me most. I'm not a very political or cause-minded person. When I look at the newspaper, I'm not worrying about nuclear war; I'm looking for things about child abuse or latch-key children. Those issues would stick in my mind and probably become the theme of another story.

"I don't really worry about keeping up with the pace of the world or whether I'm totally capable of adjusting to the times. I don't think of myself as a chameleon. I pretty much stay who I am and write the kind of thing I write, doing my best to understand people around me.

"We live in a fast-paced society. Living and living well becomes more difficult as things change faster and faster. We have all these environmental concerns and world problems, and this pile-up of problems puts pressure on everyone, kids and adults. Although we have huge pockets of the country where the child is still the most important thing in town, I think what we have is a tendency to be less child-oriented as a society. I know a great many families who haven't changed over the years, where the main concern of the parents is still their children. But I know other families where parents seem

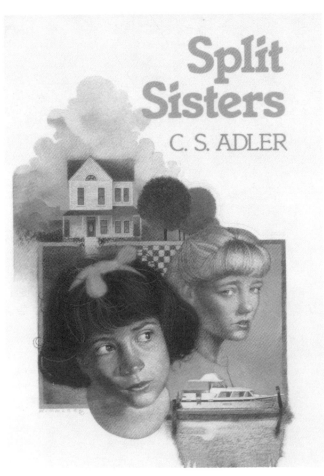

(Jacket illustration by Mike Wimmer from *Split Sisters* by C. S. Adler.)

more concerned with their own careers and children become secondary.

"I note from my fan mail that children find bits and pieces of their own problems and themselves in my books. Kids claim that my books are realistic and that they see their friends in some of my characters. Maybe they'll also see ways of dealing with life that they hadn't thought of before. Hopefully, I'm transmitting good values. At least they're my values, and I think they're good. In a sense I'm still teaching. Since I am an optimist, I think things work out well for *most* people. Children tend to despair because they have no idea that tomorrow could bring a sunny day. I can remind them of that."[1]

Adler has worked as a volunteer in a child abuse and neglect program. "That was during the few years I spent at home. I gained some important relationships from that experience. It was very satisfying. I suppose I learned a lot from it. *Fly Free* and *The Cat That Was Left Behind* had to do with foster children."[1]

Down by the River, Adler's first book for older young adults was published in 1981. "A fifteen- or sixteen-year-old girl will have different interests and concerns than a twelve-year-old: boys, her future, college, and the world around her. The twelve-year-old might also be interested in boys, but it would be at a different degree of intensity. She wouldn't possibly be concerned only about sexual contact as the older girl might be. Things would be lighter. A twelve-year-old girl might be more interested in friendships, things smaller and closer to home."[1]

Reviews of the book tended to characterize the critical response to Adler's work in general. Reviewer Hildagarde Gray wrote: "It has arrived! A love story in which the man and woman learn to need and like each other and have concern for each other long, long before the meeting of the bodies in delicate heart-felt, better than heat-felt, physical love .... The nest-building urge *is* more common among women than feminists may acknowledge. Here it is given a dignity and status of a career choice acted upon by a heroine neither simple nor saccharine, but rather ordinary and appealing."[3]

To this consideration, Adler responded: "The woman's movement was very good for those of us who come from a previous generation that never even considered how debased women had been in a society where a housewife, working on full batteries, was considered less than her husband who had the unquestionable right to rule the roost. It is a positive thing that women should have a chance to use their talents and abilities as fully as men, and that a little girl be raised to consider a career as very important in her life.

"However, there were also negative aspects to the women's movement. It's very difficult to make everything perfectly equal in any relationship. By setting up expectations of total equality—that a woman needs to have a successful career and shouldn't stay home and have children at all—that makes marriage and babies very hard to fit into a life. So many people fail at it because they can't commit to another human being, they don't want to be tied down and they can't compromise.

"Children do suffer from the uneasy relationships their parents have with each other. Where both parents are demanding, the child is caught in between. In the old relationships the woman would sacrifice, stay home, and take care of the child,

Just as Lynette started grooming her copper-colored mare.... (From *Some Other Summer* by C. S. Adler.)

maybe even stay with a man who was terrible. I don't think that was right either, but good and bad come with change. To some extent, children might be better off if somebody *did* sacrifice and stay home, whether the man or the woman. There is no question that there is extra stress on the single parent who tries to do both things."[1]

Some critics have ventured to call Adler's sensitive handling of her characters and family relationships "classy." "That's the nicest compliment I could get. I suspect that sensitivity comes from being an only child and a listener when I was young. When you are an only child, you are so lonely and interested in the outside world that you absorb a great many subtleties of life. Then you understand people better as you get older.

"I strongly believe in listening to other people's criticisms. I'm very grateful for them. I have a critiquing group and I rarely protest my editor's criticisms. I use and enjoy them. As for reviewers, since there isn't anything I can do about the book after it's published except grieve if they don't like it, I can't say that I'm thrilled when I get a negative review. I don't learn much from it. I just feel bad.

"My career is a very positive thing in my life. I have the cottage in Cape Cod because I'm a writer. I love what I'm doing. My husband and kids are proud of me. I feel comfortable, successful, and happy that my dreams actually came true. That makes me feel very, very lucky."[1]

Adler adheres to a fairly strict schedule. "In the summertime, I get up about 5:30 and work for three hours. Then I play or take care of household concerns and friends who come to visit. I have a tremendous amount of company—overnight guests. That for me is a great pleasure. In the winter I work six hours a day, usually from twelve to six. I get up a little later, play tennis or clean house in the morning, and then sit down at the computer to work all afternoon. In the summertime, I usually finish five pages a day. In the winter, ten pages a day. That may be an original or a rewrite, or a rewrite of a rewrite, or the fourth or fifth draft. I never send things out until I've gone through four or five drafts. Then an editor will usually ask for another draft and possibly another one after that. Then we go back and forth to copyediting and galleys.

"As soon as I finish one book, I sit down and start another, which I've probably been thinking about for a while. I've never been blocked and I work very quickly. I have a passion for not wasting time.

"I get inspiration wherever I can find it. I read the newspapers to pick up issues and concerns. I listen to conversations on beaches and buses and steal from them whatever I can. I listen to my friends and their stories of themselves, their childhood, and their children. Anyone who tells me a story must be aware that they may find that story used in a book. Most people don't mind. They're glad to contribute bits and pieces of their life. They're amused when it shows up in a book of mine.

"I do a fair amount of research for my books. Some require a lot, some don't require any. If I'm writing about something which I already know, I don't research. I didn't for *Magic of the Glits. Good-bye, Pink Pig* was another one. But very frequently, I end up going to the library. I check out a stack of books and take a bunch of notes from them. Then I get hold of whatever local experts I can find. Usually there are people in Schenectady who can answer my questions, whether about police procedure, environmental concerns, dyslexia, or whatever.

"One of my young-adult books, *Kiss the Clown*, dealt with dyslexia and had to do with a girl who came from Guatemala. I don't remember why she came from Guatemala, but she did. There were also horses and a boy who worked in a stable. I had to read a pile of books about Guatemala because I had never been there and I had to go down to the local stable because I don't know a great deal about horses. That book took more research than most. Right now I'm working on a book that deals with children looking for some Indians. So I've had to research Indians.

"In *Ghost Brother*, the children were interested in skateboarding which I know nothing about. I had to research skateboarding both from books and kids themselves."[1]

Ghost Brother also draws on a highly personal subject for Adler, the 1988 death of one of her twin sons. "My son, who was married, died in a car accident. I've done a lot of writing about it. The ghost who appears to the little brother is my son as he was at fifteen. It's a brother relationship story. All three of my sons were pretty close to each other. They still are. They live in different parts of the country, but we see each other as often as possible."[1]

This was a second blow. Adler's mother had died in December of 1986. "I was there with her when she died of multiple problems in the hospital. They were three terrible, painful months for her. She wanted to die and I wanted to see her out

of her misery. It was a relief when she finally let go. I had loved her very much. I keep all her things around me. She will always be part of my life as my son will be.

"A child once asked from an audience where I was speaking, 'Have you ever written about death?' I said, 'No, I'm very fortunate. I'm a middle-aged lady and I've never had any experience with death, so I don't feel confident to write about it.' Well, now I'm confident.

"I hope that my books will make kids more positive about life as well as more sympathetic to others. I also hope that I can entertain them. I'd like them to feel good about themselves when they finish one of my books."[1]

FOOTNOTE SOURCES

[1]Based on an interview by Dieter Miller for *Something about the Author.*
[2]C. S. Adler, *Something about the Author,* Volume 26, Gale, 1982.
[3]Hildagarde Gray, "*Down by the River,*" *Best Sellers,*, January, 1982.

BACKUS, James Gilmore 1913-1989
(Jim Backus)

OBITUARY NOTICE: Born February 25, 1913, in Cleveland, Ohio; died of pneumonia complicated by Parkinson's disease, July 3, 1989, in Santa Monica, Calif. Actor and author. Backus provided the booming voice of the crotchety, obstinate, and comically nearsighted cartoon character Mr. Magoo. He also appeared in such television shows as "I Married Joan" and "Gilligan's Island." His favorite role was that of James Dean's timid father in the 1955 film "Rebel without a Cause." Backus, who studied at the American Academy of Dramatic Arts, also performed on radio and the Broadway stage. He published a memoir, *Rocks on the Roof,* in 1958. With his wife, Henriette, he also wrote *What Are You Doing after the Orgy?* and two books—*Backus Strikes Back* and *Forgive Us Our Digressions*—that took a humorous view of his struggle with Parkinson's disease.

FOR MORE INFORMATION SEE:

International Motion Picture Almanac, Quigley, 1987.

OBITUARIES

Chicago Tribune, July 4, 1989.
Los Angeles Times, July 4, 1989.
Washington Post, July 4, 1989.
Times (London), July 5, 1989.
Contemporary Authors, Volume 129, Gale, 1990.

BARBOUR, Karen 1956-

PERSONAL: Born October 29, 1956, in San Francisco, Calif.; daughter of Donald C. (a physician) and Nancy B. Barbour; married Hermann Lederle (an artist), 1981. *Education:* University of California, Davis, B.A., 1976; San Francisco Art Institute, M.F.A., 1980. *Home and office:* 51 Warren St., 5th Floor, New York, N.Y. 10007.

CAREER: Free-lance illustrator, animator, and painter. *Awards, honors:* Certificate of Excellence from the American

KAREN BARBOUR

Institute of Graphic Arts Book Show, and Parents' Choice Award from the Parents' Choice Foundation, both for *Little Nino's Pizzeria.*

WRITINGS:

JUVENILE

Little Nino's Pizzeria, Harcourt, 1987.
Nancy, Harcourt, 1989.

ILLUSTRATOR

Arnold Adoff, *Flamboyan,* Harcourt, 1988.

BARGAR, Gary W. 1947-1985

PERSONAL: Born October 29, 1947, in Kansas City, Mo.; died July 29, 1985; son of Wilton H. Barger and Dorothy (Kuster) Tyler. *Education:* Attended William Jewell College, 1965-66; University of Missouri—Kansas City, B.A. (with distinction), 1969, M.A., 1972; graduate work at University of Missouri—Kansas City, 1973, and University of Iowa, 1973-74; further study at University of Chicago, 1975-77, and New School for Social Research, 1977-84.

CAREER: Smithtown Central School District 1, New York, teacher, 1969-70; Kansas City Public Schools, Mo., teacher, 1970-72; Johnson County Public Library, Shawnee Mission, Kansas, part-time librarian, 1973; Scott Foresman & Company, Glenview, Ill., started as assistant editor, became associate editor, 1974-77, senior editor, 1984-85; Harcourt Brace Jovanovich, Inc., New York, N.Y., associate editor, 1977-79;

American Book Company, New York, N.Y., senior editor, 1979; free-lance writer and editor, 1979-84. *Member:* International Reading Association, Society of Children's Book Writers, Children's Reading Round Table of Chicago. *Awards, honors:* Dorothy Canfield Fisher Children's Book Award nomination from the Vermont Congress of Parents and Teachers, South Carolina Children's Book Award nomination from the South Carolina Association of School Librarians, and Mark Twain Children's Book Award nomination from the Missouri Association of School Librarians, all 1985-86, all for *Life. Is. Not. Fair.*

WRITINGS:

What Happened to Mr. Forster, Clarion, 1981.
Life. Is. Not. Fair., Clarion, 1984.

ADAPTATIONS:

"Life. Is. Not. Fair." (cassette), 1986.

SIDELIGHTS: Dorothy Tyler, Gary Barger's mother, comments: "Gary discovered the joy of books and music early in life. During a childhood illness, they became his best friends. He liked some of the same things as most children—games, drawing, comic books, amusement parks, movies, swimming. He would entertain the neighborhood children by telling them stories. He had several small articles published in children's publications, and when he was about twelve sold a story to a national children's newspaper.

GARY W. BARGAR

"As he was growing up, he had various interests—at one time he liked to explore caves. Next he read all he could about astronomy and visited planetariums and observatories. In high school he entered speech contests, acted in school plays, and was student director of a play. His interest in writing continued to grow throughout high school.

"In college he studied to be an elementary school teacher. After teaching for three years, he decided to pursue his writing career. He worked as an editor and writer in educational publishing. He had never given up the desire to be a children's author and was able to achieve that dream with his books."

HOBBIES AND OTHER INTERESTS: Collecting children's books, reading, music, plays, musicals, and dance.

BLANCO, Richard L(idio) 1926-

PERSONAL: Born May 12, 1926, in New York, N.Y.; son of Lidio F. (an advertising manager) and Eleanor (a housewife, maiden name, Boehm) Blanco; married Irene E. Edry, June 10, 1961 (deceased); children: Richard L., Jr. *Education:* University of Maryland, B.S., 1950; Western Reserve University (now Case Western Reserve University), M.A., 1956,

(Cover illustration "Channel Bound" by Loren H. Blackburn from *The Luftwaffe in World War II: The Rise and Decline of the German Air Force* by Richard L. Blanco.)

Ph.D., 1960. *Politics:* Democrat. *Religion:* "No preference." *Home:* 51 Rush Hills Drive, Rush, N.Y. 14543. *Office:* Department of History, State University of New York College at Brockport, Brockport, N.Y. 14420.

CAREER: Duquesne University, Pittsburgh, Pa., instructor in history, 1959-60; Marietta College, Marietta, Ohio, assistant professor, 1960-63, associate professor of history, 1963-65; Frostburg State College, Frostburg, Md., associate professor of history, 1965-67, head of department, 1965-67; Rollins College, Winter Park, Fla., associate professor of history, 1967-68; State University of New York College at Brockport, associate professor, 1968-71, professor of history, 1971—, director of Overseas Study Program at University of Aberdeen, 1971-75, co-director of the Overseas Program at Brunel University, England, 1984-85. Visiting lecturer at State University of New York, Geneseo, 1957-58, Western Reserve University (now Case Western Reserve University), summer, 1963, University of Southwestern Louisiana, summer, 1965, Rollins College, Fla., 1967-68, and University of Rochester, N.Y., 1977. Consultant to American Library Association, 1967, Center for Professional Development, Wichita, Kan., 1982, and Garland Publishing, 1984—. *Military service:* U.S. Army Air Forces, 1944-46.

MEMBER: American Historical Association, Society for Social History of Medicine. *Awards, honors:* Research grants from American Philosophical Society, 1967 and 1972, State University of New York Research Foundation, 1969, 1970, 1974, and 1981, National Library of Medicine, 1974, National Endowment for the Humanities, 1976, National Institutes of Health Research, 1977-78, and National Archives, 1978; *Rommel the Desert Warrior: The Afrika Korps in World War II* was chosen an oustanding juvenile book by *Booklist,* 1983; *The War of the American Revolution: A Selected Annotated Bibliography of Published Sources* was selected a Choice Book for College Libraries by *Choice,* 1984-85.

WRITINGS:

(Contributor) Raymond F. Locke, editor, *Great Military Campaigns,* Mankind Publishing Co., 1970.
Wellington's Surgeon-General: Sir James McGrigor, Duke University Press, 1974.
(Contributor) Joseph O. Baylen and Norbert J. Gossman, editors, *Biographical Dictionary of British Radicalism,* Harvester House, 1975.
Physician of the American Revolution: Jonathan Potts, Garland, 1979.
Rommel the Desert Warrior: The Afrika Korps in World War II (juvenile), Messner, 1982.
The War of the American Revolution: A Selected Annotated Bibliography of Published Sources, Garland, 1984.
The Luftwaffe in World War II: The Rise and Decline of the German Air Force (juvenile), Messner, 1987.
Encyclopedia of the American Revolution, Garland, in press.

Contributor of articles and book reviews to professional journals including *History of Education Quarterly, Military Affairs, Mankind, Journal of the Society for Army Historical Research, Books for College Libraries, Great Military Campaigns, History Today, Societas: A Review of Social History, Enlightenment Essays, Pennsylvania History, Bulletin of the New York Academy of Medicine, New York History, War and Society in the 18th Century,* and *Medical History.*

WORK IN PROGRESS: General editor of series entitled "Wars of the United States," nine volumes, to be published by Garland.

SIDELIGHTS: "Except for the influence of my father, I am unable to discern any particular factor that helped to mold my career while growing up in a small New Jersey town. Due to my father, I was exposed to the wonders of museums, concert halls, and art galleries, and it was due to him that I read (before high school) many of the great novelists—Dumas, Zola, Hardy, Kenneth Roberts, Sinclair Lewis, John Dos Passos.

"Likewise, though army service gave me a sample of military life, I never contemplated that I would eventually become a military historian. In fact, my first college degree was in business administration, and I spent several years in the corporate world of Wall Street and one year as a salesman in Venezuela.

"Yet, I realized that I did not conform to the ideal type of a potential young business executive for I was not interested in 'making money.' I still preferred to read and read, and as members of my family commented about me: 'He always has his nose in a book.'

"Writing was still far from my mind when I changed careers at the age of twenty-seven to become a public school teacher of social studies in Cleveland, Ohio. After taking several idiotic education courses in graduate school, I virtually stumbled into history. I was twenty-nine before I finally realized that I wanted to be a historian. Fortunately for me, the history department at Case-Western Reserve University stressed excellence in writing, and I certainly benefitted from this policy.

"Although I had a yearning to begin writing at the age of thirty-four (when I received my Ph.D.), due to the heavy teaching 'loads' at various colleges where I worked, I rarely had the time, nor with a family of my own to consider, the money necessary for research. However, I did manage to write innumerable book reviews for professional journals and this task of compressing the essence of some author's work into a few hundred words taught me to be precise and concise with words, to treat words in a sentence or in a paragraph like bullets, and that I was running out of ammunition in a battle.

"Finally, due to a research grant in 1967 I was able to travel to England to begin research on British army doctors during the Napoleonic era. I have always been fascinated by the exploits of brave men whether they were generals, explorers, scientists, artists or politicians. It was this interest then that led me to write two biographies and various articles about some outstanding personages.

"Only by accident did I consider writing for high schoolers. My son and I were 'very close,' and we often played games together, particularly 'war games' and chess during the winter. One of these games (which my son invariably won) was about desert warfare in North Africa during World War II. Hence, I sent my proposal about a famous German general (Field Marshal Erwin Rommel) to a publisher who accepted it. Apparently that book—which was great fun to write—was a success, for I wrote another one about the German Air Force in World War II. I tried to make both books into lively reading for youngsters by a tight control of words, terse paragraphs, a lively style characterized by anec-dotes about brave men tested to the peak of their physical and emotional limits during combat. I kept thinking: 'would a student in the eleventh grade enjoy this?' Apparently so."

HOBBIES AND OTHER INTERESTS: Backpacking, canoeing, bird watching, trekking in South America.

BOURNE, Miriam Anne 1931-1989

OBITUARY NOTICE—See sketch in *SATA* Volume 16: Born March 4, 1931, in Buffalo, N.Y.; died of cancer, June 21, 1989, in Castine, Me. Educator, consultant, editor, and author. A respected consultant on early learning materials, Bourne wrote more than a dozen books for children during a career that spanned two decades. While living in Connecticut in the mid-70s, she owned and operated a mail-order business called the Children's Bookshop. She later taught at the Institute of Children's Literature. Among her children's books are *Emilio's Summer Day, Four-Ring Three, Bright Lights to See By,* and *White House Children.* Bourne also edited a women's history project for the Episcopal Church and wrote several adult books, including *First Family,* a study of George Washington's life.

FOR MORE INFORMATION SEE:

Martha E. Ward and Dorothy A. Marquardt, *Authors of Books for Young People,* Scarecrow, 1979.
Contemporary Authors New Revision Series, Volume 10, Gale, 1983.

OBITUARIES

Washington Post, June 24, 1989.
Contemporary Authors, Volume 129, Gale, 1990.

BRIGHT, Robert (Douglas) 1902-1988 (Michael Douglas)

PERSONAL: Born August 5, 1902, in Sandwich, Mass.; died of cancer, November 21, 1988, in San Francisco, Calif.; son of Edward (a scholar) and Blanche (Denio) Bright; married Katherine Eastman Bailey (died, 1973); children: Robert Douglas, Jr., Beatrice Ruffin. *Education:* Princeton University, B.A., 1923. *Residence:* San Francisco, Calif.

CAREER: Author and illustrator. *Sun,* Baltimore, Md., reporter, 1925-26; *Times,* Paris, France, on editorial staff, 1926-27; Conde Nast Publications, New York, N.Y., assistant to the president, 1927-28; Revillon Freres, New York, N.Y., advertising manager, 1928-36; Massachusetts Department of Education, Boston, Mass., instructor, 1948-51; Emerson College, Boston, Mass., lecturer, 1949; Department of Welfare, Taos, N.M., case worker, 1952; *New Mexican,* Santa Fe, N.M., music and art critic, 1964-65.

WRITINGS:

JUVENILE; ALL SELF-ILLUSTRATED, EXCEPT AS NOTED

The Travels of Ching, W. R. Scott, 1943.
Me and the Bears, Doubleday, 1951.
Richard Brown and the Dragon (adaptation of an anecdote from *A Tramp Abroad* by Mark Twain, pseudonym of Samuel L. Clemens), Doubleday, 1952.

ROBERT BRIGHT

(With Dorothy Brett) *Hurrah for Freddie!* (illustrated by the authors), Doubleday, 1953.
Miss Pattie, Doubleday, 1954.
I Like Red, Doubleday, 1955.
The Friendly Bear, Doubleday, 1957, reissued, 1971.
My Red Umbrella, Morrow, 1959, reissued, 1985.
My Hopping Bunny (poetry), Doubleday, 1960.
(Under pseudonym Michael Douglas) *Round, Round World* (poetry), Golden Press, 1960.
Which Is Willy?, Doubleday, 1962.
Gregory: The Nosiest and Strongest Boy in Grangers Grove, Doubleday, 1969.

JUVENILE; "GEORGIE" SERIES; ALL SELF-ILLUSTRATED

Georgie, Doubleday, 1944.
Georgie to the Rescue, Doubleday, 1956.
Georgie's Halloween, Doubleday, 1958.
Georgie and the Robbers, Doubleday, 1963.
Georgie and the Magician, Doubleday, 1966.
Georgie and the Noisy Ghost, Doubleday, 1971.
Georgie Goes West, Doubleday, 1973.
Georgie's Christmas Carol, Doubleday, 1975.
Georgie and the Buried Treasure, Doubleday, 1979.
Georgie and the Ball of Yarn, Doubleday, 1983.
Georgie and the Baby Birds, Doubleday, 1983.
Georgie and the Little Dog, Doubleday, 1983.
Georgie and the Runaway Balloon, Doubleday, 1983.

ADULT

The Life and Death of Little Jo, Doubleday, 1944, published in England as *Little Jo,* Cresset, 1946.
The Intruders, Doubleday, 1946.
The Olivers: The Story of an Artist and His Family, Doubleday, 1947.
The Spirit of the Chase (illustrated by Mircea Vasiliu), Scribner, 1956.

ADAPTATIONS:

"Georgie" (motion picture), Weston Woods Studios, 1956, (filmstrip), 1957.
"Georgie to the Rescue" (motion picture), Sterling Educational Films, 1971.
"My Red Umbrella" (filmstrip), Weston Woods Studios, 1972.
"The Life and Death of Little Jo" (opera; composed by J. Donald Robb), first performed at Albuquerque, New Mexico.

SIDELIGHTS: Robert Bright was born on Cape Cod and reared until the age of twelve, in the town of Goettingen, Germany. The Hanoverian University town was celebrated for mathematics, physics, and legend. "Baron Munchausen was a citizen of Goettingen; the Brothers Grimm, the etymologists, gathered their fairy tales there; Hamelin, the Pied Piper's town, was not far away. I suspect that the roots of my work as illustrator and author of children's books lie right there. However, it was to be many years before they were to bear fruit. My parents returned to Sandwich, and I carried on my education in New England schools and at Princeton University. I became a reporter on the Baltimore *Sun* and, abroad, on the Paris *Times,* and worked in advertising in New York City. I married, had children, and moved to the Southwest. Here, at Ranchos de Taos, New Mexico, my home for fifteen years, I began illustrating and writing books for children."[1]

It was in this intimate Mexican town that Bright received the inspiration to write his first novel *The Life and Death of Little Jo.* "Here I was in a good position because my house was right on the little narrow road between Talpa and Rio Chiquito. Officially [we] were in Rio Chiquito. Being so close to the road people stopped and chatted and presently we were exchanging problems. This was especially so between Katherine, my wife, and the women. Then there were the children. I had three. My children played with their children. Their children were all over my house and my children were all over theirs."[2]

Like their neighbors, the Brights lived as farmers, supporting themselves by cultivating the land. Without telephone, plumbing, and electricity they hauled water from a well. Under these circumstances, there was mutual support among the people. "There was an endless interchange of advice. Was I wise to plant vegetables in ridges rather than the shallow saucer method? Shouldn't I have a rooster for my chickens? One day we received the present of a brown hen that had been trained to lay eggs right in the house. She clucked at the door, we let her in. The hen laid a brown egg in Katherine's knitting basket and clucked to be let out. There were a number of such hens in the village. When our mare had a premature colt everybody was concerned. The big problem was getting the colt to nurse. So I milked the mare. At night we kept the colt in the kitchen. When we had a fire everybody came to help put the fire out. When a bad rain melted away a large piece of wall, they came to put it back into shape .... We were all happy, not because we were without our share of troubles, but because we were all getting to know so much more about ourselves from the lives of our neighbors who had so much to tell us."[2]

The Life and Death of Little Jo was published in 1944. "I honestly cannot pinpoint any character. Certainly not Jo, who was just a little boy emerging from the bushes and shooting up the road. Of course there must always have been suggestions and impressions of real people. But who were they and how many impressions and suggestions made Santiago or old Cornelio? And what does one make out of that extraordinary ballot on election day? As for the local storekeeper and his family, who were always so welcoming and indulgent to my children, especially around the candy counter, they hardly resemble the tormented characters in the novel."[2]

"One of the most flattering reactions to the book so far is the one from a lady who wrote to ask me whatever became of Jo's father, Eloy, after he escaped from prison. Well, I don't know what became of Eloy. I wonder myself.

"I think most writers know perfectly well when a book of theirs has honestly 'come off,' and must feel that their own delight and conviction in what they have accomplished will be infectious. And so most writers also know when they are resorting to flim-flam—either deliberately or because they can't do any better—and just hope and pray they can get away with it, or at least get well paid for it. So what a good critic really does is to hold the mirror up before the writer, but while he is eager to look into it, he already suspects what he is going to see. In other words, a writer can be his own most exacting critic, if he wants to take the trouble.

"Writing to me is still too much of a mysterious and exasperating process for me to know what I am going to do until I have done it. A perfectly alive and seemingly foolproof story will go dead right in the middle, for no reason. On the other hand, an insignificant incident will suddenly bring to life a whole new and exciting world. The genesis of *Little Jo* was no more than a glimpse of a very small, big-eyed boy, up to something he shouldn't have been, because he scurried away from me like a rabbit. Out of this grew a book which pleased me . . . . "[3]

"Besides *Little Jo,* I . . . published *The Intruders,* Doubleday 1946, about bigotry among doctors in a New Mexico large town; *The Olivers,* Doubleday 1947, about a very young daughter of a hedonistic [American] painter in a coastal town in Brittany; and *The Spirit of the Chase,* Scribners 1956, about the adventures of a young proper Bostonian, a collector, tracking down the whereabouts of a lost masterpiece. It is set in Paris and environs. All the novels did well except *The Olivers,* and were published in England by the Cresset Press. *Little Jo* [the book's English edition title] was translated into Hungarian, *The Intruders* into Norwegian, *The Spirit of the Chase* into Swedish and German. *The Intruders* had a paperback edition, and *Little Jo* an Armed Services Edition."[2]

"I intended to make a career as a novelist. But by the time I had published my third novel I realized that while I was gaining critical success I was not getting sufficient return to support a family. I had to be sensible, and, sensibly, I turned to writing and illustrating picture books for children whose imagination commanded my respect and affection. What I have tried to do in my books is to present fantasy in the way of good stories with interesting characters and lots of humor and fun but with no silliness. So much of fantasy is apt to be silly, but good fantasy is logical and true. It teaches without straining, and above all, it does not abuse the confidence of the reader. I like to think therefore that those who have been brought up and are still being brought up in part with my books may always look back with pleasure at the imaginary worlds to which these stories introduced them."[4]

"My specialty is picture books and I generally use acetate in two and three color separations, although I have done at least one book in four colors. I write all my own texts and generally do the layouts. I use no models and draw, not what I see, but what I feel I see. People who have watched me at work tell me that I smile as I draw. It is an indication of the pleasure and satisfaction I get from what I am doing."[5]

"In my writing I strive for lucidity and simplicity. My best writing is invariably spontaneous. I achieve form not by careful planning but by means of an original situation illustrated by long-thought-out characters. These persons are mostly entirely invented except as they have sometimes mingled traits of various living people or, more frequently, of myself. Once my characters are alive, the story almost writes itself. I can't rewrite without losing life. While each of my books is markedly different from the others, they all propound the idea that human beings are masters of their fate only in a most limited sense and that to imagine otherwise makes a man ludicrously presumptuous or pathetically and sometimes cruelly cynical. My strongest characters are those who have made their peace, innocently or wisely, with the inevitable—that is to say, with death, or with the fact that life is at best a noble or dignified tragedy."[6]

FOOTNOTE SOURCES

[1]Bertha M. Miller and others, compilers, *Illustrators of Children's Books: 1946-1956,* Horn Book, 1958.
[2]Robert Bright, *The Life and Death of Little Jo,* University of New Mexico Press, 1978.
[3]"The Life and Death of Little Jo," *Saturday Review of Literature,* February 26, 1944.
[4]D. L. Kirkpatrick, *Twentieth-Century Children's Writers,* St. Martin's, 1978.
[5]Lee Kingman and others, compilers, *Illustrators of Children's Books: 1957-1966,* Horn Book, 1968.
[6]Harry Warfel, *American Novelists of Today,* American Book, 1951.

FOR MORE INFORMATION SEE:

Saturday Review, February 12, 1944 (p. 7).
Newsweek, February 28, 1944 (pg. 94ff).
Muriel Fuller, editor, *More Junior Authors,* H. W. Wilson, 1963.
D. L. Kirkpartick, editor, *Twentieth-Century Children's Writers,* St. Martin's, 1983.

OBITUARIES

New York Times, December 3, 1988 (p. 33).
Washington Post, December 5, 1988.
Publishers Weekly, December 23, 1988 (p. 36).

CARRICK, Carol (Hatfield) 1935-

PERSONAL: Born May 20, 1935, in Queens, N.Y.; daughter of Chauncey L. and Elsa (Schweizer) Hatfield; married Donald Carrick (an artist), March 26, 1965 (died, June 26, 1989); children: Christopher, Paul. *Education:* Hofstra University, B.A., 1957. *Home:* High St., Edgartown, Mass. 02539.

CAREER: Coronet, New York, N.Y., staff artist, 1958-60; H. Allen Lightman (advertising agency), New York, N.Y., staff artist, 1960-61; free-lance artist, 1961-65; writer for children, 1965—.

AWARDS, HONORS: Children's Book of the Year Award from the Library of Congress, 1974, for *Lost in the Storm;* Children's Book Showcase from the Children's Book Council, 1975, for *Lost in the Storm,* 1976, for *The Blue Lobster,* and 1978, for *The Washout; Lost in the Storm* was selected one of Child Study Association of America's Children's Books of the Year, 1974, *The Blue Lobster,* 1975, *The Accident,* 1976, *A Rabbit for Easter* and *Some Friend!,* both 1979, *The Empty Squirrel* and *Ben and the Porcupine,* 1981, *What a Wimp!,* 1983, and *Beach Bird* and *Stay Away from Simon!,* both 1985; Outstanding Science Trade Book for Children from the National Science Teachers Association and the Children's Book Council, 1975, for *The Blue Lobster,* and 1980, for *The Crocodiles Still Wait;* New York Academy of Sciences Children's Science Book Award Junior Honor Book, 1975, and one of the Best Children's Books of the Season from *Saturday Review,* 1976, both for *The Blue Lobster;* Children's Choice from the International Reading Association and the Children's Book Council, 1975, for *The Blue Lobster,* 1978, for *Sand Tiger Shark,* 1979, for *Octopus* and *Paul's Christmas Birthday,* and 1982, for *The Empty Squirrel; The Crocodiles Still Wait* was selected one of *New York Times* Best Books of the Year, 1980; New York English-Speaking Union Books-across-the-Sea Ambassador of Honor Book, 1982, for *Ben and the Porcupine; Stay Away from Simon!* was selected one of *School Library Journal's* Best Books of the Year, 1985, and *What Happened to Patrick's Dinosaurs,* 1986; *Stay Away from Simon!* was selected one of New York Public Library's Children's Books, 1985; *What Happened to Patrick's Dinosaurs?* was selected one of *New York Times* Notable Books, 1986; California Young Readers

Carol and Donald Carrick

Medal from the California Reading Association, 1989, for *What Happened to Patrick's Dinosaurs?*

WRITINGS:

JUVENILE; ILLUSTRATED BY HUSBAND, DONALD CARRICK

The Old Barn, Bobbs-Merrill, 1966.
The Brook, Macmillan, 1967.
Swamp Spring, Macmillan, 1969.
The Pond, Macmillan, 1970.
The Dirt Road, Macmillan, 1970.
A Clearing in the Forest, Dial, 1970.
The Dragon of Santa Lalia, Bobbs-Merrill, 1971.
Sleep Out, Seabury, 1973.
Beach Bird, Dial, 1973.
Lost in the Storm, Seabury, 1974.
Old Mother Witch, Seabury, 1975.
The Blue Lobster: A Life Cycle, Dial, 1975.
The Accident, Seabury, 1976.
The Sand Tiger Shark, Seabury, 1977.
The Highest Balloon on the Common, Greenwillow, 1977.
The Foundling, Seabury, 1977.
Octopus, Seabury, 1978.
The Washout, Seabury, 1978.
Paul's Christmas Birthday, Greenwillow, 1978.
A Rabbit for Easter, Greenwillow, 1979.
Some Friend! (Junior Literary Guild selection), Houghton, 1979.
What a Wimp! (Junior Literary Guild selection), Clarion, 1979.
The Crocodiles Still Wait, Houghton, 1980.
The Climb, Clarion, 1980.
Ben and the Porcupine, Clarion, 1981.
The Empty Squirrel (Junior Literary Guild selection), Greenwillow, 1981.
The Longest Float in the Parade, Greenwillow, 1982.
Two Coyotes, Clarion, 1982.
Patrick's Dinosaurs, Clarion, 1983.
Dark and Full of Secrets, Clarion, 1984.
Stay Away from Simon!, Clarion, 1985.
What Happened to Patrick's Dinosaurs? (Junior Literary Guild selection), Clarion, 1986.
The Elephant in the Dark, Clarion, 1988.
Left Behind, Clarion, 1988.
Big Old Bones: A Dinosaur Tale, Clarion, 1989.
Aladdin and the Wonderful Lamp, Scholastic, 1989.
In the Moonlight, Waiting, Clarion, 1990.

Some of Carrick's books have been published in Swedish, Finnish, Danish, German, and Japanese.

ADAPTATIONS:

"The Accident" (videocassette), Barr Films, 1985.
"The Foundling" (videocassette), Grey Haven Films, 1986, (cassette), Houghton, 1990.
"Patrick's Dinosaurs" (cassette), Houghton, 1987.
"What Happened to Patrick's Dinosaurs?" (cassette), Houghton, 1988.
"Old Mother Witch" (videocassette), Phoenix, 1989.
"Sleep Out" (cassette), Houghton, 1989.
"Lost in the Storm" (cassette), 1990.

WORK IN PROGRESS: Banana Brew, a picture book depicting what life is like for the child of an alcoholic father: "The book is hopeful, but without easy answers." *Norman and the Tooth Fairy,* a humorous picture book about a child

Once he could grasp her harness, it was easy to sit astride her neck in the warm sun. (Illustration by Donald Carrick from *The Elephant in the Dark* by Carol Carrick.)

who tries to fool the tooth fairy before he has actually lost his first tooth; a picture book about American whaling.

SIDELIGHTS: Carol Carrick has written over thirty-seven books for children, all but one of which were illustrated by her late husband, Donald. "I met Don while working at *Coronet,* a *Reader's Digest*-type of magazine. I was working in sales promotion at the time, doing layouts and dummies of ads to help salesmen entice clients for potential ad space. For instance, when they wanted to show a liquor company how an ad would look, I would reduce it by using color photostats or drawing a rough form. When a really slick look was called for, they would hire a freelance artist. Don would come into the magazine occasionally to pick up art work, and one day he asked me out to lunch. The rest, as it goes, is history."

Although Carol Carrick grew up in Queens, New York, and Don in Michigan, she feels they had similar childhoods. "I think my husband and I grew up in the same kind of suburban neighborhood surrounded by woods, vacant lots, and trees. We both enjoyed the kind of life that doesn't exist much any more. I lived near a pond, and would bring tadpoles home and try to feed them. Today there are wonderful 'how to' books that instruct, but in those days I didn't know; I fed them bread, and they all died. I also kept baby turtles who wouldn't eat, either. My mother once gave me *Girl of the Limberlost* to read, about a girl who caught lunar moths. So I collected cocoons from the nearby woods and waited for them to hatch. Only a few of them did; I didn't realize that

they needed moisture and a certain temperature to incubate. Those early disappointments caused me a lot of grief, and prompted me to make my nature books as accurate as possible. Later, my children would have similar experiences, and I used some of them as the basis for books. *The Empty Squirrel,* for example, concerns a boy who nurses a fish back to health because his mother didn't want to cook it. That really happened to us.

"I travel a lot and don't see kids playing in the street as we did—boys and girls of all ages playing together in a very informal way. Today, kids play in organized leagues. If they're not crack ball players, they don't get up to bat. That really appalls me."

The Carricks' collaboration began with *The Old Barn.* "On our trip to Spain, a friend of Don's, Robert C. Goldston, asked my husband to illustrate a book on the Spanish Civil War. Don was basically a portrait and landscape painter, but he decided to do it. And then he did another, and another, for which he was paid by the illustration. The editors suggested that he write and illustrate picture books to get both the advance and royalties. Don didn't feel that he could write a book. In fact, neither one of us had looked at a children's book since we were children and didn't have a clue about how to begin. But it sounded like a good idea. Our friends let us use their house in Vermont for a month. Don started making sketches of a beautiful barn, and I started researching animals that lived in barns to write short texts to accompany his drawings. We were delighted when the editors accepted it."

So, Carol Carrick's career as author began quite accidentally. Her course of studies in school had been liberal arts. "I did not get the proper training to be a commercial artist, so it was very hard for me to get an art job when I graduated. Actually, I was almost totally unemployable in those days. In a career like advertising a woman had to start as a secretary to get an entry-level job. My skills were never good enough.

"I remember loving Raggedy Ann and Andy as a child. My mother read all of them to me. When I read them now, I think they're very sentimental and sticky. What I really liked about them were the illustrations, like those in *Raggedy Ann and Andy in Cookie Land.* I loved looking at those cookies with their shiny icing. And in *The Little Small Red Hen* it was the pictures not the stories that affected me as a child.

"I don't have a great sense of fantasy, so I never really thought of myself as a writer. After our first book I never believed there would be another one. As a matter of fact, I feel that every book is the last book for me. I still feel very unsure about it and remember that in those first days of living in New York, I didn't change the typewriter ribbon, even for the third, fourth, and fifth book. Later, when I invested in an electric typewriter and then a computer, it was always with the fear that now I might fail. That's a chronic problem of mine."

Neither school nor work prepared Carol Carrick for writing picture books, "but commercial art taught Donald color separation which he raised to a very high level. Most people don't realize that most of his illustrations were done in only three colors that he had to preseparate. Donald felt very limited with the process. First of all, you had to have a skin tone, or if the main character was an animal, you needed the specific color for that animal. In *Sand Tiger Shark,* for instance, if Don chose yellow and blue for water and sky, he would have no color for blood. Trying to make each book look different was a challenge. I feel very sad when I think

The dog galloped toward them. (Illustration by Donald Carrick from *Lost in the Storm* by Carol Carrick.)

about how much work it was for Don—doing over a hundred illustrations for every book. They absorbed so much of his time when he really could have been doing something more exciting.

"Donald was a person of very strong convictions and he didn't mind expressing them. He made a big distinction between painting and illustration. Painting, he felt, was under the artist's control while book illustration depended on the writer's words, the restrictions of subject matter, mood, and the very fact that you are doing it for children, although we never condescended to them. You don't have control of the size and shape of the drawings because you have to allow room for words. Then the whole thing is put into the printer's hands. In fact, Don was somewhat disappointed with the results until his last books which were in full color. Those particular books pleased him."

Donald Carrick looked for a greater range of projects. "Most of the books I wrote were about our family and the world around us, but he also wanted to do things that were more dramatic. So he accepted a lot of books from other writers because it offered opportunities to try something new. Mostly he was trying to break away, sometimes against better financial judgment—our books often sold more copies and were in print longer."

The Carricks worked out their own method of collaboration. "Actually, we didn't work together. Sometimes, we talked about an idea and I would say, 'Why don't we do a book about such and such?' and then he would agree or disagree. But we didn't sit side by side and work together on a project. I would show him a draft of my manuscript, because I respected his opinion. But he didn't work on a book until I sold the manuscript. Then he would make a mental time slot for the illustrations and on request from the editor, he'd make a dummy of the book."

Patrick was afraid to move. Out of the corner of his eyes he saw the big thing swimming along next to them. It might rise and dump them over!

"WHAT'S THAT!" he cried. "We're going to bump into it!"

"No, dopey. That's just the shadow from our boat," Hank explained.

Patrick wasn't so sure. "Let's go home now," he said. "Rowing makes me tired."

(From *Patrick's Dinosaurs* by Carol Carrick. Illustrated by Donald Carrick.)

A stickler for accuracy, Carol Carrick recalled the research the two did for the first books. "When we did *Swamp Spring,* we went to a number of swamps and took pictures. I would say, 'Well, we need a picture of skunk cabbage,' and he would take the photograph as research. We worked together in that sense."

Carol Carrick's artistic training was not for naught. She is admittedly a visual author and in particular visualized those earlier books which bore little text. "We didn't consider ourselves professional book people. I thought of my husband as a landscape painter, that's why I chose swamps, ponds, and brooks. I'd think, 'Well, this project about a brook is going to have thirteen and a half illustration spreads, so I've got to come up with thirteen things about a brook.' One could be the beginning trickle of water, another could be water flowing into a pond, and another could be a waterfall. I thought and wrote visually. There was no real story line. The book might begin with the source of the brook and finish where the brook ended, but I didn't know how to make a plot."

"The 'Dinosaur' books were the most fun. *What Happened to Patrick's Dinosaurs?* probably wrote itself more than any other book I've done. *Patrick's Dinosaurs* came about from researching Dinosaur books and my difficulty in visualizing a real dinosaur. I wanted to conjure up for kids what they really were like, and the only way to do that was to put the dinosaur in a contemporary setting."

Their own children made childhood alive for them. "My kids served more of a function in allowing me to be around children and hear their language, know what they liked and didn't like, see how they played, and feel their emotion. I would read them the manuscript to see if they understood it. I think all writers would profit by reading their work aloud because you hear the mistakes, falseness, ennui, or repetition."

But she admits, however, that one child is not representative of all children. "Our oldest son was very skinny and had a big head of hair. So if you look at Don's pictures of that period, the children have little hands and feet and big heads. Then when our other son of average build and a little heavier came along, the kids in Don's drawings began to take on little pot bellies and became a little stockier.

"I can't really think of anything I've written that's directly related to my own childhood, outside of the fact that I always felt like an outsider and a lot of my books like, *What a Wimp!* and *Some Friend!* are about kids who are not popular." *Stay away from Simon!,* set in the nineteenth century dealt with the idea of misfits. "I wrote that book because I was out of ideas and it was crisis time. My sons were getting older and I really didn't know what was going on in their lives. If I had had a daughter, I probably would have gone into writing a teenage book because she would have rekindled things from my childhood. Since children's books stay in print a long time its hard to keep them sounding contemporary. I wanted mine to have a more timeless quality so I tried setting them in an earlier period. Since I like to understand my material I read all I could about early American life. That's how I wrote *Stay Away from Simon!,* with Simon, again, as an outsider."

Writing about certain periods of time also presented obstacles for Carrick's meticulous nature. "I can never get enough research. I did a book called *The Elephant in the Dark* which takes place around 1800, and I never learned all I wanted to about training elephants. There aren't a lot of journals in that period. If I wanted to start with Will getting up in the morning, I had to think, 'Well, what did they eat then? What

(From *What Happened to Patrick's Dinosaurs?* by Carol Carrick. Illustrated by Donald Carrick.)

did they wear? Did they cook in a fireplace or in a stove?' But all those little necessities of daily life gave me the ideas for the plot.

"When I complain to my friend who is a romance writer about how I've been researching one of my books for a year, she tells me I shouldn't be worrying about that stuff, that if I'm writing 'The Princess went to the ball,' I don't have to know what kind of coach it was. But *I* feel that I do have to know that, and how many footmen it had, and what breed of horses pulled the carriage, and what kind of harnesses they wore, and how many seats the coach had, and if it had springs. I would want to write about how it felt, how it sounded, and how it smelled.

"Writing, for me, is like giving blood and I don't mean somebody draining it out through a tube in my arm. I mean that they prick my finger and squeeze it out drop by painful drop."

The loss of her husband to cancer in 1989 left Carrick with a professional as well as personal loss. "After Don was diagnosed with terminal cancer, he worked on Jim Latimer's book, *When Moose Was Young,* and had at least four more books to do at the time of his illness. I think he hoped that he would be able to do them all. He would go out to work on this happy little book, and every day he could do less and less. Sometimes, when I could see the mark on his forehead, I knew that he had fallen asleep at his drawing board.

"Donald was skilled at drawing a wide range of subjects: children, nature, humor. To find somebody else who can do all of those things is unlikely.

"I hope some of my future writing will have the fantasy element I developed with the two 'Patrick's Dinosaur' books, or the poetry of *In the Moonlight, Waiting,* or our early nature books. I find those styles wonderfully liberating. Working in longer formats has also freed me up a bit, and I find that those books give me the space to develop feelings from my own soul."[1]

FOOTNOTE SOURCES

[1]Based on an interview by Marc Caplan for *Something about the Author.*

FOR MORE INFORMATION SEE:

Doris de Montreville and Elizabeth D. Crawford, editors, *Fourth Book of Junior Authors and Illustrators,* H. W. Wilson, 1978.
Junior Literary Guild, September, 1979, March, 1981, April/September, 1986, April/September, 1988.
Children's Literature in Education, Volume 11, number 3, 1980.

COLLECTIONS

Kerlan Collection at the University of Minnesota.

SOUPS AND JUICES

Did you hear about my big brother?
The lucky stiff is sick.
All day they bring him soups and juices.
When he calls, they come running.
They keep puffing his pillow.

I'm supposed to stay out
but tonight I peeked in.
He was asleep.
The dumb kid
kicked off his blankets
so I went and covered him up.
He looked *small*.

(From *Secrets of a Small Brother* by Richard J. Margolis. Illustrated by Donald Carrick.)

CARRICK, Donald 1929-1989

PERSONAL: Born April 7, 1929, in Dearborn, Mich.; died of cancer, June 26, 1989, in Edgartown, Mass.; son of Fay and Blanche (Soper) Carrick; married Carol Hatfield (a writer), March 26, 1965; children: Christopher, Paul. *Education:* Attended Colorado Springs Fine Art Center, 1948-49, Art Students League, 1950, and Vienna Academy of Fine Art, 1953-54. *Residence:* Edgartown, Mass.

CAREER: Artist; author and illustrator of children's books. *Military service:* U.S. Army, 1950-51.

AWARDS, HONORS: The Buffalo King, Tor, and *The City in All Directions* were each selected one of Child Study Association of America's Children's Books of the Year, 1969, *The Cuban Revolution,* 1970, *The Tree* and *Journey to Topaz,* 1971, *Peter and Mr. Brandon,* and *Bear Mouse,* 1973, *Lost in the Storm,* 1974, *The Blue Lobster* and *Grizzly Bear,* 1975, *Wind, Sand and Sun, The Deer in the Pasture,* and *The Accident,* 1976, *The Blue Horse and Other Night Poems, A Rabbit for Easter,* and *Some Friend!,* 1979, *The Empty Squirrel* and *Ben and the Porcupine,* 1981, *What a Wimp!,* 1983, and *Beach Bird* and *Stay Away from Simon!,* 1985; New York Society of Illustrators Award, 1970, for *The Pond,* and 1971, for *The Tree;* Irma Simonton Black Award from Bank Street College of Education, 1973, for *Bear Mouse,* and 1986, for *Doctor Change; New York* was included in the American Institute of Graphic Arts Children's Book Show, 1970, and *Bear Mouse,* 1973-74; Children's Book Showcase selection

from the Children's Book Council, 1974, for *Bear Mouse,* 1975, for *Lost in the Storm,* 1976, for *The Blue Lobster,* and 1978, for *The Washout;* Children's Book of the Year from the Library of Congress, 1974, for *Lost in the Storm.*

Outstanding Science Trade Book for Children from the National Science Teachers Association and the Children's Book Council, 1975, for *The Blue Lobster,* and 1980, for *The Crocodiles Still Wait;* Best of the Season from *Saturday Review,* 1975, for *The Blue Lobster;* Children's Choice from the International Reading Association and the Children's Book Council, 1975, for *The Blue Lobster,* 1978, for *Sand Tiger Shark,* 1979, for *Octopus, Paul's Christmas Birthday,* and *Tawny,* 1982, for *The Empty Squirrel,* and 1985, for *Secrets of a Small Brother* and *Dark and Full of Secrets;* Children's Science Book Award Junior Honor Book from the New York Academy of Sciences, 1976, for *The Blue Lobster; Tawny* was selected one of *New York Times* Outstanding Books of the Year, 1978; *The Crocodiles Still Wait* was selected one of *New York Times* Best Books of the Year, 1980; New York English-Speaking Union Books-across-the-Sea Ambassador of Honor Book, 1982, for *Ben and the Porcupine; Alex Remembers* was selected one of New York Public Library's Children's Books, 1983, and *Stay Away from Simon!,* 1985; *More Alex and the Cat* was selected one of *School Library Journal*'s Best Books of the Year, 1983, *Stay Away from Simon!,* 1985, and *What Happened to Patrick's Dinosaurs,* 1986.

Christopher Award, 1985, for *Secrets of a Small Brother; What Happened to Patrick's Dinosaurs?* was selected one of

New York Times Notable Books, 1986; California Young Reader's Medal from the California Reading Association, 1989, for *What Happened to Patrick's Dinosaurs?*

WRITINGS:

SELF-ILLUSTRATED

The Tree, Macmillan, 1971.
Drip Drop, Macmillan, 1973.
The Deer in the Pasture, Greenwillow, 1976.
Harald and the Giant Knight (Junior Literary Guild selection), Clarion, 1982.
Morgan and the Artist, Clarion, 1985.
Milk, Greenwillow, 1985.
Harald and the Great Stag (Junior Literary Guild selection), Clarion, 1988.

ILLUSTRATOR; ALL WRITTEN BY WIFE, CAROL CARRICK

The Old Barn, Bobbs-Merrill, 1966.
The Brook, Macmillan, 1967.
Swamp Spring, Macmillan, 1969.
The Pond, Macmillan, 1970.
The Dirt Road, Macmillan, 1970.
A Clearing in the Forest, Dial, 1970.
The Dragon of Santa Lalia, Bobbs-Merrill, 1971.
The Sleepout, Seabury, 1973.
Beach Bird, Dial, 1973.
Lost in the Storm, Seabury, 1974.
Old Mother Witch, Seabury, 1975.
The Blue Lobster: A Life Cycle, Dial, 1975.
The Accident, Seabury, 1976.
Sand Tiger Shark, Seabury, 1977.
The Highest Balloon on the Common, Greenwillow, 1977.
The Foundling, Seabury, 1977.
The Octopus, Seabury, 1978.
The Washout, Seabury, 1978.
Paul's Christmas Birthday, Greenwillow, 1978.
A Rabbit for Easter, Greenwillow, 1979.
Some Friend! (Junior Literary Guild selection), Houghton, 1979.
What a Wimp! (Junior Literary Guild selection), Clarion, 1979.
The Crocodiles Still Wait, Houghton, 1980.
The Climb, Houghton, 1980.
The Empty Squirrel (Junior Literary Guild selection), Greenwillow, 1981.
Ben and the Porcupine, Clarion, 1981.
The Longest Float in the Parade, Greenwillow, 1982.
Two Coyotes, Greenwillow, 1982.
Patrick's Dinosaurs, Greenwillow, 1983.
Dark and Full of Secrets, Greenwillow, 1984.
Stay Away from Simon!, Clarion, 1985.
What Happened to Patrick's Dinosaurs? (Junior Literary Guild selection), Greenwillow, 1986.
The Elephant in the Dark, Clarion, 1988.
Left Behind, Clarion, 1988.
Big Old Bones: A Dinosaur Tale, Clarion, 1989.
Aladdin and the Wonderful Lamp, Scholastic, 1989.
In the Moonlight, Waiting, Clarion, 1990.

ILLUSTRATOR

Robert Goldston, *The Civil War in Spain* (*Horn Book* honor list), Bobbs-Merrill, 1966.
R. Goldston, *The Russian Revolution*, Bobbs-Merrill, 1966.
R. Goldston, *The Rise of Red China*, Bobbs-Merrill, 1967.
R. Goldston, *The Life and Death of Nazi Germany*, Bobbs-Merrill, 1967.

R. Goldston, *The Great Depression: The United States in the Thirties*, Bobbs-Merrill, 1968.
R. Goldston, *London: The Civic Spirit*, Macmillan, 1969.
R. Goldston, *Barcelona: The Civic Stage*, Macmillan, 1969.
Ernestine Byrd, *Tor: Wyoming Bighorn*, Scribner, 1969.
Arnold Adoff, editor, *City in All Directions: An Anthology of Modern Poems*, Macmillan, 1969.
R. Goldston, *The Cuban Revolution*, Bobbs-Merrill, 1970.
R. Goldston, *New York: Civic Exploitation*, Macmillan, 1970.
R. Goldston, *Suburbia: Civic Denial*, Macmillan, 1970.
Lee McGiffin, *Yankee Doddle Dandies*, Dutton, 1970.
Nancy Veglahn, *The Buffalo King: The Story of Scotty Philip*, Scribner, 1971.
Yoshiko Uchida, *Journey to Topaz*, Scribner, 1971.
Berniece Freschet, *Turtle Pond*, Scribner, 1971.
B. Freschet, *Bear Mouse*, Scribner, 1973.
Eleanor Schick, *Peter and Mr. Brandon*, Macmillan, 1973.
David Budbill, *The Christmas Tree Farm*, Macmillan, 1974.
B. Freschet, *Grizzly Bear*, Scribner, 1975.
Rebecca Caudill, *Wind, Sand and Sky*, Dutton, 1976.
Nathan Zimelman, *The Walls Are to Be Walked* (Junior Literary Guild selection), Dutton, 1977.
Joanne Ryder, *A Wet and Sandy Day*, Harper, 1977.
Chas Carner, *Tawny*, Macmillan, 1978.
Siv Cedering Fox, *The Blue Horse and Other Night Poems*, Seabury, 1979.
Betty Baker, *Latki and the Lightning Lizard*, Macmillan, 1979.
Helen R. Haddad, *Truck and Loader*, Greenwillow, 1982.
Helen V. Griffith, *Alex Remembers* (Junior Literary Guild selection), Greenwillow, 1983.
H. V. Griffith, *More Alex and the Cat* (Junior Literary Guild selection), Greenwillow, 1983.
Richard J. Margolis, *Secrets of a Small Brother*, Macmillan, 1984.
Marlene F. Shyer, *Here I Am, an Only Child*, Scribner, 1985.
Johanna Hurwitz, *Yellow Blue Jay*, Morrow, 1986.
Joanna Cole, *Doctor Change*, Morrow, 1986.
J. Hurwitz, *Bunkmates*, Scholastic, 1987.
Eve Bunting, *Ghost's Hour, Spook's Hour* (Junior Literary Guild selection), Clarion, 1987.
William H. Hooks, *Moss Gown*, Clarion, 1987.
Joan Hewett, *Rosalie*, Lothrop, 1987.
Jim Latimer, *Going the Moose Way Home*, Scribner, 1988.
Steven Kroll, *Big Jeremy*, Holiday House, 1989.
E. Bunting, *The Wednesday Surprise*, Clarion, 1989.
J. Latimer, *When Moose Was Young*, Scribner, 1990.

ADAPTATIONS:

"The Accident" (videocassette), Barr Films, 1985.
"The Foundling" (videocassette), Grey Haven Films, 1986.
"Patrick's Dinosaurs" (cassette), Houghton, 1987.
"What Happened to Patrick's Dinosaurs?" (cassette), Houghton, 1988.
"Sleep Out" (cassette), Houghton, 1989.
"Old Mother Witch" (videocassette), Phoenix, 1989.
"Lost in the Storm" (cassette), Houghton, 1990.
"The Foundling" (cassette), Houghton, 1990.
"Moss Gown" (cassette), Houghton, 1990.
"Ghost's Hour, Spook's Hour" (cassette), Houghton, 1990.

SIDELIGHTS: See Carrick, Carol.

(From *Doctor Change* by Joanna Cole. Illustrated by Donald Carrick.)

FOR MORE INFORMATION SEE:

Martha E. Ward and Dorothy A. Marquardt, *Illustrators of Books for Young People,* Scarecrow, 1975.
Doris de Montreville and Elizabeth D. Crawford, editors, *Fourth Book of Junior Authors and Illustrators,* H. W. Wilson, 1978.
Lee Kingman and others, compilers, *Illustrators of Children's Books: 1967-1976,* Horn Book, 1978.

OBITUARIES

Vineyard Gazette, June 27, 1989 (p. 1)
New York Times, July 3, 1989 (p. 11).
Boston Globe, July 4, 1989 (p. 17).
Publishers Weekly, July 28, 1989.
School Library Journal, August, 1989 (p. 28).
Horn Book, September-October, 1989 (p. 686).

COLLECTIONS

Kerlan Collection at the University of Minnesota.
Mazda Collection.
Pennsylvania Academy of the Fine Arts, Philadelphia, Pa.

CRABTREE, Judith 1928-

PERSONAL: Born September 23, 1928, in Melbourne, Australia; daughter of Frank Richard (a professor of economics) and Nora (a high school teacher; maiden name, Bowls) Mauldon; married Peter Crabtree (a teacher), December 12, 1954; children: Rowena Crabtree Cowan, Jonathan. *Education:* University of Western Australia, B.A., 1954; Associated Teachers' Training Institution, Certificate of Education, 1967. *Home:* 12 Bath Rd., Burwood, Victoria 3125, Australia.

JUDITH CRABTREE

CAREER: High school English and history teacher in Melbourne, Australia, 1965-79; Council of Adult Education Melbourne, teacher of writing and illustrating children's books, 1979—; writer. *Member:* Australian Society of Authors, Victorian Fellowship of Australian Writers. *Awards, honors:* Australia Council Literature Board Senior Fellowship, 1981; Critici in Erba Prize Honorable Mention, 1989, for *Song at the Gate.*

WRITINGS:

JUVENILE

Emily Jean and the Grumphfs, Wren Publishing, 1975.
Carolyn Two, Wren Publishing, 1975.
Nicking Off (self-illustrated), Wren Publishing, 1975.
The High Rise Gang (self-illustrated), Penguin Australia, 1979.
Legs (self-illustrated), Penguin Australia, 1979, Oxford University Press, 1983.
The Sparrow's Story at the King's Command (self-illustrated), Oxford University Press, 1983.
Stolen Magic (self-illustrated), Oxford University Press, 1983.
Song at the Gate (self-illustrated), Oxford University Press, 1987.
Night of the White Geese (self-illustrated), Oxford University Press, in press.

OTHER

Skins and Shells and Peelings (young adult novel), Highland House, 1979.

Author of short stories for educational publications.

ADAPTATIONS:

"The Sparrow's Story at the King's Command" (video), Reva Lee Studios, 1985.

SIDELIGHTS: "For the past few years I have worked with primary school children at writing and illustration workshops that are part of a government-funded Artists in the Community Program. I also give talks on my own working methods and the creative writing and illustration approach that I adopt when I am working with children.

"The new approach to the teaching of reading and writing, the 'Literature Scheme' whereby high calibre picture story books and junior novels are used as 'readers' and models for creative writing, has the obvious financial spin-off for the writer and illustrator guest speaker. But perhaps the best spin-off comes from 'plugging into the source,' connecting the child mind within with the magical minds of children—a marvellously energizing meeting.

"Since I began writing and illustrating fantasy stories, I have frequently been asked if I would ever consider writing for adults. My answer has always been the same. When all the universal human concerns can be woven into tales that are simple, yet endlessly varied, resonant and rich in dramatic imagery, what more could a writer-illustrator wish for?

"The best fairy tales are always allegorical. Like poetry, they are models of conciseness and address issues of the greatest importance in a form that gives clarity and vision. They are as timeless and as placeless as 'Once there was . . .' can be, and they appeal to old and young and everybody in between.

"But for me the greatest beauty of these stories is in those omissions that give them their universality, those gaps through which the reader is drawn into inner spaces that give room to intuition and creative dreaming. When a story is complete in all its details, it leaves the reader still confined within the familiar and the commonplace self. In contrast, the gaps in an allegory are byways into the reader's creative self and beyond it.

"In my last book and in the one I am working on now, I have left some incidents not fully explained and have used in my illustrations recurring images not mentioned in the text and not essential to the story line. I believe that both of these devices can give stories greater resonance, if not deeper meaning.

"When children write to ask for explanation of my stories, I hand on the ones given to me by children I have worked with. Many of their accounts are surprisingly close to my own, and even when they aren't, they are still useful because they make the story richer and more satisfying to those who give them. Some of these accounts express violence and anger, but these are feelings that the kindly fairy tale can comfortably encompass.

"Sometimes a child will ask a question with another wrapped inside it like a nighty under an overcoat.

"A year after *The Sparrow's Story* was published, my editor sent on to me a letter from the United States. It contained what seemed a simple question in large, uncertain capital letters that climbed across an otherwise blank page. IS THE SPARROW BOOK TRUE JUDITH CRABTREE.

"No punctuation, no signature. The name 'Caitlin' and an address in California had been printed neatly in an adult hand on the back of the envelope, and that was all.

"I took her question very seriously and mulled it over for most of the day. But how did I tell a five-year-old that what I value—my story—I make real, for me; that in valuing it, I'm giving my belief to it and so making it my truth, and that in this sense I choose, and make, my own 'true?'

"But it seemed obvious that this wasn't the sort of 'true' she had meant, and that if meant merely in the way that the stone and the toes it stubbed are true, then the sparrow's tale is not. But in my sense of true, without a doubt it is. And didn't she want *my* answer?

"I left the question for a while and listened closely for an inner one. It was faint, but decidely there.

"'Did the sparrow *really* die? Are you *quite* sure? Is it possibly *not* true?'

"Perhaps she was too young or too anxious to see possibilities the story already offered. Or perhaps she was asking me to lead her to options. My picture story books are rabbit-holed with them. An incident is not fully explained, a recurrent picture image is ignored in the text, a happening that is shown is not accounted for. There are holes enough for creative dreamers to enter the story and shape it to the truth they choose for it. They have sent me these stories. The few who ask me to fill the holes for them are either waiting permission to enter them or are too well taught that 'truth' is merely what you stub your toe on.

"As I listened to Caitlin's inner whisper, I realized that neither question was concerned with toes and stones. ('Did the sparrow *really* die? Are you *sure?* Is it possibly *not* true?') She was telling me that she valued the story and so had already given it truth—my sort of truth—but the shape I had given it had made her anxious, that she wanted to take it and make the shape her own.

"So I knew at last how to answer.

"Dear Caitlin,

"I have thought a lot about your question and this is what I want to tell you.

"The story didn't happen in *this* place, in our world. But it did happen in another place, in another world, in the world where fairy tales happen. This world is a real and true world. I know because I have been there many times. What the sparrow did there was brave and beautiful. And what is brave and beautiful is always true for everywhere, in all worlds.

"Some people in the sparrow's world say the sparrow didn't die. They say that three dark birds took him from the box and carried him to the forest where the storyteller waited.

"Some children who have read the book also tell me this is what happened.

"Do you think it did?'"

HOBBIES AND OTHER INTERESTS: Bush walking, meditating with trees, handcrafts, reading children's books.

FOR MORE INFORMATION SEE:

Marcie Muir, *A History of Australian Childrens' Book Illustration,* Oxford University Press, 1982.
Belle Alderman and Stephanie Owen Reeder, editors, *The Inside Story: Creating Childrens' Books,* Canberra Childrens' Book Council of Australia, 1987.
Jeffrey Prentice and Bettina Bird, *Dromkeen: A Journey into Childrens' Literature,* Dent (Melbourne), 1987.
Margaret Dunkle, editor, *The Story Makers: A Collection of Interviews with Australian and New Zealand Authors and Illustrators for Young People,* Oxford University Press, 1987.
Robert Holden, *Koalas, Kangaroos and Kookaburras: 200 Australian Childrens' Books and Illustrations, 1857-1988,* James Hardie Industries, 1988.
Walter McVitty, *Authors and Illustrators of Australian Childrens' Books,* Hodder & Stoughton, 1989.

CROWELL, Robert L(eland) 1909-

PERSONAL: Born May 11, 1909, in Montclair, N.J.; son of Thomas Irving (a publisher) and Minnie Helen (a housewife and suffragette; maiden name, Leland) Crowell; married Ruth Brown Shurtleff, December 23, 1938 (divorced, 1966); married Muriel B. Hutchinson (a writer and artist), December 19, 1967; children: (first marriage) John Leland, Timothy Adams, Benjamin Shurtleff (deceased). *Education:* Yale University, A.B., 1931. *Politics:* Independent. *Religion:* Society of Friends (Quakers). *Home address:* P.O. Box 92, Newfane, Vt. 05345.

ROBERT L. CROWELL

CAREER: Thomas Y. Crowell Co. (publisher), New York, N.Y., sales manager, 1933-37, president, 1937-72, treasurer, 1937-60, chairman of board of directors, 1960-68, principal executive officer, 1968-72, member of board of directors, 1972-79; writer, 1974—. Member of board of directors of Franklin Publications, 1952-63, treasurer, 1958-63; member of board of directors of Dun-Donnelley Corp., 1972-74; member of board of governors of Yale University Press, 1952-67; past member of board of trustees of Brattleboro Museum and Art Center and Marlboro College. U.S. State Department lecturer in India, 1957; member of U.S. Information Agency advisory committee on books abroad, 1952-63.

MEMBER: American Civil Liberties Union (past member of board of directors), American Schools of Oriental Research (past member of board of directors), American Book Publishers Council (past member of board of directors), Archaeological Institute of America (past member of board of directors), Moore Free Library Association (member of board of trustees), Century Association. *Awards, honors:* Grant from the U.S. State Department, 1957; *The Lore and Legend of Flowers* was selected one of Child Study Association of America's Children's Books of the Year, 1982.

WRITINGS:

The Lore and Legends of Flowers (ALA Notable Book; illustrated by Anne Ophelia Dowden), Crowell, 1982.
Historic Newfane Village: The Houses and the People, Moore Free Library, 1989.

WORK IN PROGRESS: Editing the diaries of a forebear who was captain of sailing ships and served in the Civil War.

SIDELIGHTS: "Four years ago the little village in which I live became a historic site and I decided to write its history from 1825 to the present. This meant reading old deeds, letters, newspaper notes, diaries and documents. I talked with dozens of people. The book tells about the architectural styles of the fifty-eight historic structures here, and the lives of the people who lived here. It is really a picture of nineteenth century life.

"Another hobby is responsible for *The Lore and Legends of Flowers*—gardening. My mother taught me to love flowers and I have been gardening since. My father taught me to love the woods, and each year since 1938 I have ordered seedling trees and planted them. The total of 'my' trees would be in the thousands."

HOBBIES AND OTHER INTERESTS: "Besides gardening, tree planting, and fixing up old houses, I love woodworking and I love to study. I dabble in languages left over from school and college: a few modern languages and Latin and Greek."

DANZIGER, Paula 1944-

PERSONAL: Born August 18, 1944, in Washington, D.C.; daughter of Samuel (worked in garment district) and Carolyn (a nurse; maiden name, Seigel) Danziger. *Education:* Montclair State College, B.A., 1967, M.A. *Residence:* New York City and Bearsville, N.Y. *Agent:* Donald C. Farber, 99 Park Ave., New York, N.Y. 10016.

CAREER: Substitute teacher, Edison, N.J., 1967; Title I teacher, Highland Park, N.J., 1967-1968; junior-high school English teacher, Edison, N.J., 1968-1970; Lincoln Junior

PAULA DANZIGER

High School, West Orange, N.J., English teacher, 1977-1978; full-time writer, 1978—. Worked for the Educational Opportunity Program, Montclair State College, until 1977.

AWARDS, HONORS: New Jersey Institute of Technology Award, and Young Reader Medal Nomination from the California Reading Association, both 1976, Massachusetts Children's Book Award, first runner-up, 1977, winner, 1979, and Nene Award from the Hawaii Association of School Librarians and the Hawaii Library Association, 1980, all for *The Cat Ate My Gymsuit;* one of Child Study Association of America's Children's Books of the Year, 1978, Massachusetts Children's Book Award from the Education Department of Salem State College, 1979, Nene Award, 1980, California Young Reader Medal Nomination, 1981, and Arizona Young Reader Award, 1983, all for *The Pistachio Prescription;* Children's Choice from the International Reading Association and the Children's Book Council, 1979, for *The Pistachio Prescription,* 1980, for *The Cat Ate My Gymsuit,* and *Can You Sue Your Parents for Malpractice?,* 1981, for *There's a Bat in Bunk Five,* and 1983, for *The Divorce Express.*

New Jersey Institute of Technology Award, and selected one of New York Public Library's Books for the Teen Age, both 1980, and Land of Enchantment Book Award from the New Mexico Library Association, 1982, all for *Can You Sue Your Parents for Malpractice?;* Read-a-Thon Author of the Year Award from the Multiple Sclerosis Society, and Parents' Choice Award for Literature from the Parents' Choice Foundation, both 1982, Woodward Park School Annual Book Award, 1983, and South Carolina Young Adult Book Award from the South Carolina Association of School Librarians, 1985, all for *The Divorce Express;* CRABbery Award from Prince George's County Memorial Library System (Md.), 1982, and Young Readers Medal, 1984, both for *There's a Bat in Bunk Five;* Parents' Choice Award for Literature from the Parents' Choice Foundation, exhibited at the Bologna International Children's Book Fair, and selected one of Child Study Association of America's Children's Books of the Year, all 1985, all for *It's an Aardvark-Eat-Turtle World.*

WRITINGS:

YOUNG ADULT NOVELS

The Cat Ate My Gymsuit (Junior Literary Guild selection), Delacorte, 1974.
The Pistachio Prescription, Delacorte, 1978.
Can You Sue Your Parents for Malpractice?, Delacorte, 1979.
There's a Bat in Bunk Five, Delacorte, 1980.
The Divorce Express, Delacorte, 1982, large print edition, G. K. Hall, 1988.
It's an Aardvark-Eat-Turtle World, Delacorte, 1985.
This Place Has No Atmosphere, Delacorte, 1986, large print edition, ABC-CLIO, 1989.
Remember Me to Harold Square, Delacorte, 1987.
Everyone Else's Parents Said Yes, Delacorte, 1989.

ADAPTATIONS:

"The Cat Ate My Gymsuit" (cassette), Listening Library, 1985, (filmstrip with cassette), Cheshire, 1985.
"The Pistachio Prescription" (cassette), Listening Library, 1985.
"There's a Bat in Bunk Five" (cassette), Listening Library, 1985.
"Can You Sue Your Parents for Malpractice?" (cassette; teacher's guide available), Listening Library, 1986.

Matthew Martin can be very organized and accurate when he wants to be. (Jacket illustration by Joe Csatari from *Everyone Else's Parents Said Yes* by Paula Danziger.)

"The Divorce Express" (cassette; teacher's guide available), Listening Library, 1986.

WORK IN PROGRESS: Sequel to *Everyone Else's Parents Said Yes,* tentatively titled *Mischief Is My Middle Name.* "I've written a third-person narrative. All my previous books are first-person. My protagonist, an eleven-year-old boy, is also a departure because most of my main characters have been girls. Writing third person was fun, a new experience. It allowed me to be more descriptive and to have a larger perspective.

"There's a book I've been wanting to do for a number of years called *Pardon My Two Left Wheels.* Its protagonist, a girl, is confined to a wheelchair. I know it will be difficult for me, as I've spent a lot of time with braces, casts, and crutches myself. But I want this to be a funny book, because laughing helps us survive adversity. The main theme I'll be exploring is the ways in which people relate and identify with abilities and disabilities. An ex-editor gave me some great advice regarding this protagonist: 'Make sure she has pimples.' And he's right, everyone who's thirteen has pimples, why shouldn't she? Because she's in a wheelchair?"[1]

SIDELIGHTS: Paula Danziger is one of the best-selling authors for young adults currently working in the United States, perhaps most widely known for *The Cat Ate My*

Gymsuit. Her characters tend to be good-hearted 'outlaws' rebelling against rigid and confused parents, dictatorial school systems and unhappy social situations.

"My life as an author began as a small child when I realized that was what I wanted to do and started mentally recording a lot of information and observations. That's also when I started to develop the sense of humor and the sense of perspective that allows me to write the way I do.

"Technically, I suppose that many people would say that I began my career as an author when I signed the contract for my first book in 1973 for *The Cat Ate My Gymsuit.*

"For years I had nightmares about the small Pennsylvania town in which I spent a substantial part of my childhood. We rented a farmhouse, unlikely as that sounds, because my mother was afraid of everything on the farm. I seem to remember that my brother and I were not allowed to touch anything, and were not encouraged to spend a lot of time outside—weird for kids living on a farm. I felt very isolated and buried myself in books. For the first time I realized that my family was hardly 'The Brady Bunch,' that, in fact, my

Now I know what the sportscasters mean when they talk about the agony of the feet. (From *Remember Me to Harold Square* by Paula Danziger.)

parents were very unhappy and that our family functioned with difficulty.

"On some level I knew I'd grow up to be a writer, especially when my father yelled at me, I'd think, 'That's fine, I'll use this in a book someday.' My favorite game was something I called the Dot Kingdom. By connecting dots, I created all the people, dogs and houses in the kingdom. If I got angry with a character, I'd erase him. Quite a power trip—creating a whole world over which I had absolute control.

"Thank goodness for the local librarian. She gave me lots of wonderful books to read and generally let me know she cared. I devoured one book after another—*Nancy Drew, Sue Barton, Cherry Ames, The Hardy Boys,* all the landmark books.

"My family moved back to New Jersey. I'd been raised to believe that I was not particularly bright, not college material. My father's refrain was, 'Paula can be a secretary.' I certainly have nothing against secretaries, except that I never wanted to be one. Family dynamics were such that I fell into fulfilling their low expectations. 'I'm not supposed to be smarter than my father, so why try,' was my thought. I wrote off-beat features for the school newspaper and a column in the town newspaper. Someone was noticing that I wasn't a total idiot.

"I think I read *Catcher in the Rye* every day for the three years I was in high school. It set me free. It told me that I wasn't alone. Other books important to me were *Pride and Prejudice, Wuthering Heights, A Tree Grows in Brooklyn, Marjorie Morningstar.*

"I desperately wanted to go to college—maybe a state teachers college. Years later I discovered that I was accepted into a special program for kids who didn't work up to their potential.

"Not surprisingly, the town librarian was important to me. One of my college projects was to find an 'average' child and do a study on him or her. The librarian put me in touch with poet John Ciardi's son, who in fact was quite brilliant. My study led to babysitting jobs with the family and attending Breadloaf Writers Conferences with them for several summers. This was no typical *au pair* situation—the kids were not supposed to bother me if I wanted to go to a lecture or a party. I used to spend Christmas with the family. The Ciardis were very special to me.

"John Ciardi taught me more than anyone else about poetry and writing. Their house was full of books, and I borrowed liberally from the shelves. I tried to read e.e. cummings' *anyone lived in a pretty how town* with no success at all. Ciardi taught its meaning to me. It was the best lesson I've ever had in my life. He read the poems and explained them, giving me a sense of language structure.

"During my third summer with the family, I came home from a party one night and Ciardi and I talked for a long, long time. Finally I got up the courage to ask him if he thought I'd ever become a writer someday. 'No, your ego's not strong enough,' was his response. Years later we laughed over the conversation."[1]

Danziger's first book, *The Cat Ate My Gymsuit,* dedicated to John Ciardi, was published in 1974. "I wrote this book in therapy, bringing newly-drafted pages to many appointments. I'd been in a very serious car accident and writing *Cat*

(Cover illustration by Robert Chronister from *This Place Has No Atmosphere* by Paula Danziger.)

was part of my coming back. The accident— actually there were two—was very freaky. In the first, I was hit from behind by a policeman and knocked into an intersection. The whiplash was immediate, but the damage took a couple of days to appear. As the pain became more severe, my mother drove me to a doctor's appointment. En route, we were hit head-on by another car and I was thrown into the windshield, cut my face and sustained some temporary brain damage. I lost the ability to read. Eventually I entered a master's program in reading. I could write backwards—a perfect mirror image of normal writing. I had recurring nightmares about the accidents and functioned with a great deal of difficulty. My feelings of helplessness and terror dredged up a lot of material from my childhood. It was time for therapy.

"*The Cat Ate My Gymsuit* is in some ways my angriest and most autobiographical book. Like Marcy, I was a fat kid who hated her father and was frustrated with her mother. My editor would say, 'Paula, the father is too one-dimensional. No father would say that to a daughter.' I'd reply, 'Wanna bet?' I don't think the father is a complete monster. Toward the end of the sequel, *There's a Bat in Bunk Five,* particularly after his heart attack, he became more sympathetic and Marcy has to confront her fear of losing him.

"I handed a set of galleys of *Cat* to my father and said, 'Daddy, I love you.' I hardly ever called him Daddy since growing up, always Sam. His reading the book made an enormous difference in our relationship.

"An important letter I've received from a reader was in response to *The Cat Ate My Gymsuit.* When I was a child, I used to ask my parents if I was adopted. And my mother, understanding the implications of my question, would respond with 'No, I love you and your father loves you.' I used those lines in *Cat.* Well, one of my reader's, who had adopted children, let me know that out of context, the lines were quite devastating in a way I had not intended. From all subsequent editions of the book, I had those lines deleted. I wrote back to her, and she answered that she was the one who was upset, not her children. Through a misunderstanding, I had caused hurt, and I didn't like that. I felt good about the revision."[1]

The Cat Ate My Gymsuit garnered its fair share of favorable reviews, and Danziger likes to point out that fifteen years after its original publication it's still going strong. But the approbation—as with all her books—has not been unanimous. "I once wrote an article, 'Why I Will Never Win the Newbery.'"[1]

Perry Nodelman, writing in *Children's Literature in Education,* finds fault with what he discerned as the willful 'typicality' of the book. "In *The Cat Ate My Gymsuit,* readers find

I hate my father. I hate school. I hate being fat.
(From *The Cat Ate My Gymsuit* by Paula Danziger.)

You'd think that by the twenty-first century someone would have invented a zit zapper. (Jacket illustration by Joe Csatari from *This Place Has No Atmosphere* by Paula Danziger.)

out many things about Marcy Lewis, her family, her appearance, and her attitudes. But interestingly enough, not one of these details is unusual or surprising; none of them separates Marcy from the vast sea of theoretically typical teenage girls we all assume exists somewhere outside our immediate acquaintance in towns we have never visited.

"In carefully avoiding distinguishing details, *The Cat Ate My Gymsuit* prevents our consciousness of otherness. In fact, we cannot possibly understand the story unless we fill in its exceedingly vague outlines with knowledge from our own experience. Marcy Lewis has no life unless we give it to her; her town and her school have no physical substance unless we provide it. The book demands, not distance, but involvement."[2]

"I basically don't listen to critics very much. I listen to my editor and to friends whose opinions I trust. If I were to define myself according to what reviewers said about my work, I'd be in deep trouble. I am aware that certain critics have said my books are 'light.' I know that certain critics have been discomforted by my sense of humor and the attention I pay to controversial matters: the Holocaust, the homeless, divorce, bi-racial kids, and so on. Sometimes I really wonder; a number of reviewers don't seem to like kids or books. Why do they do what they do?

"I don't like reviewers who don't seem to have a clear idea of the kids who will be reading the books, or I don't like reviewers who are more concerned about what they write, rather than what they read. There have been reviews that I think are good, not necessarily because they say that my books are great (although I do like those a lot), but those who offer constructive criticism, where I can learn something about becoming a better writer. I also like reviews that are written by someone that I know is a good writer. Anne Tyler once reviewed one of my books. I was so excited because I love her books and because she wrote a good review.

"I was autographing books at the American Library Association Convention and people were *actually* lining up for my signature. A librarian called out, 'I'm not going to stand in line, but I'll tell you one thing, regardless of what I may think of your books, the kids would kill me if I don't order them.' And that is what matters to me that the kids like my books, and that my books touch their lives and make them feel less alone. They are the best gauge."[1]

"If when we start to write we say, 'I'm going to teach them this,' rather than tell the story we care about, we're in trouble. But when we're telling [the story], again it comes back, for me, to survival—when we're talking about what I do, survival with a sense of humor and a sense of compassion. In [*Remember Me to Harold Square*] there's a chapter on the Holocaust. The book is set in New York City, and the kids are very affected by what they see at the Jewish Museum. I cried a lot [while I wrote] that; I cry a lot when I deal with, when I feel anything about the Holocaust. And when the kids started to talk about all the injustices that go on in the world today . . . I felt that very strongly. So personally, I feel that . . . it's important for that to be in books, for us to be witnesses. I go back to that feeling of being witnesses in a way and also, again, saying that we are survivors. So if that's bibliotherapy, I do care about it."[3]

"I get so tired of the question, 'So when are you going to do your adult book?' As though I've just been practicing all these years to become 'good enough' to write for grown-ups. One of my ex-teachers even said, 'Still writing kiddie-lit?' Children are unarguably the most important members of society—they are the future. And they can be very tough critics, particularly as they are often forced to deal with problems of their parents' making. Kids of divorces go through hell with feelings that are raw and often confused as their lives are turned upside down. Children of divorce often say they feel alone in the midst of chaos. For anyone who has ever felt alone—and who hasn't, in truth—a book can make a very good friend. Like a good friend, a book can help you see things a little more clearly, help you blow off steam, get you laughing, let you cry.

"There is a widespread misconception that it is easier to write for young people than for adults. It is not. Ask any children's or young adult writer. All writers write from deep experience. For me, that is childhood. From it flow feelings of vulnerability, compassion, and strength. Perhaps it would be better to say that I write 'of' young people rather than 'for' or 'to' them. Writers tell the best stories we possibly can, hopefully in ways that others will like. And how many books intended for a so-called specific audience are read by many age groups, generation after generation? But I must say, kids are very picky readers. They know what they like, and won't be 'conned.' They know what's authentic and what is not. If a book doesn't work for them, they chuck it no matter what the reviewers might have to say. And it is the responsibility of librarians, teachers and parents to respond to the needs of kids, not to critics. The 'dialogue,' if we may call it that, is between the writer and the reader. Reading is, after all, a deep and intimate experience.

"Young adult books are in no way marginal in terms of the commercial arena. In fact, YA books comprise the lion's share of publishers' backlists. That is to say, our sales not only justify promotion efforts on our behalf, but foot the bills for other, less marketable genres—a source of pride for those of us who write young adult books.

"It's much more enjoyable—and fruitful—to talk about writing. Our society suffers keenly from a media glut, and as an author I must say it is distressing that reviews so often become a focal point in conversations about books. Reviews are usually written within a few days, or a few hours. A book can take years. That sort of long-term, rather solitary, concerted effort deserves to be more highly valued than it currently is in our society.

"Some of the most important things I've learned about writing come from an acting course I once took. Also, Dr. Jerry Weiss once suggested I read Uta Hagen's *Respect for Acting,* which for me is still a 'Bible' for writing. Hagen lays out an acting system based on sense memory which allows an actor to know almost everything about the character. By following these sense memory exercises, the actor comes to know far more about the character than appears even between the lines of the play. I do sense memory work as a preparation for writing. I imagine what a character's closet

(Jacket illustration by Richard Lauter from *The Divorce Express* by Paula Danziger.)

might look like. For me stories begin with character rather than plot, so for a book to hang together, the characters must be fully imagined.

"Being a teacher was absolutely an influence on my writing life. In the early books, some of the incidents came from real situations that happened in my classes. Some of my characters did the same things that my students did (like crazy-gluing down desks, saying things like 'I cried all the way through the movie "Gone with the Wind," and someone stole my popcorn.') I also spent a lot of time listening to my students and their concerns about appearance, parents splitting up, fighting in the family, dating, school pressures, and tried to include a lot of that in my writing.

"I still spend a lot of time in classrooms. Sometimes I go to a school and speak for the day. As much as I like doing that, it doesn't give me the chance for real dialogues with the kids. So there are some places where I spend more time: a week in Columbus, Georgia, a week in Providence, Rhode Island, a couple of days in Los Angeles, a week at the American International School in Budapest, Hungary.

"Every once in a while, I think about going back to teach full time for a year. I miss working with the kids, but I don't miss the faculty meetings, taking attendance, and grading papers. I'm also not great about getting papers back on time. My strength as a teacher was that I really cared about kids, books and creativity. I enjoy working with teachers who work with kids, showing an easy technique I use to teach in creative writing.

"Ideas for books come to me all the time. But before I can sit down and start writing, I have to have lived with the idea for quite a while."[1]

Danziger's books carry dedications and grateful acknowledgements to a host of people. "I have a circle of several extraordinarily insightful friends to whom I read draft pages over the phone. They give me their reactions, comments and suggestions. I also read books in progress to kids, who tend to be excellent critics. Rewrites and revisions are an integral part of my process on every book. So is hysteria.

"But writing is terrific in some ways. I get a lot of sensual enjoyment from the act of writing. The feel of felt-tip pens against the paper, the movement of my hand making the letters, the look of all those marks across the page—even the way the keyboard feels.

"I do notice that my work has changed over the years. In the beginning there was a lot of anger, and the humor was more biting. The books have softened somewhat, which does not displease me. On the contrary. Writing has taught me that one can work through painful feelings and happenings, then let go of them. I think my characters have gradually become less neurotic and self-centered, and more sensual. My favorite character is Rosie from *The Divorce Express.* She dresses and thinks the way I do and sees things others often don't. This is not to say we're identical—Rosie, the product of a mixed marriage, is black, white, Protestant and Jewish while I am only white and Jewish. But Rosie has a certain light and fire that I think represents the best part of me. Phoebe, who becomes Rosie's stepsister, gave me a lot of trouble. She is so angry throughout the book that she can hardly see or speak the truth. I know about that kind of anger from experience. Originally while writing, I found myself not liking Phoebe, which of course made the work even harder. Once I changed the narrator to Rosie, it was easier to write about Phoebe.

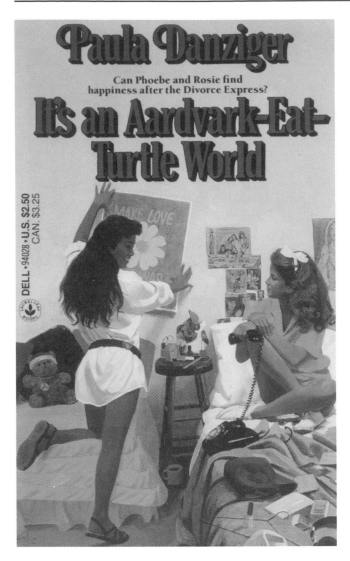

If a Prince Charming or a Prince Semi-Charming came up to my door and said, "Rosie Wilson, you are the most beautiful, individualistic fourteen-year-old in the universe," I certainly wouldn't slam the door in his face. (Jacket illustration by Hooks from *It's an Aardvark-Eat-Turtle World* by Paula Danziger.)

"I favor characters who are 'outlaws,' who want to find their own voices and their own way of looking at things. Mindy and Phoebe's father are two characters of whom I'm particularly fond. They go their own ways, able to operate without imposed structures, and have made difficult choices in order to do so. They're the gentlest of outlaws and nurture gentleness and sensitivity in their kids.

"My least favorite characters are Phoebe's mother and Marcy's father, both of whom are overly concerned with playing by the rules, not making waves, and creating a good impression. They exert a stifling influence, each in their own way.

"I've also dealt more and more with place. In *The Divorce Express,* for example, Woodstock, New York is rendered in great detail. I loved how the sights, sounds, scents, not to mention mores of the place had permeated my consciousness, and were there for me in the writing. And in *Remember Me to Harold Square,* New York City is as much a character as any

of the people in the story. The city, is filled with history, culture, ethnic and culinary variety, as well as plain old *fun.*

"A question frequently asked female authors is, 'Do you like to be referred to as a woman writer?' I'm a writer first, I have to say that. But I am a woman, and the two go together. It disturbs me to think of a hard-and-fast division between men who write and women who write. My mother's friend once said to me, 'I don't read girl writers.' I would hope that men and women would read men and women. I do consider myself a feminist and take a very strong stand on women's rights. But I also take a strong stand on the rights of girls, boys and men. There are so many struggles, so many fights to be fought: world peace, the environment, basic freedoms, education, opportunity and health care for everyone. We must stand together."[1]

Danziger is still a voracious reader. "It's gratifying that there are so many excellent writers at work today. I hesitate to begin a list of my favorites, for I'm certain I won't remember them all. Jane Austen is terrific. What a great sense of humor. I love Anne Tyler. Her characters are spun all around you. *A Mother and Two Daughters,* by Gail Godwin, is a most powerful book. Toni Morrison is a writer whose work I revere, particularly *The Bluest Eye.* Among those who write

The weekend at last. (From *Can You Sue Your Parents for Malpractice?* by Paula Danziger.)

for children and young adults, I admire Judy Blume for her gutsiness and spunk. E. L. Konigsberg's books are intelligent, elegant and diverse. Francine Pascal's novels and Lois Lowry's are also favorites.

"Writing is a lot more fun now that living is, because I know I'm going to survive. I have survived. I've got the equipment. I'm not fragile.

"I've been thinking a lot about comedy lately. In order to be really funny, I think one has to have a certain way of looking at things. It's about turning pain and anger into constructive laughter. I don't like the kind of humor that makes fun of other people, the kind that is mean spirited. (Although in my books, I do have things that aren't kind, the sort of things that brothers and sisters say to each other. It wouldn't be realistic not to include that.)

"At a Breadloaf Writer's Conference, John Ciardi taught a poem called 'Love Poem' by John Frederick Nims. Ciardi said that if you took the funny lines and underlined them in red and the serious lines and underlined them in blue, by the end of the poem, the lines would be purple. I've never forgotten that. I think there is so much in life that is hard and sad and difficult and that there is so much in life that is fun and joyous and funny. There's also a lot of in between those two extremes. As a writer, I try to take all of those things and put them together. That way people can say 'I know that feeling' and identify with it. My major ability as a writer, hopefully, is to tell a good honest story and let people laugh when it is appropriate.

"Of course my other ambition is to be a stand-up comic. But I have trick knees and can't stay up too late."[1]

FOOTNOTE SOURCES

[1]Based on an interview by Marguerite Feitlowitz for *Something about the Author.*
[2]Perry Nodelman, "How Typical Children Read Typical Books," *Children's Literature in Education,* winter, 1981.
[3]Paula Danziger, "Writing for Children," *PEN Newsletter,* September, 1988.

FOR MORE INFORMATION SEE:

New York Times Book Review, March 18, 1979, June 17, 1979, November 16, 1980, December 23, 1980.
New Yorker, December 3, 1979.
Los Angeles Times Book Review, July 25, 1982.
Contemporary Literary Criticism, Volume 21, Gale, 1982.
Washington Post Book World, May 12, 1985.
Alleen Pace Nilsen and Kenneth L. Donelson, *Literature for Today's Young Adults,* 2nd edition, Scott, Foresman, 1985.
Guardian, August 12, 1987.
School Library Journal, March, 1989 (p. 120ff).

COLLECTIONS

Kerlan Collection at the University of Minnesota.

DESAI, Anita 1937-

PERSONAL: Born June 24, 1937, in Mussoorie, India; daughter of D. N. (an engineer) and Toni (a teacher; maiden name, Nime) Mazumdar; married Ashvin Desai (an executive), December 13, 1958; children: Rahul, Tani, Arjun,

Kiran. *Education:* Delhi University, B.A., 1957. *Address:* c/o Hind Pocket Books, G. T. Rd., Shahdara, New Delhi 32, India. *Office:* Rogers, Coleridge & White, 20 Powis Mews, London W11 IJN, England.

CAREER: Writer, 1946—. Member of Advisory Board for English, Sahitya Akademi, New Delhi, India, 1972—. *Member:* Royal Society of Literature (fellow). *Awards, honors:* Winifred Holtby Award from the Royal Society of Literature (London), and Indian Academy of Letters Award, both 1978, both for *Fire on the Mountain;* Booker-McConnell Prize nomination, 1980, for *Clear Light of Day,* and 1984, for *In Custody; Clear Light of Day* was selected one of New York Public Library's Books for the Teen Age, 1981, and 1982; Guardian Award for Children's Fiction, 1983, for *The Village by the Sea; Hadassah* Award, 1989, for *Baumgartner's Bombay;* Taraknath Das Foundation Award, 1989, for enhancing understanding between the United States and India; Padma Shri Award, 1989, from the Government of India.

WRITINGS:

JUVENILE

The Peacock Garden, India Book House, 1974.
Cat on a Houseboat, Orient Longmans, 1976.
The Village by the Sea: An Indian Family Story, Heinemann, 1982, Harper, 1983, large print edition, Chivers Press, 1983.

NOVELS; UNLESS INDICATED

Cry, the Peacock, P. Owen, 1963.
Voices in the City, P. Owen, 1965.
Bye-Bye, Blackbird, Hind Pocket Books, 1968.
Where Shall We Go This Summer?, Vikas Publishing House, 1975.

ANITA DESAI

ANITA DESAI
The Village by the Sea
An Indian Family Story

The sand was washed clean by last night's tide. (From *The Village by the Sea: An Indian Family Story* by Anita Desai.)

Fire on the Mountain, Harper, 1977.
Games at Twilight and Other Stories (short stories), Harper, 1978.
Clear Light of Day, Harper, 1980.
In Custody, Harper, 1984.
Baumgartner's Bombay, Knopf, 1988.

The Village by the Sea is available in Braille. Contributor of short stories, book reviews, and articles to periodicals, including *Thought, Envoy, Writers Workshop, Quest, Indian Literature, Illustrated Weekly of India, Femina, Harper's Bazaar, New York Times Book Review, Washington Post Book World, New Republic,* and *Spectator.*

SIDELIGHTS: "Although my family was not a particularly literary one, there were a great many books in the house and we were all bookworms. What was important was that we had an immense amount of time and privacy in that large, quiet, very private house with its huge, half-wild garden in a quiet part of Old Delhi, in which to read and dream. As soon as I was taught the alphabet in the mission school to which I was sent—since it was run by English missionaries, I was taught English before Hindi—I went home and started to write, wanting passionately to create books of my own and so belong to the world of books that I loved. I wrote and illustrated stories and stitched them into books; later these were expanded into full-length novels. I started contributing to children's magazines when I was nine or ten, then wrote for adult magazines.

"After I graduated from college, I joined the Writers Workshop in Calcutta. We met on Sunday mornings and read our work to each other, again in the desire to belong to the writers' world. All this time I was working on a novel and in 1963, when I was a young married woman and a mother, had my first novel published by an English publisher who specialized in foreign and unknown authors. Later my books were taken up by larger publishing firms.

"I grew up in a home where three languages were spoken together—Hindi, English and German—but English was my literary language—the one I read and wrote in. I am grateful for that because it opened to me the literature of the world and I made myself at home in it and was not restricted to any one region. I read Russian and French and German literature in English and, of course, the English classics—fiction to begin with, then biography and finally, more and more, poetry.

"English seems to me the most flexible of languages, the most adaptable, capable of taking on the tones and resonances of any part of the world, and my effort is to convey the rhythms, accents, tones, and pace of Indian life in that language. More than that, to convey the inner life through outer images and metaphors, and find some balance between the two, and a harmony. Also, to dispel the notion that fiction is untruth and lies, because I believe literature and art really contain the essence of life and the world, uncover its innermost secrets and present those truths that one might ordinarily miss or ignore, and so is closer to the truth than life itself."

FOR MORE INFORMATION SEE:

K. R. Srinivasa Iyengar, *Indian Writing in English,* Asia Publishing House, 1962.
Paul Verghese, *Indian Writing in English,* Asia Publishing House, 1970.
Meena Bellioppa, *The Fiction of Anita Desai,* Writers Workshop, 1971.
Meenakshi Mukherjee, *The Twice-Born Fiction,* Heinemann, 1972.
New York Times Book Review, November 20, 1977.
Contemporary Literary Criticism, Gale, Volume 19, 1981, Volume 37, 1986.

EMERSON, Kathy Lynn 1947-
(Kaitlyn Gorton)

PERSONAL: Born October 25, 1947, in Liberty, N.Y.; daughter of William Russell (a manager) and Theresa Marie (a beautician; maiden name, Coburg) Gorton; married Sanford Merritt Emerson (in law enforcement), May 10, 1969. *Education:* Bates College, A.B., 1969; Old Dominion University, M.A., 1972. *Politics:* Independent. *Religion:* Protestant. *Home:* P.O. Box 156, Wilton, Maine 04294. *Agent:* Lettie Lee, Ann Elmo Agency, 60 East 42nd St., New York, N.Y. 10165.

CAREER: Tidewater Community College, Portsmouth, Va., instructor, 1972-73; Franklin County Community Action Program, Wilton, Me., tutor and counselor, 1974-75; Wilton Academy, Wilton, language arts teacher, 1975-76; free-lance writer, 1976—; University of Maine at Farmington, library assistant, 1979-85, lecturer, 1985-87. Presents lectures and workshops at schools and libraries. *Member:* Society of Children's Book Writers, Mystery Writers of America, Romance Writers of America.

WRITINGS:

YOUNG ADULT NOVELS

The Mystery of Hilliard's Castle, Down East, 1985.
Julia's Mending, Orchard Books, 1987.
Someday, Cora Verlag, 1990.
The Mystery of the Missing Bagpipe, Avon, 1991.

JUVENILE BIOGRAPHY

Making Headlines: A Biography of Nellie Bly, Dillon, 1989.

OTHER

Wives and Daughters: The Women of Sixteenth Century England, Whitston, 1984.
(Under pseudonym Kaitlyn Gorton) *Cloud Castles,* Silhouette, 1989.

Contributor of articles and stories to periodicals, including *Highlights for Children, Primary Treasure, D.A.R., Renaissance Studies,* and *Notes on Teaching English.*

KATHY LYNN EMERSON

Julia gripped the small book so tightly that her fingertips made little pockmarks in its soft brown-leather cover. (Jacket illustration by Toby Gowing from *Julia's Mending* by Kathy Lynn Emerson.)

WORK IN PROGRESS: An adult mystery novel; several historical novels, some for children and some for adults, including one gothic.

SIDELIGHTS: "I grew up in Sullivan County, New York, where my family settled in 1793, and inherited a dual interest in genealogy and writing from my grandfather, Fred 'Scorcher' Gorton. Grampa penned his memoirs when he was in his eighties, paying special attention to stories from his boyhood in what was then called Strongtown. After I sold a short story, 'Runaway,' based on one of his experiences, I decided to try a novel set in the period when he was growing up.

"*Julia's Mending* is fiction, but Julia's broken leg is treated just as Grampa's was when he fell through the hay hole in his father's barn at age five. In those days people didn't know much about emergency medical care. My great-grandfather, Nathaniel Gildersleeve Gorton, carried his son to the house just as Gil Tanner does Julia, with no idea he might be making the injuries worse. Many other incidents in the novel are based on Grampa's memoirs too, and on stories about his contemporaries. The maternal side of my family tree is represented as well, contributing both character names and the story of the lost Indian lead mine. My great-grandfather Hornbeck once had a map but never located the actual mine.

"Grampa Gorton told me once that he wanted 'some noted writer' to use his life story as the basis for a book. I think he had Ernest Hemingway or John Steinbeck in mind, but I hope he'd be pleased with *Julia's Mending.* "My favorite historical period is the sixteenth century, in which I have set several unsold adult novels. For younger readers I've been working on books set in 1643, 1922, and 1947. The 1880s have provided background for *Julia's Mending,* the biography of Nellie Bly, and *Century to Century* (in progress) which takes place at a living history center.

"If there is any single theme running through my work, it concerns the dangers of jumping to conclusions about people. My protagonists frequently must learn to be more open-minded and fight unintentional prejudices they discover within themselves."

HOBBIES AND OTHER INTERESTS: History, genealogy, cats.

FOR MORE INFORMATION SEE:

Linda L. Sudlow, compiler, *Notable Maine Children's Authors and Illustrators,* Maine State Library, 1989.

FRANK, Josette 1893-1989

OBITUARY NOTICE—See sketch in *SATA* Volume 10: Born March 27, 1893, in New York, N.Y.; died of pneumonia, September 9, 1989, in Alexandria, Va. Consultant, administrator, lecturer, editor, and author. Frank, an expert on children's literature, began her longtime position as director of children's books and mass media for the Child Study Association of America in 1923. She gave frequent lectures and wrote and edited several books in her field, including *Your Child's Reading Today, Poems to Read to the Very Young,* and *Television: How to Use It Wisely with Children.* Frank oversaw the publication of other children's books, including editions of J. M. Barrie's *Peter Pan and Wendy,* Anna Sewell's *Black Beauty,* and Lewis Carroll's *Alice in Wonderland.* She also acted as a consultant for radio and television programming, and served on the book selection committee for the National Conference of Christians and Jews and the National Committee for Program Services of the Campfire Girls.

FOR MORE INFORMATION SEE:

OBITUARIES

New York Times, September 14, 1989.
School Library Journal, November, 1989 (p. 21).
Contemporary Authors, Volume 129, Gale, 1990.

GANTNER, Susan (Verble) 1939-

PERSONAL: Born March 13, 1939, in San Francisco, Calif.; daughter of Henry and Cecily (Jones) Verble; married John Gantner (a lawyer), 1968; children: Benicia, Florence. *Education:* University of California, B.A., 1961, attended Art Institute, Berkeley Campus, 1962-63. *Religion:* Unitarian. *Home and office:* 140 Jordan Ave., San Francisco, Calif. 94118. *Agent:* Toni Mendez, 141 East 56th St., New York, N.Y. 10022.

CAREER: Art teacher, 1965-79; Creative Workshop, San Francisco, Calif., owner, 1968-79; Jordan Press (greeting card company), San Francisco, artist, 1970—. *Exhibitions:* Jean Miller Gallery, San Francisco, Calif., 1972.

ILLUSTRATOR:

Judy Taylor, *Sophie and Jack,* Bodley Head, 1980, Philomel, 1983.
Stephanie Calmenson, *Where Is Grandma Potamus,* Grosset, 1981.
S. Calmenson, *The Birthday Hat,* Grosset, 1981.
J. Taylor, *Sophie and Jack Help Out,* Bodley Head, 1982, Philomel, 1984.
J. Taylor, *Sophie and Jack in Snow,* Bodly Head, 1983.
Carol Greene, *The Insignificant Elephant,* Harcourt, 1985.
J. Taylor, *Sophie and Jack in Rain,* Bodley Head, 1989.

SIDELIGHTS: "I grew up in California and lived in Fresno until I went off to college. I come from a large family and at one time I counted forty first cousins. We went to Sierra, Nevada all summer and my sisters had cousins the same age. Somehow there was not a cousin my age and I was alone a great deal. I painted for hours and copied playing cards. I never went anywhere without a set of watercolors.

"When I was in the fourth grade my teacher, Miss Geodan said 'Susan you are an artist!' She let me draw a mural about early California for the Fresno County Fair. In any case, I never wavered in my career choices—they were always in the arts. I taught children for years and when I became pregnant myself, I drew hippos doing human things. I used to give these drawings as baby presents. Partal Publications saw one of these and asked me to design twenty greeting cards. I did and they were very popular. Since the cards were distributed nationally I began to receive many requests from publishers.

SUSAN GANTNER

Judy Taylor, the children's editor at Bodley Head in England, was the first inquiry and we did a book together without ever meeting. *Sophie and Jack* was very popular in Europe and was picked up by Philomel in New York. After *Sophie and Jack* came other books and then *The Insignificant Elephant.* I have never written a story and desperately need the *words* so I can illustrate. I consider myself a painter and never seem to have time to paint in oils as I used to do. I have two daughters, Benicia, currently at Bowdoin College and Florence, on her way to college. They are a great help to me.

"I have been painting out-of-doors. The longer I live in California the more I realize how rich and varied the landscape is. One can go twenty miles north, east, and west and be at the sea, the mountains and the gentle countryside. I enjoy painting California landscapes in watercolor."

GAUL, Randy 1959-

PERSONAL: Born November 28, 1959, in Pittsburgh, Pa.; son of Louis M. (a businessman) and Joanne (a secretary; maiden name, Hartnett) Gaul; married Doretta Ruzzier (a teacher), July 2, 1983. *Education:* Pratt Institute, B.F.A. (cum laude), 1981. *Home and office:* 2079 Ostwood Terrace, Maplewood, N.J. 07040.

CAREER: Free-lance illustrator, 1981-84; woodworking teacher in New York, N.Y., 1983-87; furniture maker and carpenter, Maplewood, N.J., 1987—. *Exhibitions:* Pratt Institute Gallery, New York, N.Y., 1980-81; Creative Corners Gallery, 1985. *Member:* Shotokan Karate Club, Manhattan Beach Volleyball Team. *Awards, honors: Coming-and-Going Men* was selected one of Child Study Association of America's Children's Books of the Year, 1986.

ILLUSTRATOR:

Paul Fleischman, *Coming-and-Going Men: Four Tales,* Harper, 1985.

Also illustrator of *Devils Race.* Contributor of illustrations to periodicals.

SIDELIGHTS: "Most of my illustrating career was between 1980-84. Within those years I supported myself with illustration and teaching. My feelings about those years are mostly positive. I have had much more work published in magazines, however. Drawing is still one of my greatest loves and I do still find some time to do it. These days are spent building furniture and doing contracting work. My recent interests are beginning to turn towards woodworking and the natural aesthetic beauty of wood."

GILL, Stephen 1932-

PERSONAL: Born June 25, 1932, in Punjab, India; son of Matthew (in the military) and Christina (a teacher) Gill; married Sarala (a college teacher), February 17, 1970; children: Rekha, Ajay, Sarita. *Education:* Punjab University, B.A., 1956; Agra University, M.A., 1963; attended University of Ottawa, doctoral program, 1967-70 and Oxford University, 1971. *Religion:* Christian. *Home address:* P.O. Box 32, Cornwall, Ontario, Canada K6H 5R9.

STEPHEN GILL

CAREER: Writer. Has taught in India, Ethiopia and Canada; editor for *Canadian World Federalist,* 1971-73, 1977-79; editor and publisher of *Writer's Lifeline,* 1982—. *Member:* Canadian Authors Association (president of Cornwall branch, 1977-78); Canadian Society of Children's Authors, Illustrators and Performers; Educational Press Association of America; World Academy of Arts and Culture; United Poets Laureate International; PEN (Canada); Canadian Poetry Association; International Academy of Poets (fellow); Co-ordinating Council of Catalyst 87 Clubs of Canada E; Movement for Political World Union in Canada; World Federalists of Canada (vice-president, 1979-81); Indo-Asian Association of Cornwall (vice-president, 1986); Multicultural Council of Stormont and Dundas (vice-president, 1987). *Awards, honors:* Ontario Graduate Fellowship, 1968, 1969, 1970; Honorary Doctorate in Literature from World University, 1986, for distinguished achievements as a writer; Volunteer Service Award from the Ministry of Citizenship and the Ministry of Culture and Communication, 1989; Honorary Doctorate in Literature from the World Academy of Arts and Literature, 1990, for devotion to writing and the literary field.

WRITINGS:

JUVENILE

(Editor) *Tales from Canada for Children Everywhere* (anthology), Vesta, 1979.
Simon and the Snow King, Vesta, 1981.
The Blessings of a Bird (illustrated by Asoka Weerasinghe), Vesta, 1983.

OTHER

English Grammar for Beginners, S. Chand (India), 1966, Vesta, 1977, third edition, 1982.

Six Symbolist Plays of Yeats, S. Chand, 1968, Vesta, 1978.

Life's Vagaries: Fourteen Short Stories, Vesta, 1974.

(Compiler with Frank Tierney) *Poets of the Capital* (anthology), Borealis, 1974.

(Editor with Roland C. Hamel) *Seaway Valley Poets* (anthology), Vesta, 1975.

The Discovery of Bangladesh (history), Venton, 1975.

Scientific Romances of H. G. Wells: A Critical Study, Vesta, 1975, 2nd edition, 1977.

Why?: A Novel, Vesta, 1976.

(Editor) *Green Snow: Anthology of Canadian Poets of Asian Origin,* Vesta, Volume I, 1976, Volume II, 1988.

Reflections and Wounds (poems; illustrated by Barbara Yerxa), Vesta, 1978.

The Loyalist City (novel), Vesta, 1979, reissued, 1988.

Sketches of India (essays), Vesta, 1980.

Political Convictions of G. B. Shaw, Vesta, 1980.

Immigrant: A Novel, Vesta, 1982, revised edition, 1989.

(Editor) *Anti-War Poems* (anthology), Vesta, Volume 1, 1984, Volume 2, 1986.

Moans and Waves and Other Poems, Vesta, 1989.

The Dove of Peace (poems), M.A.F. Press, 1989.

The Flowers of Thirst (poems), Vesta, 1990.

(Editor) *Who's Who of North American Poets,* Vesta, 1990.

Contributor of numerous articles and poems to periodicals, including *Journal of Modern Literature, Books in Canada, Calcutta Review, Literary Half-Yearly, Canadian World Federalist, Ottawa Journal, Quill & Quire, Christian Science Monitor, India, International Journal on World Peace, Sandesh,* and *Canadian India Times.*

WORK IN PROGRESS: A Critical Study of Canadian Poets of Asian Origin, an evaluation; *An Inquiry into World Peace.*

SIDELIGHTS: "I have often been asked why, how, and when I became a writer, and I have always said 'go and ask any flower why it spreads its fragrance around,' or 'ask the moon why it delights people with its silvery beams,' or 'ask the birds why they sing early in the morning.' It is like asking me why I breathe. It may be a compulsion or a deep desire to share my ideas, knowledge and experiences with others. I don't know the answer in a simple and straightforward way. However, when I began going deep within me to analyze this question, I started sensing that it may be a touch of my parents which has shaped me as a writer.

"My mother was a school teacher and a good storyteller. She was very particular about our education and, therefore, gave special attention to our regular attendance at school and tried her utmost to keep us away from the influence of the children who were disinterested in their studies. My father, a good bread-earner, edited a religious magazine for a while and was unusually interested in writing letters.

"Yet, I hated school and played truant whenever I could. I hated my curriculum and classroom, but that does not mean that I hated books. Rather, I loved to read anything, except the text books. I loved to read, especially fiction. Our home was full of books, and my father was a zealous subscriber to several dailies and monthlies. In that environment, I became a voracious reader from my early childhood. When nothing was available, I would borrow or buy materials to satisfy my

thirst. This habit remained a part of me for my whole life. I read the *Bible* several times.

"In the later part of my teens, I began to move among writers and would-be writers; nearly all of them were older than I was. Some of them had published material to their credit. Our chats often ended in discussing literary topics, and I always listened attentively to their comments on a story, a poem, or an author. I still cherish some of their ideas.

"Due to my unusual zest for books and the protective nature of my mother, which kept me away from other children, I became lonely which helped to sharpen my thinking and imagination. I never felt loneliness because I enjoyed dwelling in the domain of my fancy, like Simon who dreams of the Snow King and his castle.

"My aloofness during my childhood and later, to some extent, in my teens, may be largely responsible for my feeling ill-at-ease in a dialogue when I am alone with a stranger. I am reasonably relaxed when I give a talk or a lecture to a crowd and more so when I am behind a public-address system.

"It may be a factor that has affected my writing in one area at least. A reader may not be able to detect it. I am not reluctant to admit that I find it difficult to develop a conversation in a story between two or more characters. I have to do much thinking and rewriting to do this. I lose my patience because I

(Cover illustration by Bob Eadie from *Simon and the Snow King* by Stephen Gill.)

prefer to describe or narrate. Consequently, I use dialogues or conversations sparingly, enough to break the monotony of continuous narration.

"On the other hand, ideas appear to me easily. They are diamonds, rough in their original form; I have to chisel and polish them in order to make them presentable. Though it is a painful process, I do not give up easily. I keep revising and editing them till I am nearly satisfied; usually it takes six to ten times of rewriting or editing. My next step is to let my writing simmer or settle down for weeks or months before I take it up again to read it afresh to polish it further. I consider this to be an important stage, because it breaks my emotional bonds with that particular piece of writing. Once I feel somewhat happy over the outcome of my labour, I begin showing it to others—two or three friends—asking them for their blue pencilling. I enjoy doing revisions.

"I believe that a writer for children should not forget that his or her readers, the future citizens of their country, are passing through a most formative period of their lives. This thought is ever present in my mind when I write. Therefore, I do not hesitate to sprinkle hints wherever it is possible for the self-improvement of my readers.

"The story of *Simon and the Snow King* did not occur to me suddenly over a cup of tea, or while driving, or having a shower. It was in my mind for a long time. I carried its seeds as a pregnant woman would her fetus. It began to take shape when my son Ajay, during his childhood, insisted that I tell him a story every night. The well of my imagination soon went dry. That was the time when I began to admire the fertile imagination of my mother, who used to tell me always something new with a moral before I fell asleep. Because my son was the source of inspiration for this story, I introduced the real names of my children, Ajay and Rekha, which blend very well with the ingredients of the tale.

"*The Blessings of a Bird* also contains a moral—more obvious this time. The story was inspired by a newspaper article about birds and flowers and their psychological impact on the environment. The leading characters I modeled on the lives of some welfare recipients who were my neighbours when I was a student and rented a cheap room in Montreal. I molded everything in the smithy of my imagination.

"My friends and the people I meet even most casually, often appear in one form or another in my writing. I am sure most writers do the same. After all, we writers have to borrow material from somewhere to build our worlds. However, the real persons have to pass through the chamber of the writer's mind where their clothes and costumes are changed—sometimes to such an extent that even the proto-types fail to recognize themselves."

HOBBIES AND OTHER INTERESTS: Giving talks, promoting world peace and understanding.

FOR MORE INFORMATION SEE:

Rick Gamble, "Literature Said Vital Force for World Peace," *Expositor*, September 8, 1976.
Canadian India Times, November 18, 1976 (p. 9).
Ottawa Citizen, April 12, 1977 (p. 37).
Ottawa Journal, October 29, 1977 (p. 26).
Mary Green, "Cornwall Publisher Makes Mark," *Montreal Star*, February 21, 1978.
At Your Leisure, April 9, 1978 (p. 2).

Gazette, January 29, 1979 (p. 75).
Indian Teacher, January/February, 1979 (p. 14ff).
Review Journal, October, 1979 (p. 35ff).
Standard-Freeholder, October, 1979 (p. 6).
Asia Week, February 6, 1981 (p. 38).
Christian Monitor (India), April 16, 1981 (p. 6).
George Hines, *Stephen Gill and His Works* (an evaluation), Vesta, 1982.
Writer's Lifeline, February, 1982 (p. 19ff), number 5, 1986 (p. 28ff).
Ed Press News, October, 1986 (p. 2).

GOLD, Robert S(tanley) 1924-

PERSONAL: Born June 19, 1924, in New York, N.Y.; son of Albert (a shoe salesman) and Frances (a housewife; maiden name, Frey) Gold; married; children: (first marriage) Eva, Joshua. *Education:* Syracuse University, B.S., 1949; New York University, M.A., 1955, Ph.D., 1962. *Politics:* "Left Liberal." *Home:* 62 Leroy St., New York, N.Y. 10014. *Office:* Department of English, Jersey City State College, Jersey City, N.J. 07305.

CAREER: Queens College of the City University of New York, New York, N.Y., lecturer in English, 1958-63; Hunter College of the City University of New York, New York, N.Y., instructor, 1962; Jersey City State College, Jersey City, N.J., assistant professor, 1963-68, associate professor, 1968-73, professor of English, 1973—. *Military service:* U.S. Coast Guard, signalman, 1943-45. *Awards, honors:* Cited for Outstanding Reference Work by the *Library Journal*, 1964, for *A Jazz Lexicon*.

WRITINGS:

A Jazz Lexicon, Knopf, 1964.
(Editor) *Point of Departure: Nineteen Stories of Youth and Discovery* (young adult), Dell, 1967.
(Contributor) Barnet Kottler and Martin Light, editors, *The World of Words*, Houghton, 1967.
(With Sanford R. Radner) *Controversy* (textbook for college freshmen), Holt, 1969.
(Editor) *The Rebel Culture*, Dell, 1971.
Jazz Talk, Bobbs-Merrill, 1975, reissued, Da Capo Press, 1982.
(Editor) *The Roar of the Sneakers* (sports fiction anthology), Bantam, 1977.
(Editor) *Stepping Stones: Seventeen Powerful Stories of Growing Up* (young adult; short story anthology), Dell, 1981.

Contributor of drama reviews to *Jersey Journal*, 1964-65. Contributor of articles on literature and jazz to *Encyclopedia of World Biography*, McGraw Hill, Volumes 1-12, 1973, literature consultant, Volumes 13-15, 1987-88, and Volume 16, in press. Contributor of jazz articles to *Travel & Leisure*.

WORK IN PROGRESS: Two story anthologies: one a sports fiction anthology (a revised, updated version of *The Roar of the Sneakers*, with a new title), the second, quality short stories of the past forty years.

SIDELIGHTS: "Somewhere early in my teaching career, the not-so-original thought occurred to me that in this television-blasted age, special inducements were needed to inspire reading on the part of young people (high school students

ROBERT S. GOLD

and college freshmen, in particular). I had observed difficulty and even failure of identification of my students with the adult characters and problems that dominate most fiction anthologies. I therefore conceived a short story anthology built exclusively around adolescent characters, problems, situations: the result was *Point of Departure,* still in print! Its success inspired a companion volume, *Stepping Stones,* which is doing nicely, though not spectacularly.

"*The Roar of the Sneakers* is sports fiction—mostly short stories, but also some novel excerpts—and was intended to appeal to both younger and older readers. In fact, my controlling belief is that young readers will respond favorably to quality stories if the subject matter is more familiar and therefore accessible, but in no case did I want to 'crowdplease' and sacrifice quality for relevance."

HOBBIES AND OTHER INTERESTS: Jazz, sports (handball, tennis, watching football, basketball, and hockey), reading, movies.

FOR MORE INFORMATION SEE:

Newark Star-Ledger, March 3, 1974.
Jersey Journal, March 5, 1974.

GRAHAM, Bob 1942-

PERSONAL: Born October 20, 1942, in Sydney, Australia; married Carolyn Smith (a bookseller), 1968; children: Naomi, Peter. *Education:* Attended Julian Ashton Art School. *Home and office:* Blackbird Design, Lot 8 Main Road, Mt. Dandenong, 3767 Victoria, Australia.

CAREER: Illustrator and author of children's books, 1981—; Blackbird Design, Victoria, Australia, owner and director, 1983—. *Member:* Australian Society of Authors. *Awards, honors:* Picture Book of the Year Commendation from the Children's Book of the Year Awards (Australia), 1986, and Certificate of Honour for Illustration from the International Board on Books for Young People, 1988, both for *First There Was Frances;* Shortlisted for the Picture Book of the Year Award, 1987, for *The Wild,* and 1989, for *Grandad's Magic;* Picture Book of the Year Award 1988, for *Crusher Is Coming.*

WRITINGS:

SELF-ILLUSTRATED

Pearl's Place, Blackie, 1983, Bedrick Books, 1985.
(With Peter Smith) *Pete and Roland,* Collins (Australia), 1983, Viking, 1984.
Here Comes Theo, Hamish Hamilton, 1984, Little, Brown, 1988.
Here Comes John, Hamish Hamilton, 1984, Little, Brown, 1988.

BOB GRAHAM

Libby, Oscar and Me, Bedrick Books, 1985.
Where Is Sarah?, Hamish Hamilton, 1985, published as *Where's Sarah,* Little, Brown, 1988.
Bath Time for John, Hamish Hamilton, 1985, Little, Brown, 1988.
First There Was Frances, Blackie, 1985, Bradbury, 1986.
The Junk Book: A Guide to Creative Uses of Recycled Materials for Children, Sterling, 1986.
The Red Woollen Blanket, Walker Books (London), 1987, published as *The Red Woolen Blanket,* Little, Brown, 1988.
The Wild, Bedrick Books, 1987.
Crusher Is Coming!, Lothian, 1987, Viking, 1988.
Walking, Five Mile Press (Australia), 1988.
Playing, Five Mile Press, 1988.
Helping, Five Mile Press, 1988.
Sleeping, Five Mile Press, 1988.
The Adventures of Charlotte and Henry, Penguin, 1987.
Has Anyone Here Seen William?, Walker, 1988, Little, Brown, 1989.
Grandad's Magic, Little, Brown, 1989.
Waiting for the New Baby, Walker, 1989.
Visiting the New Baby, Walker, 1989.
Bringing Home the New Baby, Walker, 1989.
Getting to Know the New Baby, Walker, 1989.
Greetings from Sandy Beach, Lothian (Australia), 1990.

ILLUSTRATOR

Peter Smith, *Jenny's Baby Brother,* Collins, 1982, Viking, 1984.
Roland Harvey, *Roland Harvey's Incredible Book of Almost Everything,* Sterling, 1985.
Anne Bower Ingram, *Making a Picture Book,* Methuen (Australia), 1987.
Iona Opie and Peter Opie, *Babies: An Unsentimental Anthology,* John Murray (London), 1990.

WORK IN PROGRESS: Wintergarten.

SIDELIGHTS: "I lived for the first few years of my life in a Sydney suburb called Beverly Hills. Not the glamour and glitz of its namesake in Los Angeles, but in those days at least it was on the outskirts of the rapidly expanding city and still afforded small patches of bush and forest where I could play.

"Actually, I would never have admitted to 'playing.' 'Mucking about' would probably have been more acceptable to me I think. But I can only imagine what I might have said. I can really only invent it because here I am writing this and looking back along a path of some forty years. It disappears over the horizon and I am unable to focus very clearly. Small glimpses maybe.

"This is important to me, because if I think about it, it is a strange affair—a man of nearly fifty writing stories and drawing pictures which will be of interest to children, some of them fresh from the egg.

"There is a phrase often used in these circumstances, 'you must never write *down* to children,' but I can't think of any other way to do it. It has nothing to do with condescension. That is another matter.

"So because of this gap, I am left as an outside observer, a spectator who gathers as many details as I can, and by a combination of observation and intuition, shuffle them into a story which I hope will be of interest to the picture-book set and their parents.

"Having just cast aspersions on my memory, I *can* remember that I have always drawn pictures, even from a very early age. I did a pretty reasonable Mickey Mouse (when he was much leaner and didn't wear long trousers).

"I also remember at ages eight, nine, and ten religiously copying a daily newspaper cartoonist who portrayed slices of life in an inner-city working-class area. His name was Emile Mercier and he drew every character with such precision and economy that it has left a stamp on me to this day. This quality was instantly recognizable to me when I first saw the pictures of James Thurber and many other illustrators from the *New Yorker.*

"It was not until 1980, when I was married with two children of eight and ten, that it occurred to me to make a picture book. Looking back now, it seems a perfectly logical thing to have done. My wife, Carolyn, and I had shared a good ten-year apprenticeship in all child matters, I had done some four years training in painting and drawing at art school, and a story had presented itself. Our son, Peter, wandered in early one morning with a small parakeet that he had found in the garden. That was my first book, *Pete and Roland.*

"And that is how most of my books have proceeded. Not from any big conscious decisions (I try to make very few of those), but letting them happen as naturally as I can.

"My life and my work are rather tangled. I work in a little room at home and I sometimes find it difficult to know when I am at work and when I am at home. But meanwhile I have time to go to concerts (I particularly like Early Music), cook the daily meal (I like cooking Southeast Asian food), take our two dogs for two walks a day (they demand it), and being caught up around the edges of some very loud Blues music coming from Peter's room. Perhaps one day I can take him to Chicago, but it seems a very long way from here.

"I am now living and working happily on top of a mountain some forty-five kilometers outside Melbourne with huge trees towering overhead. My wife, who I am indebted to for her insights and good humour, works in a bookshop. My son is an art student. My daughter has graduated with a music degree and plays the recorder like you wouldn't believe.

"So I just work on my books all day and talk to the dogs a lot."

GRAHAM, Lawrence (Otis) 1962-
(Larry Graham)

PERSONAL: Professionally known as Larry Graham; born December 25, 1962, in New York, N.Y.; son of Richard C. (a businessperson) and Betty J. (a clinical social worker and lecturer; maiden name, Walker) Graham. *Education:* Princeton University, B.A., 1983; Harvard Law School, J.D., 1988. *Religion:* Roman Catholic. *Home:* 133 Miles Ave., White Plains, N.Y. 10606. *Agent:* Perry Knowlton, Curtis Brown Ltd., 10 Astor Place, New York, N.Y. 10005.

CAREER: Writer, 1981—; FLYERS Services, Inc., (a consulting firm), Scarsdale, N.Y., president, 1985—; Weil Gotshal & Manges, New York, N.Y., attorney, 1988—. Host of weekly cable television program "The Larry Graham Show," 1984. Intern at White House Office of Women's Affairs, 1980, and WNBC-Radio, 1981; research assistant at Ford Foundation, 1982. Member of board of directors of

Lawrence Graham with mother, Betty.

Foundation for Youth Involvement, and Entrepreneurial Institute at Manhattanville College. *Member:* Authors Guild, Society of Professional Journalists, National Association for the Advancement of Colored People. *Awards, honors:* National Essay Contest First Place from the National Association for the Advancement of Colored People, 1979, for "Behind the Mask"; named one of "Ten Most Interesting Young Men in America" by *Mademoiselle,* 1985; Entrepreneur of the Year Award from Manhattanville College, 1988.

WRITINGS:

Ten Point Plan for College Acceptance, Putnam, 1981.
Jobs in the Real World, Putnam, 1982.
Conquering College Life: How to Be a Winner at College, Simon & Schuster, 1983.
Your Ticket to Law School, Bantam, 1984.
Your Ticket to Medical School, Bantam, 1985.
Your Ticket to Business School, Bantam, 1985.
(With mother, Betty J. Graham) *The Teenager's Ask and Answer Book,* Simon & Schuster, 1985.
(With Lawrence Hamdan) *F.L.Y.E.R.S.: Fun Loving Youth En Route to Success,* Simon & Schuster, 1985.
Youth Trends, St. Martin's Press, 1987.
(With B. J. Graham) *How to Be Your Child's Best Friend,* Dodd, 1989.

Author of television scripts for Highgate Pictures. *Youth Trends* has been translated into Japanese. Contributor to magazines, including *Good Housekeeping, Reader's Digest—Families,* and *Crisis.* Syndicated columnist, "Betty and Larry Talk," Gannett Newspapers, 1988—, and "What's Hot, What's Not," United Feature Syndicate, 1990—.

WORK IN PROGRESS: A book about the history of trends and fads of American and Japanese young people.

SIDELIGHTS: "I sold my first book at age seventeen, and now, several books later, I have the same philosophy about writing. If someone perseveres, he can lead any life he wants to without sacrificing the opportunity to take a few minutes out of each day in order to make note of an experience or an idea.

"When I was a freshman in college, I decided to write a book and came to New York City with two chapters written. With two rolls of dimes, I went into a phone booth on East Fiftieth Street and began calling publishers, alphabetically, from the Manhattan phone book. Most of the receptionists, secretaries, and four editors thought it was very amusing to hear me say, 'Hi, I'm a freshman at Princeton, and I am writing a book on how to get into college .... ' After I had been laughed at for about forty-five minutes, two editors were kind enough to tell me that I was wasting my time. They both said I needed an agent. With that same phone book, those two rolls of dimes, and the same brazen ambition, I began calling literary agents, alphabetically, in the New York listings. I ended up being invited over by 'Zeckendorf, Susan.' Now I can laugh at the fact that there was only one more agent listed after Zeckendorf, but at the time I was desperate, ambitious, and determined to write and to be published. It was the greatest feeling that I have ever experienced.

"Perhaps some writers will disagree, but I find every aspect of the publishing business an exciting one—from idea, to contract, to research, to typing and arranging, to helping with the publicity and promotion. I suppose that I was fortunate to be able to publish at such an early age, but I can honestly say that I am extremely grateful that the public, the editors, my agent, and the media have felt that my work and my career are worthy of some attention.

"My situation is especially unusual because I am still young and because I managed to publish one book each year as a student at Princeton and Harvard Law School. Because of this, my books have received attention through my appearances on more than 250 television and radio shows, including the 'Phil Donahue Show' and the 'Today Show.'

"The most ambitious book I've written was a humor book, *F.L.Y.E.R.S.,* which labeled the new generation of thirteen- to twenty-five-year-olds that were replacing the yuppies with their love of Madonna, Swatch watches, junk food, and hanging out at the mall. FLYERS, an acronym for Fun Loving Youth En Route to Success, was my label for over fifty million young people, and it soon became a marketing strategy to understand a group that spent over $200 billion. Once my Harvard classmate and I came up with this new name, both American and Japanese companies started calling and asking us to help them market and understand this trend-setting FLYERS generation. I thought they were crazy. We gave them the data and they gave us the money! We had discovered a group that every company wanted to sell products to. I never thought that this or any of my books would spin off and cause me to launch a line of clothing, or that I would be advising Nestle Foods and MTV, or that I would be called the guru of the youth generation, but I've learned that I should go wherever my writing takes me. Some things just shouldn't be questioned."

FOR MORE INFORMATION SEE:

Seventeen, May, 1981.
New York Times, June 14, 1981.
Good Housekeeping, August, 1981.
People, January 25, 1982.
San Francisco Chronicle, March 25, 1982.
Us, May 25, 1982.
Philadelphia Enquirer, May 30, 1983.
Marilyn Machlowitz, *Success at an Early Age,* Arbor House, 1985.
Boston Globe, January 11, 1985.
Fortune, May 13, 1985.
Mademoiselle, November, 1985.
San Francisco Examiner, November 5, 1985.
USA Today, July 28, 1987.
Inc., October, 1987.
Boston, November, 1987.
Adweek, Febuary 2, 1988.
Daily News, September 7, 1989.
Women's Wear Daily, November 29, 1989.

GRAHAM, Lorenz (Bell) 1902-1989

OBITUARY NOTICE—See sketch in *SATA* Volume 2: Born January 27, 1902, in New Orleans, La.; died of cancer, September 11, 1989, in West Covina, Calif. Probation officer, social worker, missionary, educator, and author. Graham is best remembered for his award-winning "Town" series of young people's books, including *South Town,* which won the Follett Award and the Child Study Children's Book Award, both 1959, and *Whose Town?,* about a black youth's encounters with racism as he strives to become a doctor. This second book in the series won *Book World*'s Children's Spring Book Festival Award in 1969. Graham's varied career included positions as a lecturer at California State Polytechnic College (now University), a probation officer in Los Angeles, a social worker in New York City, and, during the 1920s, a teacher and missionary in Liberia. While in Liberia he learned a local dialect of the English language that he used in writing children's stories based on the Bible, many of which are included in the collection *How God Fix Jonah.* He also wrote young people's novelettes, including *Detention Center* and *Runaway.* He received a special citation from the Thomas Alva Edison Foundation for his 1956 adaptation of the biblical story *The Ten Commandments,* and in 1968 he received the Southern California Council on Literature for Children and Young People Award for his significant contribution to literature for young people.

FOR MORE INFORMATION SEE:

Kenneth L. Donelson and Alleen Pace Nilsen, *Literature for Today's Young Adults,* Scott, Foresman, 1980.
Rudine Sims, *Shadow and Substance: Afro-American Experience in Contemporary Children's Fiction,* National Council of Teachers of English, 1982.
Children's Literature Review, Volume X, Gale, 1985.
Something about the Author Autobiography Series, Volume 5, Gale, 1988.
Contemporary Authors New Revision Series, Volume 25, Gale, 1989.

OBITUARIES

New York Times, September 14, 1989.
Los Angeles Times, September 15, 1989.

School Library Journal, November, 1989.
Contemporary Authors, Volume 129, Gale, 1990.

GRIGSON, Jane 1928-

PERSONAL: Born March 13, 1928, in Gloucester, England; daughter of George Shipley (a town clerk) and Doris (Berkley) McIntire; married Geoffrey Grigson (a poet; died, November 28, 1985); children: Hester Sophia Frances. *Education:* Newnham College, Cambridge, B.A., 1949. *Home:* Broad Town Farm, Broad Town, Swindon, Wiltshire, England. *Agent:* Harold Ober Associates, Inc., 40 East 49th St., New York, N.Y. 10017; David Higham Associates, 5-8 Lower John St., Golden Square, London W1R 3PE, England.

CAREER: Heffers Art Gallery, Cambridge, England, assistant, 1950-51; Walker's Art Gallery, London, England, assistant, 1952-53; George Rainbird Ltd (publishers), London, assistant, 1953-54; Thames & Hudson Ltd. (publisher), London, assistant, 1954-55; editor, translator, writer. Associate of Newnham College. Trustee, Caroline Walker Trust. *Member:* Guild of Food Writers, Parson Woodford Society, Amnesty International (associate), Garden History Society, McCarrison Society. *Awards, honors:* John Florio Prize, 1965, for translation of *On Crimes and Punishments;* Glenfiddich Trophy, 1978, and 1982; Andre Simon Prize, for *Jane Grigson's Vegetable Book* and *Jane Grigson's Fruit Book.*

WRITINGS:

JUVENILE

(With husband, Geoffrey Grigson) *Shapes and Stories: A Book about Pictures,* J. Baker, 1964, Vanguard, 1965.
(With G. Grigson) *Shapes and Adventures,* Marshbank, 1967, published as *More Shapes and Stories: A Book about Pictures,* Vanguard, 1967.

Also author with G. Grigson of *Shapes, Animals and Special Creatures,* Vanguard.

OTHER

(Translator) Giovanni A. Cibotto, *Scano Boa,* Hodder & Stoughton, 1963.
(Translator) Cesare Beccaria, *On Crimes and Punishments,* Oxford University Press, 1964.
Charcuterie and French Pork Cookery, M. Joseph, 1967, published as *Art of Charcuterie,* Knopf, 1968.
Good Things, Knopf, 1971.
Fish Cookery, Wine and Food Society, 1973.
The Mushroom Feast, Knopf, 1975.
Cooking Spinach, Abson Books, 1976.
The Art of Making Sausage, Pates, and Other Charcuterie, Knopf, 1976.
English Food, Penguin, 1977.
Jane Grigson's Vegetable Book, Atheneum, 1979.
Food with the Famous, Atheneum, 1980.
Jane Grigson's Fruit Book, Atheneum, 1981.
Jane Grigson's Book of European Cookery, Atheneum, 1982 (published in England as *"Observer" Guide to European Cookery,* Macdonald, 1983).
(With Anne Willan) *"Observer" French Cookery School Edition,* Macdonald, 1983.
Jane Grigson's British Cookery, Atheneum, 1984 (published in England as *"Observer" Guide to British Cookery,* M. Joseph, 1984).

Cookery correspondent, *Observer Colour Magazine,* 1968—.

WORK IN PROGRESS: A revision of *Fish Cookery.*

FOR MORE INFORMATION SEE:

New York Times, March 7, 1984.

GUTHRIE, Donna W. 1946-

PERSONAL: Born May 15, 1946, in Washington, Pa.; daughter of Wallace Lyde (a lumberman) and Opal (a homemaker; maiden name, Daque) Winnett; married Michael Beck Guthrie (a physician), June 8, 1973; children: Carly Elizabeth, Colin Wallace. *Education:* Rider College, B.A., 1968; Ravenhill Academy, AMI Montessori Degree, 1971. *Politics:* Independent. *Religion:* Methodist. *Home and office:* 15 East Fontanero St., Colorado Springs, Colo. 80907.

CAREER: Teacher in Paulsboro, N.J., Colorado Springs, Colo., and Philadelphia, Pa., 1968-75; Colorado Springs Montessori School, Colorado Springs, vice-president of education, 1976-77; scriptwriter of pilot series about hospitalization for a video, 1979; Kids Corner Ltd. (audio visual company), Colorado Springs, founder and president, 1980-90; free-lance writer and author of children's books, 1980—. President, Board of Trustees, Pikes Peak Library District, Colorado Springs, Colo; lay member, El Paso County Bar Association Fee Dispute Committee. *Member:* Society of Children's Book Writers. *Awards, honors:* Best Parenting Video, 1982, and Best Video, 1982 and 1983, all from the National Council of Family Relations, all for "I'm a Little Jealous of That Baby"; *The Witch Who Lives Down the Hall* was selected one of *School Library Journal*'s Twenty Best Children's Books, 1985; Arts Business Education Award of Colorado Springs, 1985, for "A Visit from History."

WRITINGS:

JUVENILE

The Witch Who Lives Down the Hall (Junior Literary Guild selection; illustrated by Amy Schwartz), Harcourt, 1985.
Grandpa Doesn't Know It's Me (illustrated by Katy Keck Arnsteen), Human Sciences Press, 1986.
This Little Pig Stayed Home (illustrated by K. K. Arnsteen), Price Stern, 1987.
While I'm Waiting (illustrated by Marsha Howe), Current Press, 1988.
A Rose for Abby (illustrated by Dennis Hockerman), Abingdon, 1988.
Mrs. Gigglebelly Is Coming for Tea (illustrated by K. K. Arnsteen), Simon & Schuster, 1990.
The Witch Has an Itch (illustrated by K. K. Arnsteen), Simon & Schuster, 1990.

Contributor of stories and articles to *Turtle, Fifty Upward Network, American Library Journal, Parent's Plus, L.A. Parent, Network, Magazine for Colorado Women, Sunday Digest,* and *Denver Post.* Author of radio program "Mr. Vanatoli and the Magic Pumpkin Seeds," aired on "Children Unlimited," 1983; of videos "Jasper Enters the Hospital," "The Day of Jasper's Operation," "I'm a Little Jealous of That Baby," and "My Brother Is Sick"; of classroom presentations "Make Mine a Mystery!," "Nine Nice Newberys and a Couple of Caldecotts," and "A Visit from History"; and a series of public service announcements and health spots for the National Poison Control Center.

WORK IN PROGRESS: Two Steps Forward and *The Great Cake Bake War* are the first two books in a series about three boys who encounter all kinds of fun and mischief during their grade school years; *My Aunt Meg and Me,* a middle-grade novel about a young girl and her eccentric aunt who become involved in saving the city park; *Frankie Peferetti's Kiss List,* a fifth-grade novel about a boy who wants to kiss all the girls in the sixth grade before he goes to junior high; *102 Steps,* a picture book about a child's adventure visiting her beloved grandmother; *Not for Babies,* a picture book about a little boy's first overnight in a tent.

SIDELIGHTS: "'Book worm' is the word my family used to describe me as a child. By their standards, I was a hopeless 'ding bat.' I always had my nose in a book. Every time they turned around, I was off in some corner reading.

"My parents, were conservative farmers from western Pennsylvania. I was the fifth of six children (three girls and three boys), and according to my family, I lived with my head in the clouds. They had difficulty understanding my vivid imagination and love of reading. They saw it as a waste of time when there was so much work to do.

"As I grew older, it was just a short hop from reading stories to writing them. In fifth grade, I adopted a pen name of my own 'Kim Wayne.' I wrote stories about my family, my

DONNA W. GUTHRIE

friends, and even the animals on our farm. Everyone and everything became fair game for my wild and crazy imagination.

"But it wasn't until high school that I began to think seriously about a career in writing. My English teacher, Margaret Wylie, loved literature and language. And she had the wonderful ability to pass her interest and excitement for good writing on to others. Mrs. Wylie praised my writing and read some of it aloud in my junior English class. She was the first person in my life to encourage my writing. And her kind words made me begin to think about writing as a possible career.

"When I went to college I majored in journalism. My parents, who felt teaching and nursing held more promise for a girl, weren't happy with my decision. But that choice was my first in a long line of resolutions to take my writing seriously.

"For the past eight years, I've been writing professionally. When my children were young and our house was small, I wrote in a refurbished clothes closet.

"At that time I tried to juggle the roles of wife, mother, friend, community volunteer, business woman, and writer. Notice that writer is last. I used to tell myself that when everything else was accomplished, then and only then, could I turn on my electric typewriter and write.

"Finally, after a few unpublishable books about talking teeth and shoe laces, I joined the Society of Children's Book Writers (SCBW). Their publications were filled with all kinds of important information that as a beginning writer I needed to know.

"In 1983, I scraped together the airfare for the annual SCBW summer writers conference in California. I left my young family with a freezer full of casseroles and headed west with my latest manuscript. I'd made a firm decision that unless I received a 'sign' of some sort at that conference, I would unplug my electric typewriter and go back to being a full-time wife, mother, friend, and volunteer.

"When I arrived in California, I found I wasn't alone. There were a lot of other struggling writers at that conference in Los Angeles. I shared a room with four would-be writers. It was great fun, staying up late and reading other people's work, attending lectures, having coffee with people like Tomi de Paola and Paula Danziger. Everyone I met was open and generous with advice and encouragement and willing to share their personal experiences in writing.

"At every SCBW conference, there is the opportunity to send a manuscript ahead to be read by one of the conference's featured authors, illustrators, or editors. I had sent a copy of a manuscript titled *The Witch Who Lives Down the Hall.*

"When they posted the names of the manuscript consultants I found Kathleen Krull, the children's book editor at Harcourt Brace Jovanovich, next to my name. She was going to critique my manuscript. I called home to tell my husband that maybe this was 'the sign' I had been waiting for. I would finally have the opportunity to talk to a 'real' editor about my work.

"The next morning I waited outside Ms. Krull's door. I was so nervous that I was sweating to my waist. When it was my turn, Ms. Krull, an attractive young woman in her late twenties, invited me into her room. She was friendly, positive,

and encouraging about my manuscript. She told me 'The readers at Harcourt liked your story, they think you have talent. You understand how to write a picture book. But . . . they think that the plot, concerning a little boy who thinks the old lady who lives next door is a witch, is just too predictable a story line.'

"'What if the lady down the hall wasn't old,' I replied. 'What if she were in her late twenties, owned a cat, a computer, and did yoga every morning on her balcony?'

"'That book,' said Ms. Krull, 'I would be interested in reading.'

"Home I went to Colorado with a clear idea of how to rework *The Witch Who Lives Down the Hall.* I sent the manuscript back in early September and waited. Three days before Christmas in 1983, Ms. Krull called to tell me that they were publishing my book in the fall of 1985, over a year and a half away. I continued to write, collecting more rejections, but with one book under contract, I had a new confidence about my writing.

"My writing life is much easier, now. My children are in school. I've learned to set limitations with friends and neighbors and I've learned to limit myself to only one volunteer effort a year for my community. Usually it has something to do with writing.

"Seven books later, my husband, daughter, and son have become my most supportive critics. When I'm working on a manuscript, I often read the day's work aloud at the dinner table. My children have become very involved with my various characters. And in real life they are always on the lookout for funny incidents, interesting people, and picturesque language that I can use in my stories.

"In life there are three things that are important to me, they are my family, my work, and my friends, but not always in that order. In the future, I hope to grow and mature as a writer. And I'm more than willing to risk and change, to read and study, to write and rewrite so that growth can occur in my life. My wish is to touch the minds and hearts of today's children through my writing, and with a little luck, perhaps leave something for tomorrow's 'book worms.'"

HARRISON, Sarah 1946-

PERSONAL: Born August 7, 1946, in Exeter, England; daughter of Anthony (in British Army) and Jean (a repertory actress; maiden name, Laird) Martyn; married Jeremy Harrison (a consultant in training and employment), June 7, 1969; children: Laurence, Frances, Thea. *Education:* University of London, B.A. (with honors), 1967. *Politics:* Social Democrat. *Religion:* Church of England. *Home and office:* 17 Station Rd., Steeple Morden, Royston, Hertfordshire SG8 0NW, England. *Agent:* Carol Smith, 25 Hornton Court E., Kensington High St., London W8 7RT, England.

CAREER: International Publishing Corp., London, England, magazine journalist, 1967-70; free-lance writer, 1970-77.

WRITINGS:

JUVENILE

In Granny's Garden (illustrated by Mike Wilks), Holt, 1980.

"LAURA FROM LARK RISE" SERIES; JUVENILE

Laura and Old Lumber, Century Hutchinson, 1985.
Laura and Edmund (illustrated by Kate Aldous), Century Hutchinson, 1985.
Laura and the Lady, Century Hutchinson, 1985.
Laura and the Squire, Century Hutchinson, 1985.

ADULT NOVELS

The Flowers of the Field, Coward, 1980.
A Flower That's Free, Simon & Schuster, 1984.
Hot Breath. Macdonald, 1985.
An Imperfect Lady, Warner Books, 1988.
Cold Feet, Macdonald, 1989.

Contributor of articles and stories to magazines, including *New Woman, Woman's Own, Woman,* and *Woman's Reader.*

WORK IN PROGRESS: An untitled novel, a thriller set in the present day and World War II.

SIDELIGHTS: "I was the original scribbling child, who bombarded family and friends with unsolicited manuscripts from the age of seven. These first stories were about anthropomorphic animal heroes in the Lassie mold, but at twelve I discovered romance and relationships, and have never really looked back!

"I write for children as I do for adults—characters come first, and the narrative grows naturally out of them. A firm basis in reality, if not in one's own personal experience, is essential I think. For me, empathy, identification, and credibility, even in a fantasy for children, are more important than escapism. The imagined must seem vividly real. Writing's a branch of show business and I'm happiest telling a story in a graphic, entertaining way. I read avidly, anything and everything, after all, as a writer, you are what you read, so a good mixed diet's important! As a result of my novels I now do a lot of public speaking, and broadcasting, and the experience of learning to *talk* concisely and entertainingly has (I think) helped my writing. Variety's important to me—it's nice to try something new all the time."

HEILBRONER, Joan (Knapp) 1922-

PERSONAL: Born March 13, 1922, in Garden City, N.Y.; daughter of Robert Cole and Jessie (Allen) Knapp; children: Peter Louis, David Robert. *Education:* Western Reserve University, B.A., 1945; Columbia University, School of Library Service, M.S., 1979. *Home:* 145 East 74th St., New York, N.Y. 10021. *Agent:* Sandra Hardy, Tenth Avenue Editions, Suite 903, 625 Broadway, New York, N.Y. 10012.

CAREER: Writer; Town School, New York, N.Y., librarian, 1963-82. *Member:* International Library Science Honorary Society, Beta Phi Mu.

WRITINGS:

The Happy Birthday Present (illustrated by Mary Chalmers), Harper, 1962.

Robert the Rose Horse (illustrated by P. D. Eastman), Random House, 1962.
This Is the House Where Jack Lives (illustrated by Aliki), Harper, 1962, large print edition, Harper, 1962.
Meet George Washington (illustrated by Victor Mays), Random House, 1965.
Tom the TV Cat: A Step Two Book (illustrated by Sal Murdocca), Random House, 1984.

ADAPTATIONS:

"Robert the Rose Horse" (cassette; filmstrip with cassette), Random House, 1974.

SIDELIGHTS: "In 1982 I retired from the Town School in New York City where I had been librarian for nineteen years. Since then I have spent most of my time playing chamber music on the piano, and I recently began to study the viola. I also enjoy learning languages and am studying French and Spanish. Peter and David, about whom I wrote in The Happy Birthday Present, are now grown up. Peter is studying medicine and David is a lawyer and writer."

HOGARTH, Burne 1911-

PERSONAL: Born December 25, 1911, in Chicago, Ill.; son of Max (a carpenter) and Pauline (a housewife; maiden name, Lerman) Hogarth; married Rhoda Simons, February 29, 1936 (divorced); married Constance Green, June 27, 1955 (divorced); children: (first marriage) Michael Robin; (second marriage) Richard Paul, Ross David. *Education:* Attended Crane College, 1928-30, University of Chicago, 1930-31, Northwestern University, 1931-33, and Columbia University, 1956-58. *Home:* 6026 W. Lindenhurst Ave., Los Angeles, Calif. 90036. *Office:* Art Center College of Design, Pasadena, Calif. 91103.

CAREER: Bonnet-Brown, Inc., Chicago, Ill., artist and illustrator, 1933; WPA Arts Project, teacher at Erie Chapel Institute and Sholem Aleichem Academy, 1933-35; Leeds Features, Chicago, editor, 1935; McNaught Syndicate, Inc., New York, N.Y., staff artist, 1935; Transamerica Syndicate, Chicago, cartoonist and illustrator, 1935; King Features Syndicate, New York, N.Y., staff artist, 1936; United Feature Syndicate, Inc., New York, N.Y., illustrator and cartoonist for "Tarzan," 1937-50, and "Miracle Jones," 1946-48; Academy of Newspaper Art, New York, N.Y., founder, 1944-46; Post-Hall Syndicate, New York, N.Y., illustrator and cartoonist for "Drago," 1946-48; Cartoonists and Illustrators School (now School of Visual Arts), New York, N.Y., co-founder and vice-president, 1947-70, curriculum coordinator and instructor of anatomy, drawing, art history, and design analysis, 1947-50; Parsons School of Design, New York, N.Y., instructor of anatomy and interpretive and conceptual drawing, 1976-79; Otis Art Institute, Los Angeles, Calif., instructor in anatomy and illustration, 1981—; Art Center College of Design, Pasadena, Calif., instructor of analytical drawing, 1982—. Participant in comics conferences and conventions, 1967-77. President of Pendragon Press, 1975-79.

EXHIBITIONS: "National Cartoonists Society Exhibition," Metropolitan Museum, New York City, 1950; "Ten Millions d'Images," Societe Francaise de Photographie, Paris, France, 1965; "Burne Hogarth," Societe Francaise de Photographie (one-man), Paris, 1966; "Bande Dessinee et

BURNE HOGARTH

Figuration Narrative," Musee des Arts Decoratifs (Louvre), Paris, 1967; "Science-Fiction," Kunsthalle, Berne, Switzerland, 1967; "Science-Fiction," Musee des Arts Decoratifs, Paris, 1967-68; "Scarp Awards," New York Comicon, New York City, 1968; "Exposition de Bandes Dessinees," Palais des Beaux-Arts, Brussels, Belgium, 1968; "La Bienal Mundial de la Historieta," Instituto di Tella, Buenos Aires, Argentina, 1968; "Fourth Salone Internazionale dei Comics," Bastione San Regolo, Lucca, Italy, 1968; "Panorama de la Bande Dessinee," Maison de la Culture de Nevers, France, 1968-69; "Burne Hogarth" (one-man), Escola Panamericana de Arte, Sao Paulo, Brazil, 1969; "Fifth Salone Internazionale dei Comics," Teatro del Giglio, Lucca, 1969; "Le Monde de la Bande Dessinee," Musees Royaux de'Art et d'Histoire, Brussels, 1969; "Comic Strip," America House, Munich, West Germany, 1969; Lausanne, Switzerland, 1969; "Comic Strip," Akademie der Kunst, Berlin, West Germany, 1969-70.

"Exposicao de Quadrinhos," Museu de Arte, Sao Paulo, 1970; "Sixth Salone Internazionale dei Comics," Lucca, 1970; "The Art of the Comic Strip," University of Maryland Art Gallery, College Park, Md., 1971; "Strip 71" Nederlands Persmuseum, Amsterdam, The Netherlands, 1971; "Seventy-five Years of the Comics," New York Cultural Center, New York City, 1971; "The Comics," Kennedy Cultural Center, Washington, D.C., 1972; "Burroughs Bibliophiles Awards," Los Angeles Comicon, Calif., 1972; "First Internationale Salon," Angouleme, France, 1973; Dallas Comicon, Tex., 1973; San Diego Comicon, Calif., 1974; "International Comics," Montreal, Canada, 1975; "Four Masters of Nar-

rative Art—Opper-McCay-Foster-Hogarth," Graham Gallery, New York City, 1977; "Burne Hogarth" (one-man), Museum of Cartoon Art, Portchester, N.Y., 1978; Graham Gallery, New York City, 1979.

"The Comic Art Show," Whitney Museum of American Art, New York City, 1983; "Festival of Cartoon Art," Ohio State University, Columbus, Ohio, 1983; "Sixteenth Salone Internazionale dei Comics," Lucca, 1984; Bibliotheque Municipale, Bibliotheque Merlan, and Palais de Longchamps (one-man), all Marseille, France, 1985-86; "Life of King Arthur," Cesar Society, Paris, France, 1988; "Sites Traveling Exhibition: Great American Comics," Smithsonian Institution, 1989-90; "American Comics and Editorial Cartoons," Gallery Karikatury, Warsaw, Poland, 1990; "Tarzan Cartoons and Fine Art: Form, Structure, and Symbol," University of Colorado, Boulder, Colo., 1990. Work is included in permanent collections, including Graham Gallery, New York City; Museum of Cartoon Art, Portchester, N.Y., Smithsonian Institution, Washington, D.C.; Collector's Press, Carmel Valley, Calif.; Escola Panamericana de Arte, Sao Paulo; Musee des Bandes Dessinees, Paris; and many private collections.

MEMBER: U.S. Committee for the World Health Organization (Graphic Arts Section), Het Stripschap (Amsterdam), National Cartoonists Society (president, 1977-79), National Art Education Association, American Society for Aesthetics, Society of Illustrators, Museum of Cartoon Art, International Society for Aesthetics.

AWARDS, HONORS: Dynamic Anatomy was selected one of American Institute of Graphic Arts Fifty Best Books of the Year, 1958; Scarp Bronze Plaque Award from the New York Comicon, 1968, for "Dynamic Romanticism"; Silver Bowl Award from the Los Angeles Comicon Burroughs Bibliophiles, 1972, for *Tarzan of the Apes;* Bronze Plaque Award from the Dallas Comicon, 1973, for Excellence in Illustration; Silver Plaque Reuben Award for Best Illustration Cartoonist from the National Cartoonists Society, 1974, 1975, and 1976; Artist of the Year Award from Montreal's Man and His World Pavilion of Humor, 1975.

Ignatz Gold Brick Award from the Orlando Comicon, 1975, for Excellence in Illustration; Premio Emilio Freixas Silver Plaque Award from the V-Muestra International Salon (Gijon, Spain), 1978, for *Burne Hogarth's The Golden Age of Tarzan, 1939-1942;* Inkpot Bronze Plaque Award from the San Diego Comicon, 1978, for Achievement in Illustration; Pulcinella Award from V-Mostra Internazionale del Fumetto (Naples, Italy), 1983, for Cartooning, Art, and Illustration; Special Guest at the San Diego Comicon, 1984; Caran D'Arche (Lifetime Achievement Award) from the Salone Internazionale dei Comics del Film d'Animazione e dell' Illustrazione (Lucca, Italy), 1984; Adamson "Silent Sam" Award from the Swedish Academy of Comic Art (Helsingborg, Sweden), 1985; Edgar Rice Burroughs Bronze Plaque Award from the University of Louisville, 1985, for Excellence in Tarzan Art; Lauriers D'Or (Golden Palms) from the Cesar Society (Paris), 1988, for a Lifetime in Art and Illustration; Best in Illustration Award nomination from the National Cartoonists Society, 1989; Premio Especial from the Salo' International del Comic de Barcelona, 1989.

WRITINGS:

Dynamic Anatomy, Watson-Guptill, 1958.
Drawing the Human Head, Watson-Guptill, 1965.

AND AS HE PUZZLED OVER THE COVERED PIT, THERE LOOMED SUDDENLY BEFORE HIS MENTAL VISION A HUGE, GRAY-BLACK BULK WHICH LUMBERED PONDEROUSLY ALONG A JUNGLE TRAIL.

INSTANTLY TARZAN TENSED.

DECISION AND ACTION USUALLY OCCURRED SIMULTANEOUSLY IN THE LIFE OF THE APE-MAN, AND NOW HE WAS AWAY THROUGH THE LEAFY BRANCHES ERE THE REALIZATION OF THE PIT'S PURPOSE HAD SCARCE FORMED IN HIS MIND.

(From *Jungle Tales of Tarzan* by Edgar Rice Burroughs, adapted by Burne Hogarth and Robert M. Hodes. Illustration by Burne Hogarth.)

Dynamic Figure Drawing, Watson-Guptill, 1970.
(Author of preface) Francis Lecassin, *Tarzan ou le chevalier crispe* (title means "Tarzan; or, The Intense Knight"), Union generale d'editions, 1971.
Drawing Dynamic Hands, Watson-Guptill, 1977.
Dynamic Light and Shade, Watson-Guptill, 1981.
Dynamic Wrinkles and Drapery, Watson-Guptill, in press.

ILLUSTRATOR

Robert M. Hodes, *Tarzan of the Apes* (based on the original text by Edgar Rice Burroughs), Watson-Guptill, 1972.
R. M. Hodes, *Jungle Tales of Tarzan* (based on the original text by E. R. Burroughs), Watson-Guptill, 1976.
E. R. Burroughs, *Burne Hogarth's The Golden Age of Tarzan, 1939-1942,* Chelsea House, 1977.
Life of King Arthur, Collector's Press, 1984.

Tarzan of the Apes has been published in eleven languages. Contributor of articles to periodicals, including *American Artist.*

WORK IN PROGRESS: A book of personal sketches, art, comments, and theory, tentatively titled *A Hogarth Sketchbook,* for Fantagraphics; *Kitzel the Lackwit,* an illustrated book; an autobiography (text and pictures), tentatively titled *The Elliptical Eye,* including theories on humor, symbolism, style, art history, and contemporary criticism, for Savoy Books.

SIDELIGHTS: Burne Hogarth was born on **Christmas Day, 1911,** in Chicago, Illinois. He began studying art while still in high school; though at first uncertain what direction his career would take, necessity prompted the artist's move into cartoon work. "For the greater part of my life, it would appear I have pursued an activity which would not sustain the notion of a 'fine arts' career. While my training and orientation originated in the fine arts as a prior and continuing commitment, I had, as an art student entering the workaday world, never thought to pursue a career without expecting to make a decent living from my professional work. It never entered my mind to take a monastic stance of ascetic self-denial and sacrifice like some inspired artist afflicted with a 'divine madness' .... As much as I may stand in awe or admiration of such dramatic integrity, this kind of sacrifice ... does not excite my imagination.

"Nevertheless, the path I chose was perhaps equally austere as that of our artistic visionary and laid down for much the same reasons: my father died when I was fifteen because of unrelieved physical difficulties aggravated under the duress of sustained hard work to keep our family from want. This is dull stuff and nobody cares about silent heroism anymore—except when the obscure paint radiant sunflowers and commit suicide or die building Chartres cathedral. My brother and I stepped into the breach. What does a 'fine arts' student do in a time of personal disaster? Like my father who set the example, you become a good workman, you sell honest art like a professional, if that's your job.

"But what could I sell, still in high school, studying art? Almost by instinct I turned to an art I could perform without effort: cartoons. I could free-lance, work uniquely to myself ... and, raw as it might be, reflect my own style and signature."[1]

Hogarth first served as assistant cartoonist at Associated Editors Syndicate while still in school. Within the year, the syndicate gave him his own panel, "Famous Churches of the World," and assigned him to illustrate two sports features. In **1933,** the artist attempted his first comic strip, "Ivy Hemmanhaw" for the Bonnet-Brown Company, without success. The following year, Hogarth worked on a panel entitled "Odd Occupations and Strange Accidents" for Leeds Features. The most notable of Hogarth's early cartoon work appeared in **1935,** when the McNaught Syndicate hired the artist to draw "Pieces of Eight," a pirate story by the celebrated author Charles Driscoll.

Nonetheless, Hogarth's turning point to immortality occured in 1936, when Harold Foster announced his decision to leave the "Tarzan" strip. This cartoon, based on Edgar Rice Burroughs' 1912 novel, *Tarzan of the Apes,* debuted in England on October 20, 1928, and in the United States three months later. Foster, the original artist, collaborated on the strip with a fellow veteran of the advertising world, Joseph H. Neebe. Foster in fact had tried to return to advertising as early as 1931, but the mediocrity of his successor, Rex Maxon, prompted a renewal of his contract. Within five years however, Foster had tired of drawing Burroughs' creation, and was ready to launch his own strip, the equally renowned "Prince Valiant."

By that time, Foster had established "Tarzan" as the finest and most dynamic adventure strip in cartooning to date. Competition for his replacement was therefore extremely intense; Hogarth, however, was accepted on the strength of his first submission. His debut with the "Tarzan" strip occured on **May 9, 1937.** "As the illustrator of the Sunday newspaper feature 'Tarzan,' it was clear to me from the start that I had in my hands not merely a popular comic figure, but an epic personality, a latter-day analog of those age-old mythic culture heroes of antiquity; a modern man belonging to that class of universally-recognized beings who leap to magical life in daydreams, the emancipated other side of ourselves. I was intrigued with the idea that this archetypal man, who came into his realm naked like Adam, learns that his inherited dawn-world is no Paradise or primeval Arcadia, but a jungle of ordeal, trial, and adversity. Like the Osiris-Adonis/Hercules-Samson mythic heroes with their labors and tribulations, here was a theme for a civilization in the dust, a paradigm for a nation and a people caught in a web of turmoil and depression—wherein a man-not-god fights in a fang and claw environment and survives, a totem symbol of the victory of intelligence over malice and brute force."[1]

By the time Hogarth began "Tarzan," he had already started teaching, and his influence as an educator was perhaps equal to his success as an artist. He received his first posts, at the Erie Chapel Institute and the Sholem Aleichem Institute, through the Federal WPA Arts Project and Emergency Education Program. Here, Hogarth taught drawing, cartoons and gag humor for adolescents and young adults. The artist resumed his teaching career in **1944** when he founded the Academy of Newspaper Art. "I instituted a targeted curricular program aimed at developing art for journalistic endeavors in newspapers, magazines ... humor books and comics. Students learned drawing, characterization, idea development, finished rendering for humor, gag, caricature, satire, sports, humorous light touch, editorial/political, human interest, serious adventure, romantic-realist cartoons and illustrations.

"The Cartoonists and Illustrators School, which I co-founded in **1947,** developed as an outgrowth and natural expansion from the successful premise of the earlier Academy. It was a more sophisticated school which advanced a broad-based curriculum, both in extent and depth, under

A FEW MORE STEPS WOULD PRECIPITATE TANTOR UPON THE SHARPENED STAKES; TARZAN FAIRLY FLEW THROUGH THE TREES UNTIL HE HAD COME ABREAST OF THE FLEEING ANIMAL AND THEN HAD PASSED HIM. AT THE PIT'S VERGE, THE APE-MAN DROPPED TO THE GROUND IN THE CENTER OF THE TRAIL. TANTOR WAS ALMOST UPON HIM BEFORE HIS WEAK EYES PERMITTED HIM TO RECOGNIZE HIS OLD FRIEND. "STOP!" CRIED TARZAN, AND THE GREAT BEAST HALTED TO THE UPRAISED HAND.

(From *Jungle Tales of Tarzan* by Edgar Rice Burroughs, adapted by Burne Hogarth and Robert M. Hodes. Illustration by Burne Hogarth.)

AS TARZAN ENTERED THE CABIN, TWO SMALL, BLOODSHOT EYES WATCHED HIM FROM THE CONCEALING FOLIAGE OF THE JUNGLE CLOSE BY.

HERE HE COULD CURL UP AND LOOK AT THE PICTURES IN THE STRANGE THINGS WHICH WERE BOOKS.

HE COULD PUZZLE OUT THE PRINTED WORDS HE HAD LEARNED TO READ WITHOUT KNOWLEDGE OF THE SPOKEN LANGUAGE THESE REPRESENTED. HE COULD LIVE IN A WONDERFUL WORLD OF WHICH HE HAD NO KNOWLEDGE BEYOND THE COVERS OF HIS BELOVED BOOKS.

NUMA AND SABOR MIGHT PROWL ABOUT CLOSE TO HIM, THE ELEMENTS MIGHT RAGE IN ALL THEIR FURY; BUT HERE AT LEAST, TARZAN MIGHT BE ENTIRELY OFF HIS GUARD IN A DELIGHTFUL RELAXATION WHICH GAVE HIM ALL HIS FACULTIES FOR THE UNINTERRUPTED PURSUIT OF THIS GREATEST OF ALL HIS PLEASURES.

(From *Jungle Tales of Tarzan* by Edgar Rice Burroughs, adapted by Burne Hogarth and Robert M. Hodes. Illustration by Burne Hogarth.)

AND WHAT WAS GOD?

OF THAT TARZAN HAD NO
CONCEPTION ; BUT HE WAS
SURE THAT EVERYTHING GOOD
CAME FROM GOD. HIS GOOD
ACT IN REFRAINING FROM
SLAYING THE DEFENSELESS OLD
GOMANGANI ; TEEKA'S LOVE
THAT HAD HURLED HER INTO THE
EMBRACE OF DEATH ; HIS OWN
LOYALTY TO TEEKA , WHICH HAD
JEOPARDIZED HIS LIFE THAT SHE MIGHT
LIVE . THE GOOD AND BEAUTIFUL
TREES AND FLOWERS ,
GOD HAD MADE THEM .

(Full-page illustration from *Jungle Tales of Tarzan* by Edgar Rice Burroughs, adapted by Burne Hogarth and Robert M. Hodes. Illustration by Burne Hogarth.)

expert professional teachers geared to the new demands of the bourgeoning magazine, syndicate and comic book industry. The school grew in numbers, and took its place as a major specialized art institution in the United States . . . . It became a first class phenomenon, and soon drew students from all over the world.

"I count my contribution to this School as fundamental to its growth and importance. I had initiated the concept of the school, had set up its curricula and had written all its courses on every level from the Foundation Year, to the Intermediate Studies and the Advanced Workshops of completion and certification of student professionals. My position in the school was not limited to administration as a principal owner, Vice President, Coordinator of Curriculum, and Art Supervisor. I not only carried a full time teaching load, but I taught courses in Journalistic Art in areas not given by teachers who disavowed or abjured the unfamiliar.

"I taught the classic, analytical human figure in Anatomy and Drawing; developed Nine Principles of Foreshortening in human form; defined the multi-phase, sequential action systems of figures in deep space visual viewpoints. I taught conventional measured perspective and creative non-gravitational concepts, as well as illustrational eyeball systems of direct, intuited perspective drawing. I taught the structure and schema of story creation, characterization and personification, plotting, pacing, tempo; dialogue and caption, verbal and pictorial interaction; synoptic and finished script development. Withal, I taught five categories of humor—comedy, slapstick, caricature, wit, satire—from a 'tension theory of the absurd/ridiculous polar relationship' leading to the comic and the ludicrous."

Though Hogarth's teaching career at this point was well underway, his work as a cartoonist was hindered for a number of years. In 1945, the artist left "Tarzan" because of conflicts over creative control. He then created two short-lived strips, "Drago" (1946-48) for the Post-Hall Syndicate and "Miracle Jones" (1946-48), a humor strip for United Features Syndicate. Hogarth returned to "Tarzan" in **1947** with a guarantee of more favorable conditions, but after a dispute over foreign rights, in **1950**, he left the strip, and syndicated cartoon work, for good. Over the next two decades, he produced mostly freelance adventure illustrations for magazines such as "Argosy," "Field and Stream," and "Saga."

The Cartoonists and Illustrators School opened in **1955-56** under a new name, the School of Visual Arts of New York. "We were moving into national prominence . . . qualifying soon to give a degree, and shortly to become the largest private art school in the world by numbers of students and faculty.

"In the mid-fifties and later, a great debate split the art world and schools where Fine Arts were taught. The rise of Abstract Expressionism and rebellion against figural conventions and illusionist 'subject matter' created quite a predicament.

"The School of Visual Arts came up against a powerful contradiction: the Fine Arts sector and the practical and technical sector were in a collision of theory and opinion on the *concept* and *practise* of *teaching figure drawing*. The slogan that rose through every discussion, "the figure is dead," manifested a disagreement that was not mere academic argument.

"The problem, as it came to be identified in the Drawing Department faculty was simply: What do we *teach* in *Basic Drawing*? If not the *figure*, *what*? Aside from the School and faculty, even the administration at the top was split on the issue.

"From this time forward in art teaching . . . the figure came to be minimized, disparaged, denigrated as academic formalism, regressive philistinism, dogmatic conservatism. The human figure as a study . . . was *disabled* . . . . It was relegated to a second class use by an inferior caste of cartoonists, illustrators, and advertising specialists—and held in contempt by the Fine Arts sector. And those protagonists who upheld the prime human form became defensive, apologetic, and carried out subservient team-play duty to a domineering in-group adversary class.

"My part in all this was not passive. During this challenging period, I was at work producing a book on figure drawing. It was published in **1958** (at the height of the controversy), titled *Dynamic Anatomy* . . . . It was, I believe, a seminal study of the figure, which opened on an argument as to why the anatomical figure was the prior requirement of art study in an advanced, analytical, technological, scientific culture. The *anatomical, scientific figure* . . . was the pivotal, anthropocentric form analogue of our culture in the modern age.

"Through the middle sixties, while the cross-fire in the arts continued, I published another book . . . titled *Dynamic Figure Drawing* (1965), which advanced dozens of new perceptions and insights of the *action* figure in multiple sequence and creative inventions of forms in space. I followed this with *Drawing the Human Head* (1968). This book was distinguished by its information and visualization of progressive aging of the head, the systematic wrinkle patterns, ethnic types and racial differentia."

While debate in America raged over the relevance of the figure in general, a group of French critics began to take notice of Hogarth's individual artistic strengths. "A group of art historians from the Sorbonne, scholars, writers, aficionados of the Comic Strip in Paris, seemed to have 'discovered' me . . . . They had formed a society for a study of the Ninth Art, Pictorial Literature: the Comic Strip. They called themselves *Socerlid*—Societe d'Etudes et de Recherches de Litteratures Dessinees. In June of '65, a delegation of the Society came to visit me in New York . . . . They proposed a comprehensive exhibit of my work in Paris, a one-man show.

"The exhibit was a radical digression, an innovation of a kind not seen before; it created a flurry of excitement and enthusiasm among its viewers, and widespread critical praise and acceptance from art critics in the Paris press."

The exhibition opened at the Louvre's Museum of Decorative Arts in **February, 1966**, and prompted a flood of articles on Hogarth. As one critic wrote, "Comic art follows in the wake of narrative realism, now in fashion in the art world. Since the 'pop artists' have taken to reproducing the contents of the comics as a part of what is popularly called reality, why shouldn't the original comics be worthy of consideration? Burne Hogarth . . . started as a comic strip artist; collectors are now buying his works as a painter. It seems that today's realism is yesterday's academicism. However, as a cartoonist, Hogarth deserves more than this and his work reveals numerous aesthetic sources.

(Contemporary poster in *Dynamic Light and Shade* by Burne Hogarth. Illustrated by the author.)

"Cinema has influenced both the technique by which he frames each illustration, and the sequence in which he illustrates the narration. But at the core of Hogarth's style is the combination of text-image .... Tarzan, Burne Hogarth's central character, is seen within a space which is constantly changing. There are downward or upward shots, close-ups or long shots. The image is modified to serve the story, but the rhythm of images becomes more and more dynamic. Deprived of this tense and expressive 'motion,' the comic strip would disintegrate.... The convolutions of Tarzan's athletic body, presented in anatomically descriptive panels, show in every muscle. The figure's poses are taken from the subjects of Michelangelo and Leonardo da Vinci. It is indeed in the work of these great artists, and in the work of Rembrandt, Goya, Brueghel ... that Hogarth finds his models .... However, the over-all execution clearly reveals other influences as well— expressionism, baroque dynamism, and surrealism."[2]

The artist himself responded enthusiastically to these critical evaluations, and provided his own detailed reflections on the relationship between his art and modern culture. "Cezanne is right; the artist does not learn from nature, he learns in the museum. With the emergence of Pop art, the New Realism,

the Neo-Dada, I have been forcibly struck with the fact that our art can never again promote the Precious Object as the lodestone of forms, as the magnetic center ... around which all modern concepts turn. The nature of form is not the form of Nature; nor is it the form of Beauty ... nor is the beautiful implied in the Ugly. Today the form of art is in the nature of Ruin—*Technological Ruin*.

"We are a society whose cultural format is a gathering together of wealth in such abundance that any measure by past standards is meaningless .... No past period of history has produced a society ... whose wealth and opulence is *not* measured by accumulation, but by *discard*. The Affluent Society has produced a culture of *planned waste*.

"In the society of planned waste, the making of commodities must be conceived from the proposition of continual change; not revision, but total replacement is the goal because superabundance needs ever-increasing change to keep pace with the computerized instant schedules of superproductive machines. As planned waste and instant objects become social necessity, a new reorientation must occur in relation to custom, religion and history. Because all religion is based on austerity and need and promises a return to eternal good

Sandstorm
The camel riders are heading into a blinding sandstorm. It is broad daylight under a cloudless sky, but the sweeping sand begins to blot out all knowledge of the source of the light. Note the difference in values between the foreground and the distance. In the distance, the storm is coming on with a vengeance, and the values are paler. The near riders, drawn with stronger contrasts of tone, have yet to feel the full impact of the storm.

Underwater
Under bright sunshine, water is permeated by light. But, below ten feet, the failing light becomes flat and diffused—a twilight zone that darkens as we go deeper. As the swimmer moves through the turgid, murky water, the light plays on the whorls, air bubbles, and drifting weeds. The flow overrides the figure, which seems to dissolve, appearing and disappearing in the diffused, uncertain light. Notice how the head, lower arm, and other parts of the body tend to flow away into the darkness.

Uneven Light
As we have seen in the preceding example of underwater light, diffused light can be uneven. Such light is still flat in the sense that there remains very little difference between light and shadow. But the tones may vary with the caprice of the atmosphere—or the water. This medieval craftsman sits in a recessed, shady area not illuminated by direct light. The values are generally low in contrast, so that most of the forms of the figure and background seem to melt together. But random patches of light break through from overhead, brightening minor areas on the head, hands, legs, and foreground. At these places, there is marked contrast, suggesting touches of warm sunlight.

(From *Dynamic Light and Shade* by Burne Hogarth. Illustrated by the author.)

beyond mortal time and space; and because history is a reaction in the search of a great myth-man, an ancestor, a hero, or god who possesses the Tree of Life and shows how to reach its everlasting abundance—today such needs are gone. Man, not God, creates superabundance. If the needs are gone, the myth of the hero and the god must die.

"Man as the arbiter of push-button superabundance has redefined slow-time transformation-evolution into instant-time creation-annihilation. As these overturn the old myths of history and speed toward unimpeded chaos, chaos in its finite term is infinite good. Waste and chaos as Infinite Good become analogous to God. In the era of waste, we see the wreck of the Hero and the death of God . . . . This is why we delight in the wreck. This is why great concretions of junk abound in our world . . . . The equivalent of technological hyperproduction can only be *technological ruin* . . . . Against all progress, Technological Ruin is the paradox of our time, the precious ideal form of the perverse Cybernetic Society."[1]

Eager to again illustrate his theories, and exhausted by years of academic debate, Hogarth retired from the School of Visual Arts in **1970**. "I was ready to . . . sell my interest to a clan of hostile rivals, a clique of self-styled 'culture shapers' who saw their educational mission through conceit of saving the culture from chronic confusion and aesthetic decline.

"For me, the situation was repugnant, non-viable and pernicious. I sent a note saying I deplored seeing the school identified with the 'culture-shaper-caper.' I had reached my point of decision not without some pain; it was my time to go

. . . . I left the School . . . to bend my efforts fully to painting, drawing, etching and writing books.

"In **1972** . . . I produced a pictorial narrative novel, *Tarzan of the Apes* . . . . This form is *not* an illustrated book. Like an expanded 'comic strip' it is a sequential narrative produced for *adult* readership, a first of its kind. It carried implications of a new wave genre in book publishing that was not 'comic,' juvenile, or hebephrenic; it was not a nostalgic retreat to the past. Published, it achieved international visibility, printed in eleven languages around the world.

"In **1976**, I produced an adaptation of Edgar Rice Burroughs' *Jungle Tales of Tarzan*, a follow-up pictorial narrative which contained four stories . . . and was laced through with a series of subliminal, cryptesthetic symbolic devices, not seen or even attempted by any artist working in this genre."

These books again attracted the critical zeal of Hogarth's followers, and at last his work received widespread recognition in the United States. In the forward to *Jungle Tales of Tarzan*, New York University Professor Walter James Miller wrote, "Hogarth's continuous studies in symbolism and iconography make this his most intricate work so far . . . . We sense that there is always much more there than we have so far absorbed. He uses *covert* symbols to suggest *struggle* (toward an insight, for example), and *overt* symbols to indicate *achievement* (say, of an insight). This is directly akin to the composer's use of the teasing, unresolved seventh versus the slide home into the tonic.

Profile in Equal Light. (From *Dynamic Light and Shade* by Burne Hogarth. Illustrated by the author.)

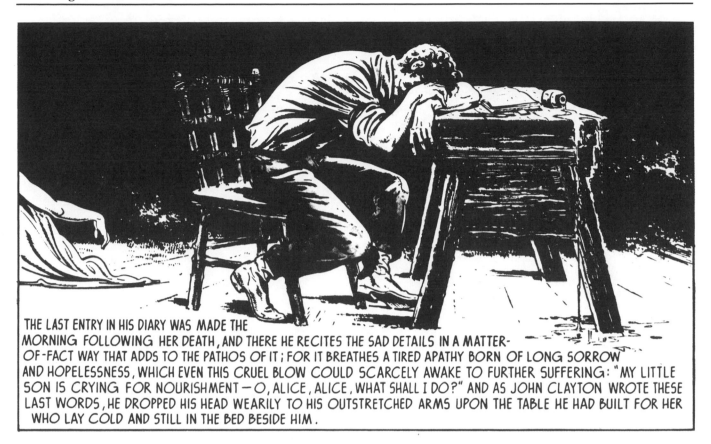

THE LAST ENTRY IN HIS DIARY WAS MADE THE MORNING FOLLOWING HER DEATH, AND THERE HE RECITES THE SAD DETAILS IN A MATTER-OF-FACT WAY THAT ADDS TO THE PATHOS OF IT; FOR IT BREATHES A TIRED APATHY BORN OF LONG SORROW AND HOPELESSNESS, WHICH EVEN THIS CRUEL BLOW COULD SCARCELY AWAKE TO FURTHER SUFFERING: "MY LITTLE SON IS CRYING FOR NOURISHMENT — O, ALICE, ALICE, WHAT SHALL I DO?" AND AS JOHN CLAYTON WROTE THESE LAST WORDS, HE DROPPED HIS HEAD WEARILY TO HIS OUTSTRETCHED ARMS UPON THE TABLE HE HAD BUILT FOR HER WHO LAY COLD AND STILL IN THE BED BESIDE HIM.

(Half-page illustration panel from *Tarzan of the Apes: Book One* by Burne Hogarth. Original text by Edgar Rice Burroughs, adapted by Robert M. Hodes. Illustrated by the author.)

"Thus, when Tarzan is still embroiled in the agonies of the search for meaning, there are likely to be disembodied eyes concealed somewhere in the frame. We sense them, but we might not see them or even feel prompted to find them .... But when Tarzan's probing verges close to resolution, the symbols are deliberately out in the open.

"Always on good terms with his unconscious—as an artist, that's his greatest strength, no matter how much he loves to verbalize—Hogarth felt the need to plunge anew into that real jungle—that jungle where the struggle is for insight into the self. He had long known that that was what the Tarzan story is really all about."[3]

With his creative energies renewed, and his critical reputation at last vindicated in America, Hogarth returned to academics, teaching Anatomy and Drawing at New York's Parsons School of Design in **1975**. Two years later, the artist published his fourth text book, *Drawing Dynamic Hands*. "It carried a minimum of 300 illustrations along with a carefully developed text. I must say now, having experienced the widespread loss in drawing sensibility and experience, I recommend my books with a fervent, even messianic enthusiasm.

"In the succeeding period, I published, for Chelsea House ... a collector's edition, in elephant size, of 155 full color "Tarzan" pages, called the *Golden Age of Tarzan*. Released before Christmas in **1979**, it sold for $200 a copy.

"I was now making plans to relocate to Los Angeles where my son, Michael, lived .... I was hard at work on ... a concept of 'light and shade.' It was a subject which had never been breached before .... The book was published in **1981** as *Dynamic Light and Shade*. It is a sleeper, not fully recognized as a breakthrough effort .... But someday it will be recognized as one of the first on the subject.

"When I came to Los Angeles in 1981, I contacted the Otis Art Institute of the Parsons School ... as a courtesy call from a faculty member of the parent school in New York. They asked me to join the faculty.

"In **1982**, I received a call from the Illustration Department at Art Center College of Design, in Pasadena. The Head of the Department, Phil Hays, was an excellent friend from the earlier days when *he* taught ... in my school, the School of Visual Arts. He was enthusiastic about my presence in Los Angeles, and instantly offered me a post in his Department.

"My latest creation since 1981 ... has been the publication of a Collector's Special Edition Portfolio on the *Life Of King Arthur* .... This is a series of ten large drawings in black and white, with a special cover drawing from which I have sculpted a deep relief medallion model, converted into bronze .... I expect them to produce a powerful visual impact when seen as a group exhibition of the pieces."

In *Tarzan*, *Seigneur de la Jungle*, Maurice Horn summarized the artist's career, writing, " ... Burne Hogarth has covered the entire range of artistic fields; he has been illustrator, cartoonist, engraver, teacher, school founder, art theorist, painter and writer. In all these disciplines, Hogarth has left his personal mark; in all of them he has succeeded and, at times, excelled. If he has gone from one mode of expression to another, relentlessly starting afresh, relentlessly experimenting, his career did not reflect discouragement or failure,

IN THE WINDOW OPENING HE SET BRANCHES, SO WOVEN
THAT THEY FORMED A SUBSTANTIAL GRATING THAT COULD
WITHSTAND THE STRENGTH OF A POWERFUL ANIMAL. THE
DOOR HE BUILT OF PIECES OF THE PACKING BOXES
WHICH HAD HELD THEIR BELONGINGS, NAILING
ONE PIECE UPON ANOTHER UNTIL HE HAD A
SOLID BODY OF GREAT STRENGTH, HUNG ON
TWO MASSIVE HARDWOOD HINGES. THE
BUILDING OF A BED, CHAIRS, TABLE,
AND SHELVES WAS A RELATIVELY EASY
MATTER, SO THAT BY THE END OF THE
SECOND MONTH THEY WERE WELL SETTLED,
AND, BUT FOR THE CONSTANT DREAD OF
ATTACK BY WILD BEASTS AND THE EVER GROW-
ING LONELINESS, THEY WERE NOT UNCOMFORTABLE OR UNHAPPY.

(From *Tarzan of the Apes: Book One* by Burne Hogarth. Original text by Edgar Rice Burroughs, adapted by Robert M. Hodes. Illustrated by the author.)

but the will to proceed ever further: 'to forever push on,' as Andre Gide recommended.

"A work of singular genius, Hogarth's 'Tarzan' marks one of the supreme moments of the comic strip."

FOOTNOTE SOURCES

[1]Frances Locher, editor, *Contemporary Authors,* Volumes 93-96, Gale, 1980.
[2]Jacques Michel, *Le Monde* (Paris), March 11, 1966.
[3]Walter James Miller, "Introduction," *Jungle Tales of Tarzan* by Robert M. Hodes, Watson-Guptill, 1976.

FOR MORE INFORMATION SEE:

Bizarre (Paris), numbers 29-30, 1963.
Francis Lacassin, "Hogarth Between Wonder and Madness," *Giff-Wiff,* number 13, 1965.
Pierre Couperie and Maurice Horn, *A History of the Comic Strip,* Crown, 1968.
Harry E. Habblitz, "Hogarth," *Heroes Illustrated,* spring, 1969.
Paul Spencer, "Hogarth's Monsieur Tarzan," *ERBdom,* November, 1969.
Nation, August 30, 1971.
Francis Lacassin, *Tarzan ou le chevalier crispe,* Union generale d'editions, 1971.
Jerry Robinson, *The Comics: An Illustrated History of Comic Strip Art,* Putnam, 1974.
"Burne Hogarth and German Expressionism," *Crimmer's: The Harvard Journal of Pictorial Fiction,* winter, 1975.
Ron Goulart, *The Adventurous Decade,* Arlington House, 1975.
M. Horn, editor, *The World Encyclopedia of Comics,* Chelsea House, 1976.
Arts/Lettres (Paris), June, 1977.
"Burne Hogarth," *Daybreak,* November, 1978.
"Burne Hogarth, World's Greatest Comic Artist," *Comics World,* September, 1982.
Denis Gifford, *The International Book of Comics,* Crescent Books, 1984.
5000 Personalities of the World, 3rd edition, American Biographical Institute, 1990.

HOLLANDER, Zander 1923-
(Alexander Peters)

PERSONAL: Born March 24, 1923, in New York, N.Y.; son of Herman (a salesman) and Tobye (a housewife; maiden name, Karesh) Hollander; married Phyllis Rosen (a writer and editor), December 13, 1951; children: Susan, Peter. *Education:* Attended City College (now of the City University of New York), and Queens College (now of the City University of New York). *Religion:* Jewish. *Home:* Indian Lake, Millerton, N.Y. 12546. *Office:* Associated Features, Inc., 240 East 35th St., New York, N.Y. 10016.

CAREER: United Press International, New York, N.Y., staff member on foreign desk, 1946-47; *New York World-Telegram,* New York, N.Y., sports writer, 1947-56; Associated Features, Inc. (publishers) New York, N.Y., president, 1955-90. *Military service:* U.S. Army; served as correspondent for *Brief* magazine. *Awards, honors: More Strange but True Football Stories* was selected one of Child Study Association of America's Children's Books of the Year, 1973, and *Roller Hockey,* 1975.

WRITINGS:

(With Joe Carrieri) *Yankee Bat Boy,* Prentice-Hall, 1955.
Famous Sports Moments, Associated Features, 1958.
(With Larry Fox) *The Home Run Story,* Norton, 1966.
(With Paul Zimmerman) *Football Lingo,* Norton, 1967.
(Under pseudonym Alexander Peters) *Heroes of the Major Leagues,* Random House, 1967.
(With Sandy Padwe) *Basketball Lingo,* Grosset, 1971.
(With Steve Clark) *Roller Hockey: Of Sticks and Skates and City Streets,* Hawthorn, 1975.
(With Phil Pepe) *The Book of Sports Lists,* Pinnacle Books, 1970.
(With P. Pepe) *The Book of Sports Lists II,* Pinnacle Books, 1980.
(With P. Pepe) *The Book of Sports Lists III,* Pinnacle Books, 1981.
(With David Schulz) *Sports Teasers: A Book of Games and Puzzles* (illustrated by Marsha Cohen), Random House, 1982.
(With P. Pepe) *The Baseball Book of Lists,* Pinnacle Books, 1983.
Record Breakers: One Hundred and One Winning Streaks in Sports, Scholastic, 1985.
(With wife, Phyllis Hollander) *Sports Bloopers: Weird, Wacky and Unexpected Moments in Sports,* Scholastic, 1985.

EDITOR

(And compiler) *Great American Athletes of the Twentieth Century,* Random House, 1966, revised edition, 1972.
Baseball Lingo, Norton, 1967.
Strange but True Football Stories, Random House, 1967, reissued, 1983.
Improve Your Sport, Popular Library, 1968.
Ballantine Beer Pro Football TV Manual, Popular Library, 1969.
The Modern Encyclopedia of Basketball, Four Winds Press, 1969, 2nd revised edition, Dolphin Books, 1979.
Great Moments in Pro Football, Random House, 1969.
Great Rookies of Pro Basketball, Random House, 1969.
(With Hal Bock) *The Complete Encyclopedia of Ice Hockey,* Prentice-Hall, 1970, revised edition published as *The Complete Encyclopedia of Ice Hockey: The Heroes, Teams, Great Moments, and Records of the National Hockey League Plus the World Hockey Association,* 1974, 3rd edition, New American Library, 1986.
Pro Basketball: Its Superstars and History, Scholastic Book Services, 1971.
Basketball's Greatest Games, Prentice-Hall, 1971.
Madison Square Garden: A Century of Sport and Spectacle on the World's Most Versatile Stage, Hawthorn, 1973.
More Strange but True Football Stories, Random House, 1973.
(With D. Schulz) *The Sports Nostalgia Quiz Book,* New American Library, 1975, revised edition, 1985.
(With D. Schulz) *The Illustrated Sports Record Book,* New American Library, 1975.
The Olympic Handbook, New American Library, 1976.
The Encyclopedia of Sports Talk, Corwin, 1976.
The Pro Basketball Encyclopedia, Corwin, 1977, revised edition published as *The NBA's Official Encyclopedia of Pro Basketball,* New American Library, 1981.
(With D. Schulz) *Complete Book of Jai-Alai,* Corwin, 1978.
Lake Placid, 1980: The Complete Handbook of the Olympic Winter Games, New American Library, 1979.
(With Bud Collins) *Bud Collin's Modern Encyclopedia of Tennis,* Dolphin Books, 1980.
The American Encyclopedia of Soccer, Everest House, 1980.

The Baseball Book: A Complete A to Z Encyclopedia of Baseball, Random House, 1982.
Home Run: Baseball's Greatest Hits and Hitters, Random House, 1984.

EDITOR; WITH WIFE, P. HOLLANDER

They Dared to Lead: America's Black Athletes, Grosset, 1972.
It's the Final Score That Counts, Grosset, 1973.
Touchdown!: Football's Most Dramatic Scoring Feats, Random House, 1982.
Winners under Twenty-One: America's Spectacular Young Sports Champions, Random House, 1982.
The Masked Marvels: Baseball's Great Catchers, Random House, 1982.
Dan Fouts, Ken Anderson, Joe Theismann, and Other All-Time Great Quarterbacks, Random House, 1983.
Sarajevo, 1984: The Complete Handbook of the Olympic Winter Games, New American Library, 1983.
Los Angeles 1984: The Complete Handbook of the Olympic Games, New American Library, 1984.
Amazing but True Sports Stories, Scholastic, 1986.

EDITOR OF ANNUALS

The Complete Handbook of Pro-Hockey, Lancer, 1972, New American Library, 1973-88.
The Complete Handbook of Baseball, Lancer, 1973, New American Library, 1974-90.
The Complete Handbook of Pro-Basketball, Lancer, 1973, New American Library, 1974-90.
The Complete Handbook of Pro-Football, Lancer, 1973, New American Library, 1974-90.
The Complete Handbook of College Football, New American Library, 1974-79.
The Complete Handbook of Soccer, New American Library, 1975-80.
The Complete Handbook of College Basketball, New American Library, 1977-80.

SIDELIGHTS: "I guess as soon as I was able to hold a pencil and throw a ball, I thought of becoming a sports writer. Actually, I broke in by manning the crank on a mimeograph machine which turned out the P.S. 106 school paper in the seashore village of Edgemere, Long Island, New York. But even before that, I'd become addicted to the delicious smell of newsprint from the magazine (*Saturday Evening Post*) I delivered by bike to a territory running from the Atlantic Ocean to Jamaica Bay.

"When I was fourteen I landed a whopping assignment, sports columnist for the local weekly newspaper, the *Rockaway Journal,* and after that I was never far from a typewriter or a playing field. My pay came from (1) the ownership of a press pass that got me into the games free and (2) the excitement of seeing something I wrote in print, and with my name on it. Later I was to earn twenty cents an inch for stories I wrote for the *Long Island Daily Press* and a trifle more when I became high school correspondent for a big city newspaper, the *New York World-Telegram.* I continued to write sports for the *Telegram* for two decades covering everything from baseball, football and basketball to tennis, boating and skiing.

"Today I am president of my own company, Associated Features, for whom I write, edit, compile and produce sports books, booklets and magazines."

FOR MORE INFORMATION SEE:

New York Times Book Review, November 6, 1966, January 5, 1975, June 17, 1979.
Commonweal, November 21, 1975.
Los Angeles Times Book Review, September 28, 1980.

HOUGH, Judy Taylor 1932-
(Judy Taylor)

PERSONAL: Surname rhymes with "plow"; born August 12, 1932, in Murton near Swansea, South Wales; adopted daughter of Gladys Spicer Taylor (a teacher); married Richard Hough (a writer and naval historian), June 6, 1980. *Education:* Educated until the age of sixteen in the United Kingdom. *Politics:* Socialist. *Religion:* Church of England. *Home and office:* 31 Meadowbank, Primrose Hill Rd., London NW3 1AY, England.

CAREER: Bodley Head, London, England, general assistant, 1951-55, specialist in children's books, 1955-80, director, 1967-84, deputy managing director, 1971-80; Chatto, Bodley Head & Jonathan Cape Ltd., London, England, director, 1973-80; Chatto, Bodley Head & Jonathan Cape Australia Pty Ltd., Sydney, Australia, and London, England, director, 1977-80; Frederick Warne, London, England, consultant on the licensing and commercial use of Beatrix Potter's creations, 1981-87; writer, 1982—; Weston Woods Institute, Weston, Conn., associate director, 1984—; Reinhardt Books, London, England, consulting editor, 1988—. *Member:* Publishers Association (chairman of children's book group, 1969-72; member of council, 1972-78), Beatrix Potter Society (chairman, 1990—). *Awards, honors:* Member of the Order of the British Empire for services to children's publishing, 1971.

WRITINGS:

UNDER NAME JUDY TAYLOR

My First Year: A Beatrix Potter Baby Book, Warne (England), 1983, Warne (U.S.), 1989.
Beatrix Potter: Artist, Storyteller, and Countrywoman, Warne (England), 1986, Warne (U.S.), 1987.
That Naughty Rabbit: Beatrix Potter and Peter Rabbit, Warne (England), 1987, Warne (U.S.), 1988.
(With others) *Beatrix Potter, 1866-1943: The Artist and Her World,* Warne, 1988.
Beatrix Potter's Letters: A Selection, Warne (England), 1989, Warne (U.S.), 1990.

"SOPHIE AND JACK" SERIES; JUVENILE; UNDER NAME JUDY TAYLOR; ALL ILLUSTRATED BY SUSAN GANTNER

Sophie and Jack, Bodley Head, 1982, Philomel, 1983.
Sophie and Jack Help Out, Bodley Head, 1983, Philomel, 1984.
Sophie and Jack in the Snow, Bodley Head, 1984.
Sophie and Jack in the Rain, Bodley Head, 1989.

"DUDLEY DORMOUSE" SERIES; JUVENILE; UNDER NAME JUDY TAYLOR; ALL ILLUSTRATED BY PETER CROSS

Dudley Goes Flying, Putnam, 1986.
Dudley and the Monster, Putnam, 1986.
Dudley in a Jam, Walker, 1986, Putnam, 1987.
Dudley and the Strawberry Shake, Walker, 1986, Putnam, 1987.

JUDY TAYLOR HOUGH

Dudley Bakes a Cake, Putnam, 1988.

JUVENILE; UNDER NAME JUDY TAYLOR; ILLUSTRATED BY REG CARTWRIGHT

My Dog, Walker, 1987, Macmillan, 1988.
My Cat, Walker, 1987, Macmillan, 1988.

SIDELIGHTS: Judy Taylor Hough was born on **August 12, 1932** in South Wales. Her mother died five weeks later of childbirth fever, leaving infant Hough in the care of her maternal aunt, a nursery school teacher. "I spent the first year of my life, until my aunt could make the right arrangements, in Welbeck Nursery Training College in Hampstead, London. They had to have babies to practice on and presumably they practiced on me. My aunt had great difficulty finding a place for me to live. She was twenty-eight and unmarried, and she had this tiny baby to look after. 'It's my sister's baby,' she would say. And everybody would answer, 'Oh yeah?'"

With the start of World War II, Hough and her aunt, "who I called Mother," were still in London. "The war was very exciting. At night, we would get out of bed and go downstairs, with the great noise from the air raids all around, and sit under the stairs obeying the official instructions to put cotton wool in our ears and a cork between our teeth to stop us from biting our tongues. The cork had to have a string on it in case we swallowed it. Imagine what a picture we must have made, sitting with our gas masks on our laps. The next morning we would go out and look for the places that had been bombed

the night before. The only time I remember ever being afraid was when it was my mother's turn for fire-watch duty. She would disappear up onto the roof—and that frightened me. She was my only security."

A few months later, Hough and her mother were evacuated with their school to Hampshire. "I was seven. The whole school stayed at the house of Sir Thomas and Lady Royden, who owned a shipping line." But soon the pair moved on to Liverpool in an attempt to gain passage to America or Canada for the duration of the war.

"I had a passage on a ship called 'The City of Benares,' but I couldn't accept it because my mother was not allowed to accompany me. The boat was sunk, with the loss of over 200 children, and all further evacuation of children to America was cancelled." Hough and her mother remained in Cheshire. "Lady Bibby [with whom the two were staying] asked my mother if she would help to look after the fifteen evacuees from Liverpool who were living in the servants' wing of the gigantic house, and also to be governess to the Bibby children before the youngest three went to school. My mother accepted the arrangement, on condition that I would be treated as part of the family.

"It was a wonderful time for me. I went from a solitary life in London to this magnificent house. The nursery was well stocked with books. I learned to ride, skate, and to drive a tractor—all things I never would have done in London.

"During the war there was strict sweet rationing. We were allowed only one sweet a day after lunch and we were then read to for an hour. We had to lie flat on our backs on the floor in the sitting room in the hope that we would grow up with straight backs. My mother or Lady Bibby would read *White Fang* or Dickens to us, books that were much too difficult for us to try by ourselves. It was a marvellous introduction to so many good books.

"John Bibby and I were very close in age and we did everything together, but when we were eight, we were sent off to separate boarding schools. Mine was a girls' school in the Lake District, in Ambleside. It was the practicing school of a training college for teachers (I've been practiced on all my life). Every week we had a new, young student teacher and we were horrible to her, seeing how quickly we could make her cry.

"The training college was for teachers in the Parents National Educational system (PNEU), a method of teaching invented by Charlotte Mason and designed specifically for those children whose parents are continually on the move—diplomats, army families, etc. Anywhere in the world PNEU children were studying the same syllabus at the same time, with timetables and examinations centrally set and corrected. The system could, therefore, also be used by families where there might be no school at all within reach, the lessons supervised by the parent or governess, and the examination papers sent to Ambleside for correction. It also meant no interruption in education should continuous school changes be necessary.

And Dudley had settled down for his long winter sleep before the jam had even begun to cool. (Illustration by Peter Cross from *Dudley in a Jam* by Judy Taylor.)

We were taught a little of everything, excluding such specifics as chemistry and physics. It gave us a very wide general knowledge but of a nonacademic nature. No one ever thought about the possibility of going on to university."

Although desperately homesick and unhappy at first, as time went on, Hough adjusted and began to make friends. "I'm afraid I became a ring leader. We used to do crazy things, like taking over an attic room in an old, broken-down cottage in the garden and making it into a den. All of this was done in the middle of the night, climbing out the window and down the drainpipe. We'd also creep out and meet the boys of the village. The school was quite worried when that was discovered.

"Then we were caught drawing pictures of sexual organs and functions, but we had got some of it all wrong and a letter was sent home asking our parents to please explain to us the facts of life. I suppose my mother felt she was in a rather difficult situation being unmarried, so Lady Bibby took the explaining upon herself. I don't remember much about it except thinking, 'What's she telling me all this for?' After all, I had been brought up with John and shared baths with him. Anatomy was no problem."

When she was thirteen, Hough was asked to leave the school. "I was always being hauled up in front of the headmistress, Miss Moffatt, and lectured for hours, about being uncooperative. Nobody ever thought that I might be unhappy or even bored.

"The war was ending and my mother announced one day that we were going back to London. But when we got back, she couldn't get a job. I can still hear her saying, 'I'm forty-two and no one wants to employ me.' She eventually landed a good job as warden of a residential girls' hostel in Lancaster Gate, in West London.

"I attended St. Pauls Girl's School, an expensive day school for which I took the scholarship exam and failed. I had to work very hard to keep up, but I loved the challenge. I was introduced to chemistry, biology, and physics and to academic competition. When I turned sixteen, my mother admitted that she could no longer afford to keep me at school any more. It was a great disappointment because by now I desperately wanted to go to university."

Hough's mother had arranged for her to go to Canada to look after the two 'babies' of friends for a year. "The babies turned out to be children of seven and nine and I was only sixteen. Their father was a circuit judge who was away most of the time, their mother an ex-concert pianist who needed a lot of rest. I had to get the children off to school every morning, even on my day off. I did a certain amount of housework, ironing, cooking, and so on, and took the children to the park or off to their friends' houses.

"Canada was very different from England, mainly in the extremes of weather. I'd never been so cold in my life. I was also lonely and homesick, but my mother always kept in touch by letter. By the end of the year, I hadn't saved nearly enough money to pay for my fare home, as I was paid only forty dollars a week, and after eighteen months, my mother had to send me the money. If she hadn't, I think I'd still be there."

Back in London Hough found a temporary position in the book department of Harrods' Department Store. "But the job didn't start immediately, so Dick Hough, an old family

(From *My Dog* by Judy Taylor. Illustrated by Reg Cartwright.)

friend who worked at Bodley Head publishers, asked if I could help put the next season's catalogs into envelopes. I must have done it quite well because he asked me to return after I finished the Harrods' job to stuff envelopes permanently. And that's how I became a publisher.

"I was just eighteen. I made the tea and worked the Addressograph machine. In those days, the whole company was virtually in one room, and you had the feel of what was happening in every department. We used to pack all our own books, too, and I learned how to do a packer's knot.

"Quite soon I was given the children's books to read, presumably because I was the youngest person in the building. Then I took over the advertisements and learned about laying them out—and they always make the youngest, most inexperienced person in every publishing house responsible for sending out review copies."

Dick Hough left the Bodley Head and Hough began her association with Max Reinhardt when he bought the Bodley Head in 1957. "Max became a very dear friend. He always had total faith in you—until you did something wrong. He put me to work with Barbara Wilson, the Bodley Head's first children's editor.

"It was a very healthy time for children's books and we had come through the shortages and strict paper rationing of the war. Dick Hough had established the children's list at Bodley, taking a number of picture books from America, like *The Happy Lion,* and starting some series publishing: *Great Men of the Counties, Great Men of Kent,* and *Great Inventors.* He had also started a series of career novels for girls, like *Air Hostess Ann,* and *Juliet in Publishing.* We then took that idea

further and published some nonfiction career books. Slowly the children's list began to grow.

"When Barbara Wilson left, Kathleen Lines was appointed as children's editorial advisor, Max deciding that I was too young to be the children's editor. K (as we knew her) instilled in us that only the best was good enough for children and that one must never lower one's standards for commercial reasons. It was the working credo.

"I was then joined by Jill Black and Margaret Clark and the three of us worked together to build the Bodley Head list. We wanted to make it the best list ever. We were proud to publish Rosemary Sutcliff and Henry Treese. We took more picture books from America—Roger Duvoisin, Paul Galdone, Pat Hutchins, Maurice Sendak. We originated picture books and I was lucky enough to work with Edward Ardizzone on his last 'Little Tim' books. His method of working was interesting. He used to write his texts by hand, at considerable length. Then he'd sketch the pictures, and after that he'd go back and take things out of the text that were in the pictures. Then he'd go back to the pictures and put things into them that weren't in the text. He'd go back and forth all the time."

Hough's work allowed her to travel all over the world for a number of years. "As Bodley Head's children's editor, I went to America (sometimes twice a year), to Bologna, to Frankfurt, to Australia, to Canada, to South Africa. I grew to love travelling.

"I was so nervous when I went to America for the first time in 1961 that I hardly left my hotel room. When I did go out, I got lost, and as I had always been taught at home, I asked a policeman the way. 'What the hell do you think I am?' he said. 'A tourist guide?' And I burst into tears."

My cat was chased
up a tree...
and got stuck there.

(From *My Cat* by Judy Taylor. Illustrated by Reg Cartwright.)

In 1980, after twenty-nine years with Bodley Head and having attained the level of deputy managing director, Judy married Richard Hough and moved to the country. "We had a large old farmhouse in the middle of Gloucestershire, miles from anywhere. We went there primarily because my husband's previous marriage had broken up and he wanted to get away from London completely. So we buried ourselves in the country.

"I soon discovered that it was physically impossible for me to commute every week to London so I resigned from the Bodley Head. Instead I became a consultant to them, though they didn't consult me very often! But one thing they did consult me about was American artist Susan Gantner. She had been doing some lovely greeting cards with hippos on them, and we all decided that we would ask her if she'd do a picture book for us. She was delighted, but when she submitted her ideas, we couldn't find one that we thought would work well.

"It was while I was playing hide and seek at home with our youngest grandson (who was just at that age where he believed that if he shut his eyes he couldn't be seen) that it suddenly clicked with me: what a wonderful theme for a hippo book, made more ridiculous because hippos are so big. Hence, *Sophie and Jack*. Sophie is the name of one of the children's ponies. Jack is the name of our grandson.

"I hadn't even met Susan, but I sent the text and a very rough layout to her in San Francisco. Because of my publishing experience, I knew that an economic format for the book would be thirty-two pages including the end-papers. I didn't actually say what should happen on each page, but I did make some suggestions, and Susan met the challenge wonderfully.

"When you have been an editor, particularly of books for small children, you have worked on many picture book texts. I don't mean that you have necessarily created them from scratch, but you have worked with artists on getting the words right. It's one of the anomalies of publishing: you never expect an author to be able to draw, but you always expect an artist to be able to write! Most artists, with a few notable exceptions, find texts very difficult. What I was doing with *Sophie and Jack* was what I had been doing for years, but now it was me who was having the ideas, too."

Sophie and Jack led to a series of books, the last of which was published in 1989. "Sequels come about usually because the first book has done so well that everyone wants more. I liked doing them very much, but I think four in a series is probably enough. I suspect that most of the present children's editors would see *Sophie and Jack* as being somewhat old-fashioned.

"Publishing in the last ten years has changed very much, and the commercial element is now overpowering. However, I'm still convinced that quality will always surface, although, at the moment, we're pretty short of it."

In 1984 Walker Books approached Hough to do some books for them. "Sebastian Walker, who I had known when he was the European salesman for the Bodley Head/Cape/Chatto

Potter on spring holiday, 1894. (From *Beatrix Potter: Artist, Storyteller, and Countrywoman* by Judy Taylor.)

commissioned me to do four picture book texts. I chose as my main theme the way children are always competing with one another, and the four texts featured counting, colors, opposites, and sibling rivalry. One of the texts was based directly on the time I was working with a play group of under-fives. One child asked another, 'How many legs has a cow?' The answer came, 'Two at the front and two at the back,' an entirely original way of looking at numbers!

"Strangely enough, those four texts have never been published. They turned out to be very difficult to illustrate, and we failed to find an artist who wanted to do them. It took months and months of trying. There must have been something odd about those stories of mine.

"Then Walker said he'd got this talented young artist named Peter Cross who had come up with a marvelous idea for a series of picture books about a dormouse called Dudley, but needed help with the texts. I met Peter and liked him very much, and we worked together on the first four *Dudley* books.

"We didn't meet often. As an editor, I never thought it particularly important for an artist and author to meet. What is important is for the artist to interpret the words as he sees them and not be told by the author: 'A character should look like this.' It was different, anyway, with Dudley as he was Peter's invention in the first place.

"The other books I did for Walker, *My Dog* and *My Cat*, were very basic picture books about a child's first pet, ideas that I had had for a long time. Walker chose Reg Cartwright to illustrate them. His illustrations are what I would call 'French primitive,' not a tiny bit the way I'd imagined them, but I find them very interesting, and the books have done well."

After seeing an advertisement in *The Bookseller* in 1981 from Frederick Warne Publishers, which indicated that they wanted to resuscitate their children's list, Hough had written to ask if she could help. "I couldn't possibly be a full-time children's editor living in the country, but I wanted to be involved in publishing children's books in some way. The Warne children's list used to be absolutely wonderful: Caldecott, Greenaway, Brooke, and of course, Beatrix Potter. I had a telephone call the next morning, saying that they needed someone to help with Beatrix Potter. The whole thing is becoming enormously complicated and we need advice about the publishing and the merchandising.

"I agreed then and there to come up to London once every six weeks to attend a Beatrix Potter meeting. I had no idea what I was going to do, but to work with anything connected with Beatrix Potter was the answer to a dream. I have always been a Potter fan, and the Warne files were full of letters from me over the years, complaining about the poor reproduction of the illustrations. I had seen Potter's artwork once or twice when I'd been in the Lake District, and knew just how beautiful it was. The current editions were a travesty. We talked about all this at our meetings and, as a committee, we also fought for better standards of merchandise reproduction.

"One day, at almost my first meeting, a Warne salesmen had come back from the Frankfurt Book Fair saying that everybody was asking for a Beatrix Potter birthday book. 'But baby books are always vulgar,' was the response. 'Well, let's make one that isn't,' was my reaction. So I accumulated all the baby books I could find, which were not very many and were indeed all terrible, and I planned a Beatrix Potter baby book called *My First Year*. I designed the page, because I knew in my mind exactly how it should be, and I did the layout." (*My First Year* has sold over one-half million copies and has even been translated into Japanese.)

"When Warne was bought by Penguin in 1984, the new owners asked me to continue as an artistic guide for the merchandising, and they then uncovered a proposal I had made some years earlier for an illustrated Potter biography, using the many early photographs taken by Beatrix Potter's father. The idea was that we should commission an established author to do the book, so when the suggestion was made that *I* should do it, my first reaction was to say no. It was my husband who said I would be crazy to refuse and just to get on with it! It was the beginning of a whole new life, a life with Beatrix Potter."

The time Hough had spent at boarding school, near the home of Potter, proved to be invaluable in tackling the book. "I can't imagine what it would have been like if I hadn't known the Lake District already. I searched out various people, family members, photographic collections, and anybody who might possibly have more photographs. I collected an enormous number of pictures and started making notes around them, realizing very quickly that I would need more room for the text than just extended captions. I did a sample spread and discussed it with Warne. 'Fine,' they said. 'Do whatever you like.'

"It was exciting when I found the full manuscript of Potter's journal in the Victoria and Albert Museum and discovered that the published version of it had been cut. I subsequently found out that the cuts had been made at the request of Potter's trustees and the remaining family members, mainly because the journal revealed that her brother and uncle had been alcoholics.

"But the most amazing thing I unearthed while I was researching was that Harold Warne, Potter's publisher, had been sent to prison for embezzling the company's money. I can't believe Margaret Lane hadn't known about this for her original biography, but presumably it was suppressed by the family publishing firm. But it was an important factor in Potter's literary life because she had unaccountably stopped receiving royalties from Warne, and was therefore reluctant to do another book for them. Margaret Lane implied that there was no new book because Potter's eyesight was failing and because she was busy doing other things.

"I discovered this quite by chance. I had talked with Winifred Warne, the little girl for whom *Two Bad Mice* was written, and she had mentioned something about 'the trouble in 1917.' When she realized that I didn't know what she was talking about, she quickly changed the subject.

"I happened to be reading one of Potter's letters in the Warne archives the next day, in which she had written, 'I've managed to keep the report in the *Times* away from my mother.' Seeing that the date was 1917 I went to the London Library and looked up the *Times* for that year. I didn't know exactly what I was looking for, but I was prepared to wade through the whole thing if necessary. So I started with Warne and there it was in the index: 'Warne, Harold, criminally convicted,' and then I found the report. It was extraordinary the way it all fell into place."

Beatrix Potter: Artist, Storyteller, and Countrywoman was published in 1986, followed closely by *"That Naughty Rabbit": Beatrix Potter and "Peter Rabbit,"* a book written at the request of Warne to mark the complete reorganization of the illustration artwork in all Potter's 'little books.' Hough and her husband then moved back to London. "We'd kept my old flat in London all along and we were now spending two nights in London and the others in the country. I liked living in the country, but I couldn't bear the continual pressure of having two homes and of spending two days on the motorway running between them. There's no fun in that. You're worried about what's happening down there when you're up here, and about what's happening up here when you're down there. I honestly never mind where I live. A home is a home. This house seems to combine everything: we've got the country feeling of Primrose Hill, and yet we are near the center of London. I miss the big garden, but the country is within easy reach by car or train, and now I have my greenhouse on the roof!

"My husband and I both go to our desks immediately after breakfast—a very strict discipline because otherwise I would never get anything done. Dick has a desk on the ground floor and mine is two floors up at the top of the house. That way we can't hear each other bashing away at our typewriters."

In 1987 Hough resigned her position as merchandise adviser to Warne. "That year Ladybird Books published a retelling of *Peter Rabbit* illustrated with photographs of stuffed toys, a book aimed at children 'to whom the original Beatrix Potter was inaccessible.' I felt it was unnecessary and diluting to the mind. The book was published just as I had arrived in America to promote my Potter biography and it was extremely embarrassing. Warne had, after all, licensed the publication. I was so angry that I resigned my appointment in protest on my return to London."

Hough's old colleague, Max Reinhardt, had just started a new publishing company Reinhardt Books, and "invited me to be consulting editor, to start a children's list, and to bring along anything I wanted to publish. I was delighted. We have a small list. One of our first books was the British edition of my old friend Maurice Sendak's *Caldecott and Co*, a collection of his writings concerning children's books, authors, and artists. We have also published children's picture books by Dick's oldest daughter, Sarah Garland, and by the Japanese artist, Mitsumasa Anno, whose books I had published at the Bodley Head."

Hough's devotion to children's literature has earned her much respect. "I should like to write more children's books, and maybe one day an adult novel. It could be an autobiographical novel because I think the story's there: I have led an extraordinary life with an extraordinary background."[1]

FOOTNOTE SOURCES

[1]Based on an interview by Cathy Courtney for *Something about the Author*.

(From *Dudley Bakes a Cake* by Judy Taylor. Illustrated by Peter Cross.)

FOR MORE INFORMATION SEE:

Publishers Weekly, July 22, 1983 (p. 78), September 25, 1987 (p. 25).
Robert D. Hale, "Musings," *Horn Book,* January, 1988 (p. 100).

HUGGINS, Nathan I(rvin) 1927-

PERSONAL: Born January 14, 1927, in Chicago, Ill.; son of Winston John (a waiter) and Marie (a homemaker; maiden name, Warsaw) Huggins; married Brenda Carlita Smith (an actress and writer), July 18, 1971. *Education:* University of California, Berkeley, A.B., 1954, M.A., 1955; Harvard University, A.M., 1957, Ph.D., 1962. *Home:* 14 Scott St., Cambridge, Mass. 02138. *Office:* Department of History, Harvard University, Cambridge, Mass. 02138.

CAREER: Long Beach State College (now California State University, Long Beach), assistant professor of history, 1962-64; Lake Forest College, Lake Forest, Ill., assistant professor of history, 1964-66; University of Massachusetts at Boston, assistant professor, 1966-69, associate professor of history, 1969-70; Columbia University, New York, N.Y., professor of history, 1970-80; Harvard University, Cambridge, Mass., W. E. B. DuBois Professor of History and Afro-American Studies, 1980—, chairman, Afro-American Studies department, 1980-84. Visiting associate professor, University of California, Berkeley, 1969-70; guest professor, Heidelberg University, summer, 1979; Fulbright senior lecturer in Grenoble, France, 1974-75.

Founding president, American Museum of Negro History, Boston, 1966-69; Howard Thurman Educational Trust, trustee, 1969-85, vice-president, 1969-80; director, Upward Bound Project, University of Massachusetts, 1966-69, Library of America, 1978—, American Council of Learned Societies, 1980—, and W. E. B. DuBois Institute for Research in Afro-American Studies, Harvard Univeristy, 1980—; commissioner, Massachusetts Teacher Corps Commission, 1967-69; council member, Smithsonian Institution, 1974—; board of directors, New York Council on the Humanities, 1978-80, Library of America, 1979-86, and American Council of Learned Societies, 1982—; chairman, Whitney M. Young Advisory Committee, Columbia University, 1978; member of advisory board, President's Panel on International Exchange of Scholars, 1982-84; trustee, Radcliffe College, 1984—.

Consultant to various organizations, including Danforth Foundation, 1970-74, Educational Testing Service, 1970-71, Anti-Defamation League, Brooklyn Educational and Cultural Alliance, 1977-80, White House Library Group, 1980, and Eakins Press Foundation, 1980-83. Consultant to broadcast productions, including "On Being Black," WGBH-TV, 1968-69; "Sesame Street," 1970—, and "The Best of Families," 1975-77, both Children's Television Workshop; "Twentieth-Century Humanists," National Public Radio, 1976-78; "Look Away: The Old South," South Carolina Educational Television, 1977-80; "Chance and Destiny," WNET-TV, 1977; "America in Chains" series, WPBT-TV, 1981-84; "Booker," film for television series "Wonderworks," 1983-84. Juror for awards and prizes, including Francis Parkman Prize, Dunning Prize, Ford Foundation Nonfiction Book Award, and National Endowment for the Humanities Awards. *Military service:* U.S. Army, 1945-46.

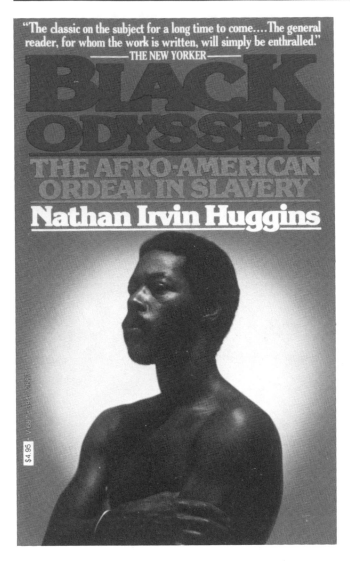

"The classic on the subject for a long time to come....The general reader, for whom the work is written, will simply be enthralled."
—THE NEW YORKER—

BLACK ODYSSEY
THE AFRO-AMERICAN ORDEAL IN SLAVERY
Nathan Irvin Huggins

(Cover illustration from *Black Odyssey: The Afro-American Ordeal in Slavery* by Nathan Irvin Huggins.)

MEMBER: American Historical Association, Association of American Historians (program committee member, 1971-72), Organization of American Historians (executive council member, 1972-80), Association for the Study of Afro-America Life and History (executive council member, 1972-75), PEN, Author's Guild, Southern Historical Association, Antiquarian Society, Council on Foreign Relations. *Awards, honors:* Guggenheim Fellow, 1971-72; Ford Foundation Research and Travel Grant, 1971-72; National Book Award nomination, for *Harlem Renaissance;* American Specialist Award from the United States State Department, 1976; Center for Advanced Study in the Behavioral Sciences Fellow, 1979-80; *Black Odyssey* was selected one of New York Public Library's Books for the Teen Age, 1980, 1981, and 1982; Rockefeller Foundation Humanities Fellowship, 1983-84.

WRITINGS:

Protestants against Poverty: Boston's Charities, 1870-1900, Greenwood Press, 1971.
(Contributor and editor with Martin Kilson and Daniel Fox) *Key Issues in the Afro-American Experience,* two volumes, Harcourt, 1971.

Harlem Renaissance, Oxford University Press, 1971.
(Author of foreword) Marina Wikramanayake, *A World in Shadow: The Free Black in Antebellum South Carolina,* University of South Carolina Press, 1973.
(Contributor) Daniel Aaron and others, editors, *American Issues Forum,* Volume I, Publishers, Inc., 1975.
(Editor) *Voices from the Harlem Renaissance,* Oxford University Press, 1976.
Black Odyssey: The Afro-American's Ordeal in Slavery, Pantheon, 1977, new edition, 1990.
(Contributor) John Higham, editor, *Studies in Ethnic Leadership,* Johns Hopkins University Press, 1978.
Slave and Citizen: The Life of Frederick Douglass, Little, Brown, 1980.
Afro-American Studies: A Review, Ford Foundation, 1985.
(Editor) W. E. B. Du Bois, *Writings* (annotated), Library of America, 1986.
(Editor) W. E. B. Du Bois, *The Suppression of the African Slave-Trade, the Souls of Black Folk and Dusk of Dawn: An Essay toward an Autobiography of a Race Concept,* Library of America, 1986.

Black Odyssey has been published in French, Danish, and German. Contributor of articles to periodicals, including *New York Times,* and *Center.* Member of editorial board, *American Historical Review,* 1979-81, *Journal of Ethnic History,* 1980—; *Reviews in American History,* 1980-85, *Journal of American History,* 1986—; consulting editor, "Foundations in Social Sciences" textbook series, Harcourt, 1974-78.

Huxley in the 1920s.

HUXLEY, Aldous (Leonard) 1894-1963

PERSONAL: Born July 26, 1894, in Godalming, Surrey, England; died November 22, 1963, in Los Angeles, Calif.; came to the U.S. in 1937; son of Leonard (an editor) and Julia Frances (Arnold) Huxley; married Maria Nys, July 10, 1919 (died, February 12, 1955); married Laura Archer, March 20, 1956; children: Matthew. *Education:* Balliol College, Oxford, B.A., 1917.

CAREER: Employed in government office during World War I; Eton College, Eton, England, schoolmaster, 1917-19; staff member of *Athenaeum* and *Westminster Gazette,* 1919-24; writer. Lecturer; visiting professor, University of California, 1959; Carnegie visiting professor, Massachusetts Institute of Technology, 1960. *Member:* Athenaeum Club. *Awards, honors:* James Tait Black Memorial Prize for Fiction from the University of Edinburgh, 1939, for *After Many a Summer Dies the Swan;* Award of Merit and Gold Medal from the American Academy and Institute of Arts and Letters, 1959; D. Litt., University of California, 1959; Companion of Literature from the British Royal Society of Literature, 1962.

WRITINGS:

NOVELS

Crome Yellow, Chatto & Windus, 1921, Doran, 1922, reissued, Chatto & Windus, 1963, Harper, 1965.
(Translator) R. de Gourmont, *A Virgin Heart,* N. L. Brown, 1921.
Antic Hay, Doran, 1923.
Those Barren Leaves, Doran, 1925, reissued, Avon, 1964.
Point Counter Point, Doubleday, 1928, reissued, Harper, 1969.
Brave New World, Doubleday, 1932, reissued, Bantam, 1960, large print edition, Ulverscroft, 1983.
Eyeless in Gaza, Harper, 1936, reissued, Bantam, 1968.
After Many a Summer Dies the Swan, Harper, 1939, reissued, 1965.
Time Must Have a Stop, Harper, 1944.
Ape and Essence, Harper, 1948.
The Genius and the Goddess, Harper, 1955.
Antic Hay and the Gioconda Smile, Harper, 1957.
Brave New World and Brave New World Revisited, Harper, 1960.
Island, Harper, 1962.

SHORT STORIES

Limbo: Six Stories and a Play, Doran, 1920.
Mortal Coils: Five Stories, Doran, 1922.
Little Mexican and Other Stories, Chatto & Windus, 1924.
Young Archimedes and Other Stories, Doran, 1924.
Two or Three Graces: Four Stories, Doran, 1925.
Brief Candles, Doubleday, 1930.
The Gioconda Smile, Chatto & Windus, 1938.
Collected Short Stories, Harper, 1957.
The Crows of Pearblossom (illustrated by Barbara Cooney), Random House, 1968.

POETRY

The Burning Wheel, B. H. Blackwell, 1916.
Jonah, [England], 1917.
The Defeat of Youth and Other Poems, Longmans, Green, 1918.
Leda and Other Poems, Doran, 1920.
Selected Poems, Appleton, 1925.
Arabia Infelix and Other Poems, Fountain Press, 1929.

a new edition of a famous novel with a special introduction by the author

BRAVE NEW WORLD BY ALDOUS HUXLEY

(Jacket illustration by E. McKnight Kauffer from *Brave New World* by Aldous Huxley.)

Apennine, Slide Mountain Press, 1930.
The Cicadas and Other Poems, Doubleday, 1931.
Donald Watt, editor, *The Collected Poetry of Aldous Huxley,* Harper, 1971.

PLAYS

Francis Sheridan's The Discovery, Adapted for the Modern Stage, Chatto & Windus, 1924, Doran, 1925.
The World of Light: A Comedy in Three Acts, Doubleday, 1931.
The Gioconda Smile (adapted from the short story; produced in New York, N.Y. at Lyceum Theater, October, 1950), Harper, 1948 (also published as *Mortal Coils,* Harper, 1948).

NONFICTION

Along the Road: Notes and Essays of a Tourist, Doran, 1925, reissued, Books for Libraries Press, 1971.
Jesting Pilate: An Intellectual Holiday, Doran, 1926 (published in England as *Jesting Pilate: The Diary of a Journey,* Chatto & Windus, 1957).
Essays New and Old, Chatto & Windus, 1926, published in America as *Essays Old and New,* Doran, 1927.
Proper Studies: The Proper Study of Mankind Is Man, Chatto & Windus, 1927, Doubleday, 1928.
Do What You Will, Doubleday, 1929.
Holy Face and Other Essays, Fleuron, 1929.
Vulgarity in Literature: Digressions from a Theme, Chatto & Windus, 1930, Haskell House, 1966.

Music at Night and Other Essays, Chatto & Windus, 1930, Doubleday, 1931, reissued, Books for Libraries Press, 1970.
On the Margin: Notes and Essays, Doran, 1932.
Beyond the Mexique Bay: A Traveller's Journal, Harper, 1934, reissued, Vintage, 1960.
1936 . . . Peace?, Friends Peace Committee (London), 1936.
The Olive Tree and Other Essays, Chatto & Windus, 1936, Harper, 1937, reissued, Books for Libraries Press, 1971.
What Are You Going To Do about It? The Case for Constructive Peace, Chatto & Windus, 1936.
An Encyclopedia of Pacifism, Harper, 1937, reissued, Garland, 1972.
Ends and Means: An Inquiry in the Nature of Ideals and into the Methods Employed for Their Realization, Harper, 1937, reissued, Greenwood, 1969.
The Most Agreeable Vice, [Los Angeles], 1938.
Words and Their Meanings, Ward Ritchie Press, 1940.
Grey Eminence: A Study in Religion and Politics, Harper, 1941, reissued, 1966.
The Art of Seeing, Harper, 1942.
The Perennial Philosophy, Harper, 1945, reissued, Books for Libraries Press, 1972.
Science, Liberty and Peace, Harper, 1946.
(With Sir John Russell) *Food and People,* [London], 1949.
Prisons, with the 'Carceri' Etchings by G. B. Piranesi, Grey Falcon Press, 1949.
Themes and Variations, Harper, 1950.
(With Stuart Gilbert) *Joyce, the Artificer: Two Studies of Joyce's Method,* Chiswick, 1952.
The Devils of Loudun, Harper, 1952.

Huxley, about age five.

(With J. A. Kings) *A Day in Windsor,* Britannicus Liber, 1953.
The French of Paris, Harper, 1954.
The Doors of Perception, Harper, 1954, reissued, 1970.
Heaven and Hell, Harper, 1956, reissued, 1971.
Tomorrow and Tomorrow and Tomorrow and Other Essays, Harper, 1956 (published in England as *Adonis and the Alphabet and Other Essays,* Chatto & Windus, 1956).
A Writer's Prospect—III: Censorship and Spoken Literature, [London], 1956.
Brave New World Revisited, Harper, 1958.
Collected Essays, Harper, 1959.
On Art and Artists: Literature, Painting, Architecture, Music, Harper, 1960.
Selected Essays, Chatto & Windus, 1961.
The Politics of Ecology: The Question of Survival, Center for the Study of Democratic Institutions (Santa Barbara, Calif.), 1963.
Literature and Science, Harper, 1963.
New Fashioned Christmas, Hart Press, 1968.
America and the Future, Pemberton Press, 1970.

COLLECTIONS

Texts and Pretexts: An Anthology with Commentaries, Chatto & Windus, 1932, Harper, 1933, reissued, Norton, 1962.
Rotunda: A Selection from the Works of Aldous Huxley, Chatto & Windus, 1932.
Retrospect: An Omnibus of His Fiction and Non-Fiction over Three Decades, Harper, 1947, reissued, Peter Smith, 1971.
The Letters of Aldous Huxley, Chatto & Windus, 1969, Harper, 1970.
Great Short Works of Aldous Huxley, Harper, 1969.
Collected Works, Chatto & Windus, 1970.
Science, Liberty and Peace (includes *Literature and Science*), Chatto & Windus, 1970.

SCREENPLAYS

(With others) "Pride and Prejudice," starring Laurence Olivier and Greer Garson, Metro-Goldwyn-Mayer, 1940.
(With others) "Jane Eyre," starring Joan Fontaine and Orson Welles, Twentieth Century-Fox, 1944.
"Madame Curie," Metro-Goldwyn-Mayer, 1943.
"A Woman's Vengence" (based on *The Gioconda Smile*), starring Charles Boyer and Jessica Tandy, Universal, 1948.

CONTRIBUTOR

Edward P. Morgan, editor, *This I Believe,* Simon & Schuster, 1952.

Contributor to numerous periodicals, including *Life, Playboy, Encounter,* and *Daedalus.*

ADAPTATIONS:

"Point Counter Point" (play), London, 1930.
"Prelude to Fame" (motion picture; based on short story "Young Archimedes"), Universal, 1950.
(Co-author) "The Genius and the Goddess," starring Nancy Kelly, first produced in New York, N.Y. at Henry Miller's Theatre, December 9, 1957.
"Brave New World" (television movie; adapted by Robert E. Thompson), NBC-TV, 1978, (cassette; filmstrip with cassette), Current Affairs and Mark Twain Media, 1978.

(From the movie "Pride and Prejudice," starring Laurence Olivier and Greer Garson. Co-scripted by Huxley, it was produced by MGM, 1940.)

SIDELIGHTS: Born on **July 26, 1894,** at Laleham, Godalming, Surrey, England, Aldous Huxley spent his formative years attending Eton, one of England's most prestigious schools. "There were funny things about it, I mean it was in many respects still a *renaissance* education. We used to spend the whole of every Tuesday from 7 in the summer and 7.30 in winter till 10.30 at night composing Latin verses—we were given a piece of Tennyson or something and were told to turn it into elegiacs or hexameters or Alcaics or Sapphics, and if you were a little further advanced Greek iambics ... which was a sort of *immense* jig-saw puzzle game ... it was the most *extraordinary* proceeding."[1]

"I left at seventeen owing to an affliction of the eyes which left me practically blind for two or three years, an event which prevented me from becoming a complete public-school English gentleman. Providence is sometimes kind even when it seems to be harsh. My temporary blindness also preserved me from becoming a doctor, for which I am also grateful. For seeing that I nearly died of overwork as a journalist, I should infallibly have killed myself in the much more strenuous profession of medicine. On the other hand, I very much regret the scientific training which my blindness made me miss. It is

ludicrous to live in the twentieth century equipped with an elegant literary training eminently suitable for the seventeenth."[2]

"Many things that I liked doing, like mountain climbing and so on, became difficult or impossible for me. I couldn't practise any kind of sport requiring a ball, because ... I couldn't *see* the balls.

"On the other hand ... if the handicap isn't too great and overwhelming, it can also stimulate one to do things which in other circumstances one wouldn't do.

"I *did* read a great deal. And I am extremely astonished at how much I was able to read. Because ... for about two years after this thing came upon me ... I couldn't read at all. Well, little by little I was able to read again—but I did all my reading ... with a powerful magnifying glass—I must say I am amazed that I did get through as much as I did. It must obviously have been rather tiring, this whole process: but *I managed to do it*."[1]

Despite these difficulties, Huxley began writing a novel, which "I never subsequently read. It disappeared. I rather regret that .... I would be interested to know what it was like now.

"It was sort of romantic—no it wasn't romantic—it was a rather *bitter* novel about a young man and his relationship to two different kind of women, as I remember it."[1] Resuming his schooling at Oxford, he earned his degree in English literature; holidays were spent in France and Italy.

Despite his impaired eyesight, when England entered the war against Germany in **1914,** Huxley was "called up" for service. "Just that day they had issued quite the most senseless of all the orders, to the effect that men must be attested, sworn in, assigned to the groups etc. *before* seeing the doctor. The process of filling up all the papers takes a good half hours work and of course, when a man is unfit, that is all wasted. Thus in my papers I was elaborately put down as belonging to group S4—according to which I should be already serving. However, when I went to the major who was to swear me in, he refused to do it, saying it was the most abject folly to go thro' all the farce with someone so almost certainly unfit: so I was sent to the doctor unsworn—who made me take all my clothes off, to examine my eyes, and declared me totally unfit."[3]

In **September, 1917** after finishing academics at Oxford, he took a post as schoolmaster at his Alma Mater, Eton. "I am glad that teaching makes you a child—I was about to say more of a child; I am always afraid of being made old by the continual assumption of superiority, the unceasing pretence of knowing better, of being respectable and a good example, which has to be kept up. I do my best to make my boys have no respect for me whatever. Most of my work this term consists in going over essays with a number of the elder boys. I have some fifty a week of them coming in for half an hour each to have their essays corrected and commented on. It is quite interesting at times and preferable to doing much work with large forms in school."[3]

Huxley became a regular at the home of Lady Ottoline Morrell, a wealthy patroness who brought together many of the literary, artistic, and political avant-garde of her time. "I had the extraordinary fortune to meet a great many of the ablest people of my time. There were the Bloomsbury people .... There was Virginia [Woolf] and Vanessa, there was Maynard Keynes .... *He* was always fascinating—he had this immense range of knowledge, and he would come out with these *curiously* elliptical remarks about things: he was a very fascinating character .... [Bertrand] Russell I met them and Roger Fry— .... He was very kind to me. And then Clive Bell— ... from them I learned a great deal about art which I really didn't know anything about at all before. They introduced me to modern art, to Post-Impressionism, Cubism and so on ....

"The meeting of all these people was of capital importance to me."[1]

But more important, he met a young woman from Flanders named Maria Nys. "I have at last discovered a nice Belgian: wonders will never cease."[1]

"The fundamental fact about her, I think, is that her aesthetic sensibility is very great; she has—hideous expression-the artistic temperament to an advanced degree. Aestheticism is a dangerous thing; in fact I dont [sic] believe that anyone who lives wholly on sensations is safe; it leads almost inevitably in

Huxley in his sixties.

the end to a sort of corruption and deliquescence of the character. What I have tried to persuade Maria to do is to centre her life on thought rather than on sensation, to adopt some fixed intellectual occupation, involving a certain amount of effort and mental concentration, and not merely to live on the aesthetic sensations of the moment. She is educating herself—in a rather desultory way perhaps—but the process gives her a solid foundation for her existence. When she first went out to Italy she was so completely bowled over by the wealth of beauty round her that she could hardly think of anything else; her life was a mere series of sensuous enjoyments. But she has, to judge from her letters, settled down a good deal since then. I think she will grow up all right. 'Grow up,' for you mustnt [sic] forget how absurdly young she is, only nineteen. When one considers how infinitely half-baked, jejune and unhealthy one was at that age, one's surprise is, not that she shouldnt [sic] have achieved more, but that she should be as much developed as she is. I only wish I was with her, for I think I could be of help to her in growing up—not to mention the fact that she would help me out of the curiously unpleasant slough of uncertainty in which one seems to wallow so hopelessly these days."[3]

1919. Huxley and Nys were married in July, and the following year became parents. "My wife has just had a son and has, I am thankful to say, weathered the tempest safely and auspiciously. These works of nature really do put works of art in the shade."[1]

The next two years brought the publication of Huxley's first two novels, *Chrome Yellow,* and *Antic Hay.* Both sold well, and with the latter he began to have his longstanding reputation as a cynic. Many readers, including his own family, disapproved of the book. "[*Antic Hay*] is intended to reflect—fantastically, of course, but none the less faithfully—the life and opinions of an age which has seen the violent disruption of almost all the standards, conventions and values current in the previous epoch.

"The book is, I may say without fatuity, a good book. It is also a very serious book. Artistically, too, it has a certain novelty . . . all the ordinarily separated categories—tragic, comic, fantastic, realistic—are combined . . . into a single entity, whose unfamiliar character makes it appear at first sight rather repulsive."[1]

The Huxleys traveled to Italy, India, and the Far East. In 1930 they returned to London when Huxley's highly successful novel *Point Counter Point* was adapted and produced for the stage. "The first night was a little painful, as the actors were so nervous that they forgot most of their lines and ranted all those they could remember. Which was a pity, as the dress rehearsals had really been rather good . . . . They got much better again after the first night and the play goes on, doing moderate and (surprisingly) slightly improving business. It may run only three weeks, unless the improvement continues. If it had been produced in a small theatre with a fairly cheap cast of stock actors it might have done quite well. But it's being given in one of the largest theatres in London with very expensive actors-so that it can only survive by doing very good business. Some of the scenes turned out finally very well indeed, particularly the last where they play the Beethoven A minor quartet, while the audience waits in a long-drawn anticipation for the man to be killed. The effect was exceedingly good, theatrically, and the music created an extraordinary atmosphere of mystical tranquillity in the midst of the prevailing horror. It showed me what very astonishing things can be done on the stage by somebody with a little imagination and the necessary minimum of technique. If I could have gone over the last scene, rewriting the whole thing, I could have made it quite prodigious, I believe. Even as it was—a kind of patchwork made up of fragments of the book more or less ingeniously stitched together and not in any sense an organic whole—even as it was it went remarkably well and held the audiences—even the popular Saturday night audience— absolutely spellbound. The only thing that deters one from experimenting much with the theatre is the theatrical world. The instruments one must use are so hopelessly unsatisfactory. Have you ever had anything to do with actors and producers? It's an eye-opener!"[3]

Thereafter, Huxley began his best known work, *Brave New World.* "[It] started out as a parody of H. G. Wells' *Men Like Gods,* but gradually it got out of hand and turned into something quite different from what I'd originally intended. As I became more and more interested in the subject, I wandered farther and farther from my original purpose."[4]

"In **1931,** when *Brave New World* was being written, I was convinced that there was still plenty of time. The completely organized society, the scientific caste system, the abolition of free will by methodical conditioning, the servitude made acceptable by regular doses of chemically induced happiness, the orthodoxies drummed in by nightly courses of sleep-teaching— these things were coming all right, but not in my time, not even in the time of my grandchildren. I forget the exact date of the events recorded in *Brave New World;* but it was somewhere in the sixth or seventh century A.F. (After Ford). We who were living in the second quarter of the twentieth century A.D. were the inhabitants, admittedly, of a gruesome kind of universe; but the nightmares of those depression years was radically different from the nightmare of the future, described in *Brave New World.* Ours was a nightmare of too little order; theirs, in the seventh century

A.F., of too much. In the process of passing from one extreme to the other, there would be a long interval, so I imagined, during which the more fortunate third of the human race would make the best of both worlds—the disorderly world of liberalism and the much too orderly Brave New World where perfect efficiency left no room for freedom or personal initiative.

"In the course of evolution nature has gone to endless trouble to see that every individual is unlike every other individual. We reproduce our kind by bringing the father's genes into contact with the mother's. These hereditary factors may be combined in an almost infinite number of ways. Physically and mentally, each one of us is unique. Any culture which, in the interests of efficiency or in the name of some political or religious dogma, seeks to standardize the human individual, commits an outrage against man's biological nature.

"*Brave New World* presents a fanciful and somewhat ribald picture of a society, in which the attempt to recreate human beings in the likeness of termites had been pushed almost to the limits of the possible. That we are being propelled in the direction of Brave New World is obvious. But no less obvious is the fact that we can, if we so desire, refuse to co-operate with the blind forces that are propelling us.

"The prophecies made in 1931 are coming true much sooner than I thought they would. The blessed interval between too little order and the nightmare of too much has not begun and shows no sign of beginning. In the west, it is true, individual men and women still enjoy a large measure of freedom. But even in those countries that have a tradition of democratic government, this freedom and even the desire for this freedom seem to be on the wane. In the rest of the world freedom for indivuals has already gone, or is manifestly about to go. The nightmare of total organization, which I had situated in the seventh century After Ford, has emerged from the safe, remote future and is now awaiting us, just around the next corner."[5]

Many years later, George Orwell wrote *1984,* a story of the future, born of the threat of totalitarianism. Inevitable comparisons between this 1949 publication and *Brave New World* arose. Huxley himself addressed the issue. "George Orwell's *1984* was a magnified projection into the future of a present that contained Stalinism and an immediate past that had witnessed the flowering of Nazism. *Brave New World* was written before the rise of Hitler to supreme power in Germany and when the Russian tyrant had not yet got into his stride. In 1931 systematic terrorism was not the obsessive contemporary fact which it had become in 1948, and the future dictatorship of my imaginary world was a good deal less brutal than the future dictatorship so brilliantly portrayed by Orwell."[5]

During the next few years, conditions became increasingly grim in Europe. Hitler and Mussolini were gaining political power. Huxley believed that a war would exacerbate these conditions, rather than put an end to them. "Man is a profoundly social animal . . . nothing brings [men] together more effectively than a common dislike for someone else . . . . War strengthens [this] sense of group consolidation to the pitch of intoxication . . . . War produces a certain simplification of the social structure . . . and men are on the whole happier in a simple than in a complicated society . . . . War begets and justifies . . . violence, delight in destruction . . . all the anti-social tendencies we have been so carefully trained to repress . . . . The Barbarian and the sadist are strong within us."[1]

(From the movie "Jane Eyre," starring Joan Fontaine and Orson Welles, produced by Twentieth Century-Fox, 1944.)

In the same year, he had finished *Eyeless in Gaza,* a story which contained several characters that both resembled himself, and people in his life. Many suspected that the protagonist's father was based directly on his own father. "I made use of mannerisms and phrases some of which were recognizably father's. I had not thought that they would prove recognizable to others and I am most distressed to find that they should have been."[1]

"I try to imagine how certain people I know would behave in certain circumstances. Of course I base my characters partly on the people I know—one can't escape it—but fictional characters are oversimplified; they're much less complex than the people one knows."[4]

By **1938** the Huxleys became residents of the United States while Europe was at war. "The thing that strikes me most about this country is its hopefulness. In spite of the depression, in spite of everything, I find an extraordinary hopefulness running through people. It is this quality that distinguishes your continent from Europe, where there is a hopeless depression and fear. It makes for a comfortable atmosphere, and, from a practical point of view, it is sound."[6]

Content to live temporarily in the semi-tropical climate of California, Huxley investigated the lucrative movie industry. "I've done a fair amount of work: a 'treatment,' as they call it in the jargon of the films, of the life of Mme Curie for Garbo.

Rather an amusing job—tho' I shdn't [sic] like too many of the kind, since this telling a story in purely pictorial terms doesn't allow of any of the experimentation with words in their relation to things, events and ideas, which is *au fond* my business. They gave me 8 weeks to do the job and I turned in what is, I think, quite a good script in which the scientific processes used by the Curies and the trains of reasoning they pursued are rendered in pictorial terms (all within the space of about 5 minutes, which is about all the public will tolerate of this kind of thing!). It now remains to be seen whether the studio will preserve anything of what I've done. They have followed their usual procedure and handed my treatment over to several other people to make a screen-play out of. By the time they are ready to shoot it may have been through twenty pairs of hands. What will be left? One shudders to think. Meanwhile they have paid me a lot of money and I find myself able to go on for a year, I should think, without further worry about finance. Always a pleasant state of affairs.

"War is beginning to produce dislocations even here. The food situation is startlingly much worse than anybody suspected it could be, largely owing to indiscriminate conscription of farm labour, but also to transportation difficulties and shipment of food abroad on a greater scale than even this land of plenty can afford. Also there seems to have been a lot of mismanagement combined with wishful thinking. The Sec: of Agriculture has been saying for several months that 1943 production would be eight percent above

1942. And now suddenly a questionnaire issued to the agricultural inspectors on the ground elicits the forecast that, in nine tenths of the counties in all the States, there will be a decline, in 1943, of thirty percent.

"Other curious and rather ominous consequences of war are the increased anti-Semitism which one meets with in all classes, particularly the common people, and the strong recrudescence of anti-negro passions in the South. The first is due to the age-old dislike of a monied, influential and pushing minority, coupled with a special grudge against the Jews as being chiefly instrumental, in popular opinion, in getting America into the war. The second is due to the negroes' position being improved and to white resentment of the fact (there are no more coloured servants to be had in the South), coupled with general Southern dislike of racial equality as a war aim. The result is a strong Southern-Democratic reaction in Congress and out of it against the administration and the New Deal. Meanwhile intelligent negroes with whom I've talked are very gloomy about the prospects of their people in the immediate future."[3]

After the war, Huxley took on a new challenge: the film adaptation of one of his own stories, *The Giaconda Smile.* "It's my only murder story. I was very fortunate, because Zoltan Korda, its director, bought it on his own. We worked on it and then sold it to Universal. We didn't suffer from the extraordinary Hollywood assumption that twelve incompetent writers equal one competent one."[7]

During the fifties, Huxley began work on an extremely complicated project involving the psychological study of a true event in French history—the demonic possession of the nuns of Loudun. "[The story] . . . begins with fraud, hysteria, malicious plotting; goes on with the commission of a monstrous judicial crime, the burning of Urbain Grandier, as the supposed author of the possession; continues posthumously with more diabolic manifestations and the bringing on to the scene of Father Surin, one of the most saintly ecclesiastics of his age, who tries to exorcise the Abbess of the convent . . . [and] by a kind of psychological infection, himself succumbs to possession and becomes half mad, but with perfectly lucid intervals, in which he realizes the full extent of his misfortune. Surin remains in this state for nearly twenty years, but finally emerges into a serene old age of something like perfected sanctity, during which he writes some of the most important spiritual works of his period.

"If you take the case of Grandier, and then the case of Surin. Between them, the two episodes describe the religious life on every level—from the most horrible to the most sublime. The whole gamut of religious life is set forth in a kind of parabola in these two episodes. Now the really extraordinary thing is that as far as I know I was the first person to bring these two episodes together in a single volume. Plenty of French people have written about Grandier, and in recent times about Surin, but nobody has thought fit to put the two cases together.

"This is the whole message of this extraordinary episode— religion is infinitely ambivalent. It has these wonderful sides to it, and these appalling sides.

"And here is a story which is strictly historical—and I really never departed from the historical documents—which is at the same time a parable. And *this* is what I'm looking for: an historical or biographical medium in terms of which I can think about all sorts of general subjects.

"I do strongly feel that philosophical and religious ideas are better expressed not in abstract terms but in terms of concrete case histories.

"If you can find the right kind of case history . . . . And this . . . is why I am looking for another biographical historical personage or episode on which to hang my ideas."[1]

In **1952,** Huxley's wife was diagnosed with cancer and succumbed to the disease in February, 1955. In **1956,** he married Laura Archer. Four years later, Huxley was also diagnosed with cancer, he died on **November 22, 1963.** "The most comforting lesson . . . is that the human race is tougher than we thought. Man has lived through two world wars, he can live at the poles and the equator. There is no reason to be boundlessly pessimistic although there's lots to be alarmed at, but we are not yet at the abyss. After all, it's amazing that only a small proportion of mankind breaks down and goes mad."[8]

FOOTNOTE SOURCES

[1]Sybille Bedford, *Aldous Huxley: A Biography,* Carroll & Graf, 1973.
[2]Press release, Harper, September, 1964.
[3]Grover Smith, editor, *Letters of Aldous Huxley,* Harper, 1969.

Quaint native cities hearken far back into old-world history. (Jacket illustration by Jose A. Velasquez from *Beyond the Mexique Bay* by Aldous Huxley.)

[4]Van Wyck Brooks, author of introduction, *Writers at Work: The "Paris Review" Interviews,* Viking, 1963.
[5]Aldous Huxley, *Brave New World Revisited,* Harper, 1958.
[6]Thomas Barensfeld, "Aldous Huxley's Seven Years in America," *New York Times Book Review,* June 27, 1943.
[7]"After Ten Years," *New Yorker,* October 25, 1947.
[8]*New York Times,* August 25, 1957.

FOR MORE INFORMATION SEE:

BOOKS

Jocelyn Brook, *Aldous Huxley,* Longmans, Green, 1954.
A. Huxley, *The Doors of Perception,* Harper, 1954.
Harvey Breit, *The Writer Observed,* World Publishing, 1956.
Julian Huxley, *Aldous Huxley: A Memorial Volume,* Harper, 1965.
Stephen J. Greenblatt, *Three Modern Satirists: Waugh, Orwell, and Huxley,* Yale University Press, 1965.
Peter Bowering, *Aldous Huxley: A Study of the Major Novels,* Athlone (London), 1968.
Ronald W. Clark, *The Huxleys,* McGraw, 1968.
John Atkins, *Aldous Huxley,* Orion Press, 1968.
Laura Archera Huxley, *This Timeless Moment,* Farrar, Straus, 1968.
Jerome Meckier, *Aldous Huxley: Satire and Structure,* Barnes & Noble, 1969.
Laurence Brander, *Aldous Huxley: A Critical Study,* Bucknell University Press, 1970.
Charles M. Holmes, *Aldous Huxley and the Way to Reality,* Indiana University Press, 1970.
Milton Birnbaum, *Aldous Huxley's Quest for Values,* University of Tennessee Press, 1971.
Peter Firchow, *Aldous Huxley: A Satirist and Novelist,* University of Minnesota Press, 1972.
George Woodcock, *Dawn and the Darkest Hour: A Study of Aldous Huxley,* Viking, 1972.
Peter Thody, *Huxley: A Biographical Introduction,* Scribner, 1973.
Contemporary Literary Criticism, Gale, Volume 1, 1973, Volume 3, 1975, Volume 4, 1975, Volume 5, 1976.

PERIODICALS

Aldous Huxley, "Sure Pre-Slump Era Can't Return, Pins Hopes to Liberalism, Dismissing Communism," *New York World-Telegram,* May 18, 1933.
Saturday Review of Literature, March 19, 1938 (p. 10ff).
Sydney Morning Herald, December 16, 1939.
New York Times, June 20, 1948, August 19, 1948, August 24, 1955, March 21, 1956, May 29, 1956, May 19, 1958, May 21, 1959, November 24, 1963.
New York Herald Tribune, August 19, 1948, May 8, 1950, July 20, 1952, May 24, 1952, June 5, 1955.
Saturday Review, August 21, 1948 (p. 8ff), May 2, 1970.
Time, August 23, 1948, October 3, 1960, December 2, 1974.
New York Herald Tribune, May 8, 1950.
New York Times Book Review, May 21, 1950, October 5, 1952 (section 7, p. 1), June 27, 1968.
New York Herald Tribune Book Review, February 7, 1954, August 24, 1965.
Listener, December 12, 1957 (p. 977ff), September 11, 1958 (p. 373ff).
Newsweek, October 3, 1960 (P. 80ff), May 4, 1970, December 9, 1974.
Midwest Quarterly, April, 1964 (p. 223).
United Asia, July/August, 1964 (p. 257ff).
New Leader, November, 1968.
New Statesman, November 28, 1969.
Times Literary Supplement, December 18, 1969.

(From the television-movie "Brave New World," presented on NBC, 1978.)

Economist, December 20, 1969.
New Republic, May 16, 1970, November 16, 1974.
Book World, May 31, 1970.
Nation, June 8, 1970.
New Yorker, July 18, 1970, February 17, 1975.
Choice, November, 1970.
Books and Bookmen, March, 1971.
Observer Review, October 21, 1973 (p. 29ff).
Saturday Review World, November 16, 1974.
Atlantic, January, 1975.
National Review, January 31, 1975.
Review America, February 22, 1975.
Commonweal, March 28, 1975.
Esquire, April, 1975.
Teachers Guide to Television, fall, 1978.
Starlog, October, 1978 (p. 34).

OBITUARIES

New York Times, November 24, 1963 (p. 1ff).
New York Herald Tribune, November 24, 1963.

JOHNSON, Fred 19(?)-1982

PERSONAL: Died February 16, 1982.

WRITINGS:

The Big Bears (illustrated by Lorin Thompson and Frank Fretz), National Wildlife Federation, 1973.

The Foxes (illustrated by L. Thompson and F. Fretz), National Wildlife Federation, 1973.

Turtles and Tortoises (illustrated by L. Thompson and F. Fretz), National Wildlife Federation, 1974.

Jim Boy (illustrated by Eideen Molloy), Vantage, 1977.

KALMAN, Bobbie 1947-

PERSONAL: Surname rhymes with tallmen; born August 29, 1947, in Mosonmagyarovar, Hungary; daughter of Imre (an engineer) and Valerie (Varaljai) Kalman; married Peter Adams Crabtree (a publisher), December 21, 1977; children: Samantha. *Education:* University of Toronto, B.A., 1968, B.Ed., 1969, elementary education teaching certificate, 1974. *Religion:* Catholic/Anglican. *Home:* 2 Christopher Court, Niagara-on-the-Lake, Ontario, Canada. *Office:* Crabtree Publishing, 350 Fifth Ave., Suite 3308, New York, N.Y. 10118.

CAREER: Stapledon School, Nassau, Bahamas, teacher of mentally impaired children, 1969-71; Berlitz School, Karlsruhe, Germany, English teacher, 1971-72; Fitzhenry & Whiteside (publisher), Toronto, Canada, marketing representative, 1973-74; McGraw Hill (publisher), Toronto, Canada, marketing representative, 1974-75; English teacher in North York, Ontario, 1976-78; Crabtree Publishing, New York, N.Y., author and editor-in-chief, 1978—.

WRITINGS:

"EARLY SETTLER LIFE" SERIES

Early Christmas, Crabtree, 1981.
Early Stores and Markets, Crabtree, 1981.
Early Travel, Crabtree, 1981.
Early Village Life, Crabtree, 1981.
Early Schools, Crabtree, 1982.
The Early Family Home, Crabtree, 1982.
Early Settler Children, Crabtree, 1982.
Early Settler Storybook, Crabtree, 1982.
Food for the Settler, Crabtree, 1983.

Bobbie Kalman with her daughter, Samantha.

Early City Life, Crabtree, 1983.
Early Artisans, Crabtree, 1983.
Early Health and Medicine, Crabtree, 1983.
Early Pleasures and Pastimes, Crabtree, 1983.

"HOLIDAYS AND FESTIVALS" SERIES

We Celebrate Christmas (illustrated by Lisa Smith and Lynne Carson) Crabtree, 1985.
We Celebrate Easter (illustrated by Maureen Shaughnessy), Crabtree, 1985.
We Celebrate Hallowe'en (illustrated by Allan Drew-Brook-Cormack and Deborah Drew-Brook-Cormack), Crabtree, 1985.
We Celebrate New Year (illustrated by Tina Holdcroft), Crabtree, 1985.
We Celebrate Spring (illustrated by Karen Harrison), Crabtree, 1985.
We Celebrate Family Days (illustrated by K. Harrison), Crabtree, 1986.
We Celebrate Hanukkah (illustrated by Cecilia Ohm-Eriksen), Crabtree, 1986.
We Celebrate Valentine's Day (illustrated by A. Drew-Brook-Cormack and D. Drew-Brook-Cormack), Crabtree, 1986.
We Celebrate the Harvest (illustrated by Janet Wilson and Greg Ruhl), Crabtree, 1986.
We Celebrate Winter (illustrated by Brenda Clark and Elaine Macpherson), Crabtree, 1986.

"IN MY WORLD" SERIES

The All about Me Activity Guide, Crabtree, 1985.
Come to My Place, Crabtree, 1985.
Fun with My Friends, Crabtree, 1985.
Happy to Be Me, Crabtree, 1985.
My Busy Body, Crabtree, 1985.
I Like School, Crabtree, 1985.
People in My Family, Crabtree, 1985.
Animal Worlds (illustrated by K. Harrison and D. Drew-Brook-Cormack), Crabtree, 1986.
The Food We Eat (illustrated by K. Harrison), Crabtree, 1986.
I Live in a City (illustrated by K. Harrison and D. Drew-Brook-Cormack), Crabtree, 1986.
People at Work (illustrated by K. Harrison and Victor Gad), Crabtree, 1986.
Time and the Seasons (illustrated by K. Harrison and D. Drew-Brook-Cormack), Crabtree, 1986.
How We Communicate, Crabtree, 1986.
How We Travel, Crabtree, 1986.
Life through the Ages, Crabtree, 1986.
People at Play (illustrated by K. Harrison and D. Drew-Brook-Cormack), Crabtree, 1986.
Natural Resources (illustrated by Halina Below and K. Harrison), Crabtree, 1987.
Our Earth (illustrated by H. Below and K. Harrison), Crabtree, 1987.
People and Places (illustrated by H. Below and K. Harrison), Crabtree, 1987.

"NORTH AMERICAN WILDLIFE" SERIES; ALL ILLUSTRATED BY GLEN LOATES

Animal Babies, Crabtree, 1987.
Birds at My Feeder, Crabtree, 1987.
Forest Mammals, Crabtree, 1987.
Owls, Crabtree, 1987.

"ARCTIC WORLD" SERIES; ALL WITH WILLIAM BELSY

Arctic Animals, Crabtree, 1988.
An Arctic Community, Crabtree, 1988.

This young raccoon has not had much experience catching live food. She wonders how to grab this leopard frog.

(From *Animal Babies* by Bobbie Kalman. Illustrated by Glen Loates.)

The Arctic Land, Crabtree, 1988.
Arctic Whales and Whaling, Crabtree, 1988.

"LANDS, PEOPLES AND CULTURES" SERIES

The Culture of China, Crabtree, 1988.
The Culture of Japan, Crabtree, 1988.
The Land of China, Crabtree, 1988.
The Land of Japan, Crabtree, 1988.
The People of China, Crabtree, 1988.
The People of Japan, Crabtree, 1988.
Tibet, Crabtree, 1989.
The Land of India, Crabtree, 1990.
The People of India, Crabtree, 1990.
The Culture of India, Crabtree, 1990.

"HISTORIC COMMUNITIES" SERIES

The Gristmill, Crabtree, 1990.
The Kitchen, Crabtree, 1990.
Home Crafts, Crabtree, 1990.
Visiting a Village, Crabtree, 1990.

Contributor of articles to periodicals.

WORK IN PROGRESS: An adult popular novel; four more titles in the "Historic Communities" series, *Fort Life, Tools and Gadgets, A School Day,* and *A Colonial Town;* "Crabtree Environment" series, *Buried in Garbage,* and *Reducing, Reusing, and Recycling.*

SIDELIGHTS: "Being an author of educational books is a lot like being a teacher. Your books must be planned out meticulously and every detail must be correct. This process requires endless rounds of rethinking and rewriting. Anything before the twentieth draft is usually not even worth reading. Being an editor-in-chief (as well as an author), my job also includes originating artwork, researching photographs, proofing every stage of production, and supervising print-runs. Besides all that, I also do market research, talk to teachers and librarians about their needs, and test books with students. I have a big job!

"Did I always want to be a writer? Truthfully, I never even gave it a second thought. My father told me from the moment I was born that I would be a pharmacist. I don't know how he got fixed on that one, but I always thought I would be a pharmacist, too, until I realized that my mathematical skills were never going to back me up. Being a people-person I switched gears and decided I would be a psychologist. I started first year university as a psychology major, but ended up with a passion for literature. No matter how many psychology courses I tried, my English courses always seemed more interesting to me. I think it was my grade ten teacher who brainwashed me into thinking I was a good writer, when in reality, writing scared me to death. English, after all, wasn't even my first language!

"After university, I gave writing a brief try. I failed miserably. The newspaper for which I was working told me that I sounded too much like a teacher. So, I thought I should stop fighting it and decided to get my high school teaching degree. I was a natural as a student teacher and received a lot of praise for my efforts. However, I discovered that I really did not want to teach high school because I loved little kids. Through an incredible set of circumstances, starting with spring break in Fort Lauderdale, I found myself over in Nassau, Bahamas, where a man accidentally knocked me down a set of stairs, dusted me off, and offered me a job teaching children with special needs. I was delighted and scared at the prospect, but it turned out to be the most wonderful two years of my life! I loved teaching and I loved Nassau. However, as all good things must come to an end, I headed off to Europe in search of new challenges. I traveled all over Europe for ten months and then found a job teaching English in Karlsruhe, Germany. I learned to speak fluent German while I was there, and also improved my knowledge of French.

"After I returned home, I decided that my life would always include travel and that I would use my travel experiences to teach children about the cultures of others. I started working for various publishing companies as a marketing representative and conducted workshops on social studies topics. At night I studied to earn my elementary teaching certificate and a specialty in Teaching English as a Second Language. In three years I got a job in this field. I loved being involved with people from different cultures. I remembered the days that I could not speak English, and no one took an interest in me at school. I tried to give my students a feeling of confidence and security. I also set up a program at the school through which all the other students could learn about the cultures of my English as a second language students. My books have come out of these experiences. I see a need for certain types of books, and I write the books.

"I have been an author for twelve years and enjoy my work very much. In total, more than a million copies of my books are in circulation at the present time. Apart from my profession as an author, I lead a very fulfilling life. I am married and have a twelve-year-old daughter, Samantha, as well as three stepchildren: Caroline, Marc, and Andrea. I love being with my family and friends and entertain a lot. People from all over the world visit us. We also travel a lot and try to take Samantha with us as often as possible.

"My daughter Samantha is a very creative child. She is a talented actress, singer, dancer, and artist. She also writes great stories, but is not always motivated to doing so. I am encouraging her to become an author/illustrator, but Samantha has a mind of her own, so we'll have to wait and see the outcome. On a recent vacation, she mastered a very difficult trapeze act and, for all we know, she may run away and join the circus!

"As for my ambitions, I hope to spend more time writing and less editing. I am currently working on a novel for adults, but do not have as much time to devote to it as I would like. One thing I do know about my future is, that writing will always be a part of it. I can't think of a more fascinating vocation or pastime. I really love being an author!"

HOBBIES AND OTHER INTERESTS: Travel, swimming, biking, gourmet cooking, photography, and antique hunting.

KARLIN, Nurit

PERSONAL: Born in Jerusalem, Israel. *Education:* Graduated from Bezalel School of Art, Jerusalem; attended School of Visual Arts.

CAREER: Free-lance artist, cartoonist and illustrator. *Military service:* Israeli Army.

WRITINGS:

SELF-ILLUSTRATED

No Comment: Cartoons, J. Murray, 1978.
The Blue Frog, Coward, 1983.
A Train for the King, Coward, 1983.
The Tooth Witch, Lippincott, 1985.
The Dream Factory, Lippincott, 1988.

ILLUSTRATOR

David Cleveland, *The April Rabbits* (Junior Literary Guild selection), Coward, 1978.
Stephen Manes, *Socko: Every Riddle Your Feet Will Ever Need,* Coward, 1982.
Slim Goodbody, *The Force Inside You* (with photographs by Bruce Curtis), Coward, 1983.
S. Goodbody, *The Healthy Habits Handbook* (with photographs by B. Curtis), Coward, 1983.

Cartoons and illustrations have appeared in *New Yorker, Audubon, Science, Ladies' Home Journal, Saturday Review, National Enquirer, Fantasy and Science Fiction, New York Times, Gourmet, Time, Business Week, Changing Times,* and anthologies.

WORK IN PROGRESS: Little Big Mouse.

SIDELIGHTS: Considering herself basically a cartoonist, Karlin illustrated her first children's book in 1978. "*The April Rabbits* was my first attempt at illustrating a children's book.

The Tooth Witch was bored. (From *The Tooth Witch* by Nurit Karlin. Illustrated by the author.)

Messrs. Ferdinand Monjo and Jim Bruce at Coward, Mc-Cann invited me to do this book and gave me a lot of encouragement along the way. It was a great experience."

KENNEDY, Robert 1938-

PERSONAL: Born May 18, 1938, in Munich, Germany; son of William (a teacher) and Doris-Mary (a teacher; maiden name, Burwood) Kennedy; married Lynda Jackson (an office manager), February 13, 1986; children: Braden Robert James. *Education:* Norwich College of Art, National Diploma in Design, 1960. *Office: Musclemag International,* 2 Melanie Dr., Unit 7, Brampton, Ontario, Canada L6T 4K8.

CAREER: Totenham Technical College, lecturer, 1961-67; Brampton Centennial College, lecturer, 1968-72; writer; photojournalist; *Musclemag International,* Brampton, Ontario, Canada, publisher, 1974—. Director of exercise videos. *Awards, honors:* Publisher of the Year from the World Bodybuilding Guild, 1975; Award of Merit from the International Federation of Bodybuilders (Montreal), 1985, Silver Medal, 1988.

WRITINGS:

Shape Up, Frederick Fell, 1972.
Bodybuilding for Women, Emerson, 1979.
Natural Body Building for Everyone, Sterling, 1980, revised and enlarged edition published as *Start Bodybuilding: The Complete Natural Program,* 1984.
Hardcore Bodybuilding: The Blood, Sweat and Tears of Pumping Iron, Sterling, 1982.
Beef It! Upping the Muscle Mass, Sterling, 1983.

(With Vivian Mason) *The Hardcore Bodybuilder's Source Book,* Sterling, 1984.
(With Vince Gironda) *Unleashing the Wild Physique: Ultimate Bodybuilding for Men and Women,* Sterling, 1984.
Reps! The World's Hottest Body Building Routines!, Sterling, 1985, published in England as *Reps! Building Massive Muscle,* 1986.
(With Ben Weider) *Pumping Up! Supershaping the Feminine Physique,* Sterling, 1985.
Hardcore Action Bodybuilding: Pumping Iron to Sculpt a Winning Body, Sterling, 1985.
(With B. Weider) *Superpump! Hardcore Women's Bodybuilding,* Sterling, 1986.
(With Dennis B. Weis) *Mass! New Scientific Bodybuilding Secrets,* Contemporary Books, 1986.
Rock Hard! Supernutrition for Bodybuilders, Warner, 1987.
Awesome Arms!, Sterling, 1987.
Ultra-Ripped Abs, Sterling, 1987.
Maxi-Cut Legs, Sterling, 1987.
(With Maggie Greenwood-Robinson) *Built! The New Bodybuilding for Everyone,* Perigee Books, 1987.
(With Joe Gold) *The World Gym Musclebuilding System,* Contemporary Books, 1987.
Super Chest! Deeper, Thicker, More Ripped-Up Pecs, Sterling, 1987.
Herculean Back! Power-Packed Ultra-Wide Lats, Sterling, 1988.
Cuts!, Perigee Books, 1988.

ROBERT KENNEDY

Barn Door Shoulders! Superstriated, Melon-sized Delts!, Sterling, 1988.
(With Don Ross) *Muscleblasting! Brief and Brutal Shock Training*, Sterling, 1988.
Posing: The Art of Hardcore Physique Display, Sterling, 1988.
Body Parts, two volumes (includes *Barn Door Shoulders! Superstrained Melon-Sized Delts,* and *Herculean Back! Power-Packed Ultra-Wide Lats*, Sterling, 1988.
Rip Up! Get Rock Hard and Supercut Now!, Sterling, 1988.
Savage Sets! The Ultimate Pre-Exhaust Pump Out, Sterling, 1989.
(With D. B. Weis) *Raw Muscle*, Contemporary Books, 1989.

Author of exercise video on women's bodybuilding. Contributor of articles to periodicals. Foreign correspondent, *Sport Salute* (Italy), *Fit* (Holland), *Le Monde du Muscle* (France), *Bodybuilding Kraftsport* (Sweden), *Fitness* (Hungary), and *Power and Fitness* (Finland), all 1988—.

WORK IN PROGRESS: Researching world's most perfect, ideal diet/exercise program.

SIDELIGHTS: "I have a specific plan once the book contract is signed. I write 500 words per day, every day, until the manuscript is completed. I never delay waiting for inspiration to strike.

"I do not believe in using agents. I feel strongly that writers should learn to tackle business with the publishers. No one has your interest at heart more than you do.

"I have a small degree of competence in the French and German languages. I love to travel, especially to Cote D'Azure, Japan and Scandinavia.

"I admire clever language, whether it's written or spoken, and marvel at writers who observe minute details that we only 'notice' when we read their words. One of the most useful tips I ever had was 'write about what everyone knows but is afraid to say.'"

HOBBIES AND OTHER INTERESTS: Travel, oil painting, bodybuilding, sailing, skiing.

KILLINGBACK, Julia 1944-

PERSONAL: Born April 17, 1944, in Sevenoaks, Kent, England; daughter of Terence A. (a pediatrician) and Yvonne (an artist; maiden name, Martin) Brand; married Norman Killingback (an orthodontist), June 2, 1967; children: Laura, Tanya. *Education:* West of England College of Art (now Bristol Polytechnic), N.D.D., A.T.D., 1965. *Religion:* Church of England. *Home:* 6 Canynge Rd., Clifton, Bristol BS8 3JX, England. *Office:* The Very Busy Bear Company, Ltd., 6 Canynge Rd., Clifton, Bristol BS8 3JX, England.

CAREER: Free-lance textile designer, 1967-83; free-lance author and illustrator, 1983—. *Awards, honors:* Textile Council Design Scholarship, 1970; *Monday Is Washing Day* and *What's the Time, Mrs. Bear?* were each selected one of Child Study Association of America's Children's Books of the Year, both 1986.

JULIA KILLINGBACK

WRITINGS:

JUVENILE; SELF-ILLUSTRATED

Monday Is Washing Day, Methuen, 1984, Morrow, 1985.
What's the Time, Mrs. Bear?, Methuen, 1984, Morrow, 1985.
Catch the Red Bus!, Morrow, 1985.
One, Two, Three, Go!, Morrow, 1985.
Rain, Rain Go Away!, Methuen, 1986.
Stars, Squares and Busy Bears!, Methuen, 1986.
Follow that Bear!, Oxford University Press, 1987.
Wake Up, Busy Bears!, Oxford University Press, 1987.
Busy Bears at the Fire Station, Oxford University Press, 1988.
Watch Out, Busy Bears!, Oxford University Press, 1988.
Busy Bears Picnic, Oxford University Press, 1988.
Busy Bear to the Rescue, Oxford University Press, 1988.
Busy Bear Firefighter Counterpack, Oxford University Press, 1988.

ILLUSTRATOR

Good Housekeeping Cooking with Herbs and Spices, Ebury Press, 1975.

Killingback's books have been published in England and France.

ADAPTATIONS:

"Monday Is Washing Day," Video Books (New Zealand), 1985.
"What's the Time, Mrs. Bear?," Video Books (New Zealand), 1985.
"Follow That Bear!" (pilot film based on the "Busy Bears"), 1990.

WORK IN PROGRESS: Illustrating *Littlest Book*, for Ragged Bears Ltd.; marketing her books.

SIDELIGHTS: "When I was small I had the good fortune to have a large and beautiful garden in which to roam, and, on rainy days, a tempting pile of freshly-slitted envelopes (just waiting to be drawn on!) left on my father's desk!

"My mother, an artist, took us on long country walks. She often drew our attention to the changing skies, or the light across the landscape—to the detail of patterns and richness of colour in the hedgerows. *This* is how my career in art began!

"At art college (in Bristol) I became interested in textile design, and on leaving, designed for a well known dress-textile studio in Paris. I learned a lot—very quickly (since I was paid on commission!) and to speak French too!

"On returning to Britain, I married and worked as a free-lance designer selling my own work all over Europe and in the United States—designs for all sorts of products, from co-ordinated bedding ranges to packaging for cosmetics. It was hard work, but fun.

"Our daughters, Laura and Tanya, were born and I decided to write and illustrate a children's book on a topic I knew well for them. Hence, *Monday Is Washing Day,* a book about bears ('Busy Bears') since everyone seems to love them!

"I was lucky to have it accepted in its original form for publication by Methuen and it became the first of a series of twelve 'Busy Bear Books.'

"Each book has a learning theme (numbers, colours, etc.) and I was, at last, able to indulge my love of detail, hoping to create the sort of books that children would want to return to over and over again. Our children's toy mouse is included in every picture to be 'discovered' while adults can search out the ghastly 'grin and bear it' puns.

"I dug deep into my 'synonym finder' and found a fascination in balancing the picture against the words on each page.

"Being constantly surrounded by small children made me aware of how important the 'sound' of the words are—I quickly started to write in rhyme for this reason.

"The 'Busy Bear' family is both chaotic and lovable. They sometimes make mistakes but whatever happens they make the most of things with their cheerful nature.

"Read the books, and feel 'at home' with them. There might be a new picture on the wall, or a new toy in the cupboard, but a feeling of 'homeliness' and continuity pervades!

"When I was eight books into the series, I was contacted by our local fire brigade for some drawings to help with their fire prevention campaign in primary schools.

"This led to Mr. Bear happily having joined the "Fire Beargade" and appearing, along with the rest of the 'Busy Bears,' in a series of four books based on—the Brigade, safety at home, in the town, and in the countryside! These are intentionally *not* about the *drama* of fire, but more about the everyday risks that both we (and the bears) can avoid.

"Having researched very carefully the grim statistics of fire accidents, and with the help of my local Fire Brigade (Avon), I had a very clear picture of what their problems are in the fire prevention field. As ever, the bears have fun, and adventures, but behind the story, in the detailed pictures there are important lessons to be learned. The books have received much praise from fire chiefs, the medical profession, teachers, and librarians (and children, too!).

"The Fire Brigade has made me a 'larger-than-life Busy Bear Firefighter' to help promote their work. To children he is REAL! (My friend, inside the costume, nearly expired when a tiny child filled the only air vent at the back of the mouth, with chocolate cake at a Teddy Bear's picnic!) To me he is a great companion. Can you imagine travelling on a crowded train with a membear of the fire brigade sitting beside you?"

HOBBIES AND OTHER INTERESTS: Skiing, mountain walking, building dry stone walls.

KUKLIN, Susan 1941-

PERSONAL: Born September 6, 1941, in Philadelphia, Pa.; daughter of Albert E. (a builder) and Bertha (Gussman) Greenbaum; married Bailey H. Kuklin (a law professor), July 7, 1973. *Education:* New York University, B.S., 1963, M.A., 1966; also attended Herbert Berghof Studio, 1960-64. *Politics:* Liberal. *Home:* New York City. *Office:* 436 West 23rd St., New York, N.Y. 10010.

CAREER: New York City Public Schools, New York, N.Y., English teacher, 1965-74; New York City Board of Education, New York, N.Y., curriculum developer, 1970-74; University of Tennessee, Knoxville, teacher of film studies, 1974-76; photojournalist, 1974—. Member of executive committee, Works Ballet Company. *Exhibitions:* "Fifty Years at the New York City Ballet," Lincoln Center Library, 1973; "Camera Infinity— Fourteen Photographers," Lever House, New York, N.Y., 1986. *Member:* PEN, Society of Children Book Writers, Authors Guild.

AWARDS, HONORS: Outstanding Science Trade Book for Children from the National Science Teachers Association and the Children's Book Council, 1980, for *The Story of Nim;* Notable Children's Trade Book in the Field of Social Studies from the National Council for Social Studies and the Children's Book Council, 1984, for *Mine for a Year; Thinking Big* was selected one of *School Library Journal*'s Best Books of the Year, and one of International Board on Books for Young People Honor Books, both 1986, and one of Child Study Association of America's Children's Book of the Year, 1987; *Reaching for Dreams* was selected one of American Library Association's Best Books, and one of New York Public Library's Books for the Teen Age, both 1987, and *Fighting Back,* 1989; Association of Children's Librarians of Northern California Best Book, 1989, for *Fighting Back.*

WRITINGS:

SELF-ILLUSTRATED WITH PHOTOGRAPHS

Mine for a Year (Junior Literary Guild selection), Coward, 1984.
Thinking Big: The Story of a Young Dwarf, Lothrop, 1986.
Reaching for Dreams: A Ballet from Rehearsal to Opening Night, Lothrop, 1987.
When I See My Doctor, Bradbury, 1988.
When I See My Dentist, Bradbury, 1988.
Taking My Cat to the Vet, Bradbury, 1988.
Taking My Dog to the Vet, Bradbury, 1988.

SUSAN KUKLIN

Fighting Back: What Some People Are Doing about AIDS, Putnam, 1989.
Going to My Ballet Class, Bradbury, 1989.
Going to My Nursery School, Bradbury, 1990.
Going to My Gymnastics Class, Bradbury, in press.

ILLUSTRATOR WITH PHOTOGRAPHS

Herbert Terrace, *Nim,* Knopf, 1979.
(With H. Terrace) Anna Michel, *The Story of Nim: The Chimp Who Learned Language,* Knopf, 1980.
Paul Thompson, *The Hitchhikers,* F. Watts, 1980.
Linda Atkinson, *Hit and Run,* F. Watts, 1981.
Gene DeWeese, *Nightmare from Space,* F. Watts, 1981.
(Contributor) *How Animals Behave,* National Geographic Society Books, 1984.
(Contributor) Robert Lacy, *Balanchine's Ballerinas,* Simon & Schuster, 1984.
(Contributor) Frank C. Taylor, *Alberta Hunter,* McGraw, 1987.
(Contributor) Terry Miller, *Greenwich Village and How It Got That Way,* Crown, 1990.

Contributor of photos and photographic essays to magazines and newspapers including *Time, Newsweek, Psychology Today, Der Spiegel, Science et Avenir, Science 80, Viva, MD, New Brooklyn, Pan Am Clipper, New York, Science, Dance, Discovery, Junior Scholastic, Family Weekly, New York Sunday News, New York Times, Perspectives, Us, Pegasus, Parenthood Review, Discover, Travel and Leisure, Cricket, Appalachian Studies, Appalachian Heritage* and *Woman.*

WORK IN PROGRESS: A young adult book about teenage pregnancy, for Putnam.

SIDELIGHTS: "At a very early age I was introduced to art, theater, and books. Going to the opera, ballet, or theater with my family was my idea of a wonderful time. At night my grandmother would read to me Russian fables and short stories, and I spent a great deal of time at the public library. I fondly remember looking at long wooden shelves filled with books thinking that I must read all of them before I grow up. Perhaps I should begin with A? But then there was the problem that new books were always added to the shelves, and I abandoned the 'start with A' idea. Through books I could visit other places and meet interesting people that I would not otherwise have contact with. I loved dance, especially ballet, and wanted to become a dancer. Once I became a teenager my pursuit of dance shifted to audience appreciation but my quest to be part of the performing arts remained strong. I became an actress.

"My summers were spent as an apprentice at Philadelphia's Playhouse in the Park, a summer stock theater, working backstage or in minor roles in productions with Steve McQueen, Geraldine Page, Jessica Tandy, Hume Cronin, and Joseph Papp's New York Shakespeare Festival. They were inspiring.

"Once in college I majored in theater at New York University. Although NYU's drama department has an excellent reputation, I took additional acting classes at the Herbert

With such short legs holding up her average-size body, it is hard for Jaime to stand or walk for a long time. When she goes on hikes with her class, the other children usually get way ahead. Sometimes, when Jaime runs to catch up, she loses her balance and falls forward. Jaime falls a lot, but she never cries.

(From *Thinking Big: The Story of a Young Dwarf* by Susan Kuklin. Illustrated with photographs by Susan Kuklin.)

Berghof Studio. Learning to interpret a role by growing into the character and losing 'me' and becoming 'another' was exhilarating. It wasn't that I didn't like *me,* I was simply curious about *them.* I continued an academic appreciation of the theater by taking a master's degree in World Theater (also at NYU).

"While in graduate school my interest in acting began to wane and I became fascinated with the backstage features of the art. I began to direct plays. While acting taught me how to interpret a part, directing forced me to look at the big picture which included a visual application of the art. I learned about framing, position, lighting, movement, etc. These fundamentals later became intrinsic aspects of my approach to photography and non-fiction writing.

"After college I supplemented my income from acting by teaching English in the New York City public schools. I taught and wrote curriculum for the New York City Board of Education, I stressed drama in the classroom, particularly Shakespeare. My students—all inner city kids—were wonderfully receptive. I travelled as much as I could taking photographs that I would later show after family holiday dinners. I am grateful that my family encouraged me and rarely fell asleep during all those pictures of 'landmarks.'

"In 1973 I married and moved to Knoxville, Tennessee where my husband and I were offered teaching positions at the University of Tennessee. He as a law professor, while I taught film studies in my old stomping grounds, the theater department.

"While in Knoxville we took trips into the Cumberland and Smoky Mountains. I was intrigued with the rugged individuality of the people who lived there. My first reaction was, 'I would love to photograph these people.' For years photography had been a pleasurable pastime. I photographed friends' weddings, their children, and the already mentioned trips. It was fun for me to *see* photographically. My theater background enabled me to understand the fundamentals of composition and lighting. I loved photography but never thought of it as a profession.

"But how to meet the mountain people? They were an in-bred group who have given of themselves only sparingly to the outside world. A person cannot simply walk up the back roads and film people in their homes. Planned Parenthood of the Southern Mountains opened their doors by arranging for me to accompany their out-reach volunteers as they made weekly visits to families in remote parts of the mountains. In return I provided them with photographs that they would use to describe their work. The result of this alliance was a photo essay called 'Appalachian Families.'

"Eventually editors of various literary publications saw my work and bought several photographs. I was hooked. I took courses in printing, read books on photography, and most important, studied the photographs of the masters.

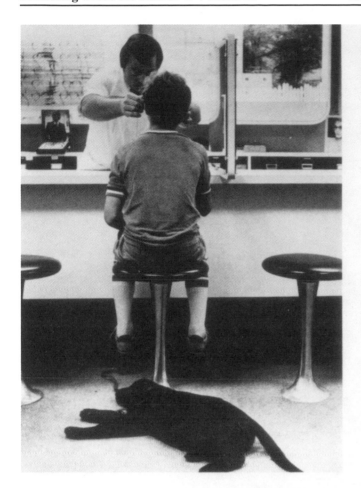 

It was hot when we came out of the optician's office and I worried about Doug burning his paws on the asphalt. I picked him up and carried him to Ev's van. "See, Doug, I'll take care of you now and later you'll take care of me, right?"

Doug liked it when I carried him places. In fact, I was learning that Doug's two favorite activities were being carried and sleeping. A puppy needs lots of sleep.

(From *Mine for a Year* by Susan Kuklin. Illustrated with photographs by the author.)

"When we returned to New York, I showed my Tennessee photographs to magazines and publishers and began to get assignments. About that time Dr. Herbert Terrace, a professor of behavioral psychology at Columbia University, was teaching language to a young chimpanzee called Nim Chimpsky. I became the photographer on his project and from that came my first illustrated children's book, *The Story of Nim: The Chimpanzee Who Learned Language.* Nim was a far cry from Appalachia. He lived in a mansion, wore clothes from Bloomingdales, and drove to class with his trainers in a BMW. Terrace urged me to learn at least ten words of sign language before I met Nim. (He said that he didn't want his chimp to think he was hiring a dummy.) I liked learning to sign. Actually, I like learning.

"After Nim, I was given many unusual assignments. For example, I rode in police cars and with undercover cops in the South Bronx. There were some dangerous moments. After one particularly tough day I met with an art director who

asked, 'If you could do any assignment, what would that be?' Without missing a beat I said, 'The New York City Ballet.' *Pegasus* magazine (Mobil Oil Ltd.) arranged for me to photograph a new ballet by George Balanchine. Mr. B. let me photograph his company as he created one of his last great ballets, 'Robert Schumann's "Davidsbundlertanze."' Working with Mr. Balanchine was a great experience and I continue to photograph the company as often as possible.

"Assignments from major magazines were very exciting. Getting a story in fast, very fast, was a challenge. After a while, though, I missed not being able to delve into a subject in great detail. Children's books enable me to spend lengthy periods of time with a specific subject. Having the opportunity to meet and become close to people who I would not otherwise have the opportunity to meet is fascinating and fun. My books are generally subjective and personal. Because I believe that my subjects are my partners, I become very close to the people with whom I work and try to interpret who

Nim's seventh word: hug. (Photograph by Susan Kuklin from *The Story of NIM: The Chimp Who Learned Language* by Anna Michel.)

they are, not who I want them to be. Though the books are nonfiction, they were written like a story with a beginning, a middle, and end, instead of a series of interviews. Hopefully the photographs and text compliment each other, but also can stand alone.

"Here is a little background about the making of some of my books.

"*Mine for a Year:* As a photographer, sight, obviously is essential. What would it be like to not have sight? I searched for an interesting approach for a book about blindness. My love of animals led me to explore the possibilities of a story about guide dogs. Part of that exploration was a blindfolded walk through Morristown, New Jersey, aided by a guide dog, under the supervision of a trainer from the Seeing Eye. However, another writer/photographer beat me to it and had already published a book about guide dogs. My project was

about to be abandoned when an acquaintance called to tell me about George Creed, a young foster boy. It was thought that George was slowly going blind. He was active in a 4-H group that raised puppies for one year to socialize them before they were trained to be guide dogs. Would I like to meet him? Indeed. From that meeting came *Mine for a Year.*

"*Thinking Big* is the story of eight-year-old Jaime Osborn, a dwarf. I interviewed a number of people before meeting Jaime. I was immediately taken with her positive attitude and fierce determination to be her own person. Jaime's parents, brothers, and friends were extremely supportive and accepting about what she was able to do and what she was not. I think of this book as a collaboration between the Osborn family and me. Jaime and I outlined all the things that *she* wanted people to know about dwarfism. We carefully went over each sentence and photograph.

"*Reaching for Dreams:* Based on my photographs of the New York City Ballet, I was asked to author a book about how a ballet is made. My subject was the Alvin Ailey American Dance Theatre. Choreographer Jennifer Muller had been asked to 'set' her signature ballet, 'Speeds,' on the Ailey company and I thought the elements in that work would serve as a perfect example of the intricacies of creating dance. All my books are important to me but *Dreams* is especially from the heart. It was wonderful to return to performing arts and be included in a very special production with a very special company.

"Every day I taped and photographed Jennifer Muller's rehearsals. Afterwards I would meet with one, two, or three dancers during their lunch break and interview them. Everyone had a lot to say. There was not one dancer who wasn't wonderful and interesting to work with and I miss not travelling with them. The fact that the ballet turned out to be a hit was icing on the cake.

"*Fighting Back: What Some People Are Doing about AIDS* is a young adult book which depicts a team of volunteers, known as buddies, who help people with AIDS with their day-to-day chores and offer support as they fight this dreadful disease. A more extraordinary group of people I have never met. Working with them has reaffirmed my faith in the human spirit.

"Another recent project was a series of full color books for preschoolers for Bradbury Press. By combining photojournalism techniques with medium format photography, actual experiences of a young child going to the doctor, the dentist, etc. are portrayed. The first two books, *When I See My Doctor* and *When I See My Dentist* were followed by *Taking My Dog to the Vet* and *Taking My Cat to the Vet.* These books, great fun to do, are a departure from my other work and give me an opportunity to stretch."

HOBBIES AND OTHER INTERESTS: Dance, traveling, gardening (in pots on her roof terrace), reading (especially Chinese and Japanese fiction and the classics), visiting museums, theater, concerts, opera.

LANTZ, Francess L(in) 1952-
(Lance Franklin, Fran Lantz, Jamie Suzanne)

PERSONAL: Born August 27, 1952, in Trenton, N.J.; daughter of Frederick W. (an architect) and Dorothea (a company treasurer and housewife; maiden name, Lingrell) Lantz; married John M. Landsberg (a physician and writer), April 30, 1984. *Education:* Dickinson College, B.A., 1974; Simmons College, M.L.S., 1975. *Home and office:* 1069 Veronica Springs Rd., Santa Barbara, Calif. 93105. *Agent:* Ginger Knowlton, Curtis Brown Ltd., 10 Astor Place, New York, N.Y. 10003.

CAREER: Semi-professional musician in Boston, Mass., 1974-79; Dedham Public Library, Dedham, Mass., children's librarian, 1976-79; writer, 1979—; "nanny" in Boston, 1979-83; teacher of writing courses for adults and children, Santa Barbara City College, and Montecito Union School, 1989—. *Member:* Author's Guild, Society of Children's Book Writers. *Awards, honors: Double Play* was selected one of *Booklist*'s Recommended Books for the Reluctant Young Adult Reader, 1988.

WRITINGS:

JUVENILE AND YOUNG ADULT NOVELS

Good Rockin' Tonight, Addison-Wesley, 1982.
A Love Song for Becky, Berkley, 1983.
Surfer Girl, Berkley, 1983.
Rock 'n' Roll Romance, Berkley, 1984.
Senior Blues, Berkley, 1984.
Can't Stop Us Now, Dell, 1986.
Making It on Our Own, Dell, 1986.
Woodstock Magic, Avon, 1986.
Star Struck, Avon, 1986.
All Shook Up, Avon, 1987.
(Under pseudonym Lance Franklin) *Take Down,* Bantam, 1987.
(Under pseudonym Lance Franklin) *Double Play,* Bantam, 1987.
(Under pseudonym Jamie Suzanne) *Center of Attention,* Bantam, 1988.
(Under pseudonym Jamie Suzanne) *Jessica's Bad Idea,* Bantam, 1989.
The Truth about Making Out, Bantam, 1990.
Mom, There's a Pig in My Bed!, Avon, 1991.
Dear Celeste, My Life Is a Mess (sequel to *The Truth about Making Out*), Bantam, 1991.

OTHER

(With husband, John Landsberg and April Rhodes) *The One and Only, No-Holds-Barred, Tell-It-Like-It-Is Santa Barbara Restaurant Guide,* Elan Press, 1988.

FRANCESS LANTZ

"Hey," called Annette, "What are you waiting for, a formal invitation?" (Cover illustration from *Making It on Our Own* by Fran Lantz.)

Lantz's books have been published in West Germany and England. Contributor of articles and reviews to *Kliatt*. With husband, author of movie column, "Over Coffee after the Movie," 1987-89, and of restaurant reviews, "The Three Little Pigs," 1989—, both for *Santa Barbara Independent*.

WORK IN PROGRESS: Novel for middle-grade readers; a screenplay; a picture book.

SIDELIGHTS: "As a small child I loved to write stories and illustrate them. My father was an architect, and we spent long hours drawing together, including creating 'tatoos' on each others hands and arms with ballpoint pens.

"I was an ardent tomboy. My stories were usually about war, or spies, and they were always violent. Despite this, my fifth grade teacher encouraged my talent and allowed me to stay inside during recess to tape record my stories with my friends.

"In 1964, the Beatles came to America and I chucked literature in favor of rock 'n' roll. I took guitar lessons, wrote songs, and soon began performing. After college, I moved to Boston to become a rock star. It never happened, but I had

fun trying. Since I also needed to eat, I earned an M.L.S. and landed a job as a children's librarian.

"When I worked as a children's librarian I used to put on a graveyard story-hour every year (yes, I took the kids to a nearby graveyard and scared the pants off them). After a couple of years I was having trouble finding new stories that were short, easy to read aloud, and really scary. In desperation, I wrote some myself. They were a big hit with the kids and that was when I first thought, hey, maybe I could write children's books. My first attempts were picture book texts. After a few of those I wrote a scary fantasy novel, followed by two mysteries. None of those sold and my next try was a young adult novel, *Good Rockin' Tonight*. Like many early novels, it was loosely based on my own life.

"For some reason I find it very easy to remember my childhood. I can vividly recall my feelings when I first heard the Sergeant Pepper album, when the cute older boy I had a crush on turned to me in the hall and patted me on the head, when I learned that my father had died. At the same time, I can now view these events from an adult perspective.

"Both these views, I feel, are required to write young children's novels. If the author can see the world through a child's eyes and nothing more, his book will be one-dimensional and claustrophobic. If he can only view children from an adult perspective, his story will be manipulative and didactic. So far I think I've been able to integrate both perspectives. If I ever lose that ability, it will be time to stop writing children's novels and move on to something else.

"I'm still interested in writing for children and teenagers, but in the last few years I've also tried my hand at journalism. I've written movie reviews for a local weekly paper, travel articles for the local daily, and restaurant reviews for a Santa Barbara restaurant guide. I've also been working on a screenplay and an adult novel.

"I live in Santa Barbara with my husband. No children (yet). When I'm not writing I like to bodyboard, listen to rock music, watch movies, and travel."

LEE-HOSTETLER, Jeri 1940-
(Jeri Marsh)

PERSONAL: Born August 16, 1940, in Mansfield, Ohio; daughter of Robert E. (a teacher) and Geraldine (a teacher; maiden name, Hostetler) Lee; divorced; children: Rob, Randy, Rusty, Dinah. *Education:* Pacific University, B.A., 1962, M.A., 1966; Portland State University, graduate study, 1980-85. *Home:* 1271 Northwest Keasey, P.O. Box 328, Roseburg, Ore. 97470.

CAREER: Has taught in junior high school, high school, and college, during the 1960s and 1980s; writer, 1970—; staff member at a shelter/home for battered women in Washington County, Ore., 1987-80; Custom Cleaners, Portland, Ore., owner-manager, 1988-1990. Woman's advocate, Oasis Shelter, Roseburg, Ore.

WRITINGS:

(Under name Jeri Marsh) *Hurrah for Alexander* (juvenile; illustrated by Joan Hanson, Carolrhoda, 1977.
Seasons of Change, Brethren Press, 1988.

PLAYS

If I Hold His Hands in Mine (one-act; first produced in Omaha, Neb., at Grace Brethren Bible Church, Easter Sunday, 1972), Baker's Plays, 1972.

Contributor of more than one hundred stories and articles, some under pseudonyms, to magazines, including *Better Camping, Young World, Woman's Life, Power for Living,* and *Guideposts.*

WORK IN PROGRESS: A novel which deals with social problems such as wife abuse in the early west.

LEVY, Nathan 1945-

PERSONAL: Born March 27, 1945, in Brooklyn, N.Y.; son of Morris and Hilda (Schieber) Levy; (divorced); children: Michele, Lisa, Marci, Joanne. *Education:* Queens College, B.A., 1967, M.S., 1968, Certificate, 1972; University of Connecticut, Ph.D., 1982. *Home:* 3 Marilyn Court, Lawrenceville, N.J. 08648. *Agent:* N. L. Associates, Inc., P.O. Box 1199, Lawrenceville, N.J. 08648. *Office:* Monmouth Junction School, Ridge Rd., P.O. Box 184, Monmouth Junction, N.J. 08852.

CAREER: New York Public Schools, New York, N.Y., teacher, 1967-73; Barkhamsted School, Pleasant Valley, Conn., elementary school principal, 1973-76; Orchard Park Central School District, Orchard Park, N.Y., supervisor of elementary education, 1976-77; Center for Intellectual Achievement, Inc., Princeton, N.J., founder, 1977-82; Monmouth Junction School, Monmouth Junction, N.J., elementary school principal, 1977—; N. L. Associates, Inc., Hightstown, N.J., founder and consultant, 1982—. Curriculum consultant to National Convention of the National Association of Elementary School Principals, 1979, 1981, 1983-85; served as National Elementary Education Expert on Accreditation Team, Boys Town, Neb., 1979; reviewer of materials for *GIC/T* (gifted, creative, talented magazine),

NATHAN LEVY

1979—; South American Consultant for American Schools, 1985. *Member:* National Association for Gifted Children, National Association for Supervision and Curriculum Development, National Association of Elementary School Principals.

AWARDS, HONORS: Public School 20 (New York, N.Y.) Parent Association Award, 1973, for extra service to school and community; Outstanding Young Man of America, 1974; Recognition from Barkhamsted Community, 1976, for service to the school community; National Endowment Award from the National Endowment for the Humanities, 1981.

WRITINGS:

Stories to Stretch Minds, four volumes, Tillium Press, 1981.
(With Janet Levy) *There Are Those* (illustrated by Joan Edwards), N. L. Associates, 1982.
Nathan Levy's Stories with Holes, Volumes 2-5, N. L. Associates, 1990.
"Guess Who" series, N. L. Associates, 1990.

CASSETTES

"Practical Ideas in Teaching Math in the Elementary Schools," Jab Press.
"Teaching Mathematics to the Gifted Child," Jab Press.
"Teaching Gifted Children in the Regular Classroom," Jab Press.

Contributor to periodicals, including *Teaching Gifted Children.*

WORK IN PROGRESS: Stories to Stretch Minds, book 5.

SIDELIGHTS: Nathan Levy went through the New York City school system as an underachiever. "At least once a year a school official would have me in for a conference to discuss my ability to do better. I was doing 'better!' My afterschool hours abounded with friends, activity, and conversation with all kinds of people. It was not until the world of teaching captured my heart that learning became relevant to me in the school setting and I could use my success out of the school for success in school.

"Shortly into my teaching career, it became obvious to me that pupils did not think critically very often. Thus began my search for ways to challenge and motivate young learners. The *Stories to Stretch Minds* and *Nathan Levy's Stories with Holes* are part of the result.

"Having been a child who found school irrelevant, I could relate to the boredom of inner city students (being only twenty-two years old when they were twelve and thirteen, I was not that far removed from them). We began to read novels, newspapers, sports information, and magazines instead of dull texts.

"After six years of teaching, I moved to rural Connecticut where I became a principal in a town called Pleasant Valley. It was no longer sufficient to use what I knew in one classroon, my ideas had to be disseminated. Verbally, I was a master, but none of my ideas, or uses of them, had been written down. I began to save more of my work (which is something I advise all teachers and writers to do). There must have been twenty books worth of ideas that were nonchalantly tossed away during my early teaching years.

"I left the principalship to try my hand as a central office administrator. It was a mistake. The children were too far away. When there were no pupil Valentine Day cards on my desk on February 14th, the mistake became very obvious.

"I returned to a principalship in Monmouth Junction, New Jersey, where I have been since July of 1977. It has been during this past decade plus years that my writings have been put into book form. *There Are Those* was a poem I had been using during my educational and management consulting. Joan Edwards, the art teacher in my school, was asked to illustrate the work. Little did we know what an inspiration the book would be for educators, artists, and business people. It felt wonderful to share in this collaborative effort.

"As I do communication and thinking skills workshops around the world, my writings gain increasing exposure. The successful thinking stories will continue to be written as long as people ask for them.

"Despite the books that appear under my name, I am first and foremost an educator who writes, not a writer who educates. People who invest their hearts and egos as pure writers have my utmost respect. One day, time permitting, I, too, will lock myself away for a period of time, set a schedule, and try to create a character 'not yet born,' a setting that will be 'real' for others, and/or a plot that may forever be remembered. It is in my plans. I wonder if the world is ready?"

LIDDELL, Kenneth 1912-1975

PERSONAL: Born January 2, 1912, in Regina, Canada; died July 7, 1975; son of Edith Liddell (a librarian); married Evelyn Ellison, July 11, 1936.

CAREER: Worked for twenty-five years as a journalist for the *Calgary Herald*, Canada; writer.

WRITINGS:

This Is British Columbia, Bailey & Swinfen, 1958.
Alberta Revisited, Bailey & Swinfen, 1960.
I'll Take the Train, Western Producer, 1977.
Exploring Southern Alberta's Chinook Country, Heritage House, 1981.

Also author of *This Is Alberta,* 1952.

LINDGREN, Barbro 1937-

PERSONAL: Born March 18, 1937, in Stockholm, Sweden; daughter of George (a civil engineer) and Maja (an artist; maiden name, Loefstedt) Enskog; children: Andreas, Mathias. *Education:* Attended Konstfackskolan Art School, 1954-58, and Konstakademin Academy of Arts, 1959. *Home:* Garvar Lundinsgraand 10, 11220 Stockholm, Sweden. *Agent:* Raben & Sjoegren, Box 45022, S 10430 Stockholm, Sweden; Eriksson & Lindgren Books, Box 22108, 10422 Stockholm, Sweden.

CAREER: Author, artist, and designer. *Awards, honors:* Swedish Foundation of Authors Labor Scholarship, 1967; Literary Promotion Scholarship, 1967, and 1971; Swedish Foundation of Authors Scholarship, 1968-69; "Gramo-

phone-70" Award, 1970, for children's song texts; Marsta Municipal Culture Prize, 1970; Swedish Foundation of Authors Five Year Labor Scholarship, 1971-1975; Literary Promotion Scholarship, 1971; *Expressen*'s Heffaklump Award (Sweden), 1971, for *Jaettehemligt;* Astrid Lindgren Award, 1973, for honorable authorship; Nils Holgersson-Plaketten from the Swedish Library Association, 1977, for *Lilla Sparvel;* Premio Europeo "Citta di Caorle" (picture book category), 1980, for *Sagan om den lilla farbrorn; The Wild Baby* was selected one of *School Library Journal*'s Best Books, 1981; *The Wild Baby Goes to Sea* was selected on of *School Library Journal*'s Best Books, 1983; Hans Christian Andersen Award nomination, 1988.

WRITINGS:

Mattias sommar (illustrated by Stan Tusan), Raben & Sjoegren (Stockholm), 1965, reissued, 1980, published as *Hilding's Summer,* translated by Annabelle MacMillan, Macmillan, 1967.
Mera om Mattias (title means "More about Mattias"), Raben & Sjoegren, 1966, reissued, 1980.
Hej, hej Mattias (title means "Hi, Hi, Mattias"), Raben & Sjoegren, 1967, reissued, 1980.
I Vaestan Grind (title means "Westwind Gate"; illustrated by Monica Schultz), Raben & Sjoegren, 1968, reissued, 1980.
Loranga, Masarin och Dartanjang, (title means "Loranga, Masarin, and Dartanjang"), Raben & Sjoegren, 1969, reissued, 1980.
Loranga Loranga, Raben & Sjoegren, 1970, reissued, 1984.
Nu har Kalle faatt en liten syster (title means "Kalle Now Has a New Little Sister"), Raben & Sjoegren, 1970, reissued, 1976.
Jaettehemligt (title means "Giant Secret"; illustrated by Olof Landstrom), Raben & Sjoegren, 1971, reissued, 1985.
Goda goda: Dikter (title means "Good, Good: Poems"), Raben & Sjoegren, 1971, new edition, 1976.
Nu aer vi gorillor laassas vi, Raben & Sjoegren, 1971, published as *Let's Be Gorillas!,* translated by Suzanne Carlson (illustrated by Susan Acker), Clamshell Press, 1976.

A bath is fun. (Illustration by Eva Eriksson from *Sam's Bath* by Barbro Lindgren.)

Vaerldshemligt (title means "World Secret"), Raben & Sjoegren, 1972, 4th edition, 1979.

Alban: Popmuffa foer smaa hunder (title means "Alban: A Muff Hat for Small Dogs"), Raben & Sjoegren, 1972, published in England as *Alban,* translated by Joan Tate, A. & C. Black, 1974.

Bladen brinner (title means "Burning Pages"), Raben & Sjoegren, 1973, new edition, 1978.

Groengoelingen aer paa vaeg: Dikter foer barn och andra (title means "The Green Woodpecker Is on His Way: Poems for Children and Others"; illustrated by Katarina Olausson), Raben & Sjoegren, 1974, reissued, 1980.

Babros pjaeser foer barn och andra (title means "Barbro's Plays for Kids and Others"), Raben & Sjoegren, 1975, new edition, 1978.

Lilla Sparvel (title means "Little Sparrow"; illustrated by Andreas Lindgren and Mathias Lindgren), Raben & Sjoegren, 1976.

Vad tycker du?, (title means "What Do You Think?"), Liber, 1976.

Stora Sparvel (title means "Big Sparrow"), Raben & Sjoegren, 1977.

(With L. Westman) *Hemliga laadans hemlighet* (title means "The Secret Box's Secrets"), Liber, 1978.

(With L. Westman) *Jag har en tam myra* (title means "I Have a Tame Aunt"), Liber, 1978.

(With L. Westman) *Kom ner fraan traedet* (title means "Come Down from the Tree"), Liber, 1978.

(With L. Westman) *Var aer mina byxor?* (title means "Where Are My Pants?"), Liber, 1978.

(With L. Westman) *Vaerldens laengsta korv* (title means "The World's Longest Hot Dog"), Liber, 1978.

(With L. Westman) *Laesa med varandra* (title means "Reading with Each Other"), Liber, 1978.

Garderobsbio (title means "The Movie Closet"), Raben & Sjoegren, 1978.

Bara Sparvel (title means "Only the Sparrow"), Raben & Sjoegren, 1979.

Sagan om den lilla farbrorn (title means "Story about a Little Man"; illustrated by Eva Eriksson), Raben & Sjoegren, 1979, reissued, 1985.

Nils Pantaloni Penell, Raben & Sjoegren, 1980.

Fotograf Jag (title means "Me, the Photographer"), Liber, 1980.

Mamman och den vilda bebin (illustrated by E. Eriksson), Raben & Sjoegren, 1980, published as *The Wild Baby,* adapted from the Swedish by Jack Prelutsky, Greenwillow, 1981.

Den vilda bebiresan (illustrated by E. Eriksson), Raben & Sjoegren, 1982, published as *The Wild Baby Goes to Sea,* adapted from the Swedish by J. Prelutsky, Greenwillow, 1983, large print edition, Greenwillow, 1983 (published in England as *The Wild Baby's Boat Trip,* translated by Alison Winn, Hodder & Stoughton, 1983).

Max nalle (illustrated by E. Eriksson), Raben & Sjoegren, 1981, published as *Sam's Teddy Bear*, Morrow, 1982 (published as *Sam's Teddy,* Methuen, 1984.

Max bil (illustrated by E. Eriksson), Raben & Sjoegren, 1981, published as *Sam's Car,* Morrow, 1982.

Max kaka (illustrated by E. Eriksson), Raben & Sjoegren, 1981, published as *Sam's Cookie,* Morrow, 1982 (published in England as *Sam's Biscuit,* Methuen, 1984).

Max boll (illustrated by E. Eriksson), Raben & Sjoegren, 1982, published as *Sam's Ball,* Morrow, 1983.

Max lampa (illustrated by E. Eriksson), Raben & Sjoegren, 1982, published as *Sam's Lamp,* Morrow, 1983 (published in England as *Bad Sam!,* Methuen, 1983).

Max balja (illustrated by E. Eriksson), Raben & Sjoegren, 1982, published as *Sam's Bath* (ALA Notable Book), Morrow, 1983.

OBS! Viktigt! (title means "Please Note! Important"; illustrated by Dan Jonsson), Liber, 1983.

Sagan om Karlknut, (illustrated by Cecilla Torudd), Raben & Sjoegren, 1985, published in the United States as *A Worm's Tale,* Farrar, 1988.

Vilda bebin far en hund (illustrated by E. Eriksson), Raben & Sjoegren, 1985, published as *The Wild Baby's Dog,* translated by A. Winn, Hodder & Stoughton, 1986, published as *The Wild Baby Gets a Puppy,* adapted from the Swedish by Jack Prelutsky, Greenwillow, 1988.

Max potta (illustrated by E. Eriksson), Raben & Sjoegren, 1986, published as *Sam's Potty,* Morrow, 1986.

Max dockvagn (illustrated by E. Eriksson), Raben & Sjoegren, 1986, published as *Sam's Wagon,* Morrow, 1986 (published in England as *Sam's Cart,* Methuen, 1986).

Verns lilla moessa flyger (illustrated by E. Eriksson), Raben & Sjoegren, 1987.

Sunkan flyger (illustrated by Olof Landstroem), Raben & Sjoegren, 1989.

Korken flyger (illustrated by E. Eriksson), Raben & Sjoegren, 1990.

ADULT

Genom ventilerna (title means "Through the Ventilators"), Bonnier (Stockholm), 1967.

Felipe, Bonnier, 1970.

Eldvin (title means "Winefire"), Bonnier, 1972.

Molnens broeder (title means "The Celestial Brothers"), Bonnier, 1975.

Rapporter fraan marken: Dikter (title means "Reports from the Land: Poems"), Raben & Sjoegren, 1976.

Det riktiga havet (title means "The Real Ocean"), Bonnier, 1979.

En liten cyklist (title means "The Little Cyclist"), Raben & Sjoegren, 1982.

Elegi oever en doed raatta (poems; title means "Elegy Over a Dead Rat"), Raben & Sjoegren, 1983.

Hunden med rocken: prosadikter (title means "The Dog with the Overcoat: Prose and Poems"), Raben & Sjoegren, 1985.

Vitkind. I ett barns hjaerta (roman), hoesten, Raben & Sjoegren, 1986.

Nu aer du mitt barn (illustrated by Katarina Olansson Saell), Raben & Sjoegren, 1988.

ADAPTATIONS:

"The Wild Baby" (filmstrip), Random House.

SIDELIGHTS: "You have to experience sorrow and passion to be able to write well,"[1] believes Lindgren. The author of many children's books, as well as books for young adults and adults, her stories are drawn from life experiences in which she describes the "unique" with understanding, sensitivity, love, and much humor.

Born on March 18, 1937 in Stockholm, Sweden, Barbro Lindgren has a clear recollection of her childhood, and in particular "the sounds, the scents, the feeling of security when you squeezed somebody's hand, the fear of dark corners. I recall this with happiness, sadness, and anxiety.

He was reckless, loud and wild. (Illustration by Eva Eriksson from *The Wild Baby* by Barbro Lindgren.)

"My childhood was traumatic. There weren't any horrendous happenings causing this, rather, the insignificant treacherous moments.

"I was afraid of everything when I was little. Some homes seemed unsafe to me, and I didn't want to stay in them, especially overnight. Some people seemed insecure and I didn't want to stay with them. I was scared of everything new. When my mother left me at nursery school for the first time, I huddled in the corner and stayed there until she returned. After that I didn't want to return to the school. Quite often thereafter when I attended my first class in anything, I never returned. At the same time I was also very curious and eager to learn."[2]

"I [also] experienced childhood as an adventure. I had much freedom to make my own friends and to investigate the world on my own."[3]

As it is with all children, school became a reality for Lindgren as well. Her impressions were most vividly revealed in her *Giant Secret*: "Now I have been in school for a week, the fall is approaching more each day. The leaves are falling and you can smell smoke outside. I feel so sad inside and I don't know why, but it feels like I never want to laugh again. I think it began yesterday. I was sitting in the rear of the classroom, watching leaves fly through the window. The teacher was lecturing and suddenly there was a flock of blackbirds flying by.

"Thereafter it seemed I saw the classroom for the first time; how small it was, and how hopeless it seemed with the rasping sound from the pencils while everyone sighed. And I thought: here I must sit for the rest of my life, until I'm eighteen years old and study and listen to the blackbirds chirp! Then everything truly seemed hopeless. I couldn't stay there. I got up and started walking towards the door."[3]

"I was afraid of death more than anything else. I was terrified that someone in my family would die and leave me. 'Don't bicycle so close to the edge!' I would scream at my parents when we were riding close to the edge of a pier. On a boat trip with my grandparents, I was convinced we would never reach the island alive. I was equally scared when I had my own family, worried something would happen to them, and was especially frightened when my children were ill. I was frightened to take their temperature when I knew they were burning up. If they were gone for too long, I would worry myself sick about cars, about them falling into wells. I was probably too worrisome to have a family in the first place. I have done a lot of writing about death, to get to know it and to bring it closer to life.

"I grew up during the 1940s, and I now meet women who seem to deal with the same feelings and conflicts. At that time adults were caught between their own upbringing which was very strict, highly moral with a heavy demand on obedience and the new thinking about a more liberal upbringing. So, they didn't know on which leg to stand. Just the same, this kind of upbringing produced a lot of 'split' children and I am one of them."[2]

Lindgren's writings began in her childhood diaries. "I wanted to be famous at any price—to be a child genius on the front page of newspapers was my grandest dream. I submitted fairy tales to newspapers and publishers, but my work was rejected. One day when I was thirteen years old, however, *Daily News* printed one of my stories on the children's page. A great moment.

"The years rolled on and my writing slowed. A few more stories were published but things eventually came to a halt. I decided, instead, to concentrate more on drawing and painting and attended art school for four years, where I met the man I eventually married. I worked a few years in advertising and layouts. I tried writing again, but was again unsuccessful and stopped altogether. My writing was superficial. It was not until I realized that I must write about things with which I am familiar, drawing from my own experiences, that my writing took shape.

"Astrid Lindgren (no relationship) gave me some sound advice after reading my stories: 'Do not use too many characters—one or two is enough. Keep your characterizations shorter! It's enough to use a brief description here or there. Reduce excessive action which becomes exhausting for the reader. Instead, allow the story to build slowly to a climax and then let it slowly subside.'"

The following year *Mattia's Summer* was published. Lindgren's first effort was autobiographical. "I really don't try to make up too much. I feel that real life is exciting enough."

Her childhood is the subject of *Little Sparrow, Big Sparrow, Only Sparrow, Giant Secret, World Secret,* and *Burning Pages.* Her childhood reading habits were recounted in *The Key to My Childhood,* the conception of an editor at Bromberg's. "She suggested that I try to recollect which specific books I had read as a child and gather them all together with my own comments.

"I have tried to remember the very first stories. The ones I had heard before I started school.

"All children are drawn to fright, it's always been that way,"[5] said Lindgren as she recalled the part in *The Cat Trip* where the cat splits in two. "That was the worse thing I had experienced at three years old. But when the gruesome becomes pleasurable and deep inside you have the feeling that all will be fine (in this case the cat is sewn back together at the bottom of the same page) then it becomes palatable.

"I think we all have a need for ghostliness, which is a strong characteristic trait in me. I guess it's always evident in my books."[4]

After Lindgren's first books were published, she traveled to schools to discuss her writing. "I then noticed that what I thought was important when I grew up was, in fact, just as important now. We talked about life and death, sorrow and birth, sex and about being different—such things as I would have liked to have read as a child. So I went home and wrote about my experiences: about all those difficult things in life."[5]

"I identify with people who are at a disadvantage. Those who are oppressed. I react with fury towards injustice—people who are treated unfairly in the workplace and people who misuse their power."[6]

"I have a longing to write and work with language. If children experience some relief in reading my books, it makes me happy. I pull together things that are burdensome and thorny and I peel away idyll, because that doesn't interest me . . . . I like to describe the best relationships between people, warm and friendly, but deep.

"Life is full of hardships as well as incredibly beautiful things, like small pearls. Among the beautiful things that can happen

(From *Sam's Teddy Bear* by Barbro Lindgren. Illustration by Eva Eriksson.)

are reaching for another person, feeling affection and warmth. You notice this throughout life, how complicated life is and how simple it can be."[3]

Lindgren's books deal with all ages from babies to pensioners and have a readership across the spectrum as well. "It's fun to change, it keeps things from becoming monotonous. You don't stiffen up and it's fun to improve oneself. I want to write in simple terms for all, but in the adult books I can include linguistic difficulties and such things that children have not acquired through experience and consequently don't understand. At the same time it's fun to write for children in an artistic way. Adult books require more nuances."[3]

Lindgren's personality is well-suited for the life of an author, but she feels slightly uneasy about the solitary nature that is demanded. "I liked being alone as a child. It seemed to make me strong. As an adult, however it has become a negative escape. I only had fun when I was alone in my own little fantasy world. Quite often I would become depressed and apathetic. On those days I refrained from making phone calls and talking with anyone. The wrong word would make me brood for months. I easily misunderstood a conversation and would become hurt because I was so focused on my own interests, not understanding the other person's situation.

"When there are many things that are not cleared up within you, you tend to feel insecure and fatalistic. I found it easier at

Where is Sam's cookie? (Illustration by Eva Eriksson from *Sam's Wagon* by Barbro Lindgren.)

those times to be with other children instead of my own. My own made too many demands on me."[2]

Lindgren had to learn to deal with her anger, as well, which she regarded as a burden of her guilt. She recalled the day she became enraged because her children would not clean up after themselves. She flung open a window and threw all of their toys into the snow. The toys stayed outside in the snow for a few days. Later, Lindgren herself picked them all up. This genuine anger, she recalled, was deep within her. Psychoanalysis was the key that helped her unlock all of these disturbing feelings.

"It is wonderful to have the job I do. Being able to live the way I want is the reason why I have been able to write so many books."[6]

"I've become more and more anti-social through the years. I don't behave the way I *should* and I don't fit in at social gatherings. Once I attended a party for authors held by a publisher. I couldn't stand the crowd, so I decided to sit behind the switchboard alone.

"'If anyone would like to talk to me, please tell them that I'll be sitting behind the switchboard,' I said. Food was delivered to me there. I didn't dare join the crowd and be friendly.

"Most people would behave that way if they had been used to a great deal of freedom. I have to be alone to be able to experience my freedom, or be with someone I know very well! who feels the same way.

"I have to feel completely free when I start writing a book. I have a starting point after which I don't know where it will lead. Suddenly there will be twists and turns I had never thought of before. That is fun and adventure."[6]

"I become extremely disturbed by intellectual, incomprehensible stories glossed in pleasant cultural descriptions; they are often a 'slap in the face' to ordinary people. When it comes to my odd main characters, I don't decide to write about anyone

who is different. It's just that odd people have such interesting personalities."[3]

Lindgren's thrust in her writings is the search for elemental truth. "Towards the origin, towards the 'seed' is what we all strive for. This is not easy, because we are not always honest with ourselves. Then we must start all over, like rolling yarn into a ball. It is too easy to be influenced by trends. At least I think that was the case when I was younger. Now it's easier for me to be truthful and as such I always have to be obstinate. I need tranquility and reflection .... .I find tranquility in nature."[3]

"There are certain of my books for which I have special feelings: *Felipe, Eldvin* and *The Celestial Brothers*. I wrote them in my own way with slowly evolving illustrations, where language and pictures blend.

"Writing captures everything for me: music, art, photography. What I may wish to paint, I instead translate into words. I can express myself more subtly with words, although nothing moves me as deeply as music. Mozart, Mahler, Pettersson. But I can always *listen* to music. I don't have to play it myself."[5]

FOOTNOTE SOURCES

[1]Translation of Marit Andersson's "Barbro Lindgren: Man maaste ha upplevt sorg och passion foer att skriva bra," *Femina*, September, 1981.
[2]Translation of Lena Rydin's "Minns du din barndom?" *Vi foraeldrar*, 1977. Amended by B. Lindgren.
[3]Translation of Birgitta Fransson's "Barbro Lindgren: Ocksaa en cyklist," *Opsis Kalopsis*, February, 1988.
[4]Translation of Annika Rosell's "Barbro Lindgren: Bakom idyllen lurar moerkret," *Vaar bostad*, 1986.
[5]Translation of Helena Ridelberg's "Barbro Lindgren: Jag aer en typisk bakvaegsmaenniska," *Foerfattarportratt*, March, 1986.
[6]Translation of Ann Rudberg's "Barbro Lindgren, Nu goer jag bara det jag vill!" *Vi maenskor*, 1982.

FOR MORE INFORMATION SEE:

Sally Holmes Holtze, *Sixth Book of Junior Authors*, H. W. Wilson, 1989.

LOCKE, Robert 1944-
(Clayton Bess)

PERSONAL: Born December 30, 1944, in Vallejo, Calif.; son of Clayton Eugene (a welder) and Bess (a medical records librarian; maiden name, Holt) Locke. *Education:* Chico State College (now California State University, Chico), B.A., 1966, San Francisco State College (now California State University, San Francisco), M.A., 1967; Simmons College, M.L.S., 1973. *Politics:* "Anything but Republican." *Religion:* Libertarian. *Home and office:* Locke/Bess Monsters, Inc., 900 53rd St., Sacramento, Calif. 95819. *Agent:* Scott Meredith Agency, 845 Third Ave., New York, N.Y. 10022.

CAREER: U.S. Peace Corps, Washington, D.C., volunteer in Monrovia, Liberia, Africa, 1968-71; Harvard College Library, Cambridge, Mass., intern librarian, 1971-73; California State University Chico Library, reference librarian, 1974-76; novelist and playwright, 1976—; John Purdy, Inc., Hollywood, Calif., writer and actor, 1978-83; *Hollywood Reporter*

Studio Blu-Book Directory, Hollywood, Calif., editor, 1980-83; American Conservatory Theatre, San Francisco, Calif., playwright-in-residence, 1983-84; University of California Los Angeles Extension, Los Angeles, Calif., professor, 1985; California Arts Council, Sacramento, Calif., artist-in-schools, 1986-88; California State University, Sacramento, substitute reference librarian, 1986-88, librarian, 1989—; Sacramento County Libraries, Sacramento, Calif., substitute reference librarian, 1986-88; Sacramento Area Regional Theatre Alliance, Sacramento, Calif., playwriting instructor, 1987-88. *Member:* Dramatists Guild, Actors Equity Association, Southern California Council on Literature for Children and Young People, American Federation of Television and Radio Artists.

AWARDS, HONORS: Maggie Award for Best Directory from the West Coast Publishing Association, 1982, and 1983, both for *The Hollywood Reporter Studio Blu-Book Directory;* Southern California Council on Literature for Children and Young People Special Recognition for Contribution of Cultural Significance, 1983, and Silver Medal for Best First Novel from the Commonwealth Club of California, 1984, both for *Story for a Black Night;* Best Original Script from the Bay Area Theater Critics Circle, 1984, and Best Writing Award, and Best Performance Award, both from *Drama-Logue,* both 1987, both for "The Dolly"; Diplome Loisirs Jeunes Award (Paris) for Best Novel, 1984, for *Par Une Nuit Noire* (*Story for a Black Night*); Elly Award for Original

(Jacket photograph by the author from *Story for a Black Night* by Clayton Bess.)

Script, for Performance, and for Actress, all 1986, all for "Rose Jewel and Harmony"; *Tracks* was selected one of American Library Association's Best Books for Young Adults, 1986.

WRITINGS:

YOUNG ADULT; ALL UNDER PSEUDONYM CLAYTON BESS

Story for a Black Night, Houghton, 1982.
The Truth about the Moon (illustrated by Rosekrans Hoffman), Houghton, 1983.
Big Man and the Burn-Out, Houghton, 1985.
Tracks, Houghton, 1986.

Story for a Black Night has been translated into French.

PLAYS

"Who's Richard?" (three-act), first performed as a stage reading at American Conservatory Theatre, San Francisco, Calif., 1977.
"Play" (one-act), first produced at Fifth Estate, Hollywood, Calif., 1982.
"The Dolly" (three-act), first produced at Front Row Theater, San Francisco, 1983.
"Rose Jewel and Harmony" (three-act), first produced at the Exchange for the Performing Arts, Sacramento, Calif., 1986.
"Murder and Edna Redrum" (two-act), first produced at Gateway Players in Nevada City, Calif., 1989.
"On Daddy's Birthday," first produced as a readers theater production by Gateway Players in Nevada City, Calif., 1990.

Also author of unproduced musical "A Howling Twain," and of unproduced screenplays, including "Romantasy," "China Clipper," "Blood," "Crystal," "The Monitor," and "Air."

WORK IN PROGRESS: All Ways, The Legend of Nothing, and *Suddenly the Cat,* all picture books; *Mayday Rampage,* a novel about the threat to heterosexual high school students of AIDS, and an outspoken statement on the rights of young people to intellectual freedom.

SIDELIGHTS: "I was born on December 30, 1944, to Clayton and Bess Locke. And now you know that my real name is not Clayton Bess.

"Why did I change my name from Robert Howard Locke to Clayton Bess? I didn't, not really. I kept my own name, and most people know me by that name and call me Bob, or some call me Rob or Bobby, and some even still call me Skip or Skipper. That was my nickname when I was a kid because, my dad says, I was such a bossy little kid, always trying to be skipper of the ship.

"But the reason I took my parents' first names as my pen name was that when my first book, *Story for a Black Night,* was published in 1982, my parents were both having a lot of trouble with their hearts, and I was afraid they might die soon. (I'm very happy to say that they are still alive and kicking.)

"I decided to give Clayton and Bess this tribute because they have always been such terrific parents, always very understanding, very generous, very helpful, very open minded. When I look at some of my friends' parents, I realize how

ROBERT LOCKE

lucky I was to be born to Clayton and Bess. They gave me values, but they didn't demand that I follow those values slavishly. As my own personality developed, they accepted who I was, that I was different from them. Sometimes it was a fight. My morality was so different in so many ways from theirs that it was hard sometimes for them to understand. But we worked out a truce because they trust me and I trust them.

"My moral code is very strict and very flexible at the same time. I get it from both Clayton and Bess. To me, morality has nothing to do with religion, nothing to do with sex, nothing to do with politics. I know that this thought flies in the face of most of the people of this country, but I firmly believe it. Morality is how you treat people. Morality is trying to be the best person you can be, never hurting anyone else, never doing anything underhanded or never betraying someone else. We all have to share the planet. We're all neighbors. We all must try to understand each other and accept each other.

"This is not to say that I'm a wimp. When I see hypocrisy, I stand up and fight. When I see blind hate, willing ignorance, brutality, injustice, I speak out. It's one of the reasons I write, to expose these evils and at the same stroke try to get young people to cherish the diversity of the world and its inhabitants. That's why the heroes in my books are often outsiders, Africans and blacks and okies and gays and people with AIDS. It's easy to be afraid of people who are different from you until you realize that they're just people, just one of us, just a little different, that's all.

"Jess Judd in *Big Man and the Burn-Out* is an eighth-grader who is constantly thinking hard, trying to figure out why life is so complicated. I liked Jess a lot when I created him, and so when I was ready to write *The Mayday Rampage,* this most recent novel about AIDS and censorship, I thought, 'Why not look up old Jess Judd and find out what happened to him in high school?' It was a very interesting experience for me, recreating a character. It was sort of like visiting an old friend. Jess was the same guy with the same values as in the earlier novel, but older now, and with even more serious questions, and an even greater sense of responsibility. And I still liked him.

"It was fun, too, to bring back Molly Pierce as a high school student. I always liked Molly in *Big Man,* but she didn't have a big part in Jess's life at that time. In *The Mayday Rampage* she's half the novel, just as opinionated and sharp-tongued and funny as ever. Meechum's back, too, and he was a big surprise to me. And Mr. Goodban and Vic, older. It made me very sad to see what happened to them.

"I enjoy creating characters and then looking them up at a different period in their lives. Sid, the grandfather in *Big Man,* became the narrator of *Tracks* because I liked the way he talked. Sid is based on Clayton, and a lot of the adventures that happened to eleven-year-old Sid—or Blue, as Sid was called in 1934—were inspired by stories I remember Clayton telling about hopping freights when he was young during the Depression.

"I created the Starr family in *Tracks,* based a bit on Bess's family, and a couple of years later I looked them up in the present. I wanted to see what happened between 1934 and 1984 to Marge and Rose Jewel and Violet Ruby. Boy, did they get hysterical! A lot of funny and very terrible things happened to them, and those things appear in my two plays 'Rose Jewel and Harmony' and 'On Daddy's Birthday' where we see the three sisters in their sixties.

"I write plays under Robert Locke and books for young people under Clayton Bess. Why? Am I schizoid? Maybe. It was sort of a trap I fell into. You see, when I created Clayton Bess in 1982 for *Story for a Black Night,* I really thought it would be the only book I would ever get published because it had taken me over ten years to even find a publisher for that story, and then even that publisher didn't seem very enthusiastic about me or my other stories. But when *Story for a Black Night* got such wonderful reviews, the publisher started taking me more seriously. And I began taking myself more seriously as a writer, and Clayton Bess kept writing.

"As Robert Locke, meanwhile, I had been writing plays and working as an actor in Hollywood, performing in silly musicals to drunken audiences in dinner theaters, doing ridiculous commercials for television. I didn't like spending my time like that.

"So when I was called up to San Francisco, as Robert Locke, to work on a play-in-progress production of my drama, 'The Dolly,' I jumped at the chance. And, thus, was born the Siamese twins, Robert Locke, the playwright, and Clayton Bess, the novelist for young people.

"What a difference between Hollywood and San Francisco! What a difference between real theater and dinner theater! How glad I was to leave all that television mentality and Hollywood glitter and superficiality! I was home, both literally and metaphorically. I had been raised in the Bay Area, and all through college I had studied drama. I mean real drama, theater, not the pseudo drama they deal with most in Hollywood. I felt energized to be back.

"San Francisco's American Conservatory Theatre (ACT) is one of the best companies in the United States. The play-in-progress of 'The Dolly' was a powerful, riveting production, so good that ACT decided to do it on the mainstage the following year. I was very excited because maybe after that 'The Dolly' would go on to Broadway.

"It didn't. I don't have a good explanation for this. Agents and actors and directors and producers tell me that the climate for dramas and new plays is not good in New York. New York audiences like comedies and musicals, they say.

"So I wrote the comedies 'Rose Jewel and Harmony' (1985), 'On Daddy's Birthday' (1986), and 'Murder and Edna Redrum' (1987). But I don't seem to get anyone to take them very seriously. I send the plays out all the time, every time I have a lead, to regional theaters around the country. But producers of regional theaters tell me that their audiences want plays that have already been a hit in New York. And since New York producers tell me that New York audiences don't like new plays, this is a catch-22 that I just can't figure out.

"Theater is dying. I hear that a lot. I hope it's not true because I really like writing plays, and I want to keep doing it. And I want young people to see new plays and write new plays. Maybe it's just a down cycle right now.

"One of the greatest thrills in the world is to sit in an audience and watch a really great performance of one of your plays, to feel the audience around you absorbing your work. On the verso, one of the greatest frustrations is not getting a production of your play. A play isn't finished until it's being acted in front of an audience; it's more a blueprint.

"And tomorrow night when this baby moon's bigger brother comes to follow me around the town, I will catch him too and put him in the bottle. And the next night, their sister. And all their brothers and sisters every night until I have the whole moon family in my bottle. Then I will have their light always."

"You silly-silly! There is only one moon. This I know, for our pa told me so."

(From *The Truth about the Moon* by Clayton Bess. Illustrated by Rosekrans Hoffman.)

"A novel, on the other hand, is finished when you write 'The End.' It's out of your hands then and in the hands of the reader. You never know who's reading your novel, where. You get letters from some readers after they've finished, and that gives you a very good feeling, almost like sitting in the audience, but removed.

"What I like best is reading to students from my books. I'm often invited to schools to speak and read. I get a different kick out of each grade level. For early grades I like to read from 'Suddenly the Cat,' a picture book that kids love but for which I can't find a publisher. Editors tell me that it's 'too adult' for kids. That's a criticism I get on a lot of my stories, but I disagree. I write UP to young people, not DOWN to them. When I send editors cassettes of me reading 'Suddenly the Cat' and kids howling with laughter, the editors say that the kids are just laughing at me because I ham it up so much. That's partly true; I do ham. But that's just what's so much fun about 'Suddenly the Cat'; it allows you to do funny things when you read it. Teachers and kids love it. And so do I.

"For fifth and sixth graders, I like to read from *Tracks*. The adventures are fun, and I get to use Clayton's okie accent. For junior high, I like reading from *Big Man and the Burn-out*. The classroom scenes are very popular with this age.

"I'm looking forward to reading from *The Mayday Rampage* to high schools. The response I've gotten so far is pretty fantastic. Teenagers like this book because it doesn't talk down to them. It's straight-talk, and teenagers appreciate that. One eleventh grade girl told me recently that she was sick of hearing about AIDS, but that she couldn't stop reading *The Mayday Rampage*. Suddenly she saw what all the talk, all the pamphlets, all the films were not getting across to her; she saw how easy it can be to slip into this disease.

"That's why I wrote *The Mayday Rampage* in the first place. AIDS is terrifying, and teenagers are at grave risk, and yet teenagers are not terrified. Why? Because teenagers don't know anyone personally who has AIDS, so they're not interested. What doesn't hit home with them is that they may know lots of people carrying the disease but who look healthy. They may even be carrying the disease themselves, but they won't find out until years from now.

"*The Mayday Rampage* introduces young people to the human side of AIDS, introduces them to some nice, funny, valiant teenagers who suddenly—by an accident that could happen to anyone—are exposed to AIDS. It's a good story that catches up the reader. At one senior class of a Catholic high school for girls, I read the part of the book where Jess and Molly stumble awkwardly into love. The eyes in the audience were electric, the girls holding their breaths as they listened. They really identified. That was a fun day for me.

"Writing is fun. I encourage all of you to think seriously about it for yourselves. It's always challenging to tell a good story, a meaningful story, keeping readers on the edge of their seats, involving them, moving them, making them think.

"You have to think for yourself to be a writer, keep yourself sharp, read, analyze, form opinions, change opinions. You

It was blistering hot the day I hopped my first freight. (Jacket illustration by Darryl Zudeck from *Tracks* by Clayton Bess.)

can't be complacent. I like that. I like challenging myself. And I like challenging young people.

"Advice from Clayton Bess?

"TRAVEL—See how other people live. It will change you forever. My three years living in West Africa, teaching in the Peace Corps, were perhaps the most important years of my life. I've travelled through West and East Africa, Morocco, Mediterranean Europe, England, Mexico, Guatemala, and through several states in the East, the West and the Midwest. I never took a trip which didn't improve me.

"READ—It's a way of traveling.

"LEARN OTHER LANGUAGES—It's a way of knowing other people and other lands, and other langauges can illuminate your own language. I speak French and Spanish pretty well, though I read them much better, along with Italian. I can say a greeting in a handful of West African dialects, much to the pleasure and laughter of the tribal people.

"'BE WHAT YOU WISH TO SEEM TO BE'—A maxim by somebody very noble and wise.

HOBBIES AND OTHER INTERESTS: Gardening, cats, running, bicycling.

FOR MORE INFORMATION SEE:

Sally Holmes Holtze, *Sixth Book of Junior Authors and Illustrators,* H. W. Wilson, 1989.

LUDWIG, Lyndell 1923-

PERSONAL: Born December 6, 1923, in Berkeley, Calif.; daughter of Albert Philip (a college professor) and Gladys (a child development teacher; maiden name, Newman) Ludwig. *Education:* University of Washington, Seattle, B.A., 1945; attended University of California, Berkeley, 1945-46, and California College of Arts and Crafts, 1948-56. *Home:* 15 Lenox Rd., Kensington, Calif. 94707. *Office:* Star Dust Books, 15 Lenox Rd., Kensington, Calif. 94707.

CAREER: University of California, Berkeley, secretary at Associated Students Store, 1947-64; researcher and writer, 1964— . Free-lance lettering and poster work, 1958-64. *Member:* United States-China Peoples Friendship Association. *Awards, honors: Ts'ao Chung Weighs an Elephant* was a finalist at the Prix International du Livre pour Enfants, Geneva, Switzerland, 1987.

WRITINGS:

JUVENILE; SELF-ILLUSTRATED

Ts'ao Chung Weighs an Elephant, Creative Arts, 1983.
The Shoemaker's Gift: From an Ancient Chinese Folktale, Creative Arts, 1983.
The Little White Dragon, Star Dust Books, 1989.

An abridged version of *The Shoemaker's Gift* was included in the Harcourt Brace Jovanovich Reading Program.

WORK IN PROGRESS: Children's picturebooks, based on Chinese stories: *Ring a Bell to Catch a Thief; How the Rabbit Got His Long Ears; The Country Goose; One Can Always Find a Way to Do Anything; Why the Cock Crows When the Sun Comes Up; "Kerplunk"; The Tree and the Foolish King;* forty or more Chinese tales for a collection or anthology.

SIDELIGHTS: "My father taught at Nan Kai School in Tientsin, China from 1916 to 1918, and returned with a love for the Chinese people and their culture. Exposed to things Chinese from my earliest years I, too, developed similar interests, which led to majoring in Far Eastern studies at the University of Washington and study for a year at the University of California in Berkeley.

"Paralleling this has been a fascination with drawing and art for as long as I can remember. A thoughtful third grade teacher let me sit in the back of the room and sketch as the roll and other daily classroom routines were being conducted. In the eighth and ninth grades an imaginative art teacher gave me much encouragement. Easel, paper, paintbrush, and water colors were put before me as I was given free rein to paint whatever I wanted to—nursery rhymes, *Alice in Wonderland,* and a charcoal rendition of a Chinese child which, because of the war in that country, was titled 'A Prayer for China.'

"After college the pursuit of art was furthered and enriched by attending a local art school where life drawing and art history classes gave me background and eased my curiosity about the wonders of art and artists through the ages.

LYNDELL LUDWIG

Learning to draw the human figure was like learning to write the alphabet. Once the fundamentals were mastered there was the freedom to do with it what I would.

"In my introduction to the Chinese language, I came across many intriguing stories for children, fascinating tales with basic human values. Over the years, while reading through Chinese books, I have found many more. When children know about the cultures of those in other lands, we all become the richer for it. Although the ultimate objective with the stories is to have them published, discovering the stories, interpreting them from the Chinese, and illustrating them is a delight in itself.

"Over the years I have accumulated many Chinese books, primarily literature, art, reference, and children's stories. In addition, I subscribe to several magazines and periodicals from mainland China which help me to understand present conditions there. Also, for the past several years I have been studying T'ang poems and ancient Chinese essays with a Chinese friend. Character by character, line by line, the ideas unfold, and I am continually impressed by the richness and beauty of the Chinese language."

HOBBIES AND OTHER INTERESTS: Gardening.

MANDELL, Muriel (Hortense Levin) 1921-

PERSONAL: Born August 19, 1921, in New York, N.Y.; daughter of Simon and Gertrude (Maisel) Levin; married Horace Mandell, January 23, 1945; children: Mark, Jonathan. *Education:* Brooklyn College (now Brooklyn College of City University of New York), B.A. (cum laude), 1942; Columbia University, M.S., 1943. *Home:* 72 Barrow St., New York, N.Y. 10014.

CAREER: Overseas News Agency, Washington, D.C., correspondent; *Long Branch Daily Record,* Long Branch, N.J., police reporter; *Tips* (magazine), New York, N.Y., associate editor; Radio Station WMGM, New York, N.Y., public relations, 1948-51; New York Board of Education, New York, N.Y., teacher of English, teacher-trainer, 1951-84. Adjunct, Hunter College, 1988—.

WRITINGS:

(With Robert E. Wood) *Make Your Own Musical Instruments,* Sterling, 1957, revised edition, 1959.
101 Best Educational Games, Sterling, 1958, revised edition published as *Games to Learn By: 100 Best Educational Games,* 1972.
Science for Children, Sterling, 1959, reissued as *Physics Experiments for Children* (illustrated by S. Matsuda), Dover, 1968 (published in England as *Science for Beginners,* Oak Tree Press, 1962).
Jonathan's Sparrow, Lothrop, 1963.
The Fifty-one Capitals of the U.S.A., Sterling, 1965.
(With others) *Complete Science Course for Young Experimenters,* Sterling, 1967.
Two Hundred and Twenty Easy-to-Do Science Experiments for Young People: Three Complete Books, Dover, 1985.
Fantastic Book of Logic Puzzles, Sterling, 1986.
Simple Science Experiments with Everyday Materials (illustrated by Frances W. Zweifel), Sterling, 1989.
Simple Weather Experiments, Sterling, 1990.

SIDELIGHTS: "I've been writing professionally since I was a teenager (I had a regular column in the *Paterson Morning Call* while in high school) and spent years as a journalist, magazine editor, and publicist.

"I started writing children's books when my own children were little. I wrote for, with, and about them. When it was time for them to go to college, I went into teaching full time. Children's books may be rewarding in many ways, but they don't pay tuitions. I found that teaching children wasn't so very different from writing books for them. While I worked for the New York Board of Education, I wrote and/or edited any number of manuals for teachers, but it wasn't until after I officially 'retired' that I returned to writing for children, dedicated again to making learning both challenging and joyous. In *Fantastic Book of Logic Puzzles,* I set logic problems in imaginative and humorous settings to stimulate the imagination and make it more interesting to master the verbal and mathematical skills involved. Similarly in the science experiment book, *Simple Science Experiments with Everyday Materials,* I tried to promote adaptability and originality by using ordinary materials in unusual ways.

"It may be of interest that one of my youthful collaborators (Mark) became a scientist and the other (Jonathan) a writer."

HOBBIES AND OTHER INTERESTS: Painting, sewing, swimming, cryptograms, reading, computer programming.

McCUNN, Ruthanne Lum 1946-

PERSONAL: Born February 21, 1946, in San Francisco, Calif; married Don McCunn (a writer). *Education:* University of Texas at Austin, B.A., 1968; San Francisco State College (now University), Teaching Credential, 1969.

Finally, after many months, Spanish Louie spoke the words Pie-Biter had been working and waiting for. "There's nothing more I can teach you. You're ready to run your own pack train."

(From *Pie-Biter* by Ruthanne Lum McCunn. Illustrated by You-shan Tang.)

Politics: Independent. *Religion:* Independent. *Home:* 1007 Castro, San Francisco, Calif. 94114.

CAREER: Librarian at public school in Santa Barbara, Calif., 1969-70, teacher, 1970-73; teacher in San Francisco Unified School District, Calif., 1974-78; writer, 1979—. Visiting lecturer, University of California at Santa Cruz, 1988, and Cornell University, 1989. Member, California State Committee for Evaluation and Selection of Texts for State Adoption, Committee for Library Services, Committee for Legal Compliance, and California Arts Council; member of advisory board, Asian Women United, Chinatown YWCA, and Chinese Historical Society of America; consultant on bilingual and bicultural education and on teaching English as a second language. *Member:* Chinese Historical Society, Chinese for Affirmative Action, American Civil Liberties Union, Amnesty International, Chinese Culture Center, Asian Women United. *Awards, honors:* American Book Award from the Before Columbus Foundation, 1984, for *Pie-Biter;* Best Book of Nonfiction Adventure from the Southwest Booksellers Association, 1985, for *Sole Survivor.*

WRITINGS:

An Illustrated History of the Chinese in America, Design Enterprises, 1979.
Thousand Pieces of Gold (biographical novel), Design Enterprises, 1981, reissued, Beacon Press, 1989.

Pie-Biter (picture book; illustrated by You-shan Tang), Design Enterprises, 1983.
Sole Survivor (nonfiction novel), Design Enterprises, 1985, reissued, Scholastic, 1990.
Chinese American Portraits: Personal Histories 1828-1988, Chronicle Books, 1988.

An Illustrated History of the Chinese in America, Thousand Pieces of Gold, and *Sole Survivor* are available in Braille. Contributor to periodicals, including *Yihai.*

ADAPTATIONS:

"Thousand Pieces of Gold" (film), American Playhouse/ Motherlode Productions, aired on American Playhouse, fall, 1991.

WORK IN PROGRESS: A novel, as yet untitled.

SIDELIGHTS: "I grew up in Hong Kong during the 1950s. As an Amerasian child I did not belong anywhere. In the Chinese neighborhood where we lived, my white skin and blond hair made me a *faan gwai mui,* foreign devil girl. At school, I was a 'ching chong Chinaman' because I couldn't speak English. Books quickly became my escape, a lifeline to the possibilities beyond the tiny island. But books were too expensive to buy. The school 'library' was a single shelf of dog-eared discards. And there were no public libraries. Only when I came to America did books finally become easily accessible, and I was so overwhelmed by my sudden wealth that years passed before I began to recognize that there are serious 'poverty pockets.' Among the impoverished areas of particular interest to me is the dearth of books by and about Chinese Americans.

"What helps to disguise the paucity of such titles is that people—Chinese and Chinese Americans as well as non-Chinese-often fail to distinguish between Chinese and Chinese Americans, so bibliographies combine books about the two groups into a single category. One recent bibliography, for example had only three titles about Chinese Americans—the other twenty-six books were about Chinese. Yet Chinese Americans are not Chinese anymore than Polish Americans, German Americans, or Afro Americans can be considered Poles, Germans, or Ghanians.

"Perhaps a brief review of history will clarify just who Chinese Americans are. Chinese from southern China began emigrating to California in large numbers during the Gold Rush. Mexicans and South Americans who preceded the Chinese had been driven out of the gold fields by a Foreign Miners' Tax, and in 1852, the California State Legislature tried to drive the Chinese out by reenacting this law. The Chinese—most of them laborers—stayed, working the tailings of white miners, in service occupations such as restaurants and laundries, in shoe and cigar factories; building the railroad and the fishing and agriculture industries—indeed, the west.

"Punitive taxes against the Chinese were extended from mining to other industries in which they worked. And when the country hit an economic slump in the late 1870s, politicians initiated a violent anti-Chinese crusade that culminated in passage of the Chinese Exclusion Act in 1882. For the next sixty years, only Chinese merchants, teachers, students, and diplomats were permitted entry into the United States; none could become naturalized citizens. Moreover, Congress enacted a series of increasingly harsh laws designed to prevent the creation of Chinese families and to exterminate Chinese from America. So effective were these laws that by the time Exclusion was repealed in 1943, the population of Chinese in America had been reduced from a peak of 107,488 in 1890 to 77,504.

"Chinese who have emigrated since are diverse. The political refugees of the 1950s were students, officials, and supporters of the Nationalist government in Taiwan. Most were wealthy non-Cantonese speakers from northern and eastern China. Those who emigrated after the abolishment of the National Origins Quota in 1968 were usually from Hong Kong and Taiwan, educated and often cosmopolitan. In the 1970s, overseas Chinese, many of whom had never lived in China, emigrated from Cuba, Burma, and Indochina. And since 1979, Chinese have emigrated directly from China as well.

"The new immigrants quickly out-numbered the small American-born population descended from Cantonese laborers. As a result, many people look on all Americans of Chinese descent as foreign. Certainly the books available reflect this viewpoint, for almost all of them are about China, and of these, the large majority are Chinese mythology.

"I'm certainly not saying that children don't need mythology or to learn about China. But they also need to read realistic stories, stories with Chinese American characters, stories with contemporary settings, stories that reflect our diversity. How else can children in America find out about Chinese Americans today? How else can Chinese American children find books that have characters with whom they can fully identify? And children surely need books that relate an accurate history of the Chinese in America. How else will the cycle of confusion born of ignorance be broken?

"Sadly, even the books about China are by and large so archaic that they are about a country that no longer exists. Just look at the illustrations and you will see what I mean. The kinds of illustrations that still prevail show Chinese men and boys with queues in long robes and skull caps, hands tucked in their sleeves, and bowing. These pictures have the same degree of authenticity as illustrations of English men and boys with powdered wigs, pantaloons, and high heeled shoes. Yes, both existed. But both belong to history.

"While we are discussing illustrations, let us consider the stereotypes that still proliferate. Squinty eyes and buck teeth are almost as prevalent and accepted today as 50 years ago. In Bishop's *The Five Chinese Brothers* (Coward, 1938), not only are the illustrations stereotypic, but the plot—which I agree is an interesting story—pivots on the premise that all Chinese look alike. Yes, I realize that the book was written and published 50 years ago. But the point is that it is still being reprinted and sold and is almost always included in bibliographies on books about Chinese.

"The reason generally given for its inclusion is that there are so few books about Chinese and Chinese Americans available. But I wonder if that is reason enough. If all that children see of Chinese and Chinese Americans is stereotype, that stereotype will become their reality.

"There are three schools of thought on books which portray negative or inaccurate images. The first is that there is nothing wrong with the books. The civil rights movement, which raised the consciousness of the general public with regard to stereotypes of African-Americans, did not, unfortunately, create a similar change with regard to Chinese and Chinese Americans. Even librarians who do care and want to 'do the right thing' often feel uncertain as to what may be offensive.

"In such cases I would say: go by the same criteria that you would use for any book. Ask yourself, do the characters seem like real people? Do I, as a reader, care about them? Is the dialogue smooth or stilted? Is the plot credible? If the illustrations were of my own people, would I be offended? You might also consider how the book measures up with regard to some of the issues raised here.

"A second alternative is to leave the books on the shelf, but use them only with guidance and discussion. This is generally more practical in a classroom than in a school or public library. However, there is no reason why such books should not sometimes be used during story hours. Children are bombarded daily in the media with stereotypes—sexual as well as racial—and discussions on stereotypic images can help them to develop their critical faculties. In the long run, this approach can possibly be more beneficial than the third alternative, which is to 'dump' all such books.

"The greatest problem with this last alternative is that what is offensive to one person may not be offensive to another. For example, I wince when the term *Oriental* is used instead of *Asian*. Yet there are many Asian Americans who refer to themselves as Oriental, just as there are blacks who prefer the term Negro, Chicanos who prefer to be called Mexican American, and so on.

"Any dumping of books must therefore smack of censorship. On the other hand, publishers are businesses first and last. This means that they will publish only what they think they can sell. So if libraries continue to purchase books which portray negative or inaccurate images, publishers will continue to publish them.

"The library market for children's books is significant enough that librarians can influence publishing decisions and bring about change by proving that there is a market for 'ethnic' titles. Unfortunately, librarians sometimes confirm publishers' worst marketing fears.

"For example, I wrote a book, *Pie-Biter,* about a Chinese American Paul Bunyan/John Henry character who lived in the frontier west. The book was well reviewed and appeared on many lists of recommended books. Yet I can't tell you the number of times librarians have said to me, '*Pie-Biter* is wonderful, but we don't serve any Chinese children so it isn't appropriate for our collection.'

"My response to such statements is that the story takes place in America; the hero, Pie-Biter, is a Chinese American; and the other main character is Hispanic. In short, it reflects America's pluralistic society; it's an American story.

"Besides, if we read books only about people exactly like us, what are libraries doing with books about China and other countries? And that is what's so curious. Publishers, librarians, and teachers would never argue against the need to learn about China. Yet Chinese Americans continue to be ignored.

"Not surprisingly then, when Jesse Jackson first formed his Rainbow Coalition, he left out the color yellow, For not only are Chinese Americans absent from many library shelves but we also rarely appear on television or in newspapers, magazines, or books. So it's easy for anyone who doesn't live in one of the few areas of the country with sizable Chinese American populations to forget we exist. But we are here, and our numbers are rapidly increasing.

"Jesse Jackson has since rectified his error. Publishers, librarians, and writers must follow suit by working hand in hand to acknowledge the existence of Chinese Americans, Asian Americans, indeed all Americans, in books."[1]

FOOTNOTE SOURCES

[1]Ruthanne Lum McCunn, "Chinese Americans: A Personal View," *School Library Journal,* June/July, 1988. Amended by R. L. McCunn.

FOR MORE INFORMATION SEE:

Sampan, January, 1982.
San Francisco Chronicle, September 21, 1983.
Los Angeles Times, September 25, 1983.
Womanews, November, 1985.
San Francisco Examiner, December 8, 1985.

McRAE, Russell (William) 1934-

PERSONAL: Born January 1, 1934, in Winnipeg, Manitoba, Canada; son of William Daniel (a purchasing agent) and Agnes Jean (a homemaker; maiden name, Russell) McRae; married Mary Evelyn Courtis (a homemaker), July 1, 1956. *Education:* University of Toronto, B.A., 1961;

York University, M.A., 1971, Ph.D., 1975. *Home:* R.R.6, Gardner Rd., Thunder Bay, Ontario, Canada P7C 5N5. *Agent:* Nikki Smith, 23 East Tenth St., 712, New York, N.Y. 10003.

CAREER: Cochrane High School, Cochrane, Ontario, Canada, English teacher, 1963-65; Wheable Secondary School, London, Ontario, English teacher, 1965-67; Thornhill Secondary School, Thornhill, Ontario, English teacher, 1968; Sir John A. MacDonald Collegiate Institute, Toronto, Ontario, English teacher, 1968-70; York University, Toronto, Ontario, teaching assistant, 1971-75; Geraldton Composite High School, Geraldton, Ontario, English teacher, 1975-89; free-lance writer, 1989—. *Awards, honors:* Norma Epstein Creative Writing Award from the University of Toronto, 1960; Canada Council for the Arts Literary Award, 1987-88; *Going to the Dogs* was short-listed for Governor-General's Literary Award for Children's Literature, 1987.

WRITINGS:

Sam for Sure (illustrated by Louise Roy), Roundstone Council for the Arts, 1975.
Going to the Dogs, Viking, 1987.

Also author of unpublished plays, including "Conestoga," "Frankie and Johnny," and "Playboy," and a musical adaptation of John Millington Synge's play "Playboy of the Western World."

WORK IN PROGRESS: An adult novel.

SIDELIGHTS: "I wrote a lot of pop songs (music and lyrics) in my late teens and early twenties. I wrote full time for about three years after marrying in 1956—plays, short stories and television scripts. I came close to success occasionally. I had a song accepted by a popular male quartet, moments before they disbanded forever. There was quite a bit of interest in a three-act play called 'Conestoga,' which was about the Donner party's tragic wagon train to California; a television musical play, based on the folk song 'Frankie and Johnny';

RUSSELL McRAE

and a musical play 'Playboy,' based on Synge's 'Playboy of the Western World.'

"In 1959 I abandoned writing, then earned a B.A. and taught English in high schools in Cochrane and London, Ontario. In 1968 the desire to write returned and I quit teaching. My wife and I lived in Manhattan for a few months until we ran out of money and I was unable to complete my first attempt at novel writing. So, it was back to Canada and the classroom in 1969. I did not write again until the early 1980s when I found myself writing songs again. One of the songs I wrote was called 'Going to the Dogs' and from that, the novel was born with the same name— the first that I was able to complete.

"I plan to write full time now that I've retired from teaching."

FOR MORE INFORMATION SEE:

Globe & Mail (Toronto), January 23, 1988.

MENZEL, Barbara J(ean) 1946-

PERSONAL: Born February 16, 1946, in Brooklyn, N.Y.; daughter of Harvey E. (in sales) and Dorothea (Roberts) Hurst; married John Paul Menzel (a librarian), April 2, 1966; children: Kristina, John, Timothy. *Education:* Drew University, B.A., 1968; Hofstra University, M.S., 1974; Rutgers University, Psy.D., 1986. *Politics:* Democrat. *Religion:* Society of Friends (Quaker). *Home:* 8 Suttie Ave., Piscataway, N.J. 08854. *Office:* Community Mental Health Center, Piscataway, N.J. 08854.

CAREER: Community Mental Health Center, Piscataway, N.J., coordinator of early prevention program, 1974—; writer.

WRITINGS:

Would You Rather (illustrated by Sumishta Brahm), Human Sciences Press, 1982.

WORK IN PROGRESS: Books for preschool-aged children.

SIDELIGHTS: "My writings grow out of my work with emotionally disturbed preschool children and their families at the mental health center. I work with children who are reacting to the stresses of life: hospitalization, divorce, death, etc. The children's book manuscripts I am working on reflect my attempt to help children understand events around them and their reactions to them."

MILLER, Madge 1918-

PERSONAL: Born May 31, 1918, in Pittsburgh, Pa.; married Howard R. Eulenstein, (a lawyer), 1955; children: Rob, Betsy Eulenstein Arthur. *Education:* Pennsylvania College for Women (now Chatham College), B.A., 1939; Case School of Applied Science (now Case Western Reserve University), A.M., 1940. *Home:* 324 Mill St, Williamsville, N.Y. 14221.

CAREER: Teacher of English, Spanish, and French at public schools in Pittsburgh, Pa., 1941-45; Fillion Studios, Pittsburgh, teacher of speech and drama, 1946-49;

Knickerty-Knockerty Players, Pittsburgh, playwright and director, 1950-71. Playwright with Pittsburgh Children's Theatre, 1947-50; lecturer on playwriting and theatre for professional clubs, national children's theatre conferences, and college drama groups; director of church plays and pageants and amateur adult group. *Awards, honors:* Chorpenning Cup from the American Theatre Association, 1970, for excellence in playwriting.

WRITINGS:

PLAYS FOR CHILDREN

The Land of the Dragon (first produced in Pittsburgh, Pa., 1945), Anchorage Press, 1946.
The Princess and the Swineherd (first produced in Pittsburgh, Pa., 1953), Dramatic Publishing, 1946.
The Pied Piper of Hamelin (first produced in Pittsburgh, Pa., 1948), Dobson, 1948, Anchorage Press, 1951.
Hansel and Gretel (first produced in Pittsburgh, Pa., 1949), Dobson, 1949, Anchorage Press, 1951.
Alice in Wonderland (first produced in Pittsburgh, Pa., 1951), Anchorage Press, 1953.
Pinocchio (first produced in Pittsburgh, Pa., 1950), Anchorage Press, 1954.
Puss in Boots (first produced in Pittsburgh, Pa., 1950), Anchorage Press, 1954.
Snow White and Rose Red (first produced in Pittsburgh, Pa., 1951), Anchorage Press, 1954.
Robinson Crusoe (first produced in Pittsburgh, Pa., 1951), Anchorage Press, 1954.
The Emperor's Nightingale (first produced in Richmond, Va., 1962), Anchorage Press, 1961.
The Unwicked Witch: An Unlikely Tale (first produced in Pittsburgh, Pa., 1964), Anchorage Press, 1964.
OPQRS, Etc. (first produced at University of Kansas, 1985), Anchorage Press, 1984.

Also author, with Larry Villani, of plays "Ali Baba," "Beauty and the Beast," "The Emperor's New Clothes," "The Little Mermaid," "Merlin the Magician," "The Red Shoes," "The Elves and the Shoemaker," "Hok Lee and the Dwarfs," "Princess Pocahontas," "Rapunzel," "The Sleeping Beauty," and "St. George and the Dragon." Some of Miller's plays have been translated into Japanese and Afrikaans.

SIDELIGHTS: "I am an advocate of fantasy. The fairy tales which make up the bulk of my playwriting material are to me the best possible literary form with which first to delight the child, then, when he is emotionally ready, to help him experience a greater awareness of the inner problems of human beings. He learns that he is not alone in his fears and his confusions. He identifies with those on stage who fight against great odds to win independence and 'live happily.' As a subtle dividend he receives a valuable moral education which suggests to him the advantage of right behavior. The universality and timelessness of these age-old themes furnish his mind with valuable inner resources to last a lifetime. I write to create a real world of make-believe from which the child can gain a better understanding of the sometimes unbelievable world of reality."[1]

FOOTNOTE SOURCES

D. L. Kirkpatrick, *Twentieth-Century Children's Writers*, St. Martin's, 1978, 2nd edition, 1983.

MINARD, Rosemary 1939-

PERSONAL: Born July 5, 1939, in Houston, Tex.; daughter of Alton Keith (a lawyer) and Rosamunde (a teacher; maiden name, Strozier) Stewart; married Bernie Minard (a hospital administrator), March 17, 1962; children: Keith, Evan. *Education:* Newcomb College, Tulane University, B.A., 1961; University of Houston, M.A., 1969; University of Texas, M.L.I.S., 1987. *Home:* 2639 Pemberton Dr., Houston, Tex. 77005.

CAREER: Librarian. Co-owner of writing, editing and research business, Houston, Tex., 1978-84; Episcopal High School, Houston, teacher and head of English department, 1984-86; Fisher, Gallagher, Perrin & Lewis, Houston, law librarian, 1988—. *Awards, honors: Womenfolk and Fairy Tales* was selected one of *New York Times* Outstanding Books of the Year, 1975; Texas Bluebonnet Award Nominee, 1984-85, West Virginia Children's Book Award Nominee, 1985, Ann Martin Award from the Catholic Library Association (Houston, Tex.), 1987, all for *Long Meg.*

WRITINGS:

(Editor) *Womenfolk and Fairy Tales* (illustrated by Suzanna Klein), Houghton, 1975.
Long Meg (Junior Literary Guild selection; illustrated by Philip Smith), Pantheon, 1982.

ROSEMARY MINARD

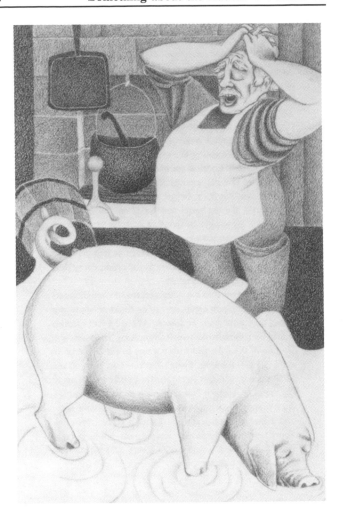

The pig had already knocked the churn over and stood there, rooting and grunting amongst the cream which was running all over the floor. (Illustration by Suzanna Klein from *Womenfolk and Fairy Tales,* edited by Rosemary Minard.)

WORK IN PROGRESS: A young adult novel based on a legendary incident that took place in Texas during the Civil War.

SIDELIGHTS: "I grew up in Conroe, Texas, about fifty miles northeast of Houston. Today, the town is quickly being swallowed up by Houston-area sprawl, but when I was a child Conroe was a sleepy, insular, East Texas town, much more Southern in its culture and traditions than 'cowboy' or 'wild West.' The families of both my parents had moved to southeast Texas several generations earlier and so we had many family stories that were told again and again. An uncle (I forget how many 'greats' should come before) died in the Alamo, a great-grandfather was a colorful east Texas sheriff, and one of my grandfathers, a country doctor in his younger days, often had to take a railroad hand-car on an icy winter night to get to a patient.

"Many relatives and family friends also had the gift of gab and the ability to turn the most ordinary, everyday incident into high drama. It seems that someone was always around our house telling an earth-shaking story.

"I never thought of being a writer when I was small, but I think all the story-telling in my background helped to train my ear. To this day I enjoy listening for the rhythms, accents, and figures of speech that characterize different ways of speaking.

"I also liked to read when I was young, which was a good thing, I guess, because there was not much else to do.

"My maternal grandparents lived in Houston and I visited them often. As a result I learned early that there was more to the world than the piney woods and I decided I wanted to see it. My family also placed a high value on education, so when the time came for college, I decided to leave Texas and study in New Orleans. At Newcomb College my world became much wider. I received a good liberal arts education and came to really enjoy studying and learning. Consequently I always look forward to the reading and research my writing requires.

"*Womenfolk and Fairy Tales* grew out of a parents' meeting at my older son's school. One of the mothers at the meeting objected to the teachers' reading fairy tales to the children because all the female characters (such as Snow White, Sleeping Beauty, and Rapunzel) were passive characters and, therefore, unsuitable role models for young girls. As I listened, I agreed that she had a valid point, yet I felt that to do away with reading fairy tales altogether would be throwing out the baby with the bath water. Furthermore, I remembered immediately one tale that had a strong female leading character, and thought that if I did some research I would surely find others. My first thought was to turn my idea into an article with a bibliography of the stories I found. I had several friends who had published books, however, and they encouraged me to create an anthology with the stories I found.

"I came across the stories about Long Meg when I was working on *Womenfolk and Fairy Tales.* The stories of Meg's 'merry pranks' had been great favorites in the sixteenth and seventeenth centuries, and it seemed to me that several of the episodes might form the kernel for a story that boys and girls today would enjoy. From there the story began to grow with a life of its own. Meg became a younger and more complex character than the 'female Robin Hood' of the original stories. My research about the era and the Battle of Boulogne kept turning up more and more interesting details about King Henry VIII until it seemed inevitable that he would become an important character in Meg's story. One of the most interesting things about writing fiction, I think, is the way a story takes life and seems to grow almost as much in spite of you as because of you."

HOBBIES AND OTHER INTERESTS: History, especially cultural history; French language, achieving fluency; gardening.

MOYES, Patricia 1923-
(Patricia Moyes Haszard)

PERSONAL: Born January 19, 1923, in Bray, Ireland; daughter of Ernst (a judge in the Indian Civil Service) and Marion (Boyd) Pakenham-Walsh; married John Moyes (a photographer), 1951 (divorced, 1959); married John S. Haszard (an official of the United Nations), October 13, 1962. *Politics:* Liberal (non-party). *Religion:* Church of England. *Home address:* P.O Box 1, Virgin Gorda, British Virgin Islands, West Indies. *Agent:* Curtis Brown Ltd., 162-168 Regent St., London W1, England.

CAREER: Peter Ustinov Productions Ltd., London, England, secretary, 1947-53; *Vogue,* London, assistant editor, 1954-58; writer, 1956—. *Military service:* British Women's Auxiliary Air Force, Radar Section, 1940-45; became flight officer. *Member:* Mystery Writers of America, Crime Writers Association, Detection Club, Lansdowne Club. *Awards, honors:* Edgar Allan Poe Award from the Mystery Writers of America, 1970, for *Many Deadly Returns.*

WRITINGS:

Time Remembered (play; first produced in London, 1954; first produced in New York, 1957), Methuen, 1955.
(With Peter Ustinov and Hal E. Chester) "School for Scoundrels" (screenplay), Continental Pictures, 1960.
Helter-Skelter (juvenile), Holt, 1968.
(Contributor) *Techniques of Novel Writing,* Writer, 1973.
After All, They're Only Cats, Curtis Books, 1973.
How to Talk to Your Cat, Holt, 1978.

MYSTERY NOVELS

Dead Men Don't Ski, Collins, 1959, Rinehart, 1960, large print edition, Ulverscroft, 1983.
Down among the Dead Men, Holt, 1961 (published in England as *The Sunken Sailor,* Collins, 1961).
Death on the Agenda, Holt, 1962.
Murder a la Mode, Holt, 1963.
Falling Star, Holt, 1964.
Johnny under Ground, Collins, 1965, Holt, 1966.
Murder by 3's (omnibus volume), Holt, 1965.
Murder Fantastical, Holt, 1967.

PATRICIA MOYES

You've got more than a murderer, Captain. You've got several million pounds' worth of stolen diamonds. (Jacket illustration by Richard Mantel from *Night Ferry to Death* by Patricia Moyes.)

Death and the Dutch Uncle, Holt, 1968.
Many Deadly Returns, Holt, 1970 (published in England as *Who Saw Her Die?,* Collins, 1970).
Season of Snows and Sins, Holt, 1971.
The Curious Affair of the Third Dog, Holt, 1973.
Black Widower, Holt, 1975, large print edition, Ulverscroft, 1981.
The Coconut Killings, Holt, 1977 (published in England as *To Kill a Coconut,* Collins, 1977, large print edition, Ulverscroft, 1981).
Who Is Simon Warwick?, Collins, 1978, Holt, 1979.
Angel Death, Holt, 1980, large print edition, Ulverscroft, 1982.
A Six-Letter Word for Death, Holt, 1983, large print edition, Ulverscroft, 1984.
Night Ferry to Death, Holt, 1985, large print edition, Ulverscroft, 1987.
Black Girl, White Girl, Holt, 1989.

Many of Moyes' books have been translated into fifteen languages and have been recorded on tape for the blind. Contributor of short stories and articles to periodicals, including *Women's Mirror, Evening News* (London), *Writer,* and *Ellery Queen Mystery Magazine.*

WORK IN PROGRESS: A mystery novel set in England at a country hotel featuring the Tibbetts.

ADAPTATIONS:

"A Sad Loss" and "Hit and Run" (short stories) were made into episodes of the British television programme "Tales of the Unexpected."

SIDELIGHTS: "I find it difficult to write about my own work, which in many ways is as much of a mystery to me as to anybody else. The most I can say is that I choose my settings first— sailing, skiing, places I know, etc.—and then try to work out a plot which arises out of the background, rather than being tacked on to it. I love humour, and try to slip it into my mysteries. I think dialogue is terribly important, maybe because of my theatrical experience, and I love writing in the first person, which means that virtually the whole book is dialogue: however, in a detective story this can raise difficulties, as the 'I' character has to be everywhere and see everything. In *Season of Snows and Sins,* I got around this by writing in three different first persons.

"I get very attached to my characters, which is why not only the Tibbets but other characters as well tend to recur in subsequent books. I am currently finishing a new one set in the Caribbean again, in which old friends like Sir Edward Ironmonger and Miss Lucy Pontefract-Deacon reappear. I also find that, within the limits of the plot, it is wise to let the characters behave as they want to, rather than pushing them into a pre-formed mould. This way, they take on a sort of life of their own."

HOBBIES AND OTHER INTERESTS: Skiing, sailing, good food and wine, travel.

FOR MORE INFORMATION SEE:

New Times Book Review, July 26, 1964, May 31, 1970, February 22, 1981, May 16, 1982.
Times Literary Supplement, August 13, 1964, July 16, 1970, November 12, 1971, October 3, 1980, June 20, 1986.
Observer, July 5, 1970, February 6, 1977.
Saturday Review, December 25, 1971.
Spectator, August 18, 1973.
Washington Post Book World, November 18, 1973, July 20, 1975, January 21, 1979.
Listener, April 7, 1977, January 11, 1979.
Los Angeles Times Book Review, October 6, 1985.

MURRAY, Marguerite 1917-

PERSONAL: Born December 21, 1917, in Chicago, Ill.; daughter of Ira Lee (a salesman) and Ruth (a writer; maiden name, Herrick) Myers; married James J. Murray (in printing management), March 4, 1944; children: Jennifer Murray Lapp, Alan, Priscilla Murray Dieterich. *Education:* Rockford College, A.B., 1939; Carnegie Institute of Technology, M.L.S., 1941. *Politics:* Democrat. *Religion:* Unitarian. *Home:* 10805 Keswick St., Garrett Park, Md. 20896.

CAREER: District of Columbia Public Library, Washington, D.C., children's librarian, 1941-46; Montgomery County Public Schools, Md., teacher, 1956-58, librarian, 1956-68; Montgomery County Department of the Public Library, Md., coordinator of children's services, 1968-78; free-lance writer, 1978—. *Member:* Children's Book Guild.

Awards, honors: Like Seabirds Flying Home was selected one of School Librarians International Best Books, 1988.

WRITINGS:

The Sea Bears, Atheneum, 1984.
A Peaceable Warrior, Atheneum, 1986.
Odin's Eye, Atheneum, 1987.
Like Seabirds Flying Home, Atheneum, 1988.

Contributor of articles to professional library and educational periodicals, including *School Library Journal* and *Instructor.*

SIDELIGHTS: "My mother wrote stories and articles for Sunday School papers. She made quite a career of it and was still writing odd pieces at the age of ninety-two. My father sold fine papers, keeping me and my mother well supplied with odd job lots. I was the envy of my schoolmates because of my own personal drawerful of assorted paper. My particular chum had a corner on art (drawing and painting) and so I inevitably turned to script. Because of all that paper!

"I was always and forever a bookworm. My career turned in the direction of library work. I worked for the Oak Park (Illinois) Public Library during high school and college and after. They gave me (in the heart of the Depression) a scholarship to library school. After Carnegie Library School I worked for five years in the District of Columbia Public Library as a children's librarian. When my husband returned

MARGUERITE MURRAY

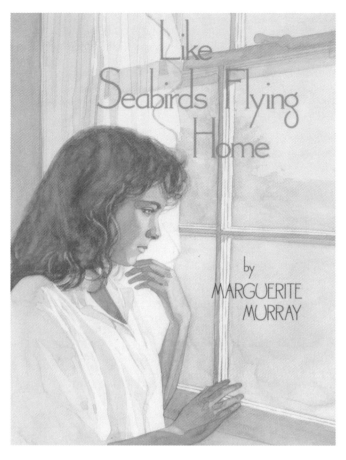

She'd waited all her life for this moment. (Jacket illustration by Deborah Chabrian from *Like Seabirds Flying Home* by Marguerite Murray.)

from the war, I devoted some years to raising a family, but I soon started substituting in the Montgomery County (Md.) Public Schools. This led to the classroom, but when the County discovered I was a qualified librarian, I found myself in the then opening up school library program. I had ten happy and exciting years in the schools, but left to take an administrative position with the Montgomery County Department of Public Libraries. I was the children's coordinator there for ten years.

"My library career was full of excitement and surprises. I was caught up in the development of the school media center, and I wrote several articles for professional journals at the time promoting the concept. Later I worked with educational television, particularly Channel 26 (WETA) in Washington, D.C. John Robbins was doing his delightful literature series, and consulting with him about books and planning the programs was great fun. I also worked hard with the Maryland State Department of Education promoting libraries and reading and taught occasional children's literature classes at various universities around Washington. Some of my students were excited enough to become librarians. (That has always been nice to hear.) During this time I even helped make a film for Encyclopedia Britannica. It was called 'The Library: A Place for Discovery" and was, I believe, quite successful. I played one of the roles (none too successfully—one of my students told me in disgust that what I needed was idiot boards). At library conferences strangers would sometimes look startled, wondering, I presume, where they had seen me before.

"During my public library years, I became a member of the Washington area Children's Book Guild. It was through the Guild that I found the inspriation and the help needed to start a writing career. I had been accepted as a member because of my qualifications as a 'children's specialist.' It was a source of great satisfaction to me when my label was changed to AUTHOR. I have held a number of offices for the Guild and served twice as president.

"The writing of children's books, a natural consequence, I suppose, of long years in the children's library field, is a retirement project and great fun. I received a batch of letters from a school I visited. One little fellow wrote: 'We didn't know you'd be that old.' I thought at first, better than dead, but I do know that one reason I write is to communicate to young people some of the insights collected from a long and happy life.

"In the hero cycles, there was always a counselor. This seems to me important still, as it was to our forebears, that a counselor advise, stand ready to pick the hero up after inevitable trials and failures, help him/her through the crisis testing and the important challenges, and be ready to fade insignificantly into the background when the hero is able to manage on his own. We aren't, in this generation, paying enough attention to the role of the counselor. The young people do not value these services: the natural counselors have not accepted the responsibility of their roles.

"I do not write instructional novels—they are meant to be fun. But in all of them, the children and young people are not alone in their struggles to grow up.

"If there is a single meaning in my life it is this, that our culture was founded through benevolence and care, and that we as adults have an obligation to pay heed to the concept of the counselor in our institutions for the young.

"Life is full of invitations, and I'm not very good at turning them down. So I garden with delight, and I have intruded on my schoolgirl chum's field and enjoy watercolor—though I wish I had some of my father's beautiful paper! Just lately I have discovered weaving. I am thinking about two books I'd like to write, but if I do that, I'll have to get started because I *am* getting up there."

NAIDOO, Beverley 1943-

PERSONAL: Born May 21, 1943, in Johannesburg, South Africa; daughter of Ralph (a composer and music copyright manager) and Evelyn (a broadcaster and theater critic; maiden name, Levison) Trewhela; married Nandhagopaul Naidoo (a solicitor), February 1, 1969; children: Praveen, Maya. *Education:* University of Witwatersrand, South Africa, B.A., 1963; University of York, B.A. (with honors), 1967, Certificate of Education, 1968. *Home:* 13 Huntly Rd., Bournemouth, Dorset BH3 7HF, United Kingdom. *Agent:* Gary Carter, Roger Hancock Ltd., Greener House, 66/08 Haymarket, London SW1Y 4QW, United Kingdom. *Office:* c/o Harper & Row, 10 East 53rd St., New York, N.Y. 10022.

CAREER: Kupugani Non-Profit Nutrition Corporation, Johannesburg, South Africa, field worker; primary and secondary teacher in London, England, 1969; writer, 1985—; researcher, 1988—. *Member:* Education Committee of the British Defence and Aid Fund for Southern Africa, Anti-Apartheid Movement. *Awards, honors:* Other Award from

Children's Book Bulletin, 1985, Children's Book Award from the Child Study Book Committee at Bank Street College of Education, 1986, one of Child Study Association of America's Children's Books of the Year, 1987, and Parents' Choice Honor Book for Paperback Literature from the Parents' Choice Foundation, 1988, all for *Journey to Jo'burg: A South African Story.*

WRITINGS:

Censoring Reality: An Examination of Books on South Africa, ILEA Centre for Anti-Racist Education and British Defence/Aid Fund for Southern Africa, 1985.
Journey to Jo'burg: A South African Story (fiction; illustrated by Eric Velasquez), Longman, 1984, Lippincott, 1985.
(Editor) *Free as I Know,* Bell & Hyman, 1987.
Chain of Fire, Collins, 1989, Harper, 1990.

WORK IN PROGRESS: Research exploring issues of racism with white students through fiction and drama for doctoral thesis prior to publication.

SIDELIGHTS: Beverley Naidoo was born on May 21, 1943 in Johannesburg, South Africa. "I was brought up with the usual conceptions most white South Africans have, completely taking for granted the services of our cook-cum-nanny, whose own three children lived more than 300 kilometers away, cared for by . . . I don't know. She provided much of my actual mothering. We knew her as 'Mary,' I don't know her real name. What I do recall, with the vivid intensity of one of those seminal childhood experiences, was how when I was perhaps eight or nine, Mary received a telegram and col-

BEVERLEY NAIDOO

lapsed. The telegram said that two of her three young daughters had died. It was diphtheria—something, for which, I as a white child, had been vaccinated.

"It was only years later that I began to realize the meaning of that scene. I must have continued to spout with the arrogance of white youth the customary rationalizations—that Mary, and those who followed her, were lucky because we gave them jobs, sent presents to their children at Christmas, and so on. I still feel intensely angry about the racist deceptions and distortions of reality which the adult society passed on to me as a child."[1]

"My own fascination with experiences which change people owes a great deal to the profound change of attitudes I underwent myself around the age of eighteen. That was when I began to become conscious of the artificially-constructed blinkers of racist prejudice which were distorting my vision as a white South African and when I began the struggle to remove them."

In 1963 Naidoo received her B.A. from the University of Witwatersrand, South Africa. In 1964 she was detained under the 'Ninety Days' solitary confinement law. At the age of twenty-two she moved to England to study at the University of York, where she received her certificate of education in 1968. Later she taught primary and secondary school in London. In 1985 Naidoo published *Censoring Reality,* a study on the image of South Africa presented to British children in nonfiction books. "The research for this study was carried out originally within the South-West Herts Anti-Apartheid Group. Over thirty book collections of nonfiction books, mainly for primary and lower secondary age children, were examined during 1982/3, in South West Hertfordshire, Barnet and Brent. They included collections in seven schools, a Teachers' Centre, a College of Education, a Schools' Library Service, and twenty-two public libraries. In some cases, as a result of the investigation and discussion, some of the books have since been withdrawn. The extent to which the sampling is representative of the situation throughout Britain is not known. However, there is no reason to suspect that the area involved in the investigation would be significantly different from the rest of the country. Nor is there any reason to suppose that the books examined at the time of the study are not still available in the majority of libraries where no such review has taken place.

"South African society is openly racist in structure, the only society in the world which discriminates in all its laws on the basis of race. Yet, as this study demonstrates, the images conveyed through most materials available in schools and public libraries suggest a quite different reality. We must then ask ourselves this: if the reality of apartheid and racist domination can be totally ignored, glossed over with passing references, and even sometimes dressed up to look positively good, what is likely to be the treatment of racism in materials on other societies and situations in which racism is far more subtly embedded? In other words, this case-study of materials on South Africa is a springboard. It is indicative of how racism is still being condoned, and indeed promoted, through what is passing for 'educational media' in this country."[2]

Bernard Newman's *Let's Visit South Africa* was one entry examined in the study. "On the fly-leaf the book is referred to as 'a sane and objective account of Apartheid' which includes the 'fascinating' subject of the Transkei— the first Bantustan.

(From *Censoring Reality: An Examination of Books on South Africa* by Beverley Naidoo.)

"Consider the different impression that would be made on Lena [the twelve-year-old fictitious reader in the study] if instead of a cover picture of bustling, prosperous Cape Town, the publishers had chosen an image of something they describe as 'fascinating'—a Bantustan—and shown lines of bare corrugated iron dwellings set in the midst of arid, barren land. From the fly-leaf alone, we might suspect that such an example of government town-planning is not going to be on the sight-seeing agenda for the young—presumably white—visitor.

"Newman omits quoting figures for actual wages and he falsifies the white/black differential. In 1974 it was certainly not 3 to 1 [in the mining industry]. In 1970 it was 21 to 1 and by 1978 (four years after this revised edition) it had only decreased to 7 to 1 . . . . He omits any information on the cost of living. He omits to say why in a country as wealthy as South Africa, black adults haven't learnt to read and write in school when they were children. But instead his message to Lena and other readers is that black South Africans are quite content with a very low quality of life. It is whites who would like to make things better for black South Africans, if only they would respond!"[2]

"It is not only the explicit, or implicit, tone of white superiority with which the young reader is faced. Books deriving their information from the South African Embassy include many unsubstantiated claims and half-truths, and omit any of the documentation which might reveal something of the reality for most black South Africans.

"Perhaps the prime example of the art of omission is provided by *South Africa in Pictures* by Peter English . . . which reads just like a South African Government handbook. Indeed, it goes further than omission, to include statements which bear little relation to reality.

"Of over 130 pictures, only 23 focus on black South Africans, and 16 of those present traditional tribal images—in line with the authorities' cultivation of 'ethnic differences.' If Lena were asked to do a visual analysis of the book, she would produce an interesting table:
40 pictures of landscape and animals
28 of industrial development
30 reflecting white South Africans
23 reflecting black South Africans
11 historical pictures—all white
1 picture of a wealthy 'Indian' home
1 picture of a 'Coloured' University.

"Not a single picture suggests any criticism of apartheid."[2]

"It is possible that some authors who sanitise reality might argue that the children for whom they are writing are too young to be told about harsh social reality. Another argument that I heard from a secondary school librarian proposed that pupils aged 11 to 14 were too young to understand or be affected by a racist portrayal of South Africa. In both

Naledi lay imagining herself in a long white coat. (Illustration by Eric Velasquez from *Journey to Jo'burg: A South African Story* by Beverley Naidoo.)

cases, I believe the reader's youth is being used to rationalise the provision of misinformation."[2]

However, Basil Davidson's *Discovering Africa's Past* presents a different perspective: "Simply, how Africans were forced by taxes into the migrant system, and how by the end of a long contract, the maximum they could afford might be a couple of blankets, or possibly a bicycle.

"Is this too hard or harsh for Lena to understand? Or do we not want her to understand this? There seems to be no problem about Lena learning of appalling working conditions, including the employment of child labour, in England during Victorian times—perhaps because that period is sufficiently distant. Why then is it so difficult for her to learn of such conditions in present day South Africa?"[2]

Naidoo also took to task well-meaning but uninformed authors: "Particularly with more recent books, it has become increasingly necessary to distinguish between an author's intentions—and perhaps own lack of awareness of bias—from the images and concepts that are actually conveyed to the young reader.

"To be blunt, it seems to me that both [Richard] Gibbs [in *Living in Johannesburg*] and [Rhoda] Blumberg, [in *Southern Africa*] while wanting to dissociate themselves morally from apartheid, are nevertheless not prepared to imagine themselves (nor to let their readers imagine themselves) in the position of black South Africans at the receiving end of a policy of unremitting violence and who decide to resist. That failure of imagination results in a censored reality too. For it means that black South Africans are allowed only to be objects of pity and sympathy. It seems that Lena can be encouraged to appreciate the convictions and courage of various Resistance fighters in the Second World War, but not to recognise these qualities where they exist in the Resistance movement in South Africa. Why?"[2]

In her "Conclusions" Naidoo wrote: "However, changes are taking place in areas where the issues are being raised. Teachers and librarians are increasingly being questioned on their own role in the propagation of racist ideas when they allow such ideas to go unchallenged. Such changes are unfortunately rather piecemeal, dependent on local circumstances and initiatives—even in areas such as ILEA where the fundamental policy statements have now been made.

"It is essential to develop the political will to combat racism in all its manifestations. We need to develop not only new policies, but also the determination to implement them. For with racism we have to choose—either to be for it or against it. Because our society has been so deeply racist for so long, being against racism involves continually examining our own perceptions as well as those of others. For those of us concerned with the transmission of what we define as 'knowledge' to young people such as Lena, this is surely a special responsibility."[2]

Journey to Jo'burg, Naidoo's first work of fiction, was inspired by her work with the Education Group of the British Defence and Aid Fund for Southern Africa. "This fund generally is concerned not only with providing legal and other help for political victims of apartheid legislation and their families, but with keeping the conscience of the world alive. Apart from the Fund's Director, Ethel de Keyser, we are mainly working teachers who started off in a small way in 1981 with an art project for nine- to eleven-year-olds, who were asked to submit drawings about children living under apartheid. It became clear that there was a great lack of material on South Africa which was directly accessible to the children. There was the straight informational material, but what we needed was fiction that could stir their imaginations and touch their emotions. Not only were we seriously lacking resources for children, but the research I was carrying out with a local anti-apartheid group revealed that any child referring to school and public library shelves for factual material would be finding and reading books which either omitted or largely distorted the reality of apartheid.

"Thus the Education Group decided to find someone who could write a work of fiction which would convey some of that reality. I think, much to the surprise of the others, I volunteered! I was given three months to come up with something. I wrote the text simply, quite deliberately. As I wrote I could hear myself telling [the story] to my own children, aged six and ten at the time. Both had been born in England, and it seemed important to be able to explain, at their level, what was happening in South Africa."[1]

The novel received the Other Award in England. In the U.S. it was a Parents' Choice honor book for paperback literature and won the Award of the Child Study Children's Book Committee at Bank Street College. "I've always regarded *Journey to Jo'burg* as a sort of window for my readers—to direct their focus onto the drama of children living under apartheid. That is why my initial tribute is to my subject matter: To those young people in South Africa who are struggling to take control of their lives and to reshape their future. They face a cruel, corrupt, relentless power . . . , but somehow they keep picking up the pieces.

"I wanted to chart a journey of two such children, on what for them is initially a simply-motivated mission, to find their mother and so save their sister's life. It is their determination, particularly that of Naledi, the older sister, which sees them through. And the journey becomes a learning process, as the nightmare complexities of apartheid in the wider society are revealed to them. By the end of the journey, Naledi has begun to realize the wider dimensions of their own particular problems. She hasn't got solutions, but she has many questions—political questions. Black schoolchildren in South Africa are probably amongst the most politically-conscious children in the world.

"My second tribute is to the people with whom I worked on the British Defence and Aid Fund for Southern Africa's Education Group.

"For years, in my teaching, I had seen children struggling with the printed word, and I wanted this story to be accessible to as wide a readership as possible. In addition, my children were living in a society in which racist ideas have flourished. I hoped that empathizing with Naledi on her psychological as well as physical journey would encourage all children to explore and help strengthen their responses to the injustice of racism.

"I learned from [the] . . . *South African Weekly Mail* that [*Censoring Reality*] joined *Journey to Jo'burg* on the regime's list of banned books. From one perspective, the notion is, of course, quite ludicrous. To know their own oppression, the majority of South Africans don't need their own lives—nor the lies told about those lives—interpreted for them. People's hearts are already like red-hot coals. As one black sixteen-year-old put it: 'They can detain me forever. That's no problem at all. Because I am going to live as other people. Because one thing I know is being locked in jail is not far different

"If only Mma was here," Naledi wished over and over. (Jacket illustration by Eric Velasquez from *Journey to Jo'burg: A South African Story* by Beverley Naidoo.)

from being outside. We are all handcuffed, inside . . . and outside the jail.'

"Most of our children are exposed to a wide range of [media] images, many of which reflect a violent world. Some of these come from South Africa. I believe we owe it to our children here to help them understand what that struggle against an evil system—from which both Britain and America have profited—is about. How can we hope for peace if we refuse to acknowledge that, and deny our children access to the knowledge? We must listen clearly to the voices of young people in South Africa. As one declared: 'One day they—the government—will do what we want . . . . We are prepared to die any moment. We are prepared to be detained any moment. As long as the government does not want to respond, we are prepared to do anything.'"[1]

"The American edition of *Journey to Jo'burg* is illustrated by Eric Velasquez, who has brought his own knowledge of the American experience—of the pain, the suffering, and the struggle for justice—into his interpretation of this South African story."

In 1987 Naidoo published *Free as I Know*. "The anthology *Free as I Know*—currently published only in the United Kingdom—derived from a strong commitment to giving young people access to writing which would encourage them to ask fundamental questions. For instance, are children simple innocents who cannot avoid contamination as they grow up into a pre-determined adult world of compromise, or are they capable of the inner strength to become as 'free as I know?'

"Each of us can probably point to some particular experiences in childhood or adolescence which we feel have played an important part in shaping our perceptions, perhaps even personality. The idea of seminal experiences—those which contain the seeds of change and which are capable of influencing us—was central to creating the collection. I consciously looked for extracts from novels and autobiographies, short stories and poems which reflected young people gaining insights into their various societies, as well as contending with powerful forces within them.

"It is, of course, not only in the white South African community that young people grow up with a narrow, blinkered view of their society and their own role within it. Any group which has advantage over another is unlikely to encourage questioning of the relationship. All over the world people who are oppressed have difficulty in making their voices heard. For every book in which one can hear such voices, there are hundreds of others in which they are completely absent.

"From this followed a second criterion in selecting texts . . . that the perspectives revealed would be those which are often passed over. I particularly looked for pieces which were challenging and which would encourage readers to clarify their own responses.

"Literature has the tremendous quality of allowing us to engage imaginatively in the lives of others. It enables us to move beyond ourselves and our own experiences. If we allow ourselves to respond to it fully, it can be a great educator. For those of us brought up monoculturally, literature which springs from outside our own boundaries can be a life-line. My final—but equally important—criterion was therefore that the collection should be internationally rich. My hope is that young readers will not only see connections between experiences which span time and place, but will respond with both emotionally and intellectually."

Chain of Fire was published in 1989. "[It] developed as a sequel to *Journey to Jo'burg.* I originally intended writing it in a similar format—an essentially simple story containing powerful undercurrents. That format has enabled *Jo'burg* to be read by a wide age range—my youngest correspondent being six. However as I began to think about and write *Chain of Fire,* I found myself increasingly drawn into the drama through the eyes of my central character, fifteen-year-old Naledi, and the story became a novel. I immersed myself in the devastating data on the mass destruction of the homes and lives of millions of South Africans by the apartheid regime through its programme of 'Removals' to so-called 'Homelands.' *Chain of Fire* is dedicated to all those who have struggled to resist and I hope it will enable young people in various parts of the world to feel links of both heart and mind to Naledi and others like her who refuse to let the flames of justice be smothered."

FOOTNOTE SOURCES

[1]Beverley Naidoo, "The Story behind *Journey to Jo'burg,*" *School Library Journal,* May, 1987.
[2]B. Naidoo, *Censoring Reality,* ILEA Centre for Anti-Racist Education and the British Defence/Aid Fund for Southern Africa, 1985.

FOR MORE INFORMATION SEE:

Bulletin of the Center for Children's Books, May, 1986.
Roy Blatchford, editor, *That'll Be the Day,* Bell & Hyman, 1986.
School Library Journal, April, 1987.

OPIE, Iona 1923-

PERSONAL: Born October 13, 1923, in Colchester, England; daughter of Sir Robert George (a pathologist) and Olive (Cant) Archibald; married Peter Opie (an author and folklorist), September 2, 1943 (died February 5, 1982); children: James, Robert, Letitia. *Education:* Attended schools in England. *Politics:* Conservative. *Religion:* Church of England. *Home and office:* Westerfield House, West Liss, Hampshire GU33 6JQ, England.

CAREER: Author. *Military service:* Women's Auxiliary Air Force, meteorological section, 1941-43; became sergeant. *Awards, honors:* Coote Lake Research Medal (joint winner with husband, Peter Opie), 1960; M.A., Oxford University, 1962; European Prize of the City of Caorle (Italy; joint winner), 1964; Chicago Folklore Prize (joint winner with P. Opie), 1970; *The Oxford Book of Children's Verse* was selected one of Child Study Association of America's Children's Books of the Year, 1973, and *The Classic Fairy Tales,* 1974; D.Litt., Southampton University, 1987; *Redbook* Children's Picturebook Award, 1988, for *Tail Feathers from Mother Goose;* May Hill Arbuthnot Lecturer, 1991.

WRITINGS:

ALL WITH HUSBAND, PETER OPIE, EXCEPT AS NOTED

(Compiler) *I Saw Esau,* Williams & Norgate, 1947.
(Editor) *The Oxford Dictionary of Nursery Rhymes,* Clarendon, 1951.
(Sole editor) *Ditties for the Nursery* (illustrated by Monica Walker), Oxford University Press, 1954.
(Compiler) *The Oxford Nursery Rhyme Book* (illustrated by Joan Hassall and others), Clarendon, 1955.
Christmas Party Games, Oxford University Press (N.Y.), 1957.
The Lore and Language of Schoolchildren, Clarendon, 1959.
(Compiler) *The Puffin Book of Nursery Rhymes* (illustrated by Pauline Baynes), Penguin (London), 1963, published as *A Family Book of Nursery Rhymes,* Oxford University Press (N.Y.), 1964.
Children's Games in Street and Playground: Chasing, Catching, Seeking, Hunting, Racing, Duelling, Exerting, Daring, Guessing, Acting, Pretending, Clarendon, 1969.
(Editor) *Three Centuries of Poetry and Nursery Rhymes for Children* (exhibition catalogue), Oxford University Press, 1973, J. G. Schiller, 1977.
(Editor) *The Oxford Book of Children's Verse,* Oxford University Press, 1973.
(Compiler) *The Classic Fairy Tales,* Oxford University Press, 1974.
A Nursery Companion, (*Horn Book* honor list), Oxford University Press, 1980.
(Compiler) *The Oxford Book of Narrative Verse,* Oxford University Press, 1983.
The Singing Game, Oxford University Press, 1985.
(Editor) *Tail Feathers from Mother Goose: The Opie Rhyme Book* (ALA Notable Book), Little, Brown, 1988.

IONA OPIE

(With son, Robert Opie and Brian Alderson) *The Treasures of Childhood: Books, Toys, and Games from the Opie Collection,* Little, Brown, 1989.

(With Moira Tatem) *A Dictionary of Superstitions,* Oxford University Press, 1989.

Contributor to reference works, including *Encyclopaedia Britannica,* and *New Cambridge Bibliography of English Literature.*

ADAPTATIONS:

"The Lore and Language of Schoolchildren," British Broadcasting Corp., 1960.

SIDELIGHTS: Iona and Peter Opie have been called folklorists, historians, and anthropologists, having compiled volumes of children's nursery rhymes, games, fairy tales, lore, and language. Their collection of children's books and toys grew so large that the Opies had to move to a new home in order to accommodate their wealth of childhood treasures.

Iona was born in Colchester, England, and was raised primarily by her mother. "My parents met when my father took part in a tennis tournament, and at the mere sight of him, my mother fell in love. When he went back to Africa, they'd known each other three weeks; she waited for him devotedly for seven years, through the entire first World War. My father returned in 1919, their wedding picture was thoroughly depressing. My father looked haggard, ill, and trapped, having married my mother because she'd waited for him.

"My father was a director of the Wellcome Research Laboratories in Khartoum, Africa, so most of his time was spent there. I worshiped him from afar and grew up wanting to become a plant pathologist, because he was a pathologist, studying tropical diseases. When my sister and I were young, he'd turn up occasionally, a complete stranger, and his arrivals disrupted the even tenor of our lives. My mother looked after us with the utmost care; my father thought we were pampered. We moved to the south coast and my mother outfitted us in knitted body belts beneath our bathing costumes to keep us from catching a chill. We were not to eat chocolate and we always wore our hats in the sun. When my father came home, he'd take us from the house weighed down with our garments and rules, then the hats flew off and out came the bars of chocolate. I was a nauseatingly obedient child, learning early on that was the popular thing to be, but I admired my father for these moments of freedom.

"Where I enjoyed being commended for good behavior, my sister was rebellious; consequently, she was often left at home while I was taken to feed the ducks in Poole Park, glowing with self-righteousness. Fortunately, she was not at all vindictive, and I adored her. Her name is Anstice which she later changed to Anne. My name, Iona, was taken off the map of Scotland. I imagine my parents poring over the map saying, 'Would this do? No. Would this?' until finally they agreed on Iona. I never felt my name had much to do with me, and I wasn't called Iona when I was small. I was called Bunty.

Iona Opie, age four.

"Growing up together, my sister and I spent hours in the kitchen garden, making little cradles out of oblong chemists' boxes, which made comfortable beds for caterpillars and other insects. We made sheets, pillowcases, and pillows of rose petals and picked raspberries and gooseberries to feed our pets. Rose beetles, being more excitable, lived in shoe boxes until unsuspecting governesses opened the lids.

"We had an endless number of pets. For a while I had a second-hand goldfish tank, and when I cleaned the tank, I put the goldfish in a jam-jar on the lawn. One evening I forgot they were there. The cat knocked the jar over, and skeletons covered the lawn in the morning. Another time my sister and I brought up some starfish from the sea in a bowlful of sea water and promptly forgot about them. They too turned into skeletons."[1]

Having little luck with live creatures, Iona fixed her affections on her thirteen teddy bears. "They were the people I *really* lived with. My first arrived when I was two but was cast aside with the arrival of a new one when I was three. When I finally missed the first, I asked, 'Where's Weeny?' and my mother produced him from the cupboard. Then there were two. Eleven more followed, living in a Bible box with the lid propped open so that they could breathe."[1]

At age six, Iona attended prep school and made her first book, "all of twelve pages about spiders, with pictures and a plaited woolen thread for binding. It was hung up on the notice board.

"The school was run on the Dalton system which meant that we had control over our own work. A week's assignment was done anytime we chose during the week. I'm sure that later helped me be more organized.

"As a child, I was known as a bookworm (which I thought a horrid word). Reading was a way of retreating from the rest of the family. I'd go into the lavatory and lock the door, losing myself so completely in a book that only anxious shouting could pull me out. Luckily, we had two lavatories.

"Consuming book after book, I loved both the pictures and the story, loved everything down to the smell of the pages. My tastes were by no means literary: I didn't read anything highfallutin', couldn't boast of having read Horace or Dickens at age seventeen. My mother was not literary in the least; most of her books were about antique furniture or gardening. She despised novels for being a waste of time and read only the very popular ones, necessary for dinner party discussion. She read Beverley Nicols because he was 'amusing.' I've avoided the word 'amusing' ever since."[1]

"When I was about fourteen I began buying antiquarian books from Commins, in Bournemouth; mostly poetry in leather or half-leather, and limited editions. My mother was tolerant, and did not press her own conviction that second-hand books harbor germs."[2]

"I was a great non-joiner, but my mother's theory was that children should be introduced to everything. We were taught to play tennis, to dance, to skate, to ride, to row, and to sail. All these experiences a child *had* to have. It wasn't necessary to be good at anything in particular but rather to know enough to do a little of each.

"When I was young, I was not, as so many real authors seem to have been, terrified or even frightened of the dark. In fact, I have always enjoyed the darkness simply because it is different from the light. How wonderfully calming it is to voyage toward the stars, right beyond the *farthest* star. Star-gazing helps put me in my own small place, lets me know that there are very few things of importance."[1]

While Iona was reading and collecting books, Peter Opie was anxious to be writing them. Much of Peter's childhood was spent in Sherborne, England, learning to lead an independent life. Iona recalled that he had "a very strong and sentimental feeling about his childhood because it was extra precious. Peter was a romantic and passionate personality: what he loved, he loved intensely, and he loved his youth. He loved the books his mother read him like *Winnie the Pooh* and Cowper's *John Gilpin.* His mother drew the whole story of *John Gilpin* for him, episode by episode, as a panorama which could be wound from one spool to another.

"He lived with his mother and father until he was seven, when he was left behind in Sherborne in the care of distant relatives while his parents went on to India. It was a complete break in his life, a barrier, a division, and he suddenly found he had to do everything on his own. Peter was always very proud of it afterwards, saying, 'From the age of seven, I made my own dental appointments and arranged all my own journeys.' He became fiercely independent, not a chink in his armour showing.

"Though his parents were away, they had a continuing relationship, because his mother wrote regularly. He knew a letter would arrive on the same day every week in which he'd find the next installment of their life in India, complete with illustrations."[1]

"At eight, when he was invited to contribute to the prep-school magazine, he discovered the joy of writing. He wrote a story about shooting tigers, which ended, 'Shoot! Bang! Fire!' 'It was,' he said, 'the most exciting thing I had ever done in my life. I couldn't understand why everybody didn't want to be a writer.'"[2] "Peter knew that writing was the only thing he wanted to do. For him, it was the sublime occupation."[1]

"He was not able to buy many books, even as a teenager because of his peripatetic existence; but looking back I can see that, not only was he a born writer, he was also a born collector. A writer records; a collector assembles, categorises, and keeps. As a child, Peter collected farm animals. He didn't have his toy farm imposed upon him; he collected it piece by piece, asking for the various animals, people, and buildings when Christmas and birthday came round, from relations who knew that he knew exactly what he wanted."[2] Peter continued his propensity for collecting at his prep school. He later recalled, "We weren't allowed money—the currency was cigarette cards—and when I left school, I had more cards than all the other boys put together .... My school report said that I was undoubtedly going to become a millionaire."[3]

"Because he had no settled home, Peter spent time with his grandparents when he was young, and it was from their house that his toys were stolen. The chauffeur went off with them, took the whole lot.

"He went to Eton when he was thirteen, I think. Loved the school, but hated wasting time on Latin verse. He didn't like

Peter Opie, age seven.

sports either, so he took up the least time-consuming one, running. He had a curious style, just lowered himself several inches and scudded. He ended up running long distance for the school."[1]

"After he left school," Iona said, "his mother wanted him to go to Cambridge as his father had, but Peter wanted to get on with being a writer. So they made a pact: he was to cram for university entrance exams while writing his first book, and if he found a publisher for the book he needn't go to university. So when he was eighteen, he wrote his first autobiography, *I Want to Be a Success* and sent it to Michael Joseph who published it. The book was very naive, very appealing, all about himself—which was all he knew about—his time at Eton, his family, and his visits to India. Peter laid himself wide open to ridicule from the critics, but the critics were completely disarmed by his honesty."[1]

Both Iona and Peter entered the services during the Second World War. Iona's decision to join up was made after a friend was killed in the Fleet Air Arm. "When I sent him a Balaclava helmet that I'd knitted, it was returned by the commanding officer. His plane had flown out to sea, never to be heard of again. I decided that if the war was going to take my friends, I wanted to have a hand in stopping it.

"So I joined the Meteorological Section and was happily, permanently, in the ranks; I rose to being a sergeant. We'd do hourly observations and send our material off on the tele-printer which was connected to all the other stations; then we'd receive material from the whole network, all over Britain. I'd set about making my map, plotting the information. The map was then taken to the forecaster who would draw in the isobars and interpret the weather information to the pilots."[1]

"[Peter's] career in the army was fairly brief. He was as eager to do well as a soldier as he was to do well in everything, and was proud of having, in spite of a natural incompetence, come top in the lorry-driving examination when training to be an officer. A lieutenant in the Royal Sussex Regiment, the stringency of Montgomery's training defeated him. He had suffered intermittent attacks of epilepsy since he was fourteen (caused, they said, by falling on his head onto an army parade ground in India when he was three); and when he was climbing over a stone wall in Sussex, carrying full army equipment, he collapsed, broke his collarbone, was nursed by VAD's in Leeds Castle, in Kent, for six weeks, and was then pronounced 'permanently unfit for military duty.' He was bitterly ashamed of what he saw as a failure. The rest of the battalion went overseas, to North Africa; and many of them were killed. Afterwards he felt he must succeed not only on his own account, but for his friends whose lives had been cut short so young.

"When I met [Peter] he had been in and out of the BBC .... He had returned to writing his own books, and was living in a small flat with his long-suffering mother, who catered for him and forbore entertaining her friends in the flat, lest their chattering should disturb his writing. He was undoubtedly on the lookout for a wife.

"One day [while still in the air force] I was desperate for a book to read, and went upstairs to ask a friend if she had one to lend me. She handed me one, saying: 'This—it's by a young man called Peter Opie.' It was, of course, *I Want to Be a Success*. Before I was half way through the book, I felt I knew Peter; and when I had finished it, I wrote to ask him, 'What happened next? Did you change? What do you think

Peter and Iona Opie

now?' My letter must be somewhere in this house, in one of the boxes marked 'PMO PERSONAL' which I have not yet had the courage to go through. I have his reply in my hand. It begins:

"'For several months I have been carrying in my mind's eye a picture symbolising our times. It is a picture of a WAAF in uniform, colourful and goodlooking, walking along by herself with a paperbacked edition of philosophy under her arm.

"'By this picture I meant four things. Her book of philosophy showed our present very conscious search for truth. Her being in uniform showed the practical[ness] to which she was ready to put her theories. Her being alone showed her independence. Yet her attractiveness showed that independence wasn't her ideal.

"'I am very fond of the person in this picture, and have been nursing her in my mind for, as I say, several months. Long before I received your letter.

"'Your letter is the only one I have had from an unknown person for a long time. My days of receiving 'fan' mail are

past . . . . Your letter has come, as it were, out of the past. And you are the age I was four years ago. Maybe you understand how pleased I am receiving your letter, and you being a WAAF.

"'I gather you're not satisfied with my decisions of before the war. That's good because neither am I. You have suggested that my opinions of three years ago may now be different. They are. You ask questions I believe all our generation is asking: Can this indescribable war fit in with a theory of human progress? Does a friendly God still guide us? Who now can say what is good and what is evil? Can we in fact hold opinions about anything?

"'I'm sunk. I can't today even make pretence at answering these questions. These are the sort of questions to which we can find answers only in that book of philosophy tucked under the arm of the beautiful girl in my imagination.'

"A forty-five page letter which made it unnecessary, after all, to write the imaginary WAAF's book of philosophy, and which warned that success is not inevitable either in war or in one's private life. The letter began, 'Dear Miss Archibald,' and ended, 'Yours, very fondly dear, Peter.'

Jackets from two Opie collaborations.

"Soon after this I hitchhiked to London, booked a bed at the Union Jack Club opposite Waterloo Station, and telephoned him in Kensington. He said, 'Come to breakfast tomorrow.' When I arrived he was on the telephone, leaning back in an armchair and waving an entrepreneurial hand in the air (something to do with a stage presentation of the news in the interval between newsreels in the News Theatres: the idea was never taken up). Years later it occurred to me that he had timed this telephone call especially to impress me: I was impressed.

"It is always disconcerting to meet in the flesh someone you have learned to know, quite intimately, by correspondence. Neither of us was attracted at first sight by the other's looks, but as soon as we continued the conversation we had started by letter we felt comfortable together.

"Forever afterwards I thought of the real Peter as being embodied in his handwriting, and this is what he would have liked. He was essentially a writer. He communicated better on paper than face to face. He transferred his own thoughts onto paper, so that he could find out exactly what he was thinking. He scarcely knew he was alive unless he was writing.

"We went on meeting, as often as I could get a forty-eight-hour pass. Looking back, I realise I was wooing him without at all knowing I was doing so.

"He was exhilarating company. A walk round the Round Pond in Kensington Gardens with him was an exploration. The world was new, that day, or it was a different world; the colours were brighter, the people were stranger, and anything might happen. Peter was quite different from anyone I had met before. He was an original. He did unexpected things, like hanging backwards out of the window (high up on the seventh floor) to see what the sunset looked like upside down. I must have been in love, but I did not recognise the state; it was not what I had been led to expect.

"It is curious how one can live simultaneously on two different levels, the cerebral and the instinctive, without either impinging on the other. Probably one deliberately keeps them separate. There was I, becoming more and more entwined with Peter, without ever thinking where I was being led. If I had thought (and in wartime people often did not think much beyond the present) I would have assumed that we would go on just as we were until, when the war ended, I would go to London University. I took it for granted that

PEDLAR'S SONG

Smiling girls, rosy boys,
Here – come buy my little toys,
Mighty men of gingerbread
Crowd my stall, with faces red;
And sugar maidens you behold
Lie about them all in gold.

(From "Pedlar's Song" in *Tail Feathers from Mother Goose: The Opie Rhyme Book* by Iona Opie. Illustration by Shirley Hughes.)

that was going to happen. I had the right qualifications. I was going to Bedford College to read botany and be a plant pathologist.

"However, Peter needed a wife; and he proposed marriage. I refused; I said there were many other things I wanted to do. He went away to Savernake Forest, to write: the classic gambit, designed to give one's lover a sense of loss and an opportunity for decision. I did, indeed, feel bereft for a while; a sinking feeling, as I remember it, in the stomach. He returned to London, and proposed again; became angry, said I had led him on; tried conventional caveman tactics. The situation blew up into chaotic farce."[2]

"I felt guilty and obliged to get married. I sat in my airforce hut with the other girls, saying 'I can't. I just can't.' They said, 'You must. You've promised him.' Feeling a frightful sense of doom, as if I'd come to the end of my life, I went up on a forty-eight hour pass for our register office wedding. Peter was so desperate to see me signed up, he altered the date of my birth, making me over twenty-one instead of under twenty-one on my identity card. That way we did not need to tell either of our parents.

"When it came time for me to return for night duty, we were standing on the platform of the tube station, and I told him, 'I just can't bear it. I want to throw myself on the rails.' Peter said, 'Oh, dear. I'm sorry you feel like that. But at any rate, you will always have been married now.' Then I was more than annoyed; I was furious.

"Later Peter said, 'You must ring up your parents.' I felt even worse, but I rang them. A terrible silence ensued. Of course my parents were hurt, and I felt dreadful. When I went to see them, they were terribly concerned with what the neighbors would think, so they had me ring up a woman who was the centre of the neighborhood to tell her I was going to get married. We then had an entirely fabricated journey. Peter's mother, my parents, and some friends attended a pretend occasion with dinner at one of the big London hotels. Then we pretended to go and get married.

"When Peter and I got married . . . it was like a death knell. (Luckily, it got a bit better.) He came down to live in a mill house at Royston, in Hertfordshire, near my air force station, where he went on writing. Then we moved into a caravan, and he did the cooking and shopping, as well. We had a tiny old-fashioned iron stove which just took a small joint of meat; Peter cooked joints of meat, put potatoes round them, sliced up a cabbage, and was very pleased with himself. Then I was posted to Canterbury, and he went back to London.

"Neither of us anticipated having children. The children decided it for themselves at regular intervals of two and a half years."[1] "James was first. As soon as he made his presence known our situation became entirely different. I had to leave the air force; and the elders of the family told Peter that now that he had responsibilities he should get a proper job so he took work at Todd Publishing, which published reference books. We also had to find a home of our own, and moved into a somewhat rickety flat near Kensington Square. Soon afterwards the firm was evacuated to Bedfordshire, because the buzz bombs made it difficult to work in London; the staff and their families were lodged in the cottages and small hotel of the remote hamlet of Waresley. We all, I think, felt rather at a loose end."

It was there, with time on their hands, that the Opies embarked upon a collaborative project which was to occupy almost all their time for nearly the next forty years. Iona describes how they became interested in nursery rhymes: "One day, Peter and I were walking alongside a cornfield, and we took a ladybird onto . . . I forget whose finger it was. But we recited the rhyme—'Ladybird, ladybird,/Fly away home,/Your house is on fire/And your children all gone'—and we wondered where the verse came from, how old was it? We got bitten by these questions."[3]

That weekend they rushed to London's Kensington Public Library, where, as Peter described, "nothing was satisfactory. We went from one place to another—finally, of course, to the British Museum, which always felt safe when the bombs were coming down. You couldn't believe a bomb would hit it . . . and, equally, one felt that if a bomb did come

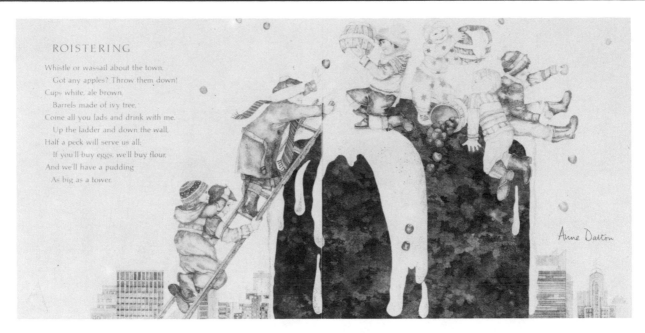

ROISTERING

Whistle or wassail about the town,
  Got any apples? Throw them down!
Cups white, ale brown,
  Barrels made of ivy tree.
Come all you lads and drink with me.
  Up the ladder and down the wall,
Half a peck will serve us all;
  If you'll buy eggs, we'll buy flour,
And we'll have a pudding
  As big as a tower.

(From "Roistering" in *Tail Feathers from Mother Goose: The Opie Rhyme Book* by Iona Opie. Illustration by Anne Dalton.)

by, what a glorious thing to go up with! It would have been marvelous!"[3]

The most recent book with information about the ladybird rhyme in the library was J. O. Halliwell's *Nursery Rhymes of England,* published in 1842. The Opies decided that there must be room for a new book on the origins of nursery rhymes. They began work on the *Oxford Dictionary of Nursery Rhymes,* which would be more than seven years in the making.

Peter later revealed, "The story about wondering about the ladybird rhyme is the superficial level. The deep level is that we were going to have a child; being the kind of people we were, we wanted to know everything one could about children and about getting ready for this awful event that we were entirely unprepared for. We were terrified of this—at least I was. . . . Hitherto, I'd always written about myself, or love, or the people I'd met . . . ; and now, suddenly, I had been brought face to face with childhood . . . . We were having a child, so our complete interest now went into the things of childhood. And everything grew from that.

"While Iona and I were working on the *Dictionary,* I won a literary prize for my autobiographical book *The Case of Being a Young Man,* which was worth five hundred pounds and a guaranteed sale of a hundred thousand copies. I was earning eight pounds a week at that time, and that check was a year's pay in front of me. So I quit my job—taking on, with Iona, the writing of an ordinary pocket dictionary—and went on with our work."[3]

The *Dictionary,* a work of unprecedented scholarship in the field, was published in 1951. *The Oxford Nursery Rhyme Book* followed in 1955, and four years later *The Lore and Language of Schoolchildren,* based on contributions from 5,000 schoolchildren, was published. Iona described the questionaires which they used in classrooms: "Our questionaires were very informal, wide open, and we never included 'yes' or 'no' questions. The idea was not that the children spelt words right or made nice sentences; they were just allowed to let rip, describing what they thought was especially good or silly or describing any games they played with a ball, etc. If they mentioned a game without fully describing it, we'd write back to that particular child, asking to know more about this game that, perhaps, we'd never heard of before. There were always several children in a class from whom I could quote in the book."[1]

While busy corresponding with school children, Iona was also engaged with caring for three of her own. "My priority remained the children and the house, which required some doing since I was not by nature a domestic person. In certain respects, I was really stretched both ways, but Peter was in the driving seat where the work was concerned.

"Peter wasn't of the generation that helped; he was of the generation that thought women's work was women's work and men did something different. He felt that he needed this regular framework for his working life so he didn't have to think about the material things at all. Everything would happen in the same way at the same time so he needn't take time to make mundane decisions. It was this sort of regularity, time ticking by in the same way each day, that allowed for original thinking.

"Because he was trying to succeed and earn his living as a writer, Peter knew that he and I needed every minute of our every day, so he had to shut people out, most of whom understood his predicament. He was like a man trying to sail round the world. I think Francis Chichester felt like that, without time for anything else. Peter was doing something that seemed almost impossible and had to conserve every ounce of energy, avoid any interruptions.

"He took the children very seriously, though; he'd sit on the drawing room sofa with a child on each side, reading them mostly Lear because both he and the children liked the bumpy sounds of Lear's alphabets.

Peter Opie taking down the box of "Crazes 1930s," early in 1964, just before the Temple was sliced horizontally to create the Archive Room above, the Temple (below), "Peter's Room" and The Great Book Case (far left). (From *The Treasures of Childhood: Books, Toys, and Games from the Opie Collection* by Iona and Robert Opie and Brian Alderson.)

"The children got along in the usual fashion; squabbling, and then closing ranks because they needed each other for mutual support. Life with the children largely involved keeping out of their way. Poor old Peter used to take refuge in the lavatory. He would take a volume of *Punch* and spend half an hour there, just to get away from work and family.

"Though there was always the pressure of the work, the sense of time passing, Peter had the ability to suddenly switch off and become utterly boyish and ebullient, rushing into the garden and inventing games. On Guy Fawkes day fallen apples covered the yard; we made them into hand grenades by sticking sparklers in them, and hurled them from one end of the backyard to the other. Despite the work, there were still times of wildness."[1]

The Opies had begun their own collection of books shortly after they married. This helped with their folklore studies. Peter recalled, "It began with nursery rhymes, but we were always looking to the future, and we realized that no one could be a proper research worker unless he possessed the books himself. So we went around to the antiquarian bookshops. We realized we'd probably someday work on fairy tales, and that, in turn, would lead to something else."[3]

POISON. The start of the game. The player who is going to chase is the boy in jeans. (From *Children's Games in Street and Playground* by Iona and Peter Opie.)

Amid the Opies' ever-increasing myriad of books, there were numerous first editions and association copies. Peter described holding "in one's hand something that the author held in *his* hand" as "wonderful," but said he didn't "care for ideas like magic. That it makes you tingle, yes. And even buying a first edition of an author whom you like is an expression of love, much like buying a ring for a lady: it's an expression of your affection and respect. And if I read an eighteenth-century book, I like to do so in an eighteenth-century edition, because this is how one gets close, you see."[3]

In 1969, the Opies published *Children's Games in Street and Playground,* based on a survey of 10,000 children. Later, Iona researched children's games by going to the playground every week for twelve years. "I never minded talking to the children, but I was a bit scared of the grown-ups.

"For me there's been excitement in communicating with the children and discovering that what they're doing now connects back with the past. It's hard not to feel the extra life and wonderful battiness of the children; they can get drunk on nothing.

"I am neither fish nor fowl nor good red herring in the playground. The children can't place me, but it doesn't bother them . . . because they know I have this special role in life, which is listening to what they explain to me. But I'm not a teacher and I'm not a parent, just an unknown species. Occasionally, a new pupil—usually a girl—will come up and say, 'That boy's been hitting me.' And all I do is guy it up, make a bit of an act of writing down what she's said; and by the time I've written it, the children think it's so funny that they've forgotten all about their complaints.

"I sort of moon about, I'm a sort of typical village idiot, really; I never even know how to play marbles, I can't always follow the game and I have to get the children to explain. And they love explaining, they know more than I do. Playtime is the one time when children are the 'superiors.' Adults sometimes ask us why we used the word 'people' in our book on children's games, 'You need six people to play a game,' for example. But that's what they themselves say. We never like to make fun of children, because this isn't what we'd want to have done to us.

"I find that my being there has no effect on the games. I've sometimes wondered when on earth the children were going to skip again, because even though I have great faith in the continuity of games, every now and then I lose faith, thinking, Has skipping disappeared forever? And then, when they think on their own that they haven't done so for a long time, they start to skip again. It's the period of time between strong crazes that interests me . . . . The children have a violent craze for hopscotch [then] all of a sudden, they won't play it anymore."[3]

(From *The Treasures of Childhood: Books, Toys, and Games from the Opie Collection* by Iona and Robert Opie and Brian Alderson.)

"If you get a long view back to the mid-nineteenth century or earlier, you can see the fluctuations in games. For instance, the great hand-clapping craze of the eighteen nineties subsided and then there was another great hand-clapping craze in the nineteen seventies, coming strongly over from America. Skipping used to be a boy's game at the beginning of the nineteenth century, then turned into exclusively a girl's game. Now it's unthinkable for a boy to be skipping rope in the playground."[1] "[Children] arrange games like lightning, then play and get tired of them. It's the speed of childhood living."[3]

Alongside their collection of books, a toy collection began to flourish. The Opies were concerned with collecting on the physical side what they were collecting on the oral side in books. "As with the games," Peter explained, "we're interested in classifying both the attraction and what makes the thing work. Toys have been looked at as sentimental objects, but we want to look at them 'scientifically.' We started by buying things that are mentioned in children's literature, to try to understand what was being made. If Iona sees children playing with some toy in the playground, we go and get one like it. So we've got her report and we've also got the object.

"This is the material side of *Lore and Language,* these are the physical jokes as opposed to the oral jokes: the stink bombs, things that go squeak when you sit down, joke pencils that collapse or explode, squirt rings, joke drinking glasses, disguises, tops from the eighteenth century, marbles with threads of twisted glass inside. We have the earliest form of dominoes, which started to be played in France at the end of the eighteenth and the beginning of the nineteenth centuries .... We've got knucklebones made from sheep or goats like those used by the ancient Greeks. We've got yo-yos from the 1850s .... We've got everything.

"We have the earliest known surviving race game, the earliest peepshow, and—from 1766—the earliest known jigsaw puzzle. It's the only copy in existence, and it's mentioned by Jane Austen in *Mansfield Park.*

"We have an electric chair from 1903, a clockwork train from 1860, a nineteenth-century Noah's Ark made in Bavaria, all kinds of movable toys and, in particular, sand toys .... One features Leotard, the man who gave his name to the garments every ballerina wears. He came to England in the 1860s, and was the first man to perform on the flying trapeze. The toy is operated by means of sand flowing down onto a wheel, and you never see Leotard doing the same action twice."[3]

In order to remain fiercely dedicated to their task, the Opies seldom left home. It is doubtful they missed socializing much as they both suffered from what Iona termed "social confusion." "This was one of the things I had in common with Peter; he was hopeless in a crowd, couldn't keep his wits about him. We made appalling *faux pas* at parties. We went to a party in London where he picked a woman out as we were leaving, raced along the pavement, and caught her at the traffic light to congratulate her on having written a book she hadn't written at all.

The Opies by their own estimation were unfit for any work other than the work they've done. "Neither of us had a decent memory, and we couldn't keep our cool with too many people or too much heat, so we stayed home, keeping as calm as we could, and plod, plod, plodded along."[1]

Peter's mother used to tell him, "You must get out and meet people, how else can you be a writer?" But he felt that "all life is within oneself. Most people are rushing about because

The Tragical Death of A, Apple Pie

WHO WAS CUT IN PIECES,

AND EATEN BY TWENTY-SIX GENTLEMEN,

WITH WHOM ALL LITTLE PEOPLE

Ought to be Very Well Acquainted

A was an
Apple pie

B
Bit it

C
Cut it

D
Dealt it

I
Inspected it

J
Joined for it

K
Kept it

L
Longed for it

E
Eat it

F
Fought for it

G
Got it

H
Had it

M
Mourned for it

N
Nodded at it

O
Opened it

P
Peeped in it

Q
Quartered it

R
Ran for it

S
Stole it

T
Took it

U
Upset it

V
Viewed it

W
Wanted it

XYZ and &
All wished for
a piece in hand

108   109

(From *The Oxford Nursery Rhyme Book* by Iona and Peter Opie.)

they're afraid of what they're carrying around in themselves. But I find that one other person is enough ... and what arrogance you have to have if you want to go against the herd! Most people try to look for ways to get through their days—does the day drag along or is it too short? Our days are so short that we don't know what's happened to them. So the only thing possible is to keep cutting down what one does."[3]

By recording essentially oral traditions, the Opies often wondered if they were damaging the very thing they loved. "We feared that by turning the oral into the literary we might spoil it for the children," said Iona, "but that never happened because the world of childhood is too independent, too large, and too vital to be affected by any book."[1]

According to Peter, to appreciate the discoveries linking contemporary nursery rhymes, games, and fairy tales to the past, required a practical mind and just a touch of romance. By example, he cited Gilbert White, author of *The Natural History of Selbourne,* who "found it almost impossible to believe that swallows migrated to Africa and then came back to this region. And he did everything he could to show that it wasn't true; he thought that in winter they hibernated in the village—he had all the thatch off of one house to find

them!—or went into the marshland. Because, being a practical man, it was much too extraordinary for him to believe that this tiny little bird could go to Africa, live there, and then fly all the way back to exactly the same place each year.

"Because we're practical, it seems utterly extraordinary that a children's rhyme or a nursery rhyme or a fairy tale—all the things we study—can come across half the world unchanged. Whereas, if you're a romantic, it's easy—you can just go through the centuries or around the world without bothering too much about it. The romantic can believe anything. If you tell him that something is one hundred or two thousand years old, it doesn't make any difference to him, he doesn't understand that that means one year or one generation after another. But if you're a practical person, and you're really looking at what actually happens, then the world is so much more marvelous. So, to me, it is more exciting to get a thing back a couple of hundred years than a couple of thousand. Of course, if a rhyme, say, has gone back two hundred years, then there's no reason why it might not have gone back a further couple of hundred, and so on. And if people say, Well, the rhymes and games deteriorate and change, it seems to us much more extraordinary that they're recognizably the same

The fox springs up, and tries to seize the last chicken in the line. (From *Children's Games in Street and Playground* by Iona and Peter Opie.)

after two centuries. To my mind, it's the similarities that are extraordinary, not the variation."[3]

In 1982, at the age of sixty-three, Peter Opie died of a heart attack. "During that last year," said Iona, "we felt he might be going to die; he seemed to be failing. He kept making last-minute pronouncements, and I never knew how to reply because I didn't want to hear even a whisper of a thought that he might soon die.

"Peter and I lived together more than most married couples, lived together and worked together; we were together all day long every day, except when once a fortnight, he went up to his library, The London Library, and I went up to mine, The British Library. His death was a total loss to me, except that I've always felt he was still here. When I want to talk to him, I talk to him. I knew his mind so well that when he had to leave *The Singing Game* half written I just went on writing in the genuine Opie style, feeling I'd inherited the family firm. In fact, as soon as I knew he was dead in the hospital, I thought, 'Now it's up to me. I've got to write the preface for the *Book of Narrative Verse*' and started writing it right then and there.

"For three years, I operated on auto-pilot. For three years, I grieved for Peter in a most energetic way. I remembered reading that mourning is like an illness; you must allow yourself to cry, cry as much as you can. Well, I practically drowned the village. I burst into tears on all occasions

without feeling the slightest bit embarrassed. And people were wonderful; I could approach someone in the carpark, tell them that I'd lost my dear husband, and they'd put their arms around me.

"After three years of total grieving, I began enjoying myself again. Now I sleep in different rooms on different nights. I spend a great deal of the day in pajamas, and luckily my neighbours don't mind a bit.

"It was not until after Peter's death that I realized how extremely hard he'd worked at what he was doing. Since then I've heard people say, 'A mistake—well, it doesn't really matter.' Never having ventured out of my secluded, studious life before, I hadn't realized that there were people who thought it didn't matter if a date was wrong. Peter and I would just worry away at something until we got it as nearly right as possible."[1]

Following Peter's death, over 20,000 volumes of the Opie's children's books went to the Bodleian Library, Oxford. Iona recalled Peter saying, "'If I die before you, you'll only have to ask Sotheby's to remove the books.' It seemed such a boring thing to do. And when he did die, that idea proved unsatisfactory. He'd amassed a collection illustrative of the whole of children's book publishing, assembled to represent every kind of children's book. In addition, everything had been documented with all his research and notes and filing systems to go with it. It was a complete collection, and I believed that was how it had to remain. I didn't want it sold at auction, split up for people assembling their own collections, and I didn't want it to go out of the country. I had an interest in leaving the collection to the Bodleian."

Discovering that she could not give the collection away to the Bodleian against death taxes, Iona decided on a compromise. "As I believe very strongly in going halves, I figured that since Peter had died half his collection should go with him, as it were. If I could just keep half the value, partially because my three dependents might expect to be left something. The Bodleian brought in someone to value the collection, and it was appraised at a million pounds. I decided that if the Bodleian could raise half a million, then I would give them the other half. The Prince of Wales graced the whole effort by becoming its patron, and in eighteen months it was successfully concluded.

"I felt a great satisfaction when the books left. Another stage in the aftermath of Peter's death was complete. I have a whole program still to go through."

(Jacket illustration from "Mother and Child" by Adam Back (1808) in *The Oxford Dictionary of Nursery Rhymes,* edited by Iona and Peter Opie.)

"Although twenty thousand volumes of children's books have gone out of the house, there are still so many books. I think it's over-earnest to make a reading plan, so I read very much at random. I still buy books and like to have plenty around, ready to be read. It doesn't worry me if I don't read them. Just to feel that they're here, that exactly the right book is ready for a particular evening, is one of the greatest luxuries."[1]

Peter Opie was a scholar, credited with having instilled new respect for the study of children's literature. He believed that it was important to look at children because they are "beautiful specimens, the stuff which tells us about the rest of life before a veneer has come over them. And, if you can understand them, you can see that a certain person is actually a certain type of child.

"I happen to believe," he said shortly before his death, "that life is nonsense, that we're an accident, that there is no life after death, and that there is no reason for one being here other than being here. Now, good nonsense is wonderful because it frees the mind, it's like one's dreams, it makes you realize that nothing matters very much. And it seems to me that if you appreciate nonsense, then you're *really* getting wise."[3]

Iona has continued researching and recording. She has published *Tail Feathers from Mother Goose, The Treasures of Childhood,* with her son, Robert, and author Brian Alderson, and *A Dictionary of Superstitions,* with Moira Tatem. Iona has said of their lifetime of strenuous work: "There shouldn't be any such thing as regrets. Life is just how it shapes itself. There came a moment . . . when I was mowing the lawn, when I suddenly had a blinding flash of realization that it had all been worth it.

"Since Peter died I've been collecting things in twos, starting—quite unconsciously—to put things in pairs: two children's chairs companionably placed close together, two white Chinese horses, nuzzling each other. I've got two celluloid ducks that I play with in my bath that sit beak to beak, two kittens from the farm, and two geese, Goosey and Gander. It goes on in the garden as well. I don't plant one rose bush. I plant two."[1]

FOOTNOTE SOURCES

[1] Based on an interview by Cathy Courtney for *Something about the Author.*

[2] Iona Opie, *Something about the Author Autobiography Series,* Volume 6, Gale, 1988.

[3] Jonathan Cott, *Pipers at the Gates of Dawn,* Random House, 1983. Amended by I. Opie.

FOR MORE INFORMATION SEE:

London Times, October 4, 1969.
Times Educational Supplement, October 10, 1969.
Observer, October 19, 1969.
Christian Science Monitor, December 4, 1969.
Contemporary Authors, Volume 5R, Gale, 1969, Volume 61, 1976.
Library Journal, January 15, 1970.
Horn Book, February, 1970.
Carlton Miscellany, Spring, 1970.
New York Review of Books, July 23, 1970.
Horizon, Winter, 1971.
Something About the Author, Volume 3, Gale, 1972.
Washington Post, December 13, 1974.

The Calendar, September 1975-February 1976.
Publisher's Weekly, July 29, 1988 (p. 134ff).
New York Times Book Review, November 13, 1988 (p. 41).
Independent, June 28, 1989, November 22, 1989.
The Independent Magazine, October 28, 1989 (p. 60ff).
School Library Journal, February, 1990 (p. 14), March, 1990 (p. 156).
Wilson Library Bulletin, March, 1990 (p. 15).

COLLECTIONS

De Grummond Collection at the University of Southern Mississippi.
The Opie Collection of Children's Literature at the Bodleian Library at the University of Oxford.

OPIE, Peter 1918-1982

PERSONAL: Born November 25, 1918, in Cairo, Egypt; died February 5, 1982, in West Liss, Hampshire, England; son of Philip Adams (a surgeon) and Margaret (Collett-Mason) Opie; married Iona Archibald (an author), September 2, 1943; children: James, Robert Letitia. *Education:* Attended Eton College. *Residence:* West Liss, Hampshire, England.

CAREER: Author and folklorist. *Military service:* Royal Fusiliers, Royal Sussex Regiment, 1939-41; became lieutenant. *Member:* Folklore Society (president, 1963-64), British Association for the Advancement of Science (president of anthropology section, 1962-63). *Awards, honors:* Chosen Book Competition (joint winner), 1944; Silver Medal from the Royal Society of Arts, 1953; Coote Lake Research Medal (jointly with wife, Iona Opie), 1960; M.A., Oxford University, 1962; European Prize of the City of Caorle (Italy; joint winner), 1964; Chicago Folklore Prize (joint winner with I. Opie), 1970; *The Oxford Book of Children's Verse* was selected one of Child Study Association of America's Children's Books of the Year, 1973, and *The Classic Fairy Tales,* 1974.

WRITINGS:

I Want to Be a Success (autobiography), M. Joseph, 1939.
Having Held the Nettle, Torchstream Books, 1945.
The Case of Being a Young Man, Wells Gardner, Darton, 1946.

ALL WITH WIFE, IONA OPIE

(Compiler) *I Saw Esau,* Williams & Norgate, 1947.
(Editor) *The Oxford Dictionary of Nursery Rhymes,* Clarendon, 1951.
(Compiler) *The Oxford Nursery Rhyme Book* (illustrated by Joan Hassall and others), Oxford University Press, 1955.
Christmas Party Games, Oxford University Press (N.Y.), 1957.
The Lore and Language of Schoolchildren, Clarendon, 1959.
(Compiler) *The Puffin Book of Nursery Rhymes* (illustrated by Pauline Baynes), Penguin (London), 1963, published as *A Family Book of Nursery Rhymes,* Oxford University Press (N.Y.), 1964.
Children's Games in Street and Playground: Chasing, Catching, Seeking, Hunting, Racing, Duelling, Exerting, Daring, Guessing, Acting, Pretending, Clarendon, 1969.
(Editor) *Three Centuries of Poetry and Nursery Rhymes for Children* (exhibition catalogue), Oxford University Press, 1973, J. G. Schiller, 1977.

PETER OPIE

(Editor) *The Oxford Book of Children's Verse,* Oxford University Press, 1973.
(Compiler) *The Classic Fairy Tales,* Oxford University Press, 1974.
A Nursery Companion (*Horn Book* honor list), Oxford University Press, 1980.
(Compiler) *The Oxford Book of Narrative Verse,* Oxford University Press, 1983.
The Singing Game, Oxford University Press, 1985.
(Editor) *Tail Feathers from Mother Goose: The Opie Rhyme Book* (ALA Notable Book), Little, Brown, 1988.

Contributor to reference works, including *Encyclopaedia Britannica,* and *New Cambridge Bibliography of English Literature.*

ADAPTATIONS:

(Also host) "The Lore and Language of Schoolchildren," British Broadcasting Corp., 1960.

SIDELIGHTS: See Opie, Iona.

HOBBIES AND OTHER INTERESTS: Collecting early children's books.

FOR MORE INFORMATION SEE:

Times (London), October 4, 1969.
Times Educational Supplement, October 10, 1969.

Observer, October 19, 1969.
Christian Science Monitor, December 4, 1969.
Library Journal, January 15, 1970.
Horn Book, February, 1970.
Carlton Miscellany, spring, 1970.
New York Review of Books, July 23, 1970.
Edna Johnson and others, compilers, *Anthology of Children's Literature,* 4th edition, Houghton, 1970.
Horizon, winter, 1971.
New York Times, June 16, 1973.
Washington Post, December 13, 1974.
Junior Bookshelf, June, 1982 (p. 87ff)
Jonathan Cott, *Pipers and the Gates of Dawn,* Random House, 1983.
Publishers Weekly, July 29, 1988 (p. 134ff).
Journal of Youth Services in Libraries, spring, 1990 (p. 177).

OBITUARIES

Times (London), February 8, 1982.
Chicago Tribune, February 9, 1982.

COLLECTIONS

De Grummond Collection at the University of Southern Mississippi.
The Opie Collection of Children's Literature at the Bodleian Library at the University of Oxford.

(Jacket photograph by Inge Aicher-Scholl from *The Short Life of Sophie Scholl* by Herman Vinke. Translated by Hedwig Pachter.)

PACHTER, Hedwig 19(?)-1988

PERSONAL: Died February 11, 1988; married; children: Renee Vera Pachter Cafiero.

CAREER: Awards, honors: Jane Addams Children's Book Award from the Jane Addams Peace Association, 1985, for *The Short Life of Sophie Scholl.*

WRITINGS:

(Translator) Hermann Vinke, *The Short Life of Sophie Scholl,* Harper, 1984.

PERCY, Rachel 1930-

PERSONAL: Born February 2, 1930, in Geraldton, Western Australia; daughter of R. G. J. (a rancher) and B. M. (a homemaker; maiden name, Mountain) Percy; married Richard Oxenburgh, April 22, 1957 (divorced, March 11, 1987); children: Dickon, Merinda, Daniel. *Education:* Attended schools in Australia. *Religion:* Church of England. *Home:* 14 Owen Rd., Darlington, Western Australia 6070. *Agent:* Currency Press, P.O. Box 452, Paddington, New South Wales, Australia 2021.

CAREER: Free-lance writer, 1954—; Richard Oxenburgh Productions, Bassendean, Western Australia, partner and producer, 1976-87. Free-lance broadcaster, Australian Broadcasting Commission, 1954-72. *Member:* Australian Writers Guild, Australian Society of Authors, Strehlow Research Foundation, Australian Stockmans Hall of Fame and Outback Heritage Centre.

WRITINGS:

(With Rod Ansell) *To Fight the Wild: A Modern Day Robinson Crusoe's True Story of Survival in the Australian Bush,* Currency Press, 1980, Harcourt, 1986.

Also author of radio talks and plays. Contributor of articles to periodicals, including *Bulletin, Australian Women's Weekly,* and *West Australian.*

WORK IN PROGRESS: A Dream of Droving (working title), a biography set mainly in the Northern Territory of Australia about experiences working in the drovers' camps and on cattle stations (ranches) from 1958 through the mid 70s.

SIDELIGHTS: "I was born in the small West Australian coastal town of Geraldton, but spent my childhood and early youth on sheep stations (ranches) near Meekatharra, and later, Mullewa, in the dry inland country. I loved the bush life, was a keen horse rider, but also spent a lot of time drawing and sketching and scribbling stories and verse!

"Education was at home by correspondence lessons, and later, at boarding school, where I became interested in drama. By 1954 I had begun, as a free-lancer, writing and broadcasting talks for the Australian Broadcasting Commission (ABC) in Perth, the capital city of Western Australia. I was also involved in theatre (mostly amateur).

"In 1957 I married a young Englishman who had migrated to Australia, and have brought up three children. I continued to

RACHEL PERCY

write as much as possible, mostly for radio, but also television scripts and articles for Australian newspapers and magazines.

"By 1978, my then husband and I were partners in his documentary film and television production business (Richard Oxenburgh Productions) and we made the documentary/drama 'To Fight the Wild.' This was a true adventure story. A young man, Rod Ansell, had been stranded in the far north of Australia, on the Fitzmaurice River, which is totally uninhabited. He had survived for about six weeks by hunting wild cattle and other game. I researched the story, wrote the script, and was mainly responsible for the production and direction of the film during eight weeks on location, five weeks of that time actually camped, with Rod and the film crew, in the remote Fitzmaurice River area.

"When it came to writing the book, *To Fight the Wild,* (in the first person, telling the story as Rod Ansell) the fact that I had spent so much time in the area where his adventure had happened, and had worked closely with him, made it much easier to 'speak' with his voice. Much of the book is in Rod's exact words, arranged from tapes I'd recorded, about what had happened, and how—but I was able to weave in more detailed descriptions and still keep 'in character.' This meant that I adopted a very different style for the introductions to parts two and three, to 'set the scene,' which I felt I could not do properly except by using an 'outsiders' voice. (The poetry in the book is, of course, Rod Ansell's own.)

"I have always had very strong feelings about the Australian bush—with all its harshness it also has great beauty and a haunting fascination—and the people who live there, with all their toughness, have very special qualities. So *To Fight the Wild* was very important to me as I felt I was speaking, not just for Rod, but for all the others who have lived in the bush.

"Since *To Fight the Wild* I have worked on a film script (set in Northern Australian cattle country) which is unfinished as yet. I've made a short, video documentary about an amateur bush race meeting ('Landor: Sixty Plus and Still Racing') which has only been sold privately, and have had a few articles published.

"I've also been involved with the West Australian branch of the Australian Stockmans Hall of Fame and Outback Heritage Centre (the Australian version of the American Cowboys Hall of Fame)—helping to raise the money to build the Hall (in Queensland, where it was opened in April, 1988) and collecting historical material.

"I would like to write another book, set in sheep-station country. I have also started to paint again—watercolours. I'd like to travel more. I've seen a lot of Australia, and have visited Singapore, Hong Kong, and Japan, but have yet to go to Europe or to the United States. I have an ambition to ride down the Grand Canyon on a mule!

(Jacket photograph of co-author Rod Ansell from *To Fight the Wild: A Modern Day Robinson Crusoe's True Story of Survival in the Australian Bush* by Rod Ansell and Rachel Percy.)

"Darlington, where I live now, is on the escarpment just beyond Perth. A hilly, bushy area with a 'villagey' sort of atmosphere. My house is over one hundred years old, which is pretty ancient by Australian standards. My youngest son is still living at home, plus two cats and one dog, and my mother (who lives next door) shares a big rambling garden with me and we both share it with three kinds of parrots (who eat all our fruit), magpies, kookaburras, and multitudes of small birds. It's a nice place in a fairly mad world."

HOBBIES AND OTHER INTERESTS: Gardening, walking the dog, painting and sketching, reading, good films and theater, horseback riding, history, especially Australian rural history.

PUNER, Helen W(alker) 1915-1989

OBITUARY NOTICE—See sketch in *SATA* Volume 37: Born June 18, 1915, in New York, N.Y.; died July 14, 1989, in Valhalla, N.Y. Journalist and author. Puner was the first woman editor at *Fortune* magazine which she joined in 1935 as a researcher. After nine years with *Fortune* she worked as a free-lance writer, becoming special editor of *Parents'* magazine in 1956. She was the author of the biography *Freud: His Life and His Mind,* and the books *Daddies: What They Do All Day, The Sitter Who Didn't Sit, Not While You're a Freshman,* and *I Am Big, You Are Little.*

FOR MORE INFORMATION SEE:

Contemporary Authors New Revision Series, Volume 2, Gale, 1981.

OBITUARIES

New York Times, July 16, 1989.

RAY, Carl 1943-1978

PERSONAL: Born January 18, 1943, in Sandy Lake, Ontario, Canada; died September 26, 1978; son of Maggie Ray; married Helen Goodwin; children: Carl, Norman, Corinna Maggie.

CAREER: Illustrator; artist. Worked in the mines in Red Lake, Canada, and was a trapper, in Sandy Lake, Canada. Publisher of newspaper *Kitawin* ("The Call"). Paintings have been exhibited in Canada.

ILLUSTRATOR:

James R. Stevens, *Sacred Legends of the Sandy Lake Cree,* McClelland, 1971.

SIDELIGHTS: Ray's mother and uncle told him many of the legends of people he later painted. He wanted to preserve the stories of his people and *Sacred Legends of the Sandy Lake Cree* was a step towards that goal. Certain stories belonged to certain families, and were handed down as heirlooms from one generation to the next. To tell these stories Ray had to get permission from each family. He wanted to preserve this inheritance for the young people through paintings and books before it was lost; old word-of-mouth pattern was no longer adequate. From the old people of Sandy Lake he collected and illustrated legends which were arranged by James Stevens.

Born in Sandy Lake, Ontario, Ray has always drawn pictures. Although he worked in the mines and later as a trapper, he continued his painting even when everyone told him an Indian boy with a sixth grade education couldn't become an artist. He sold his first two watercolors for five dollars each. "It doesn't take very long to make a painting or a drawing. But it takes a long time to think about it first."[1]

As editor of *Kitawin,* a Sandy Lake newspaper, Ray frequently highlighted a legend which he retold and illustrated. He continued to paint the legends as well as more naturalistic works such as the scene of the trapline campfire, the northern lights over the lakes, or hunting scenes in the country he knew so well. He signed his pictures with both his name and his signature in Indian syllabics.

FOOTNOTE SOURCES

[1] Irma McDonough, editor, *Profiles,* revised edition, Canadian Library Association (Ottawa), 1975.

REEMAN, Douglas Edward 1924-
(Alexander Kent)

PERSONAL: Born October 15, 1924, in Thames Ditton, Surrey, England; son of Charles Percival and Lilian (Waters) Reeman; married Kimberly Jordan, October 5, 1985. *Education:* Attended local schools in England. *Home:* Blue Posts, Eaton Park Rd., Cobham, Surrey KT11 2JH, England.

CAREER: Royal Navy, England, served on destroyers and small craft in World War II, 1940-46, became lieutenant, Royal Naval Volunteer Reserve, 1946—; writer, 1946—; London Metropolitan Police, at first on the beat and later as detective in the Criminal Investigation Division, 1946-50; London County Council, London, children's welfare officer, 1950-60. Has also worked as a book reviewer and held navigation classes for yachtsmen. Lecturer on juvenile problems and delinquency; script adviser for television and motion pictures. Director, Bolitho Maritime Productions Ltd. and Highseas Authors Ltd. *Member:* Royal Navy Sailing Association, Motor Torpedo Boat Officers Association, Royal Society for the Protection of Birds (fellow), Garrick Club (London), Officers' Club (London). *Awards, honors:* *Richard Bolitho: Midshipman* was selected one of Child Study Association of America's Children's Books of the Year, 1976; *The Inshore Squadron* was selected one of New York Public Library's Books for the Teen Age, 1980 and 1981, and *Stand into Danger*, 1982.

DOUGLAS EDWARD REEMAN

WRITINGS:

A Prayer for the Ship, Jarrolds, 1958, Putnam, 1973.
High Water, Jarrolds, 1959.
Send a Gunboat, Jarrolds, 1960, Putnam, 1961, published as *Escape from Santu,* Hamilton, 1962.
Dive in the Sun, Putnam, 1961.
The Hostile Shore, Jarrolds, 1962.
The Last Raider, Jarrolds, 1963, Putnam, 1964.
With Blood and Iron, Jarrolds, 1964, Putnam, 1965.
H.M.S. Saracen, Jarrolds, 1965, Putnam, 1966.
Path of the Storm, Hutchinson, 1966, Putnam, 1967.
The Deep Silence, Hutchinson, 1967, Putnam, 1968.
The Pride and the Anguish: Dark Days in Singapore!, Hutchinson, 1968, Putnam, 1969.
To Risks Unknown, Hutchinson, 1969, Putnam, 1970.
The Greatest Enemy, Hutchinson, 1970, Putnam, 1971.
Against the Sea (nonfiction), Hutchinson, 1971.
Adventures under the Sea, Walker, 1971.
Rendezvous: South Atlantic, Putnam, 1972.
Go in and Sink, Hutchinson, 1973, published in America as *His Majesty's U-Boat,* Jove, 1985.
The Destroyers, Putnam, 1974.
Winged Escort, Putnam, 1975.
Surface with Daring, Putnam, 1977.
Strike from the Sea, Morrow, 1978.
A Ship Must Die, Morrow, 1979.
Torpedo Run, Hutchinson, 1981, Morrow, 1982.
Badge of Glory, Hutchinson, 1982, Morrow, 1983.
The First to Land, Hutchinson, 1984, Morrow, 1985.
D-Day: A Personal Reminiscence (nonfiction), Hutchinson, 1984.
The Volunteers, Hutchinson, 1985, Morrow, 1986.
The Iron Pirate, Heinemann, 1986, Putnam, 1987.
In Danger's Hour, Heinemann, 1988, Putnam, 1989.
The White Guns, Bentley, 1989.

"RICHARD BOLITHO" SERIES; UNDER PSEUDONYM ALEXANDER KENT

To Glory We Steer, Putnam, 1968.
Form Line of Battle!, Putnam, 1969.
Enemy in Sight!, Hutchinson, 1970.
The Flag Captain, Putnam, 1971.
Sloop of War, Putnam, 1972.
Command a King's Ship, Putnam, 1973.
Signal: Close Action!, Putnam, 1974.
Richard Bolitho: Midshipman, Hutchinson, 1975, Putnam, 1976.
Passage to Mutiny, Putnam, 1976.
In Gallant Company, Putnam, 1977.
The Inshore Squadron, Hutchinson, 1977, Putnam, 1979.
Midshipman Bolitho and the "Avenger," Putnam, 1978.
Stand into Danger, Putnam, 1980.
A Tradition of Victory, Hutchinson, 1981, Putnam, 1982.
Success to the Brave, Hutchinson, 1983, Putnam, 1984.
Colours Aloft!, Putnam, 1986.
Honor This Day, Heinemann, 1987.
With All Despatch, Heinemann, 1988.
The Only Victor, Heinemann, 1990.

Also author of *Captain Richard Bolitho R.N.*

ADAPTATIONS:

CASSETTES

"Richard Bolitho: Midshipman," Listen for Pleasure, 1977.
"In Danger's Hour," Chivers Audio Books, 1988.
"The Iron Pirate," Music for Pleasure, 1988.

WORK IN PROGRESS: A book about the Battle of the Atlantic.

SIDELIGHTS: Douglas Reeman was born in Thames Ditton, Surrey, England on October 15, 1924. He left school at the age of sixteen to join the Royal Navy's war efforts. "I can well recall my early-morning gloom when roused by the twittering call and the cry to all hands to 'Lash up and stow!' That was when warships still carried hammocks for those lucky enough to find spare hooks from which to sling them! A rude awakening indeed!"[1] Following World War II, the author began writing short stories while serving with the London Metropolitan Police, first as a foot patrolman, then as detective.

Primarily known as an adventure novelist, Reeman's most popular works have been sea stories. Two of his novels, *Send a Gunboat* (1960) and *The Deep Silence* (1967) have been adapted into films in the United States. Since then, he has written, under the pseudonym Alexander Kent, more than fifteen novels in the Richard Bolitho series. These books portray the life of an eighteenth-century British sailor as he progresses from midshipman to admiral; many of the character's adventures coincide with major historical events such as the French and American Revolutions.

Reeman's illustrator, Geoffrey Huband, explained the appeal of this period by saying, "The focus of my interest centres . . . between 1700-1800, a period I regard as the peak of achievement in the combination of function and beauty in ships . . . . The fact that this was also a time of intense scientific discovery, political change and international strife offers further possibilities of material."[1] One commentator wrote of these novels, "Alexander Kent captures the excitement and detail of the times, and gives us a thrilling story for the young of all ages."[1]

"My interest is in the sea, in ships, and in maritime history," admits Reeman. "I spend every available moment, when not writing, on travel, research, and seeking out locations and situations for my books. I travel many thousands of miles per year, by sea whenever possible, for as my books are published throughout the world I feel I need to know better the people who read them. My hobbies, too, are connected with the sea: sailing, cruising, and exploring beaches are amongst them—wild birds, too, in all forms and of all countries."

Reeman has retained his commission in the Royal Navy Volunteer Reserve, and has taught navigation classes for yachtsmen. As a former children's welfare officer for the London County Council, he is also a frequent lecturer on juvenile problems and delinquency. The author's books have been translated into twenty-two languages and have sold more than twelve million copies.

FOOTNOTE SOURCES

[1]*Richard Bolitho Newsletter*, Issue XIV, Heinemann.

FOR MORE INFORMATION SEE:

New York Times, February 16, 1965, February 24, 1968.
Times Literary Supplement, May 12, 1966, July 2, 1971.
New York Times Book Review, March 3, 1968, May 24, 1970, January 27, 1974.
Top of the News, June, 1968.
Saturday Review, November 9, 1968.
Books & Bookmen, August, 1969.

Observer, August 13, 1972, November 24, 1974, December 19, 1976.
Book World, September 24, 1972.
National Observer, January 13, 1973.
America, May 5, 1973.
Christian Science Monitor, December 3, 1975.
Publishers Weekly, May 29, 1978.

RICE, Alice (Caldwell) Hegan 1870-1942 (Alice Caldwell Hegan)

PERSONAL: Born January 11, 1870, in Shelbyville, Ky.; died February 10, 1942, in Louisville, Ky.; married Cale Young Rice, 1902. *Education:* Attended private schools.

CAREER: Writer. Co-founder of Cabbage Patch Settlement House, Louisville, Ky. *Awards, honors:* D. Litt., Rollins College, 1928, and University of Louisville, 1937.

WRITINGS:

FICTION; FOR CHILDREN

(Under the name Alice Caldwell Hegan) *Mrs. Wiggs of the Cabbage Patch,* Century, 1901, reissued, Appleton-Century, 1933, reissued with an introduction by William F. Axton, University of Kentucky Press, 1979 [other editions illustrated by Everett Shinn, Grosset, 1950; Norma Garris and Dan Garris, A. Whitman, 1962].
Lovey Mary, Century, 1903, reissued, Appleton-Century, 1935.
Captain June (illustrated by C. D. Weldon), Century, 1907.

ADULT NOVELS

Sandy, Century, 1905.
Mr. Opp (illustrated by Leon Guipon), Century, 1909.
A Romance of Billy-Goat Hill (illustrated by George Wright), Century, 1912.
The Honorable Percival, Century, 1914.
Calvary Alley (illustrated by Walter Biggs), Century, 1917.
Quin, Century, 1921.
The Buffer, Century, 1929.
Mr. Pete & Co., Appleton-Century, 1933.
The Lark Legacy, Appleton-Century, 1935.
Our Ernie, Appleton-Century, 1939.

ADULT; SHORT STORIES

Miss Mink's Soldier and Other Stories, Century, 1918.
(With husband, Cale Young Rice) *Turn about Tales,* Century, 1920.
(With C. Y. Rice) *Winners and Losers,* Century, 1925.
(With C. Y. Rice) *Passionate Follies: Alternate Tales,* Appleton, 1936.

OTHER

On Being "Clinnicked": A Bit of a Talk over the Alley Fence, Eldridge, 1931.
My Pillow Book, Appleton-Century, 1937.
The Inky Way (autobiography), Appleton-Century, 1940.
Happiness Road, Appleton-Century, 1942, reissued, Books for Libraries Press, 1968.

Mrs. Wiggs of the Cabbage Patch has been translated into many languages as well as Braille.

ALICE HEGAN RICE

ADAPTATIONS:

"Mr. Opp" (play), first produced in London, England at Garrick Theatre, 1910.

"A Romance of Billy-Goat Hill" (play), first produced in Columbus, Ohio, 1913.

"Mrs. Wiggs of the Cabbage Patch" (play), first produced in Louisville, Ky. at Maculey's Theatre, (film), starring W. C. Fields and ZaSu Pitts, Paramount, 1934.

SILENT MOVIES

"Sandy," starring Jack Pickford, 1918.

"Lovey, Mary," starring Marguerite Clark, 1926.

"Calvery Alley," starring Ann Pennington.

"Mr. Opp," starring Arthur Hough.

"A Romance of Billy-Goat Hill."

SIDELIGHTS: Alice Hegan Rice was born in Selbyville, Kentucky on **January 11, 1870.** "Some are born with silver spoons in their mouths. I, more fortunate, was born with a pen in my hand.

"On my mother's side I am of typical American pioneer stock . . . . On my father's side I come of a high-living, hard-riding Celtic family.

"It was at my grandfather's, Judge James Caldwell's, six miles distant, that I spent much of my childhood . . . . A big friendly house among the trees, glowing with light and ringing with laughter, where the clan, often forty strong, foregathered every summer and at Christmas time, to hold high carnival.

"The joys of summer differed only in kind, not in degree. There was the long cellar lined with barrels full of pickles, and apples, and molasses, shelves upon shelves of preserves, jams, and jellies.

"Back of the cow pasture was a creek, clear in name only, where we waded and paddled, and on whose banks we sat spellbound while a young mulatto nurse recounted the doings of Brer Fox and Brer Rabbit a couple of years before Joel Chandler Harris put them on paper. On hot nights the grown-ups gave outdoor concerts, moving the piano to the front porch, and with the aid of a violin, a guitar, and a banjo, entertained a black and white audience which hung entranced over the entire length of the front fence.

"Is it any wonder that a city-bred little girl should have regarded these 'reunions' as periods spent in Paradise? Being the first grandchild, with a bevy of devoted young aunts and uncles and eight cousins who looked up to my few years of seniority, I occupied an enviable position in the family.

"Possessed of an energy out of proportion to my frail body, my constant demand was, 'What shall I do next?' And when sometimes impatiently advised to sit on my thumb, the insult to my infant intelligence was great. As I grew older I tried to draw, to model, to make up stories, creative efforts that were met with loving tolerance by my elders.

"The children, however, took me more seriously. They performed the plays I thought up, admired my attempts at art, and by their enthusiastic co-operation started me on my story-telling career. Long summer afternoons we spent perched in an old sycamore tree back of the hen-house while I spun endless tales for my cousins. Here my first hero, Roger Carlyle, was born, a dashing cavalier, destined to become the prince of our dreams.

"Never had a budding author such an inspiring audience! Blue eyes and brown were riveted upon mine, cheeks glowed and lips quivered, breaths were held in suspense while the tale unfolded.

"My father's business necessitated frequent trips abroad, my young mother and their two small children were parked for safety in the largest hotel in Louisville. Three years of my childhood were passed in the old Galt House, the very name of which will recall to the minds of many, palatial parlors, stately halls, imposing stairways, and 'the ambrosial entertainment' that bespoke the luxury and elegance of the old South.

"Unfortunately my personal memories of those early years spent in the hotel are less glamorous. They include high-ceilinged bedrooms, surreptitious rides on a velocipede through broad corridors, meals with a nurse in the 'Ordinary.'

"The strongest literary influence in my early life came through a spinster aunt, who came to live with us soon after we acquired a home of our own. She possessed one of the most acquisitive minds I have ever known, and almost as soon as I possessed ears, she began pouring into them a steady flow of information.

"The only two schools that I attended before I was ten were Sunday school and dancing school. The former was associated entirely with learning a Bible verse and putting a nickel in the box. I was a sort of religious maverick, wandering happily from one fold to another, Episcopal, Baptist, Presby-

'Tain't no street . . . this here is the Cabbage Patch. (Illustration by Florence Scovel Shinn from *Lovey Mary* by Alice Hegan Rice.)

terian, and Disciples of Christ, my choice controlled by the little girl who happened to be my best friend at the moment.

"Dancing school seemed a much more important institution. On Saturday afternoons I fared forth, a slim, sallow little girl with eyes much too big for the rest of her and long brown hair crimped to the bitter end. An irascible old Frenchman instructed us in the intricacies of the 'five positions,' and was not above rapping us over the toes with his fiddle bow when we proved too clumsy. Once a year we had an exhibition, and were taught to perform fearsome feats on our tiptoes before an audience of adoring parents. These occasions were rendered bleak to me because I was invariably cast in the role of a tipsy or an Indian when my whole soul longed to be on the side of the blonde angels and blue-eyed fairies.

"Being a delicate child, I was often house-bound during the winter months, and my chief joy was in being read to. I listened with avidity to anything the grown-up happened to be reading, with the result that when I started to school at the advanced age of ten, my small head was crammed with strange fancies and unrelated facts.

"The private school to which I was sent was staffed by a group of women whose charm and culture played as important a part in their equipment as their pedagogic ability. They had come to Louisville from the East and established themselves in the fine old house built by George Keats.

"During my short subjection to mental discipline I was taught less about the American Revolution than about the Peloponnesian wars, less about practical science than about English literature. Mathematics was a dark continent from the start. When the teacher confidently asserted that x plus y equals z, I accepted her ultimatum. It didn't make sense, but it was all right if she said so. But when I was called upon to say how long it would take a stone to fall a distance of one hundred feet, or how much material would be required to build a one-layer concrete floor thirty feet long, twenty-four feet wide, and five inches thick, I indignantly refused to submit to such mental cruelty.

"When it came to English, however, I promptly soared to the head of the class, and was soon writing the other girls' compositions as well as my own. Confronted with such a depressing subject as 'A Rainy Day in the Country,' I could turn off a week of rainy days if seven girls happened to need assistance. The only medal I ever received was for handwriting, which is almost as ignominious as the honor conferred on a friend 'for good intentions.'

"The most suppressed desire of my youth was the ambition to draw. I can never remember a time when a pencil and a blank sheet of paper did not offer instant provocation. To this day I make surreptitious sketches on telephone pads, market books, shopping lists, and hymnals, and frequently employ a spare hour in drawing for 'my own amazement.'

(From the movie "Mrs. Wiggs of the Cabbage Patch," starring W. C. Fields and ZaSu Pitts. Produced by Paramount Pictures, 1934.)

"So when I started to school and discovered a large, high-ceilinged studio where girls stood at easels drawing from a model, I was in a fever of impatience until I was enrolled as an art student.

"But like so many adolescent dreams its accomplishment was far from what I expected. Seated before a table on which was a cup and saucer, I was told to draw them and continue to draw them until I had mastered their ellipses.

"It was early in my school career that I first saw my name in print. It was signed to an article I had written for the school paper. The subject given me was 'The Great American Loon,' and even my lively imagination faltered before the task. I am, however, not ashamed of the result, which fortunately was preserved for posterity. In fact, I consider it a masterpiece of accuracy, brevity and honesty.

"It was not until I was nearly fifteen that I again got into print. I had read Ik Marvel's *Reveries of a Bachelor,* and so moved was I by his reflections on love and matrimony that I was impelled to write an article on the same theme from a different point of view. I called mine 'Reveries of an Old Maid,' and some one suggested that I send it to a local newspaper. Being inexperienced in submitting manuscript, I sent it unsigned, written on both sides of the paper, and with no postage for return. To the delight of myself and my classmates, it was not only published, but elicited several

printed answers, attacking the acrimonious spinster who had penned the lines.

"From that time on I never ceased trying to put my thoughts on paper, vainly endeavoring to get every experience into concrete form.

"When I was about sixteen an event occurred which changed my future life. I discovered 'the proletariat.' A friend took me to a mission Sunday school in a slum neighborhood. At the time of our arrival the services were being disrupted by the unholy activities of a gang of young hoodlums on the outside, who were terrifying the potential Christians by dangling a dead cat in at the window. I promptly offered to corral the boys on the front steps and try to hold their attention until Sunday school should be over.

"Several of the boys were about my age and inclined to be difficult. 'You ain't aimin' to talk God to us, are yer?' asked one. On being assured that such was not my intention, they condescended to suspend activities until I could show what I had to offer. Amid a barrage of jeers and spit-balls I valiantly attempted to establish a point of contact. Story-telling being my chief accomplishment, I embarked on a mystery tale which I had recently read, called 'Picayune Pete or Nicodemus the Dog Detective.' The result was so successful that I was urged to carry on throughout the summer. Surely no stranger Sunday-school class was ever conducted than that al fresco affair, where rogues and murderers, pirates and gangsters played the leading roles. There was no discipline and, alas, no uplift, but the cause of peace was promoted, and I learned a great deal about the nature of boys.

"From that time until after my marriage I was never without a boys' club, and it was in prowling about the alleys visiting their families that I acquired the first-hand knowledge of the poor that was to be the foundation of my life work.

"Armed with a decrepit typewriter and an old ledger, both borrowed from my father's office, I valiantly set to work.

"Fortunately I had a subject ready to my hand. For years a funny old woman had been coming to our back door for food, and stopping to talk to whoever would listen. She had a good-for-nothing husband who, she said, was 'just as bad as a poor man could be,' and a brood of children of whom she loved to discourse. She was dirty and improvident, but gay and courageous, and her sayings and doings became part of our family history. It was easy to build a story around her and the other characters I knew in the Cabbage Patch.

"First I wrote my manuscript in longhand, carefully skirting the entries in the old ledger and adorning the margins with sketches as I went along. When the last page was reached, I brought the tale to an end like a sculptor who must fit his subject to the size of his marble.

"Next came the far more arduous task of copying my story on the typewriter, an achievement regarded by the family as much more remarkable than the composition itself.

"Little did any of us dream that the old ledger would one day be sold at auction and later occupy an honored place in the Rosenbach Gallery; that the slight story would travel all over the world, and serve in some humble way to touch the springs

Mrs. Wiggs took pictures from her walls and chairs from her parlor to beautify the house of Hazy. (Illustration by Florence Scovel Shinn from *Lovey Mary* by Alice Hegan Rice.)

of human nature in both rich and poor, and bring them into closer understanding.

"The crudely copied manuscript was sent to my friend in New York, and in due time a note came from the Century Company saying they would like to make a book of it. Much surprise and excitement did this cause in the family! I myself sent out nineteen postcards advising absent friends of the unbelievable thing that had happened to me."[1]

December, 1901. *Mrs. Wiggs of the Cabbage Patch* published. "One thing that marred my pleasure in the unexpected success of my first professional venture was the unpleasant notoriety it brought on my humble heroine. Visitors to the Cabbage Patch descended upon her in droves and subjected her to annoyances which I was unable to spare her. They took palings from her fence and leaves from her trees as souvenirs, and made snapshots of her whenever she showed herself. In vain I offered to move her to a better house in a cleaner neighborhood. She preferred to stay where she was and enjoy the drama of fighting the intruders, sometimes with words, and sometimes, alas, with pails of slop."[1]

Married Cale Young Rice, a dramatist and poet, in 1902. "Three months later we set sail on the first of our many voyages.

Alice Hegan Rice camping in the Cumberlands, 1940.

"The times when we were not traveling abroad were spent largely in seeing our own country. We traveled from the Atlantic to the Pacific, from Canada to Florida, usually managing to spend part of each summer in what we considered an ideal spot.

"Mrs. Wiggs of the Cabbage Patch" produced as a play, first in Louisville, Kentucky, and later in New York and abroad.

February 10, 1942. Died at her home in Louisville, Kentucky. "If and when I ever reach heaven, I shall probably be found with a tablet under one wing and a pen under the other, trying to chronicle the antics of the angels."[1]

FOOTNOTE SOURCES

[1]Alice Hegan Rice, *The Inky Way,* Appleton-Century, 1940.

FOR MORE INFORMATION SEE:

David Morton, "Alice Hegan Rice: Her Work and Herself," *Book News Monthly,* April, 1918.
Stanley Kunitz and Howard Haycraft, *Junior Book of Authors,* H. W. Wilson, 1934.
Current Biography 1942, H. W. Wilson, 1943.
John Mackay Shaw, *Childhood in Poetry,* Gale, 1967.
W. J. Burke and Will D. Howe, *American Authors and Books, 1640 to the Present Day,* 3rd edition, Crown, 1972.
Barbara Bader, *American Picture Books from Noah's Ark to the Beast Within,* Macmillan, 1976.

OBITUARIES

Publishers Weekly, April 11, 1942.

ROSEN, Lillian (Diamond) 1928-

PERSONAL: Born September 10, 1928, in New York, N.Y.; daughter of William and Gladys (Gross) Diamond; married Charles E. Rosen (a company president), December 24, 1955 (divorced August, 1967); children: Eric. *Education:* New York University B.S., 1951; Columbia University, M.S., 1952. *Politics:* Independent. *Religion:* Jewish. *Home and office:* 1 Strawberry Hill Ave., Apt. 1F, Stamford, Conn. 06902.

CAREER: English teacher at public schools in New York, N.Y., 1953-56; community worker, activist, and reading tutor, 1956-66; reading consultant for public schools in Stamford, Conn., 1966-68; Lillian D. Rosen Antiques (mail order antique business), Stamford, owner and manager, 1972—. Co-founder, first president, and member of board of directors of Fairwest Society for the Deaf and Hearing Impaired (a self-help service organization), 1977. Past chairman of Stamford Integrated Housing Committee. *Member:* Writers Guild. *Awards, honors:* Woodward Park School Annual Book Award, one of New York Public Library's Books for the Teen Age, and voted Best Book of the Year by the Madison School, all 1982, all for *Just Like Everybody Else;* Fellowship from the Virginia Colony for the Creative Arts, 1982; Silver Pen Award for Juvenile Literature from the Society of German Women Physicians, 1984, for *Bright Lightning—Silent Thunder.*

WRITINGS:

Just Like Everybody Else (young adult novel), Harcourt, 1981 (published in Germany as *Bright Lightning—Silent Thunder,* Verlag Herdere, 1983).

WORK IN PROGRESS: An adult novel, tentatively titled *A Matter of Survival,* dealing with the world of the deaf and the hearing impaired.

SIDELIGHTS: In 1966, shortly before her divorce, Rosen returned to her career as an educator. Six months later, she was dismissed from her position as a reading consultant when she became totally deaf. Considered "unemployable," Rosen spent "the ensuing years . . . adapting and pursuing work that I *could* do and that was relevant, exciting, and meaningful. Rehabilitation and staying sane were my primary occupations during that period. Opportunities were extremely limited, so I finally transformed a hobby into a business. I sell antiques and collectibles."

Rosen's young adult novel springs directly from this background. The story of a girl who loses her hearing in an accident, *Just Like Everybody Else* traces the functional and emotional problems Jenny encounters as she attempts to cope with her disability. My book is for everyone who can

I lived in Millport, a small, pretty city in Connecticut. I had two special friends and reasonably decent parents. (Jacket illustration by Les Morrill from *Just Like Everybody Else* by Lillian Rosen.)

read even on a minimal level (fourth or fifth grade). Many adults have read it, enjoyed doing so, learned and written to me about it from all over the world. This book is of special value to literacy programs, also to the many who serve and deal with the hearing impaired. My next novel will go into the subject in far more depth.

"I am a writer by default. I got started after meeting and getting to know several deaf and deafened youngsters. Then intensive research made me aware of the paucity of literature about the hearing impaired, particularly work written by an 'insider.'

"Sixteen million Americans are hearing impaired. One million of these are children. At present we are an 'invisible' minority, aliens in our own land, often incompetently educated, shunned, isolated, and discriminated against. Not until 'normal' people gain some insight into who we are, in all our diversity, will the beginnings of needed change become a possibility.

"Textbooks are not enough. There are only a handful of novels written by handicapped authors about disability itself. Only one novel by a deaf writer had been published before mine, and that appeared over fifty years ago! I'd like to believe that each one published will encourage others.

"I have retained full control of my voice and have lectured and given poetry readings, which were well-received. I would like to do more of that."

FOR MORE INFORMATION SEE:

ALA Booklist, October 15, 1981.
Stamford Advocate, October 18, 1981.
Childhood Education, September-October, 1982.

SACHAR, Louis 1954-

PERSONAL: Surname is pronounced *Sack*-er; born March 20, 1954, in East Meadow, N.Y.; son of Robert J. (a salesman) and Ruth (a real estate broker; maiden name, Raybin) Sachar; married Carla Askew (a teacher), May 26, 1985; children: Sherre. *Education:* University of California, Berkeley, B.A., 1976; University of California, San Francisco, J.D., 1980. *Home:* Austin, Tex. *Agent and office:* Ellen Levine Literary Agency, 432 Park Ave. S., Suite 1205, New York, N.Y. 10016.

CAREER: Beldoch Industries (manufacturers of women's sweaters), Norwalk, Conn., shipping manager, 1976-77; writer, 1977—; attorney, 1981—. *Member:* Authors Guild, Society of Children's Book Writers. *Awards, honors:* Ethical Culture School Book Award, 1978, and Children's Choice from the International Reading Association and the Children's Book Council, 1979, both for *Sideways Stories from Wayside School;* Parents' Choice Award from the Parents' Choice Foundation, 1987, Young Reader's Choice Award from the Pacific Northwest Library Association, and Texas Bluebonnet Award from the Texas Library Association, both 1990, and Charlie May Simon Book Award from the Arkansas Elementary School Council, Georgia Children's Book Award from the University of Georgia College of Education, Indian Paintbrush Book Award (Wyoming), Land of Enchantment Children's Book Award from the New Mexico Library Association, Mark Twain Award from the

LOUIS SACHAR

Missouri Association of School Librarians, Milner Award from the Friends of the Atlanta-Fulton Public Library (Georgia), Nevada Young Reader's Award, and West Virginia Book Award from Wise Library, West Virginia University, all for *There's a Boy in the Girls' Bathroom.*

WRITINGS:

JUVENILE

Sideways Stories from Wayside School (illustrated by Dennis Hockerman), Follett, 1978, new edition (illustrated by Julie Brinkloe), Avon, 1985.
Johnny's in the Basement, Avon, 1981.
Someday Angeline (illustrated by Barbara Samuels), Avon, 1983.
There's a Boy in the Girls' Bathroom, Knopf, 1987, large print edition, Cornerstone, 1990.
Sixth Grade Secrets, Scholastic, 1987.
Wayside School Is Falling Down (illustrated by Joel Schick), Lothrop, 1989.
Sideways Arithmetic from Wayside School, Scholastic, 1989.
The Boy Who Lost His Face (young adult novel), Knopf, 1989.

He's in the basement. (From *Johnny's in the Basement* by Louis Sachar.)

WORK IN PROGRESS: Monkey Soup, a picture book, and *Will Somebody Please Laugh,* a juvenile novel, both for Knopf; a play based on *There's a Boy in the Girls' Bathroom,* to be produced by Seattle Children's Theater, spring, 1991; a series of readers for second and third graders.

SIDELIGHTS: Louis Sachar was born in East Meadow, New York. "As a child, I remember having to keep away from the woods across the street, avoiding the older, tough kids who played there. (Looking back now, those tough kids were probably only eleven or twelve years old.) Younger kids, like me, weren't allowed in the woods, making them all the more forbidden."

At age nine, Sachar moved with his family to Tustin, California in Orange County, which, at the time, was mostly orange groves. "We cut through the orange groves on the way to school, and had orange fights on the way home. Now, sadly, most of the groves have been paved over and replaced with fast food restaurants, offices, and housing developments."

While attending Barnum Woods School in East Meadow, then Red Hill School in Tustin, "nothing especially traumatic" happened to Sachar. For the most part he enjoyed school, got good grades, liked math, and played in Little League. It wasn't until high school, in the late 60s, that he began to love reading. This was during a typical teenage rebellious period. His high school had a dress code which he preferred to ignore, wearing his hair long despite reprimands and instructions to cut it off. "My parents fortunately were very understanding and gave me a lot of leeway during these difficult years."

Following high school, Sachar had started college in Ohio at Antioch when he received news of his father's sudden death. "He died when I was eighteen—seventeen years ago—and I still haven't gotten over it."

Returning to California to be near his mother, Sachar took the next semester off. "For three months I worked as a Fuller Brush Man, and I was great at it. My employers couldn't understand how I could possibly want to go back to college when I had such a great career ahead of me selling brushes."

With other aspirations, Sachar returned to school, majoring in economics at Berkeley where he also took creative writing classes. He continued to read a lot on his own, but didn't like English classes, because he "didn't like analyzing the books to death.

"I developed a particular interest in Russian literature and somehow got the rather ridiculously ambitious notion to learn the language and read my favorite Russian authors in the original. After taking over a year of Russian, I realized it was still Greek to me. A week into the semester I dropped out of Russian V and tried to figure out what other class I should take instead. As I wandered across the campus, I saw an elementary school girl handing out pieces of paper. I took one from her. It read: 'Help. We need teacher's aides at our school. Earn three units of credit.'

"Prior to that time I had no interest whatsoever in kids. However, I signed up to be a teacher's aide because I needed to take something other than Russian, and it sounded easy. It turned out to be not only my favorite class, but also the most important class I took during my college career. After I was there for a while they asked me to be the 'Noon Time Supervisor.' It was my job to watch over the kids during lunch, for which I was paid $2.04 a day. I played games with the kids who all called me 'Louis, the Yard Teacher.'

"Around that same time I came upon *In Our Town* by Damon Runyon, a book of very short stories, two or three pages each, about different characters in a town. This gave me the idea for *Sideways Stories from Wayside School,* which is a book of short stories about different kids in a school. All the kids are named after kids I knew at the school where I worked. 'Louis the Yard Teacher,' is also a character in the book. I probably had more fun writing that book than any of my others, because it was just a hobby then, and I never truly expected to be published."

After graduation from Berkeley, Sachar took a job as shipping manager for a sweater factory in Connecticut, while writing *Sideways Stories* in the evenings. He was fired from the job after about seven months.

"Thinking it was time to return to school, I sent out the finished manuscript of *Sideways Stories* to ten publishers while simultaneously sending out law school applications. My first book was accepted for publication during my first week at University of California, beginning a six-year struggle over trying to decide between being an author or a lawyer. I finished law school, passed the bar, and half-heartedly looked for a law job. Meanwhile, I wrote three more children's books. Finally, I stopped agonizing over the decision and realized it had already been made. I've been an attorney

(Jacket illustration by Alexander Strogart from *The Boy Who Lost His Face* by Louis Sachar.)

since 1981 but have chosen to devote my time to writing children's books."

Continuing part-time law work when it "didn't interfere" with his writing, Sachar wrote in the mornings and practiced law in the afternoons. "The hardest part was putting on a suit and tie at one o'clock in the afternoon and going to a deposition after a somewhat bohemian morning."

The long-awaited sequel to *Sideways Stories* did not appear for several years. "When I first received a letter from a kid inquiring about a sequel, I thought he was joking; the idea hadn't even crossed my mind. Though *Sideways Stories* wasn't highly successful when it first came out, I did receive a number of letters from students, calling it their favorite book. Several years later, after having difficulty finding a publisher for *There's a Boy in the Girl's Bathroom,* I decided it was time to try a sequel set at Wayside.

"Interestingly enough, despite the troubles with *There's a Boy,* it has since become my most popular book." The story of Bradley Chalkers, a school-room outcast who is his own worst enemy, and Jeff Fishkin, the new kid who slowly befriends him, the book was completed in 1982 but did not find a publisher until 1985. "Editors kept telling me that I switched back and forth between Jeff and Bradley's points of view too often. I wanted to alternate viewpoints to fool the reader into thinking that they were reading Jeff's story, to

lure them into Bradley's. The publishers, however, preferred that the book be written entirely from Bradley's point of view.

"While working on this novel, I wrote for about two hours every morning and then every afternoon I made up a puzzle for the sequel to *Sideways Stories* entitled *Sideways Arithmetic from Wayside School.* Having enjoyed math so much when I was in grade school, I wanted *Sideways Arithmetic* to help kids discover that math could be fun. Unfortunately, I think a lot of kids flip through the book, see all the puzzles, and automatically assume it will be too difficult, so they don't even attempt it. When I visit schools and put the first puzzle on the board, I ask the often lost-looking class to help solve it. Receiving little or no response, I go through it aloud, showing them step by step. When the next problem goes up on the board, kids start shouting answers.

"Writing for elementary school students, I've tried to recall what it felt like for me to be that age, because despite the notion that times have changed, I think that kids in grade school are basically the same as they were when I was young.

"It's difficult to say where ideas for stories come from. I brainstorm until one idea leads to another which leads to another, and often it is the third or fourth idea which proves salvageable. I've started books, worked on them for a couple of weeks, and then abandoned the story for another. Through my first drafts, I never know what's going to happen, making the story terribly disorganized and subject to re-writes."

Sachar encountered censorship for the first time while writing his most recent book, *The Boy Who Lost His Face.* "Initially the book had the 'f' word in it. My editor approved it, knowing full well I don't use words indiscriminately; but right before the book was published, a consultant informed me that if I didn't take it out, I'd be killing the sales of the book, as well as hurt my other books, and possibly kill my career in the process. Every single word in my books is important to me; however, I also know that kids don't worry about individual words as much when they're reading as I do when I'm writing. Although I believed the word belonged where I had put it, I agreed to change the text, because it would not ultimately affect how readers responded to the book. I find it very interesting that what people often object to is the word itself, rather than to content. As much as I might back down and change a word, I would never consider altering the moral or political content of a story."

Now a husband and a father, Sachar initially had doubts about the effect a family might have on his work. "When I first started writing, I spent a great deal of time alone. Solitude allowed me to think about a project at all times—even when not actually writing—and I was afraid that with someone else around, I'd lose valuable thinking time. But family life has given me a sense of stability which has improved my writing rather than hindered it."

Sachar makes it a practice never to discuss his work in progress because "by working on a book for a year without talking about it—even to my wife—the story keeps building inside, until it's bursting to be told and the words come pouring out when I sit down to write."

Regarding early works like *Sideways Stories* as "complete fantasy," Sachar believes it is more difficult to write books like *There's a Boy in the Girl's Bathroom* which strive for a deeper, more realistic level of characterization. "When you

Everybody liked Maurecia—except Kathy, but then she didn't like anybody. Maurecia only liked ice cream. (Illustration by Julie Brinckloe from *Sideways Stories from Wayside School* by Louis Sachar.)

write something like *Sideways Stories* people tend to say, 'What an imagination it takes to think of all those fantastical things.' On the contrary, I think it takes a greater imagination to write realistic stories complete with realistic details. It's simple to invent, but to get to the heart of reality takes some real creativity."[1]

FOOTNOTE SOURCES

[1] Based on an interview by Dieter Miller for *Something about the Author.*

SCHNURRE, Wolfdietrich 1920-1989

OBITUARY NOTICE: Born August 22, 1920, in Frankfurt am Main, Germany; died June 9, 1989, in Kiel, West Germany. Critic and writer. Schnurre will be remembered as a founder of "Group 47," an important German literary association that shunned the trend toward realistic writing in postwar literature for magical realism, in which poetic imagination had free reign. Drafted at nineteen to serve in Adolf Hitler's army, Schnurre was repeatedly court-martialled for "defeatism," eventually deserting in 1945. He then began to write short stories and worked as a critic. A prolific author who wrote in various genres, Schnurre took as his subject common men but described the circumstances of their lives in a highly aesthetic style that gave tension to his works. Among his writings are essays, novels, radio and television plays, animal stories, and books focusing on children, including the most famous, *I'm Just Asking,* published in 1973, in which he collected children's "innocent" questions about different subjects from war to sex. Schnurre's works translated into English include the poetry collection *Climb, But Downward* and *Twelve Stories.*

FOR MORE INFORMATION SEE:

International Who's Who, 49th edition, Europa, 1985.
Dictionary of Literary Biography, Volume 69: *Contemporary German Fiction Writers, First Series,* Gale, 1988.
Who's Who in the World, 10th edition, Marquis, 1990.

OBITUARIES

Times (London), June 26, 1989.
Contemporary Authors, Volume 129, Gale, 1990.

SCIOSCIA, Mary (Hershey) 1926-

PERSONAL: Born November 4, 1926, in Toronto, Canada; came to the United States, 1929; daughter of John Harold (a physician) and Louisa (a social worker; maiden name, Smith) Hershey; married Frank A. Scioscia (an owner of an out-of-print bookstore), 1946; children: Louisa Scioscia Stephens, John, Charles, Virginia. *Education:* Attended Reed College, Portland, Ore., 1944-46; Los Angeles State College, B.A., 1961; Teacher's College, Columbia University, M.A., 1972. *Politics:* Democrat. *Religion:* Episcopalian. *Home:* 15 Hopke Ave., Hastings-on-Hudson, New York, N.Y. 10706.

CAREER: Samuel Gompers Junior High School, Los Angeles, Calif., English, geography, and remedial reading teacher, 1962-66; Hawthorne Junior High, Yonkers, N.Y., English and remedial reading teacher, 1966-77; Whitman Middle School, Yonkers, N.Y., English and remedial reading teacher, 1977-83; free-lance writer, 1983—. Secretary and member of board of directors, Happy Harbor Day Care

MARY SCIOSCIA

Center, Hastings-on-Hudson; former president; Friends of the Library, Hastings-on-Hudson. *Member:* Westchester Pen Women, International Reading Association, Hastings Literature Club, Jean Fritz Writing Workshop. *Awards, honors: Bicyle Rider* was selected one of Child Study Association of America's Children's Books of the Year, and a Notable Children's Trade Book in the Field of Social Studies from the National Council for Social Studies and the Children's Book Council, both 1983.

WRITINGS:

Bicycle Rider (illustrated by Ed Young), Harper, 1983.

Contributor to textbooks published by Macmillan, Harcourt, Houghton, Silver Burdett, Merrill, and Holt.

WORK IN PROGRESS: Sapphire Bird, a retelling of a French-Italian fairy tale; *Scranton Cowboy,* about an Italian-American family; *Broken Bottles,* about a boy who has trouble at school after his father dies.

SIDELIGHTS: "I lived with my parents in a small farming village called Roseneath until I was nearly three years old. We moved to the United States in 1929 just before the stock market crash, and I grew up in St. Louis, Missouri. After graduating from high school, I moved with my family to Oregon. I met my husband in Portland and married him when I was nineteen. We attended Reed College together, but I dropped out of school to have my first child. Four were born and attending school before I returned to get my B.A.

"I've always loved to read. Both my parents and uncles and aunt read to me as a child. *Tom Sawyer* and *Huckleberry Finn* were read to me by my father. Once we visited Mark Twain's home town of Hannibal, Missouri and saw the cave, Becky Thatcher's house, and the typewriter Mark Twain used. We had lunch at the Mark Twain Hotel. Other books I enjoyed that my mother read to me were *Cinderella, Winnie-the-Pooh, The Secret Garden,* and *Ann of Green Gables.* Also, my grandmother and parents told me stories. Later, I told stories to my little sister and neighborhood children.

"I found one of the great joys of raising children was reading to them or telling them stories. Now, with four grown children and four grown grandchildren, we read to our fifth and youngest grandchild and to each other.

"My husband, who worked thirty years for a publisher, now runs an antiquarian bookstore in Hastings-on-Hudson where I work part-time. I taught school for twenty-one years and took an early retirement to devote more time to writing. I decided to become a writer in third grade when Miss Van Matre read my story aloud to the class.

"Besides reading and writing, we like to travel and have visited almost every state in the United States as well as some travel in Mexico. We've visited France and Italy once and England many times because my mother and stepfather lived there. Once I took a tour with reading teachers to Czechslovakia, Hungary, Romania, and Russia. We ended in Copenhagen, Denmark to attend an international reading conference. In each country we met local teachers and visited schools. Our biggest trip was to India to visit our son and his wife when they lived there."

All the racers leaned over their handlebars. (Illustration by Ed Young from *Bicycle Rider* by Mary Scioscia.)

HOBBIES AND OTHER INTERESTS: "Collecting miniatures for my three dollhouses and watching my granddaughter play with them."

SCRIBNER, Kimball 1917-
(Captain Kim Kimball)

PERSONAL: Born February 13, 1917, in Piedmont, W.Va.; son of Bourdon Walter (a scientist) and Nellie (a homemaker; maiden name, Mansfield) Scribner; married (wife died, 1987); children: Colleen, Susan M. *Education:* Attended University of Maryland, 1936-39. *Home and office:* 2828 N. Atlantic Ave., Apt. 2106, Daytona Beach, Fla. 32018. *Agent:* James Jackson, Drawer 582, Winnsboro, S.C. 29180.

CAREER: Pilot; author. Congressional School of Aeronautics, Rockville, Md., chief ground and flight instructor, 1939; National University, Washington, D.C., faculty member, 1939; taught civilian pilot training courses, George Washington University and University of Maryland, 1940; Embry-Riddle Flying School, Miami, Fla., flight instructor, 1940; Pan American Airlines, co-pilot, 1941-43, captain, master pilot, and chief pilot, 1943-77; presently vice-president of United States Overseas Airline. Lecturer, writer and producer of films and slide presentations including "Qualification of Pilots into Airports," "Utilization of Runway Barriers for Jet Aircraft," and "The Study of Clear Air Turbulence."

Inventor of first steerable parachute, known as the "Eagle Parachute." Chairman, Air Transport Association; director and vice-president, Aero Industry Youth Development Association, 1961; member of science advisory board, aviation research chairman, Explorers Club, director and vice-president of the New York chapter, chairman of Florida chapter; trustee emeritus, Embry-Riddle Aeronautical University, 1969-68, and chairman of their International Advisory Council; special advisor to the President of Daytona Beach Community College, 1983-88; director, Speakers Bureau, Daytona Beach Community College; consultant, Bendix Avionics Division, Fort Lauderdale, Fla.; first vice-president, Volusia County Chapter, United Nations Association; board of trustees, Soaring Museum, Elmira, N.Y.; board of trustees, chairman, policy and rules committee, Golden Hills Academy, Ocala, Fla. *Member:* Cosmos Club, International Platform Association, National Soaring Society of America, Aviation/Space Writers Association, Airline Pilots Association, Quiet Birdmen, International Order of Characters, Ox-S Club.

AWARDS, HONORS: World Acrobatic Sailplane Championship, Cleveland Air Races, 1947; won Middle Atlantic States Soaring Championship, 1949; "Beechcraft Speed Award," U.S. National Soaring Contest, Grand Prairie Tex., 1950; honorary doctorate in Aeronautical Science, Embry Riddle Aeronautical University, 1969, Salem College, 1984; honorary life member, Sigma Chi International Fraternity, 1971; honorary member, Alpha Rho Omega, Professional Aviation Technologists Fraternity, 1972; Champion of Higher Independent Education Award, issued by presidents of colleges and universities of Florida, 1974; honorary member, Omecron Delta Kappa, National Honorary Society, 1977; elected "Pilot of the Year," International Order of Characters, 1978; inducted into the "Hall of Fame," OX5 Aviation Pioneers, 1978; Bishop Air Industry Award, 1979; *Your Future in Aviation: In the Air* was named a New York

KIMBALL SCRIBNER

Public Library Books for the Teen Age, 1981, 1982; Madaille en Vermail, French Society for the Encouragement of Progress, 1982.

WRITINGS:

Your Future as a Pilot, Rosen, 1968.
Your Future in Aviation: In the Air, Rosen, 1979, revised edition published as *Your Future in Aviation: Careers in the Air,* 1982.
Your Future in Aviation: On the Ground, Rosen, 1979, revised edition published as *Your Future in Aviation: Careers on the Ground,* 1983.

Author of technical papers and contributor of articles to *Popular Science, Airline Pilot, Skyways,* and *Explorers Journal.* Associate editor, *Flight Operations* magazine; editorial board, *Explorers Journal.*

WORK IN PROGRESS: The Golden Age of Aviation; another book, with photographs, to illustrate the humorous incidents in his aviation career.

SIDELIGHTS: At age sixteen, Scribner made his first parachute jump and thereafter became a professional jumper. He and his buddy would "pass the hat" at airports before jumping to make money for flying lessons and college. Five years later, he invented the first steerable parachute, the "Eagle Parachute," followed by the invention and development of a parachute capable of collapsing completely and reopening close to the ground after a free fall.

The Sikorsky S-42, America's first true transoceanic transport. (From *Your Future in Aviation: In the Air* by Kimball J. Scribner.)

A professional pilot, Scribner retired from Pan American Airways after almost thirty-seven years, logging over 27,000 hours (five thousand of which in the Boeing 747).

Scribner is the author of many technical papers, magazine articles, films, and lecture presentations throughout the world on aviational subjects. *Your Future in Aviation: On the Ground* and *Your Future in Aviation: In the Air* are devoted to vocational guidance of high school and college students interested in aviation careers.

HOBBIES AND OTHER INTERESTS: Sailplane flying.

FOR MORE INFORMATION SEE:

Avion, November 18, 1981.

SHANNON, Jacqueline

PERSONAL: Born in Los Angeles, Calif.; daughter of Eugene Jack (an educator) and Louise Ann (an educator; maiden name, Garry) Farmer; married Stephen Trobaugh (a photographer/videographer), September 5, 1981; children: Madeline. *Education:* San Diego State University, B.A. (with honors), 1979. *Home and office:* 4454 Normandie Place, La Mesa, Calif. 92041. *Agent:* Lisa Bankoff, International Creative Management, 40 West 57th St., New York, N.Y. 10019.

CAREER: Fotofax (magazine), La Jolla, Calif., editor, 1979-82; *Desert* (magazine), San Diego, Calif., editor, 1982-83; free-lance writer, 1983—. *Member:* American Society of Journalists and Authors, Authors Guild. *Awards, honors:* Received several writing, photography, and editing awards from the International Association of Business Communicators as editor of *Fotofax;* Delacorte Press Prize for an Outstanding First Young Adult Novel Honorable Mention, 1984, for *Too Much T. J.*

WRITINGS:

Too Much T. J., Delacorte, 1986.
Upstaged, Avon, 1987.
Big Guy, Little Women, Scholastic, 1989.
Faking It, Avon, 1989.
Why Would Anyone Have a Crush on Horace Beems?, Scholastic, 1991.

Contributor of articles and short stories to periodicals, including *Co-ed, 'Teen, Girls Only, Sourcebook, 18 Almanac, On Your Own, College Woman, Seventeen, Working Parents, Health, Family Living, San Diego Reader, Lady's Circle, Newsday, Bestways, Writer's Digest, National Motorist, Friendly Exchange, Women's Health Adviser, Working Woman, Executive Female, Woman Engineer, Ms., California Today, Parenting, Parenting Adviser, Special Reports, Reader's Digest,* and *Air California.*

WORK IN PROGRESS: A novel for middle-grade readers tentatively titled, *I Hate My Hero;* a supernatural thriller for adults.

SIDELIGHTS: "In the last ten years, I have traveled extensively around the United States and Canada on a variety of assignments and talked to hundreds of people, but mostly teens. I have great empathy for and interest in this age group because I remember my own teen years with utter clarity (and six hundred handwritten diary pages). I could have had a charmed Southern California adolescence . . . had I not been so desperately unhappy practically every minute of it, thanks partially to raging hormones that had me shooting up eight inches and out eight bra sizes within two years. I knew by the time I was twenty that I wanted to devote several years to writing for teens. And in the last pages of that six-volume diary, I vowed that I would never write 'preachy' books or stories—because I hated them myself—unless the message was one or more of the 'three great truths' I wish I'd known as a teen: That if you hang in there long enough it gets better; that outside of high school it's actually an advantage to be different; and that despite appearances, *nobody* has it all together.

"I still believe it.

"Like most authors, the questions I am asked most by young people are 'Where do you get your ideas? Do they come from things that have happened to you?' And I tell them, no, every time I have tried to thinly disguise an incident from my own past for the purpose of fiction, it has come out too melodramatic and overwrought or the heroine (me!) is too smarmy or self-righteous or perfect to be true while everyone else is severely flawed, either in character or in the way they treat this poor girl! Maybe I am still too young to be unbiased about adolescence . . . particularly my own.

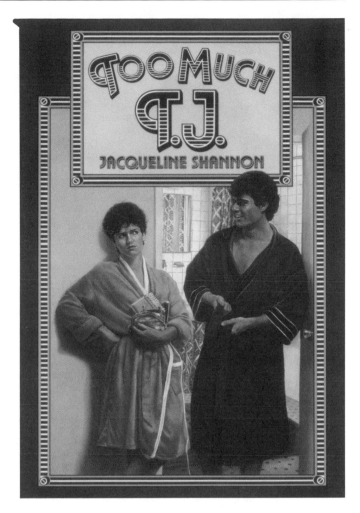

I'd have to start getting up fifteen minutes earlier so that I could beat him to the shower. (Jacket illustration by Bob Travers from *Too Much T. J.* by Jacqueline Shannon.)

"I do, however, freely use settings—as opposed to experiences—from my own past. For example, I was very active in theater in high school and I remember that each of our productions was rife with backstage backstabbing, upstaging, romances, rivalries, self-doubts, moments of soaring confidence, and sharing of long-kept secrets. In other words, every emotion was magnified by the tension and excitement of the production. I was 'collecting' settings for future use even back then and I was sure that someday I'd find the right story to fit that one . . . and I did with *Upstaged.*

"My own personal reactions and feelings when confronted with a situation are also well represented in my books. For example, I remember how horrible it was, after fighting with and suspending all communication with my best friend, to have to face the rest of our crowd the next day while in this feuding state. It was so difficult to have to go to school and pretend—for the sake of pride, especially in front of my best friend—that everything was just fine and dandy. And it was unbearable to have no special person to sit next to at lunch or to walk the halls with between classes. Though it was standard practice, attempts to temporarily latch onto someone else were viewed as pathetic and selfish and transparent. If the 'temporary' did allow herself to be used in such a fashion, I would then have to contend with my guilt feelings upon dumping her the second my 'real' best friend and I made up. I

JACQUELINE SHANNON

remember the dynamics, the importance of, and the misery of this fight-with-a-best-friend situation so well that I have purposely staged such fights in five of the six books I've written so far. (I recently wrote to a twelve-year-old aspiring writer that in some ways, being a writer makes painful feelings more bearable. Whenever something crummy happens to you, you can always think: 'There's a purpose to this. I have to live through this or I will never be able to write convincingly about the feeling.')

"Although my own experiences are off limits, I do ruthlessly steal bits and pieces of the experiences of friends and acquaintances, building on them by continuously asking 'What if . . . ? What if . . . ?' which is, to me, the foundation of fiction. My best friend in junior high, for example, was very disturbed when her divorced mother announced plans to marry a particular man. He had a very good-looking sixteen-year-old son and Annie was worried about how she and this boy would handle things if, after they moved into the same house, they became romantically attracted to each other. As it turned out, they were at each other's throats within two weeks. But my thirteen-year-old self mentally filed the possibility—What if one or both of them *had* fallen in love?—and many years later that 'What if?' was the inspiration for my first YA novel, *Too Much T. J.*

"I first considered writing as a career in junior high school, where I did a stint as the editor of the school newspaper and also contributed stories, poems, and essays to local and state literary magazines for students. But when I got to high school, the drama bug bit hard and I was convinced that acting was my destiny. It was a short-lived destiny . . . eight seconds, to be exact. That's how long it took me to open an envelope one afternoon when I was sixteen to discover that I'd sold my first short story. *Co-ed,* a magazine for teenage girls that was distributed through home economics classes, paid $300 for 'Almost.' I was hooked on writing once and for all. In the weeks after I cashed that first check, I kept thinking smugly 'Writing for money is so easy . . . . I can do this forever.' Well, it was pure beginner's luck, I would say, because although I wrote and submitted reams to scores of magazines, I didn't sell another thing for four long years."

HOBBIES AND OTHER INTERESTS: Reading, travel, "long lunches in new restaurants with old friends."

FOR MORE INFORMATION SEE:

Los Angeles Times, November 5, 1986.

SHAW, Arnold 1909-1989

OBITUARY NOTICE—See sketch in *SATA* Volume 4: Born June 28, 1909, in New York, N.Y.; died of cancer, September 26, 1989, in Las Vegas, Nev. Music publicist and publisher, composer, educator, and author. Shaw, an authority on twentieth-century American popular music, worked during the 1950s and 1960s to promote such performers as Elvis Presley, Paul Simon, and Burt Bacharach. He is credited with bringing Elvis Presley to national prominence by persuading northern radio stations to play his records. Shaw began his career in the 1940s as a pianist and composer and later taught music at the University of Nevada. He founded the Popular Music Research Center in 1985 and wrote several books about popular music, including biographies on singers Frank Sinatra and Harry Belafonte, *The*

Rock Revolution, Dictionary of American Pop/Rock, and *The Street That Never Slept: New York's Fabled 52nd Street,* a book that led to the establishment of the New York City thoroughfare—once famous for its jazz nightclubs—as an official historical landmark.

FOR MORE INFORMATION SEE:

Contemporary Authors New Revision Series, Volume 1, Gale, 1981.
Who's Who in American Music, Bowker, 1985.

OBITUARIES

Los Angeles Times, October 6, 1989.
New York Times, October 7, 1989.
Chicago Tribune, October 9, 1989.
Contemporary Authors, Volume 129, Gale, 1990.

SHIRTS, Morris A(lpine) 1922-

PERSONAL: Born April 11, 1922, in Escalante, Utah; son of Morris (a farmer) and Neta (a housewife; maiden name, Hall) Shirts; married Dorothy Maxin Baird (a business education teacher), 1945; children: Russell, Randy, Andrea, Robert, Steven. *Education:* Dixie College, A.S., 1942; Brigham Young University, B.A., 1947, M.A., 1950; Indiana University, Ed.D., 1952. *Politics:* Republican. *Religion:* Church of Jesus Christ of Latter-Day Saints (Mormons). *Home:* 570 South 580th W., Cedar City, Utah 84720.

CAREER: North Sanpete High School, Mount Pleasant, Utah, teacher of mathematics, physics, radio, and chemistry, 1947-50, district audio-visual supervisor, 1949-50; Brigham Young University, Provo, Utah, assistant professor of education, 1952-57; National Teachers College, Tehran, Iran, visiting professor of education, 1957-59; Southern Utah State College, Cedar City, associate professor, 1959-64, chairman of department, 1964-65, professor of education, 1965-83, dean of School of Education, 1965-72, professor emeritus, 1983—. Member, Utah Bicentennial Commission. *Military service:* Twentieth Air Force, 1942-45, served in Burma, China, India, and the Southwest Pacific; received Air Medal and presidential citation; Utah National Guard, 1948-50.

WRITINGS:

Warm Up for Little League Baseball, Sterling, 1971, revised edition, Archway, 1989.
Playing with a Football, Sterling, 1972.
Call It Right: Umpiring in the Little League, Sterling, 1977.

Contributor to periodicals, including *Utah Historical Quarterly, Utah Education Review, American School Board Journal, Teaching Tools, School Executive, Boston Globe,* and *National Association of Secondary School Principals Bulletin.*

WORK IN PROGRESS: The Restless Saint, the life of his great-great-grandfather; *Past Times,* true stories about the settlement of southern Utah and adjacent areas; *Trail Furnace: The Story of Iron Making in Utah 1850-1858;* with Paul D. Proctor, *Silver, Sandstone, Saints, and Sinners: The Story of Silver Reef, Utah.*

MORRIS A. SHIRTS

SIDELIGHTS: "The first experience I had with youth baseball was devastating. My first son wanted to play but lacked the necessary skills to be accepted on a team. This was my fault, as I had been too busy in my professional life to teach him. I talked with several parents with similar problems and we organized 'Peanut League' for the rejected players then took an active part in teaching them the skills. The more I worked with these kids, the more I recognized the important role adults played in the lives of young boys and girls. Many of them were really disenfranchised during summers of exciting youth programs [supervised] by uninterested or uncaring parents. I also learned that most parents lack the basic skills themselves. To compound the problem, mothers, who did not know the game nor had the necessary skills, were trying to substitute for fathers in teaching their children to play baseball.

"The idea of writing a book to help them began to develop in my mind as I struggled with these problems. My first manuscript was called 'Little League Baseball for Adults.' I could not find a publisher. Finally Sterling Publishing Company suggested that I rewrite it in the language of children. This I did using a basic word list for sixth graders. The rest is history. The book has been revised in fairness to girls and minority groups and undergone several printings.

"I get letters from young baseball players who like the book. Occasionally I get comments from mothers. One in particular said 'I taught my son how to play baseball from that book! It is my baseball Bible.'

"It gives me a deep satisfaction to learn that the book has been instrumental in improving the baseball skills of American youth and contributing to the enjoyment of the great national pastime.

"My high school teaching career was punctuated with one of my chemistry students placing among the forty National Westinghouse Science Contest winners and several students in our high school radio station gaining recognition in radio electronics and engineering. I also played a key role in getting four-year status for Southern Utah State College."

HOBBIES AND OTHER INTERESTS: Collecting and restoring Studebakers, amateur radio, KA7PUZ, scouting, restoration of Mountain Meadow Massacre monument, Boy Scout camp "Thunder Ridge."

SIMUNDSSON, Elva 1950-

PERSONAL: Born January 28, 1950, in Manitoba, Canada; daughter of Gunnar (a farmer) and Margaret (a homemaker; maiden name, Halldorsson) Simundsson; married Jerry Jonasson (a physical education teacher). *Education:* Attended University of North Dakota, 1969-70; University of

Manitoba, B.A., 1981; University of British Columbia, M.L.S., 1983. *Politics:* Social Democrat. *Religion:* Avowed Atheist. *Home:* Gimli, Manitoba, Canada. *Office:* Library, Canadian Grain Commission, 303 Main St., Winnipeg, Manitoba, Canada R3C 3G7.

CAREER: Manitoba Museum of Man and Nature, Winnipeg, Canada, cataloguer, 1983-84; Agriculture Canada, Brandon, Manitoba, Canada, information specialist, 1984-88; Canadian Grain Commission, Winnipeg, Manitoba, Canada, information specialist, 1988—. Director, Icelandic National League, Manitoba Intercultural Council, and Icelandic Language Camp. *Member:* Canadian Association of Special Libraries and Information Services (past chairman; Manitoba chapter).

WRITINGS:

Icelandic Settlers in America, Queenston House, 1981.
Fjallkonas of the Islendingadagur (title means "Women of the Icelandic Festival"), INL, 1989.

WORK IN PROGRESS: A retelling of Icelandic folktales and children's stories.

SIDELIGHTS: "I grew up on a farm in rural prairie Canada. In my community the settlement was only two generations old, our farm was homesteaded by my grandfather. The whole community was Icelandic-Canadian. Everyone in my home and all the neighbours spoke Icelandic as a first language. My whole cultural upbringing was a unique blend of Icelandic foods and traditions adapted into a prairie setting.

"Folktales told of elves and trolls in the mountains were very real in my imagination, but totally alien in reality for being brought up on the prairie flatlands. I had never seen a mountain.

"Our home was always full of friends and relatives from Iceland. My father was a well-respected member of the Icelandic cultural community and our farm was the focus of many visits from a variety of officials and important guests who wanted to meet a typical Icelandic-Canadian farm family. Myself and my six brothers and sisters were also part of the show. My mother coached us in memorizing poetry by highly respected Icelandic-Canadian and Icelandic poets and we performed on cue. The resulting brainwashing was inevitable. I will never be 'just a Canadian,' but an 'Icelandic-Canadian.' When the opportunity for a grant from the Canadian Secretary of State for Multiculturalism came about, I jumped at the chance to write about my people. Many of the stories in my book are personal recollections from my parents or friends in the neighbourhood.

"I have been a director of the Icelandic Language and Cultural Camp for Manitoba kids for many years. I have taught Icelandic language classes and am presently a director on the board of the Icelandic National League of North America. I have been appointed to a provincial government agency that advises the province of Manitoba on multicultural issues and distributes lottery funds to multicultural organizations in the province. The whole involvement sticks to me like a second skin.

"I have enjoyed my participation in conferences and events related to multicultural and cross-cultural understanding.

Discovering other cultures has been a rich and rewarding experience. I have been an avid hockey player, a swimming instructor, and golfer."

SOMMER-BODENBURG, Angela 1948-

PERSONAL: Born December 18, 1948, in Reinbek, West Germany; daughter of Karlheinz (an optician) and Anneliese (a secretary; maiden name, Steinbeck) Schockert; married Burghardt Bodenburg (a private secretary), December 27, 1978; children: Katja. *Education:* University of Hamburg, Assistant Master for Intermediate and Secondary Schools, 1972. *Home and office:* Dorfstrasse 13, 2371 Prinzenmoor, West Germany. *Agent:* Burghardt Bodenburg, Dorfstrasse 13, 2371 Prinzenmoor, West Germany.

CAREER: Assistant master for intermediate and secondary school, Hamburg, West Germany, 1972-84; free-lance writer, 1984—. *Awards, honors: If You Want to Scare Yourself* was selected one of New York Public Library's Children's Books, 1989, and a Children's Choice of the International Reading Association and the Children's Book Council, 1990.

WRITINGS:

Sarah bei den Woelfen: Gedichte (title means "Sarah and the Wolves: Poems"), Suhrkamp, 1979.
Der kleine Vampir, Rowohlt Taschenbuch, 1979, translation by Sarah Gibson published in England as *The Little Vampire,* Andersen, 1982, published in the United States

ANGELA SOMMER-BODENBURG

as *My Friend the Vampire* (illustrated by Amelie Glienke), Dial, 1984.

Der kleine Vampir zieht um, Rowohlt Taschenbuch, 1980, translation by S. Gibson published as *The Little Vampire Moves In,* Andersen, 1982, published in the United States as *The Vampire Moves In* (illustrated by A. Glienke), Dial, 1985.

Das Biest, das im Regen kam (title means "The Beast That Came in the Rain"), Rowohlt Taschenbuch, 1981.

Der kleine Vampir verreist, Rowohlt Taschenbuch, 1982, translation by S. Gibson published as *The Little Vampire Takes a Trip* (illustrated by A. Glienke), Andersen, 1984, published in the United States as *The Vampire Takes a Trip,* Dial, 1985.

Ich lieb dich trotzdem immer (poems; illustrated by H. Heine), Gertraud Middelhauve, 1982, published in England as *But Still, I Love Her Just the Same,* Burke, 1985.

Der kleine Vampir auf dem Bauernhof, Rowohlt Taschenbuch, 1983, translation by S. Gibson published in England as *The Little Vampire on the Farm* (illustrated by A. Glienke), Andersen, 1985, published in the United States as *The Vampire on the Farm,* Dial, 1989.

Der kleine Vampir: Alle vier Geschichten in einem Band (title means "The Little Vampire: Four Stories in One Volume"), Rowohlt, 1983.

Wenn du dich gruseln willst, Ravensburger Buchverlag, 1984, translation by Renee Vera Cafiero published in the United States as *If You Want to Scare Yourself,* Harper, 1989.

Der kleine Vampir und die grosse Liebe, Rowohlt Taschenbuch, 1985, translation by S. Gibson published in England as *The Little Vampire in Love* (illustrated by A. Glienke), Andersen, 1986.

Der kleine Vampir in Gefahr (title means "The Little Vampire in Danger"), Rowohlt Taschenbuch, 1985.

Die Moorgeister (title means "Moor Ghosts"), Rowohlt/Wunderlich, 1986.

Der kleine Vampir im Jammertal (title means "The Little Vampire in the Valley of Doom"), Rowohlt Taschenbuch, 1986.

Coco geht zum Geburtstag (illustrated by Agnes Mathieu), Ravensburger Buchverlag, 1986, published in England as *Coco's Birthday Surprise,* Hamish Hamilton, 1987.

Kuecuek Vampir: Der kleine Vampir, tuerkisch-deutsche Ausgabe (title means "The Little Vampire, Turkish-German Offering"), Rowohlt Taschenbuch, 1987.

Moewen und Woelfe: Gedichte (title means "Seagulls and Wolves: Poems"), Rowohlt, 1987.

Freu dich nicht zu frueh, ich verlass' dich nie! Gedichte (title means "Don't Get Happy Too Soon, I Will Never Leave You: Poems"; illustrated by Anne Wilsdorf), Rowohlt, 1987.

Der kleine Vampir liest vor (title means "The Little Vampire Reads"), Rowohlt Taschenbuch, 1988.

Die Unterirdischen (title means "The Subterraneans"; illustrated by Magdalene Hanke-Basfeld), C. Bertelsmann, 1988.

Julia bei den Lebenslichtern (title means "Julia and the Lamps of Life"; illustrated by Irmtraut Korth-Sander), C. Bertelsmann, 1989.

Anton und der kleine Vampir: Der geheimnisvolle Patient (title means "Tony and the Little Vampire: The Mysterious Patient"), C. Bertelsmann, 1989.

Anton und der kleine Vampir: In der Hoehle des Loewen (title means "Tony and the Little Vampire: In the Lion's Den"), C. Bertelsmann, 1989.

Anton und der kleine Vampir: Das raetselhafte Programm (title means "Tony and the Little Vampire: The Enigmatical Program"), C. Bertelsmann, 1989.

Anton und der kleine Vampir: Boese Ueberraschungen (title means "Tony and the Little Vampire: Bad Surprises"), C. Bertelsmann, 1989.

Anton und der kleine Vampir: Die grosse Verschwoerung (title means "Tony and the Little Vampire: The Great Plot"), C. Bertelsmann, 1989.

Anton und der kleine Vampir: Die Klassenfahrt (title means "Tony and the Little Vampire: The Class Trip"), C. Bertelsmann, 1990.

Anton und der kleine Vampir: Froehliche Weihnachten! (title means "Tony and the Little Vampire: Happy Christmas"), C. Bertelsmann, 1990.

Gerneklein (title means "He Doesn't Want to Grow Up"), C. Bertelsmann, 1990.

Florians gesammelte Gruselgeschichten (title means "Freddy's Collected Scary Stories"; sequel to *If You Want to Scare Yourself*), C. Bertelsmann, 1990.

Sommer-Bodenburg's books have been published in the United States, Iceland, Belgium, Brazil, Denmark, Finland, France, England, Greece, Indonesia, Israel, Italy, Japan, Netherlands, Norway, Portugal, Spain, Sweden, and Turkey.

ADAPTATIONS:

"Der kleine Vampir" (thirteen-part international television production; based on *Der kleine Vampir* and *Der kleine Vampir zieht um*), German Television, 1986.

"Der kleine Vampir" (play), first performed in Tampere, Finland, 1988, first performed in Cologne, Germany, 1989.

RECORDINGS

"Wenn du dich gruseln willst," Karussell/Polygram, 1987.

"Der kleine Vampir," BMG Ariola, 1989.

"Der kleine Vampir zieht um," BMG Ariola, 1989.

"Der kleine Vampir verreist," BMG Ariola, 1989.

"Der kleine Vampir auf dem Bauernhof," BMG Ariola, 1989.

"Der kleine Vampir und die grosse Liebe," BMG Ariola, 1989.

"Der kleine Vampir in Gefahr," BMG Ariola, 1989.

"Der kleine Vampir im Jammertal," BMG Ariola, 1989.

"Der kleine Vampir liest vor," BMG Ariola, 1989.

"Anton und der kleine Vampir: Der geheimnisvolle Patient," BMG Ariola, 1990.

"Anton und der kleine Vampir: In der Hoehle des Loewen," BMG Ariola, 1990.

"Anton und der kleine Vampir: Das raetselhafte Programm," BMG Ariola, 1990.

"Anton und der kleine Vampir: Boese Ueberraschungen," BMG Ariola, 1990.

"Anton und der kleine Vampir: Die grosse Verschwoerung," BMG Ariola, 1990.

"Die Unterirdischen" (title means "The Subterraneans"), German Broadcasting, 1990.

WORK IN PROGRESS: Poems about teddy bears; a picture book done in watercolors; a series about a huge dog that talks and likes chocolate; "The Little Vampire: Musical," pop music combined with classical music; "The Little Vampire: Animated Movie"; *The Little Vampire Visits Count Dracula;* "Der kleine Vampir verreist and Der Kleine Vampir auf dem Bauernhof," a thirteen-part television production for German-TV.

Then suddenly her eye fell on the closet, and with a cry of "Aha! Then what's this?" she seized a mysterious piece of black cloth, which was sticking out from under the closet door. (Illustration by Amelie Glienke from *My Friend the Vampire* by Angela Sommer-Bodenburg.)

SIDELIGHTS: "From the very beginning of my childhood I knew that I would become a writer. But I didn't know that I would finally become a writer for young readers. I first published lyrics, poems, and short stories in periodicals. Then I became a teacher, and I learned that my students weren't fond of reading. They preferred playing football instead. I didn't want to accept this behaviour and I asked them why they didn't like reading. 'Books are boring' was the most frequent answer. So I asked them what kind of books they would be willing to read. They answered, *'Books should be exciting, thrilling, creepy, and funny.'*

"From my first- to fourth-grade students I have learned what they like to listen to and read. Their imagination is peopled with monsters, Marsmen, ghosts, and vampires. They have not encountered such creatures but are quite capable of imagining that a vampire will sit on their windowsill one evening. And this is where my story of *The Little Vampire* starts. However, my vampire is not a blood-thirsty monster but rather an affectionate little vampire with fears and foibles who will perhaps help children get rid of their fears.

"In those days there weren't any books of that kind in the school libraries. So I started to write the first fifteen pages of *The Little Vampire,* chapter 1: The Thing at the Window. I sent these fifteen pages to one of the leading German publishers for young readers. His comment was 'not suitable for young readers.'

"I sent the manuscript to a second publisher, and after months, I got the answer that they would publish the story under the condition that I would write 100 pages more. What a shock! I wasn't sure whether I would be able to write so many pages, since I was only used to writing poems or short stories.

"In March of 1979 *The Little Vampire* was published, and I knew that my Little Vampire was a very strong character, like Mickey Mouse, and too good for only one book. That was the beginning of my 'Little Vampire Empire' that is spread all over the world. There have been more than 3.5 million copies of the series sold worldwide.

"Caroline Seebohm wrote in the *New York Times Book Review,* 'Angela Sommer-Bodenburg's *The Vampire Moves In* should show any anxious mother or father that horror stories are not only good clean fun, but also provide a healthy release for the inchoate fears of childhood.'

"I am happy that I have succeeded in writing books that young readers love to read, and that even their parents and grandfathers love to read too.

"Regarding the future, and the many ideas for new books I have in mind, I just do hope that I will have sufficient time in my life to realize all of them."

HOBBIES AND OTHER INTERESTS: Writing, painting, reading, her animals (a Hungarian sheepdog, a Spanish sheepdog, a sheep, a chinchilla, and a squirrel).

FOR MORE INFORMATION SEE:

Hans Gaertner, *Almanach der Kinder- und Jugendliteratur,* Neugebauer Press, 1981.
Kuerschners Deutscher Literatur-Kalender, de Gruyter, 1981.
Spektrum des Geistes, Literaturkalender 1990, Husum-Druck, 1989.

SORENSON, Jane 1926-

PERSONAL: Born May 7, 1926 in Oak Park, Ill.; daughter of Walter H. (a newspaper publisher) and Olga (a homemaker; maiden name, Volle) Buescher; married Melvin J. Sorenson (an executive), June 19, 1948; children: Stephen W., Linda Jane. *Education:* Illinois School of Journalism, B.S., 1948. *Religion:* Christian (Evangelical).

CAREER: Free-lance writer, 1948—; *Christian Advocate,* Chicago, Ill., assistant editor, 1949-52, book review editor, 1949-55; Wheaton College, Wheaton, Ill., writing instructor, 1959-70; *Trails* and *Reflection* (magazines), Wheaton, Ill., editor, 1970-72. *Member:* Society of Children's Book Writers.

WRITINGS:

(With Patricia Burke and Marie Frost) *Adventures from God's Word,* Standard, 1983.

It's Me, Jennifer (illustrated by Helen Endres), Standard, 1984.

It's Your Move, Jennifer (illustrated by H. Endres), Standard, 1984.

Jennifer's New Life (illustrated by H. Endres), Standard, 1984.

Jennifer Says Goodbye (illustrated by H. Endres), Standard, 1984.

Boy Friend (illustrated by H. Endres), Standard, 1985.

Once Upon a Friendship (illustrated by H. Endres), Standard, 1985.

Fifteen Hands (illustrated by H. Endres), Standard, 1985.

In Another Land (illustrated by H. Endres), Standard, 1985.

Time Out for God, Standard, 1985.

Time Out for God, No. 2, Standard, 1985.

Five Minutes with God, Standard, 1985.

Five Minutes with God, No. 2 (illustrated by Steve Hayes), Standard, 1985.

The New Pete (illustrated by H. Endres), Standard, 1986.

Out with the In Crowd (illustrated by H. Endres), Standard, 1986.

Another Jennifer (illustrated by H. Endres), Standard, 1986.

Family Crisis (illustrated by H. Endres), Standard, 1986.

Hi, I'm Katie Hooper (illustrated by Kathleen L. Smith), Standard, 1988.

Home Sweet Haunted Home (illustrated by K. L. Smith), Standard, 1988.

Happy Birth Day (illustrated by K. L. Smith), Standard, 1988.

Stephanie has one of those voices that isn't really loud, but it sort of stands out. (Cover illustration from *Another Jennifer* by Jane Sorenson.)

Honor Roll (illustrated by K. L. Smith), Standard, 1988.

Quiet Moments with Young Children (illustrated by Diane Johnson), Standard, 1988.

Quiet Moments with Older Children (illustrated by Rob Parker), Standard, 1988.

Angels on Holiday (illustrated by K. L. Smith), Standard, 1989.

First Job (illustrated by K. L. Smith), Standard, 1989.

Left Behind, Standard, 1989.

The New Me, Standard, 1989.

WORK IN PROGRESS: An Ordinary Woman, an autobiographical story of my spiritual pilgrimage.

SIDELIGHTS: "I wrote my first 'book' in seventh grade. Called 'Camping Out,' it described my adventures with my cousins at a state park in southern Indiana. I bound it in green. To this day, it's a source of laughter at family reunions!

"In eighth grade, I had to research a career and write a 'book' about it. With much anguish and family consultation, I decided to write about journalism. Frankly, I was in my thirties before it occurred to me that I could have changed my mind! I have no idea what happened to the 'book!'

"I guess I was a 'pathfinder' during my children's growing up years! Although I felt my family was my priority, I juggled

JANE SORENSON

babysitters like women do today! I always kept my finger in something connected with writing.

"The books are a recent career. My very first contract called for a series of four young teen novels! The resulting twelve 'Jennifer' books can be read 'in order' as a continued story. Jennifer spends most of the series in eighth grade.

"Because I have the advantage of writing about the same people, my characters experience growth and change. For example, Jennifer's mother begins the series as a stay-at-home mom, but by the twelfth book, she has a nice little career going. Meanwhile, Jennifer's father goes from east coast vice-president to losing his job!

"Each book in the series can be read independently and deals with a different theme. For example, *Jennifer Says Goodbye* deals with death; *Out with the In Crowd* is about partying; *Another Jennifer* is about prejudice.

"Starting all over with another set of characters for the new 'Katie Hooper' series was a challenge. What I did was select a minor character from the 'Jennifer' books, Aunt Elizabeth, who appears briefly in book four and has a somewhat mysterious past. I always wondered what happened and what her kids would be like! Actually, Aunt Elizabeth is the *mother* in the new 'Katie Hooper' series!

"Since I'm probably more like Jennifer, writing about Katie is stretching me! The new heroine has almost nothing in common with her cousin! She's a second child (Jennifer's the oldest); she lives in a small town in Colorado (not Philadelphia); the family is poor (the father paints mountains!); Katie's messy, irresponsible, laid back, and generous.

"I love the surprises that happen as I write! For example, when the Hoopers lose their cabin and are looking for a new place to live (in the first book), I planned to have them move into a small bi-level house on a city lot. (The challenge would be to bring all their creativity to this uncreative setting.) But while they were going through the house with a realtor, the door opened. Suddenly, January (the dog) barked! And I found the realtor unwilling to rent to anyone with pets! I was 'stuck' until they found an old Victorian wreck held by the bank. That's when I realized I had my second book in the series—a haunted house story!"

HOBBIES AND OTHER INTERESTS: Needy Third-World children, antiques, visiting historical sites, staying at country inns.

SOUSTER, (Holmes) Raymond 1921-
(John Holmes, Raymond Holmes)

PERSONAL: Surname rhymes with "Gloucester"; born January 15, 1921, in Toronto, Ontario, Canada; son of Austin Holmes (a bank employee) and Norma (a housewife; maiden name, Baker) Souster; married Rosalia Lena Geralde (a bank clerk), June 24, 1947. *Education:* Attended Humberside Collegiate Institute, 1938-39. *Politics:* New Democratic Party. *Religion:* United Church of Canada. *Home:* 39 Baby Point Rd., Toronto, Ontario, Canada M6S 2G2.

CAREER: Poet and editor. Canadian Imperial Bank of Commerce, Toronto, Ontario, accountant, 1939-84. *Military*

service: Royal Canadian Air Force, 1941-45; leading aircraftsman. *Member:* League of Canadian Poets. *Awards, honors:* Canada's Governor-General Award, 1964, for *The Colour of the Times;* President's Medal from the University of Western Ontario, 1967, for Best Canadian Poem; Centennial Medal from the Canadian Government, 1967; Canadian Silver Jubilee Medal from the Canadian Government, 1977; City of Toronto Literary Award, 1979, for *Hanging In.*

WRITINGS:

JUVENILE

The Flight of the Roller Coaster: Poems for Younger Readers, Oberon, 1985.

POETRY

When We Are Young, First Statement Press, 1946.
Go to Sleep, World, Ryerson, 1947.
City Hall Street, Ryerson, 1951.
Selected Poems, Contact Press, 1956.
Crepe-hanger's Carnival: Selected Poems, 1955-58, Contact Press, 1958.
Place of Meeting: Poems, 1958-60, Gallery Editions, 1962.
A Local Pride: Poems, Contact Press, 1962.
The Colour of the Times: The Collected Poems, Ryerson, 1964.
Twelve New Poems, Goosetree Press, 1964.
Ten Elephants on Yonge Street, Ryerson, 1965.
As Is, Oxford University Press, 1967.

RAYMOND SOUSTER

Lost & Found: Uncollected Poems by Raymond Souster, Clarke, Irwin, 1968.
So Far So Good: Poems 1938/1968, Oberon, 1969.
The Years, Oberon, 1971.
Selected Poems, Oberon, 1972.
Change-Up, Oberon, 1974.
Double-Header, Oberon, 1975.
Rain-Check, Oberon, 1975.
Extra Innings, Oberon, 1977.
Hanging In, Oberon, 1979.
Collected Poems of Raymond Souster, Oberon, Volume I: *1940-1955,* 1980, Volume II: *1955-1962,* 1981, Volume III: *1962-1974,* 1982, Volume IV: *1974-1977,* 1983, Volume V: *1977-1983,* 1984, Volume VI: *1984-1986,* 1989.
Going the Distance, Oberon, 1983.
(With Bill Brooks) *Queen City,* Oberon, 1984.
It Takes All Kinds, Oberon, 1985.
The Eyes of Love, Oberon, 1987.
Asking for More, Oberon, 1988.
Running Out the Clock, Oberon, 1990.

OTHER

(Contributor) Ronald Hambleton, editor, *Unit of Five,* Ryerson, 1944.
(Under pseudonym Raymond Holmes) *The Winter of Time* (novel), Export Publishing, 1950.
(Compiler) *Poets 56: Ten Younger English-Canadians,* Contact Press, 1965.
(Editor with John Robert Colombo) *Shapes and Sounds: Poems of W. W. E. Ross,* Longmans, Green, 1968.
(Editor) *Made in Canada,* Oberon Press, 1970.
(Editor) *New Wave Canada,* Contact Press, 1970.
(Editor with Richard Woollatt) *Generation Now* (poetry anthology), Longmans, Green, 1970.
(Under pseudonym John Holmes) *On Target* (novel), Village Book Store Press, 1973.
(Editor with R. Woollatt) *Sights and Sounds* (poetry anthology), Macmillan (Toronto), 1973.
(Editor with Douglas Lochhead) *100 Poems of Nineteenth Century Canada* (poetry anthology), Macmillan (Toronto), 1974.
(Editor with R. Woollatt) *These Loved, These Hated Lands* (poetry anthology), Doubleday (Toronto), 1975.
(Compiler and author of introduction) *Vapour and Blue: Souster Selects Campbell* (selected poetry of William Wilfred Campbell), Paget Press, 1978.
(With Douglas Alcorn) *From Hell to Breakfast* (war memoirs), Intruder Press, 1978.
(Editor) *Comfort of the Fields* (selected poetry of Archibald Lampman), Paget Press, 1979.
(Editor with R. Woollatt) *Poems of a Snow-Eyed Country* (poetry anthology), Academic Press of Canada, 1980.
Jubilee of Death: The Raid on Dieppe, Oberon Press, 1984.
(With James Deahl) *Into This Dark Earth,* Unfinished Monument Press, 1985.
(Editor with Douglas Lochhead) *Windflower: Selected Poems of Bliss Carman,* Tecumseh, 1986.
(Editor with D. Lochhead) *Powassan's Drum: Selected Poems of Duncan Campbell Scott,* Tecumseh, 1986.

WORK IN PROGRESS: Another book of verse.

SIDELIGHTS: "About the age of eight or nine I must have begun to notice the world of nature spread out all around me. Which perhaps is surprising for a big city boy to say, except that through all those growing-up years I was fortunate enough to be living in the west end of the city of Toronto, Canada. Here I was never more than a five-minute walk away

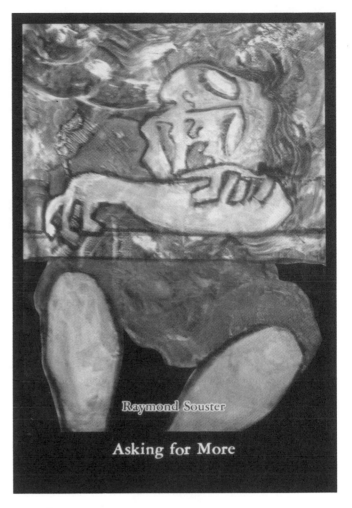

(Cover art from "Sleeping Woman" by Janet Moore in *Asking for More* by Raymond Souster.)

from what still seems to me the most beautiful river valley ever carved out of the earth.

"This was the Humber Valley, with its river completing three last lazy miles of flowing southward before emptying into Lake Ontario, the second smallest of the Great Lakes and along which Toronto was originally built. Here it passed between high rocky cliffs crowned with tall forests all the way from the Dundas Street Bridge to my favourite, the tiny Old Mill Bridge, a distance of perhaps a mile and a half. It was this small stretch of river that I made into my own little private world, first in my explorations and then, from the age of thirteen, in my first attempts at poetry. And as the boy so the man—I still return to it as often as I can sixty years later, living even closer to it now than I did in those early days.

"But there was also a second stretch of that valley, which, though I visited it much less often then, I still grew to love for its own special charm. This other part of my private childhood world began at the Old Mill Bridge and continued south past the ruins of Tom Fisher's Mill to its first landmark, the proud, newly-built giant of the Bloor Street Bridge, with its eighty-foot pillars rising up dizzily from the shallow river bed below.

"Here the Humber suddenly stretched out to a stream over twice its normal width, and with those same high wooded cliffs on either side, moved leisurely on for the best part of a mile. Then for no apparent reason it took a sharp turn left, running eastward for another half mile before straightening out for its final southerly leg. Here were huge marshlands, the haunts of strange birds with long, slender legs, filled to overflowing with wild grasses, marigolds, and acres of bullrushes a foot taller than any of us. We kids had them soon divided into three separate marshes, of which Second Marsh made the best huge natural ice-rink for our bone-chilling, mid-winter ice-hockey games. It was also down on this stretch of river in a later heat-wave summer that we stumbled across two giant mud turtles, their bodies attached to slimy, slightly-curved shells which we measured in our heads as at least four feet across. Somehow these awesome creatures had been left high and dry up on the river bank. Of course by a succession of dares hurled at each other we children eventually managed to walk across the slippery backs of those pitiful river dwellers, which very soon smelt to high heaven and proved too big an obstacle for even our eager curiosity. Then early that fall they both disappeared from that river bank as mysteriously as they had first appeared.

"Of course it was inevitable that my favourite upper part of that valley would change very much with the passing years. The Old Dundas Street Bridge was swept away like a matchstick by Hurricane Hazel in '53. The small falls not far below

GOING THE DISTANCE
RAYMOND SOUSTER

(Cover art by Jo Manning from *Going the Distance* by Raymond Souster.)

that ill-fated bridge with its six-foot drop into boiling, murky water where we skinny-dipped often in the hottest summer days, was changed by engineers into a more efficiently-flowing waterfall. Two totally man-made falls were added at intervals further down to also speed up the flow. But those wild clumps of six-foot-high willow trees where we played so many games of hide-and-seek and kick-the-can are still there. The Old Mill Bridge where we played hockey under either one of its low, echo-building arches, is still wonderfully preserved, along with herons, ducks, sounds of river water, even wild flowers if you know where to look. Only that secret wood where the trilliums came out in white Easter masses holds nothing more today than wild fern and skunk-cabbage in season. And how could one forget the Chinese market gardens with the steady summer mist of irrigation sprays that used to rise above endless rows of carrots, lettuce, and celery, their tiny farmhouses almost like the toys of children? All gone now, transformed into a very sober subdivision of homes called Warren Park.

"And although that boy who somehow made this stretch of valley his own personal preserve has long since grown to manhood and far beyond, who is to say that at this very minute another young boy isn't walking those valley paths beside the same idly-murmuring Humber River? He may even hold in his hand several stale crusts of bread for the waiting ducks, and perhaps has the first words of a verse already forming in his head. In that valley, as in my boyhood years, anything is still possible.

"My interest in writing started about the age of fourteen. I'd done a lot of reading before that, but mainly books for boys. When I was accepted as a junior high school student at the University of Toronto Schools, then a boys' private school, I found a library especially heavy in two subjects—basketball and modern literature—which was very puzzling. I had to wait two years to find out that these were the special interests of the librarian, 'Bunny' Baird, who several years later became both my form English teacher and basketball coach. Next I remember the fellow who shared the next locker to mine, Peter Dickinson, handing me one of the first Penguin paperbacks, Ernest Hemingway's *A Farewell to Arms,* and telling me I should read it. That in turn led me to *The Sun Also Rises,* which I still can reread with pleasure. Before long I encountered James Joyce's *Dubliners,* and went on to marvel at the trials and tribulations of Stephen Dedalus in *A Portrait of the Artist as a Young Man.* Then for some reason I switched to reading the poets in that friendly, second-floor library. John Masefield, D. H. Lawrence, E. J. Pratt, and Robinson Jeffers were a few of those poets, including my own personal favourite right to this day, the Canadian Archibald Lampman. It was about this time that I knew I was hooked on poetry. For me prose was dessert, poetry the meat and potatoes. And it's been that way ever since.

"Although I've published only one book specifically aimed at children, *Flight of the Roller Coaster,* I know that a large number of my poems can be read and understood by young readers. Perhaps that's because I have always looked at the world and the people around me (the writer's raw material) with what some might describe as an unaffected honesty. This simplicity of outlook I've always tried to match with an equal simplicity of verse style. Many have called this a strong limitation. I on the other hand feel that it often gives me a greater strength than a more sophisticated approach might provide. I hope I always retain this innocence of a child when either looking at a flower, a person's face, or the Berlin Wall coming down, at least as it's reflected in my poetry.

"After I left high school I tried to read the best books of both poetry and prose that I could get my hands on, with an emphasis on the twentieth century. Not only the best in English but other languages as well. At first there were few good translations available; now almost every important world writer has been well translated. I like to think I got my college education and more by my own private reading. And as writing today is much more sophisticated than ever, like everything else in this 1990s world, you should if possible try to keep abreast of the best new work of your contemporaries.

"I really believe my decision to become a writer was such a natural evolution that I was hardly aware of the process taking place. I studied poems in the classroom, and thought it might be fun to write some of my own. Even then I thought of poetry as celebration, as pure enjoyment. When I'd written twenty or so short pieces into a small notebook, I left it in the office of my history teacher, a Mr. Daniher, with a short note asking for his opinion. He returned the notebook to me several days later with another short note that said in effect: 'You know how to interest the reader. Now you have to learn about rhyme and rhythm.' Getting this first encouragement from a teacher I respected was all I needed. From then on I never looked back.

"I suspect I began to write books primarily because I wanted to share with other people the wonder and complexity of the world as I was slowly beginning to know it. Whether or not I would succeed or whether I was even fitted for that immense task never really entered my mind. The important thing seemed to be making the effort or in the words of that old cliche 'giving it your very best shot.' It's easy to say today how youthfully naive I was, how impractical, how juvenile. But the sad truth is that most writers are impractical and childlike—if they weren't they probably wouldn't be writers attempting one of the most precarious of callings. Instead they would have been salesmen and doctors, bankers and lawyers.

"Nearly all the poems I write are inspired by a certain happening, sighting, or other event going on around me in 'my world.' As such they require no research; indeed would lose all their spontaneity and freshness if that element were allowed to intrude. But for many of the poems in my on-going cycle of poems titled 'Pictures of a Long-Lost World,' research is required, as in the poems about the assassination of 'Butcher' Hydrich or in the recent 'Sinking of the *S.S. Cariboo*.' Indeed, any historical subject will benefit from a sympathetic investigation.

"I've made so many mistakes in my own life that I think it would be presumptuous of me to attempt any direct moral teaching in my own writing. But I do hope that at least some of my poems have made a reader or two take a second look at some beautiful, natural miracle of this earth that they've perhaps taken for granted. And if certain of the poems have caused readers to rethink their attitudes toward their fellow human beings, then I've been more than amply rewarded."

HOBBIES AND OTHER INTERESTS: Collecting pictures and articles about early Toronto, Canada.

FOR MORE INFORMATION SEE:

Canadian Literature, fall, 1964, autumn, 1972 (p. 27ff), winter, 1974 (p. 123ff).
Louis Dudek and Michael Gnarowski, *The Making of Modern Poetry in Canada,* Ryerson Press, 1967.

Canadian Forum, December, 1968, February, 1969, June, 1975 (p. 40ff), August, 1977 (p. 37ff).
Tamarack Review, winter, 1965 (p. 81ff).
Saturday Night, December, 1971 (p. 35ff), July, 1977 (p. 75ff).
Poetry, March, 1972 (p. 358).
Contemporary Literary Criticism, Gale, Volume V, 1976, Volume XIV, 1980.
Globe & Mail (Toronto), October 13, 1984.
Bruce Whiteman, *Collected Poems of Raymound Souster: A Descriptive Bibliography,* Oberon, 1984.

STANEK, Lou Willett 1931-

PERSONAL: Born June 5, 1931, in Vandalia, Ill.; daughter of William (a farmer and horsetrader) and Pearl (McNicol) Willett; married John R. Stanek, September 24, 1960 (divorced, 1974). *Education:* Eastern Illinois University, B.A., 1954; Northwestern University, M.A., 1963; University of Chicago, Ph.D., 1973. *Politics:* Democrat. *Home and office:* 440 East 56th St., New York, N.Y. 10022. *Agent:* Marilyn Marlow, Curtis Brown Ltd., 10 Astor Place, New York, N.Y. 10003.

CAREER: Free-lance writer; college professor. United Air Lines, Chicago, Ill., stewardess, 1956-60; Bowen High School, Chicago, English teacher, 1960-67; Demonstration Center for Gifted, Chicago, director, 1967-69; University of Chicago, director of English and educational graduate programs, 1969-74; Marymount Manhattan College, New York, N.Y., director of women in management, 1974-76, 1982—; Philip Morris, New York, N.Y., director of training and executive development, 1976-82. Trustee, Millikin University Board of Directors, Decatur, Ill, 1981—; member of board of directors, Ronald House. *Member:* Author's Guild, PEN. *Awards, honors:* Outstanding Alumni Award from Eastern Illinois University, 1981; Children's Choice from the International Reading Association and the Children's Book Council, 1983, and one of a Child Study Association of America's Children's Books of the Year, 1987, both for *Megan's Beat;* Woodward Park School Annual Book Award, 1985, for *Gleanings.*

WRITINGS:

Megan's Beat, Dial, 1983.
Gleanings, Harper, 1985.
Katy Did (young adult), Avon, 1991.

CONTRIBUTOR

Issues in Children's Book Selection, Bowker, 1973.
Books for You, National Council of Teachers of English, 1976.
Doorways, Macmillan, 1987.

Also author of *Censorship: A Guide for Teachers, Librarians and Others Concerned with Intellectual Freedom,* Dell, and other teacher's guides, articles, and promotional materials.

WORK IN PROGRESS: Memorial Days and *Clipped Wings,* both adult novels; *Sam's Girl,* a young adult novel.

SIDELIGHTS: "I was born on June 5, 1931 in the upstairs bedroom of an Illinois farm, ten miles from a library, 3000 miles from Paris and light years away from any hope of becoming a writer. Fortunately, Mother liked to read, but

LOU WILLETT STANEK

books were scarce. When she had read everything to me, including stories from ladies' magazines, we made up tales playing the characters. On that remote farm with no playmates, I was forced to live mainly in my imagination—training to be a writer unaware.

"My father was a horsetrader. With my own horse and dozens of others always in our corral, little did I know I was living out most adolescent girls' fantasy. Belle Starr, the notorious woman outlaw who led the Younger Gang, was my childhood personae as I terrorized the countryside with two red-handled cap pistols strapped on my hips. Even today I love Western movies and when I often wear a Western denim skirt and boots around Manhattan, I like to think I still have a Belle Starr stride.

"I was a published writer at thirteen. It was my first job and maybe the best. I certainly learned the power of the press. The editor of the local, weekly newspaper, the *Vandalia Leader,* asked me to write a column we called 'Lou's Teen-Talk.' That by-line did more for my self-image than the Ph.D. I earned twenty years later, and I needed all the help I could get.

"When I started high school the snooty town kids soon made it plain to those of us who rode the bus were not about to be included in any of the fun. Fortunately, everybody likes to see his name in print. 'Lou's Teen-Talk' appeared and like magic I was asked to join the Hi-Gals, an exclusive club formed by the popular town girls. A varsity basketball player developed a crush on me. I was ecstatic until my old and new friends started forcing me into some tough loyalty tests.

"But if you've read *Megan's Beat,* you already know that, of course. My first young adult novel was such a thinly disguised autobiography I could be sued for plagiarizing my own life. My friend's too, according to the feedback I received from a recent high school reunion where much time was spent figuring out whom the characters were based on. Pris is the villain. No one has ever yet guessed who she is. They all think she was the person who was mean to them when they were young.

"When I went back home to sign books, a shy woman introduced herself to me and said, 'But I guess you know me. I'm Tom's mother.' Tom was the only character in *Megan's Beat* who was total fantasy—a combination of the brother and boy-as-best-friend I never had.

"However, *Gleanings,* my second book came totally from my imagination. I have never known a Pepper, Jr. or a Frankie, but I would like to, especially Pepper, a good/bad girl with a lot of spunk. Ideas for books come from strange places. I started thinking about *Gleanings* when a child, who was all bluff, told me the biggest, most outrageous fib. My character Pepper was not anything like the real child, except both were too proud to let the world know they were in pain.

"By the time I seriously began writing stories, I had been to many strange and far away places. Even though I knew from the beginning I wanted to be a writer, I did a wide range of other things before I found the courage. Perhaps all of the great writers I read at Northwestern and the University of Chicago intimidated me. I was a horse trainer, an airline stewardess, a high school English teacher, a college professor, a business woman. What a grab bag of experiences, I have accumulated to write about.

"The story of how I finally became a writer reads a bit like a novel with a twisting and turning plot. In 1981, after having worked five years as an executive in a large New York corporation, the challenge was gone. That summer I rented a vacation house on the ocean, packed my typewriter and a ream of blank paper. I wrote a book called 'Sam's Girl,' a scrappy girl's testy relationship with a fiercely independent father, reluctant to let her go.

"After much ado and my agreeing to do revisions, 'Sam's Girl' was purchased by a major publishing house. Naively assuming I was launched, I resigned from the corporation and set up 'a room of my own' in my apartment. But my editor left, the publishing house was sold, and 'Sam's Girl' was never published.

"Eventually, *Megan's Beat* was published in 1983, *Gleanings* in 1985. Currently I am at work on an adult book called *Clipped Wings,* the story of three feisty young women who become air line stewardesses in the 60s. I am glad I did not know all of the scarey ups and downs writers encounter. If so I might still be in a career I did not enjoy, still only dreaming about writing.

"Today I live in New York City. In the summer I head for Maine. I love the ocean so much I think perhaps in another life I was a mermaid. In addition to fiction I write for magazines and newspapers and teach writing. I work early in the morning when the world and my ideas seem fresher. By noon, with a notebook in my back pocket, I hit the streets, seeing and listening as a writer where nothing can be lost. I collect words, smells, incidents. Characters sit next to me on the subway, in the movies. I keep in close touch with my nephew Dannon, a teenage athlete in the Midwest who always knows where 'it's at' for kids. One page in the notebooks lists interesting names waiting to become characters, like Hoover the midget, Skeeter and Peeler—cowboys, hot rodders, ballplayers? They will find their way into a story. When these people begin to talk in my head, they are relentless.

"I own a co-op, have friends, vote in Manhattan. I'll probably always live here. But those voices who talk in my head? They have Midwestern accents. Home is not always where we live."

HOBBIES AND OTHER INTERESTS: "Theater, films, ballet, speaking to students and reading from my work, reading, travel, friends, water sports, gardening, classical music."

STEPTOE, John (Lewis) 1950-1989

PERSONAL: Born September 14, 1950, in Brooklyn, N.Y.; died of complications from acquired immune deficiency syndrome (AIDS), August 28, 1989, in New York City; son of John Oliver (a transit worker) and Elesteen (Hill) Steptoe; children: Bweela (daughter), Javaka (son). *Education:* Attended New York High School of Art and Design, 1964-67, an afternoon art program sponsored by the Harlem Youth Opportunity Act, 1964-67, and Vermont Academy, 1968. *Residence:* Brooklyn, N.Y. *Agent:* Estate of John Steptoe, c/o Ann White, Executrix, Apt. 9-AA, 375 Riverside Dr., New York, N.Y. 10025.

CAREER: Artist; author and illustrator of children's books. Teacher at Brooklyn Music School, summer, 1970, and

Steptoe, age nineteen, about the time his first book was published.

Bemidji State University, Minnesota, summer, 1976. *Member:* PEN American Center, Amnesty International.

AWARDS, HONORS: John Steptoe Library dedicated in Brooklyn, New York, 1970; selected one of *School Library Journal*'s Best Books, 1969, Gold Medal from the Society of Illustrators, 1970, Art Books for Children Citation from the Brooklyn Museum and the Brooklyn Public Library, 1973, and Lewis Carroll Shelf Award, 1978, all for *Stevie; Train Ride* was selected one of *New York Times* Outstanding Books, 1971; *Birthday* was included in the American Institute of Graphic Arts Children's Book Show, 1971-72, and exhibited at the Biennale of Illustration, Bratislava, 1973; MacDowell Colony Fellowship, 1972, 1973, 1974, 1989; Brooklyn Arts Book for Children Citation from the Brooklyn Public Library, 1974; Irma Simonton Black Award from Bank Street College of Education (with Eloise Greenfield), and *Boston Globe-Horn Book* Award Honor Book for Illustration, both 1975, both for *She Come Bringing Me That Little Baby Girl;* Certificate of Merit from City College of New York, 1978.

Coretta Scott King Award for Illustration, 1982, for *Mother Crocodile,* and 1988, for *Mufaro's Beautiful Daughters;* Jane Addams Children's Book Award Special Recognition from the Jane Addams Peace Association, and honorable mention, Coretta Scott King Award, both 1983, both for *All the Colors of the Race;* Caldecott Honor Book from the American Library Association, 1985, for *The Story of Jumping Mouse,* and 1988, for *Mufaro's Beautiful Daughters; Boston Globe-Horn Book* Award for Illustration, Parents' Choice Honor Book from the Parents' Choice Foundation, and was named a Notable Children's Trade Book in the Field of Social Studies by the National Council for Social Studies and the Children's Book Council, all, 1987, all for *Mufaro's Beautiful Daughters* and Milner Award, 1989; Colorado Children's Book Award Nomination from the University of Colorado, 1986, for *The Story of Jumping Mouse*; Biennale of Illustration, Bratislava Award Honorable Mention in Memoriam, 1989.

WRITINGS:

JUVENILE; SELF-ILLUSTRATED

Stevie (ALA Notable Book), Harper, 1969.
Uptown, Harper, 1970.
Train Ride (*Horn Book* honor list), Harper, 1971.
Birthday, Holt, 1972.
My Special Best Words, Viking, 1974.
Marcia, Viking, 1976.
Daddy Is a Monster . . . Sometimes, Lippincott, 1980.
Jeffrey Bear Cleans Up His Act, Lothrop, 1983.
The Story of Jumping Mouse: A Native American Legend (*Horn Book* honor list), Lothrop, 1984.
Mufaro's Beautiful Daughters: An African Tale (ALA Notable Book; "Reading Rainbow" selection), Lothrop, 1987.
Baby Says, Lothrop, 1988.

ILLUSTRATOR; JUVENILE

Lucille B. Clifton, *All Us Come Cross the Water,* Holt, 1972.
Eloise Greenfield, *She Come Bringing Me That Little Baby Girl,* Lippincott, 1974.
Arnold Adoff, *OUTside/INside: Poems,* Lothrop, 1981.
Birago Diop, *Mother Crocodile = Maman-Caiman* (ALA Notable Book), translated and adapted by Rosa Guy, Delacorte, 1981.

He used to like to get up on my bed . . . and leave his dirty footprints all over. (From *Stevie* by John Steptoe. Illustrated by the author.)

Uncle Amadou puffed his pipe slowly. (From *Mother Crocodile* by Birago Diop, translated and adapted by Rosa Guy. Illustrated by John Steptoe.)

A. Adoff, *All the Colors of the Race: Poems* (ALA Notable Book), Lothrop, 1982.

ADAPTATIONS:

"Stevie" (cassette), Live Oak Media, 1987.
"The Story of Jumping Mouse" (cassette; filmstrip with cassette), Random House.
"Mufaro's Beautiful Daughters" (cassette; videocassette; 16mm film), Weston Woods, 1988.

SIDELIGHTS: Author and illustrator of several award-winning books, Steptoe wanted to share his conviction that African-Americans have a reason to be proud by reflecting the lives and experiences of black children. He began his life in the Bedford-Stuyvesant section of Brooklyn in a culture of slick talk, slick clothes, slick cars, basketball, and big legs. He was a peculiar kid because he took great pleasure in staying home painting and drawing.

He attended the High School of Art and Design until his senior year at which time he was recruited by John Torres to be a student in the 1968 eight-week summer program for minority artists at the Vermont Academy, funded by a grant from the Ford Foundation. Torres believed that "John was a fully-formed visual person at seventeen. He was creating museum quality art without the benefit of any formal training." As a matter of fact, Torres found Steptoe so promising

that he offered him the use of his own studio in the attic of the administration building.

One day, Torres noticed that the students were going in and out of Steptoe's studio in a steady stream and he thought he'd better check on the activity. He discovered Steptoe surrounded by other students engaged in teaching. John Steptoe was sharing his ability to capture what he could see from his studio window on canvas with the other students.

Torres got Philip Dubois, an instructor on staff and returned with him to Steptoe's studio and Dubois asked John what he wanted to do with his art. "I want to create books for black children," answered Steptoe.

Dubois offered John an apartment over his horse stables at the end of the summer program. *Stevie* was created there and published by Harper when Steptoe was nineteen.

Stevie, reprinted in *Life* shortly after its appearance as a book, catapulted Steptoe to national prominence. Written by a sixteen-year-old black inner-city youth, directed at inner-city black children and illustrated in a masterly style reminiscent of Rouault, *Stevie* had no precedent in American book publishing. "The story, the language . . . is not directed at white children. I wanted it to be something black children could read without translating the language, something real which would relate to what a black child would know."[1] It

It was evening before he reached the edge of the brush. Before him was the river; on the other side was the desert. The young mouse peered into the deep water. "How will I ever get across?" he said in dismay.

(From *The Story of Jumping Mouse* by John Steptoe. Illustrated by the author.)

was a tremendous incentive for Steptoe to become a pioneer in an untapped market and to realize that there was a great need for good books for black children.

The critical response was all but unanimously positive. Barbara Novak in the *New York Times* said: "*Stevie* . . . offers a subtle paradox. One of the first books set in the ghetto, using black characters, black dialogue and a presumably black life-situation, it certainly stems from black culture. But the simple story the author tells, and pungently illustrates, is of a common experience of young rivalry. Though the author writes and paints out of his own blackness, he pushes black identity beyond the 'black is beautiful' stage into a common identity. Which is as it should be. In fact, one might recommend this book for white children."[2]

Author and editor, Selma Lanes commented: "Here, at last, [is] a recognizable human being drawn from life. Steptoe's *Stevie* was not intended for white children, but the tale it tells—of sibling rivalry and the realization by an older boy that a nuisance of a small brother adds considerable spice to life—has universal appeal. After Stevie leaves, the hero of the tale recalls 'the time we played boggie man and we hid under the covers with Daddy's flashlight.' And the closing line, 'Aw, no! I let my cornflakes get soggy thinkin' about him,' brings not black or white but universal laughter."[3]

Authors Judith Thompson and Gloria Woodard wrote: "*Stevie* . . . provides black ghetto children with identification. The writer simply presents a problem familiar to all children—the intrusion of a younger child on a small boy's time, friends, and family and his ambivalent feelings about the situation. To this extent, the book reflects no peculiarly black perspective. Identification for the young black reader rests in the central character's intimate knowledge of the black sub-

culture—his use of informal grammar and idiom, his loosely structured family life, his sophistication and independence in worldly matters, and his brief sketches of the kinds of good times city children make for themselves—from the familiar game of cowboys and Indians to the less usual experience remembered nostalgically by Robert: 'And that time we was playin' in the park under the bushes and we found these two dead rats and one was brown and one was black.'

"The value of such a book is that it assures the ghetto child that he, too, is visible—that he is important enough to be reflected in that literature which has always been made to seem too cultured to admit him."[4]

"I have often been asked," said Steptoe, "'When will you grow up and write an adult book?' I think one of the real questions here, one of the underlying questions, is 'How do we really feel about children?' and consequently 'How do we really feel about ourselves?' If you said there was a particular kind of person, on a particular sort of a level, who has to write for children, as opposed to a kind of person who has to write for adults, would you say the same thing about a surgeon who's going to operate on a child? It has to be a surgeon; it has to be a full-blown person who knows what it is he's doing and who knows how to do it. That is what I feel I've been doing for the last twenty years of my career.

"It is also said that from about age one to age twelve we develop ourselves, our personality, and from then on we are dealing with those same questions and those same issues over and over again . . . . This is really where it happens; this is what we are all through our lives as children, as adults. And I don't think that we really take a good look at that; we really don't respect that particular time in our lives, we would

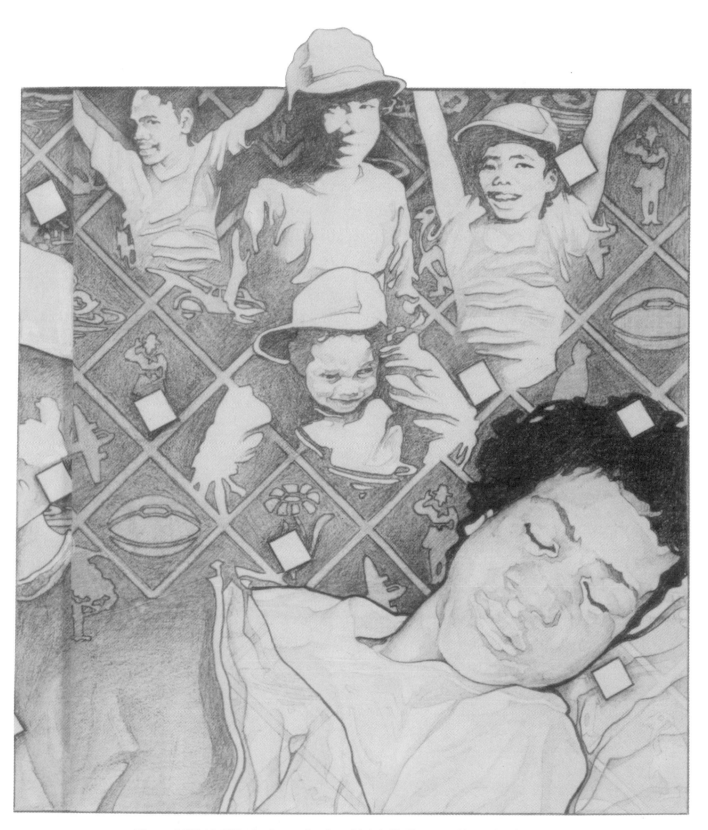

(From *OUTside/INside: Poems* by Arnold Adoff. Illustrated by John Steptoe.)

respect children, and we would respect people who write in a particular form that reaches to them.

"I have taken four, three, two and a half years to do a picture book, and I get the same amount of money I might have gotten if I took a couple of months. But I really put a lot into it, and I don't think that I'm writing or drawing pictures for people who won't necessarily understand. I'm doing something and reaching inside of myself.

"In my books and picture books I put all the things I never saw when I was a child, things I'm angry about not having seen, things that make me feel sad, things that have outraged me, and things I long to see happen. It is a beautiful, wonderfully delicious situation that I have the opportunity to go ahead and fill in those gaps. People look at the things I do, and say, 'Well, this guy jumps around from one thing to another. I couldn't necessarily tell that it's a John Steptoe picture book unless I saw his name on the title page.' And that comes from my almost feeling as though ... I have to do everything. That is nice, and it also gets to be kind of crazy because I can't do everything but I want to. There were so many things that weren't addressed for me as a child in books; there were so many things that weren't addressed and weren't dealt with for me as a black child in books. And I wanted to see those things. And I want to see them now. So I'm still working through problems I had and questions I had and angers ... that I had when I was twelve or when I was seven. So that's important. Things that I had difficulties with back at that time, I still have difficulties with. So if I go ahead and struggle through those things and get those things done, I will have moved and I will have grown. This society we live in will have grown.

"Something about me and my experience, or the experience of a Latino child, an Oriental child, a disenfranchised person, has something to do with being a white, middle-class person. You don't want to be deprived of the world that you live in; you want to know about where you are and how it relates to other people and what other people are doing and who you are. And you want to be decent. A lot of librarians and teachers ask me how they should relate to black children they are teaching or working with. I say, 'You don't need to have anybody tell you how to be decent.' ... It's very difficult for us to go ahead and deal with things we don't know how to deal with, the things we've been struggling with all our lives, but that's what it is we're talking about. That's what goes on in children's books; that's what goes on in adult novels, and that's what's happening for me. When I write and when I illustrate, I'm not condescending; I'm not taking an easy way out; I'm not doing things that are easy. I'm writing something that I will want to tell my children in a positive and a creative way. And that's hard for me to do; it's hard for me to be a parent, it's hard for me to say that that's not the place I'm at right now, and it's also very hard for me to say that still after thirty-six years that is the place I'm at.

"I think there are things we need to keep sight of, things we need to know—not so much what it is that we need to avoid saying or avoid talking about, and kids do know when we're trying to lay something on them. I like to deal with the immorality of denying information and not talking openly and honestly about certain things ... : Because we screwed up on handling a particular problem at any given age, we're going to go ahead and deny [information] to our children. There've been a lot of occasions in which my son or my daughter has come to me and said, 'Well, I see that you're doing this, Dad, and I understand that Grandma did so-and-so and such-and-such to you. We don't have those issues, and

that's not our problem. You're laying this on us, and we're entirely different kinds of people.' And I always have to remember that—everybody's not dealing with the same problems, everybody doesn't have the same fears I have. So if I go deep enough into myself, I'm going to come up with something that's basically universal, I hope, something everybody needs to see .... I don't want to be a pedant, but I need to watch out for what I don't want to talk about, things that I try to avoid dealing with constantly. And that's probably when I become—or anybody becomes—the most immoral, when I censor.

"Visual artists have a lot of different ways of handling a picture, of handling an emotion, speaking about certain things. There are line drawings; there are things with impastos that deal with light and dark. If you were going to say that, say, Frank Stella was less complex than Ad Reinhardt because in Ad Reinhardt's things you can't tell one square from another unless you squint, or that somebody like Mondrian just does lines and somebody like Rembrandt is really working hard, that's not true .... There are different vehicles, visual vehicles, to portray what you want to say .... It's very complex, and it does not have anything to do with the age of the child. Infants have to look at this world in all its complexity, and they make out of it what they make out of it.

"If you present a child with line drawings, the child is going to wonder why they're so different from everything else—when a child is used to processing other things, what Mother or Father looks like, what goes on in the home. I guess it takes a shorter amount of time to do line drawings, but it doesn't have anything to do with whether it's easy or whether you're going to make something simple for a child to absorb. It has to do with what sort of format, what kind of a feeling you want to give in your pictures, whether you want to talk about light and dark, or whether you want to talk about a literal sort of a thing with pictures. It doesn't have anything to do with age. When people see things ... it's different from what happens with words. It's a whole different sense."[5]

Steptoe with children, Bweela and Javaka.

"Okay, baby.
Okay."

(From *Baby Says* by John Steptoe. Illustrated by the author.)

Like *Stevie,* Steptoe's second and third books, *Uptown* and *Train Ride,* also feature black inner-city street jargon. A number of critics were unsettled by the uncompromising realism of *Uptown.* Selma Lanes critiqued: "Steptoe obviously does not intend [*Uptown*] as a cautionary tale for middle-class liberals, but as a mirror in which young blacks might, perhaps for the first time, recognize themselves. This they will surely do—but mirrors, unfortunately, do not transform reality into art. One gathers that Steptoe was honest enough to realize that no conventionally pleasing story could be made from his meager crumbs of spiritual sustenance. Eschewing art, he has rendered instead a sobering picture-book prognosis, ultimately beneficial, but highly painful."[6]

Mufaro's Beautiful Daughters won Steptoe the *Boston Globe-Horn Book* Award for Illustration, the Coretta Scott King Award, and was named a Caldecott Honor Book. "During the two-and-one-half years it took me to complete *Mufaro's Beautiful Daughters* I often wondered if my belief in what I was doing was justifiable. During those long months I felt I was doing something different, something bolder, something largely more sensible than any of my earlier works. My abilities as an artist were growing, and I began to realize that I was actually capable of creating images that I've wanted to see all my life. I am deeply gratified to know that others have wanted to see those images, too.

"I believe that every experience can be used as a vehicle for spiritual growth. In that light *Mufaro* was healing for me. Working on the book was a way for me to learn more about loving myself. One of the marvels of the book experience is that when it is finished, others can join in the experience, too.

"I wanted to create a book that included some of the things that were left out of my own education about the people who were my ancestors. I began with the idea of doing a Cinderella story. As I read about the story, what I suspected was confirmed: Cinderella is not just a European story. The Cinderella theme is ancient, and almost every culture has its own unique version of the tale in its storytelling tradition. My search for an African variant put me in contact with people who became excited about what I wanted to do. I have never

been to southeast Africa, but I was able to find and talk with people from there who were willing to share their personal experiences.

"The more I spoke with such people and the more I read, the more reasons I found to be proud of my African ancestors. I knew in my heart that the history of my race had to be a great history, but it wasn't easy to defend this belief against the implications in history books that the Africans of two or three hundred years ago were not as highly evolved as the Europeans who came to enslave and, later, to colonize them. My friend Naimani Mutima at the African American Institute, who was a great source of information, gave me important insights into the role that early anthropologists played in misconceptions that many people still hold about my ancestors. When colonialism was at its height, certain countries commissioned scientists to make discoveries that were meant to enhance the reputations of the countries that hired them. In the nineteenth and early twentieth centuries, many countries justified colonialism by claiming they were doing the world a service by helping non-Europeans fit into the European plan. Needless to say, an anthropologist who discovered that civilization existed in Africa before it was occupied by Europeans would not have been popular with his employers. Also, scientists who made unpopular discoveries were not likely to be paid.

"This is why, when the ruins in Zimbabwe were first discovered, they were declared to be of European origin. It was impossible for Europeans to think that an African people could have been as clever, skilled, and industrious as the builders of this ancient city must have been. It is now known that the city is of African origin. However, the implications of this knowledge have not yet displaced the old notions of Africa as a Dark Continent inhabited by backward people.

"The evidence of past grandeur that is obvious in the Zimbabwe ruins triggered these thoughts for me: a people who got together and built a city that lasted for hundreds of years must have been organized. Also, people don't build a city just to look at it, so they must have been doing something that motivated them. Artifacts found at the ruins suggest the inhabitants were involved in trade with the Orient as well as among themselves. All this suggests a society working to-

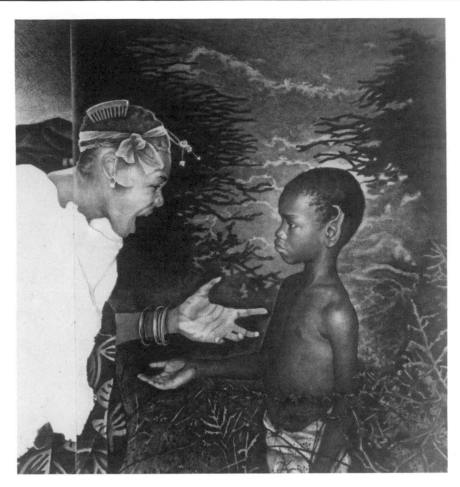

"Please," said the boy. "I am hungry." (From *Mufaro's Beautiful Daughters: An African Tale* by John Steptoe. Illustrated by the author.)

gether for a common end. Like any society, they must have had rules to govern themselves. They must have had families, and those families raised children to follow the rules that made their way of life possible. When we take away the thin layer of differences that twentieth-century technology has made in people's lives, there's no reason to think that people of a thousand years ago behaved any differently toward one another than people do today. People love, laugh, and quarrel; some are kind, and some are selfish and spoiled.

"The popularity of the Cinderella theme in so many cultures for so many centuries tells us that industrious, kind, and considerate behavior has always been an ideal to be encouraged. The presence of the story in Africa told me that my ancestors were probably very much like my own family. Once I made that connection, I knew who my characters were and that they had dignity and grace. I also knew they cared for one another as a family, for better or worse. To make the visual statement of this connection, I used actual members of my family as models for some of the characters—my mother as the queen mother; my nephew, Antoine, as the little boy in the forest; and my daughter, Bweela, as the model for both sisters. Bweela, being sixteen at the time, was an ideal model for Manyara's self-centeredness as well as Nyasha's generous nature. Telling the story was easy once I knew who my characters were. I knew the characters would have a strong sense of tradition and ceremony and that they would have expressed it in their everyday lives.

"In my first books I was primarily a colorist. When preparing the art for *Daddy Is a Monster... Sometimes,* I turned away from being a colorist to explore the technical problems of light and dark. My next books were *OUTside/INside: Poems* by Arnold Adoff and *The Story of Jumping Mouse,* which were both black and white only. Getting a firm, sure grip on black and white as a medium complemented my movement toward realism. I learned to develop clarity of image. I am very excited about that. With *Mufaro's Beautiful Daughters* I brought back the color. I added the old knowledge of coloration to my new discoveries of light and dark. I love to change and grow. I enjoy the challenge that exists in creating a new image, and I intend to continue to increase my abilities to express the many beautiful aspects of humanity.

"[The *Boston Globe-Horn Book* Award] is validation for work that has been ongoing now for almost twenty years. During those years I have learned pride and reasons to be proud. I have also learned that I am able to infuse my work with a loving sense of pride and pass it on to my children and to my readers.

"Unlike the nineteenth century, when it was thought that the Zimbabwe ruins could not have been of African origin, we live at a time when society has matured enough to accept the findings of scientists like the Leakeys, which strongly suggest that humanity itself originated in Africa. On the other hand, we haven't matured enough to fully embrace the idea that all people have a common origin. Consequently, *Mufaro's Beautiful Daughters* is said to be based on an African tale, rather

(From *Jeffrey Bear Cleans Up His Act* by John Steptoe. Illustrated by the author.)

than on a world ancestral tale. Even though I fully understand and support the reason for making this distinction, I'd like it to be known that I did not write and illustrate a special-interest picture book. I hope I have made a statement that is even greater than my discovery of reasons to be proud of African ancestors. I hope the book is also a statement of brotherhood in the wide world into which I was born.

"There is something I want to be said about me. I am not an exception *to* the rule among my race of people. I *am* the rule. By that I mean there are a great many others like me where I come from. There are hundreds of thousands of young people who want to accomplish something important with their lives and who need understanding and encouragement to seek the opportunities open to them. That you have understood and appreciated what I have put into *Mufaro's Beautiful Daughters* gives me hope that children who are still caught in the frustration of being black and poor in America will be encouraged to love themselves enough to accomplish the dreams I know are in their hearts."[7]

On August 28, 1989, John Steptoe died of complications from AIDS. His editor of seventeen years, Dorothy Briley eulogized: "Like the character in *Jumping Mouse,* John wished to reach beyond his circumstances and share with children his vision of a better world. Through his books he wanted to share his conviction that African-Americans have reason to be proud.

"All of [his] books are about family and the struggle to maintain dignity in a world that he many times perceived as being hostile."[8]

FOOTNOTE SOURCES

[1]*Life,* August 29, 1969.
[2]Barbara Novak, *New York Times Book Review,* November 30, 1969.
[3]Selma G. Lanes, *Down the Rabbit Hole: Adventures and Misadventures in the Realm of Children's Literature,* Atheneum, 1971.
[4]Judith Thompson and Gloria Woodard, "Black Perspective in Books for Children," *The Black American in Books for Children: Readings in Racism,* edited by Donnarae MacCann and G. Woodard, Scarecrow, 1972.
[5]"Writing for Children: Where Does It Come From and How Is It Different from Writing for Adults?," *Pen Newsletter,* September, 1988.
[6]S. G. Lanes, *New York Times Book Review,* November 8, 1970.
[7]J. Steptoe, *"Mufaro's Beautiful Daughters,"* *Horn Book,* January/February, 1988.
[8]Dorothy Briley, *Publishers Weekly,* September 29, 1989.

FOR MORE INFORMATION SEE:

Daily News, April 30, 1969.
Saturday Review, September 13, 1969.
New York Times Book Review, October 5, 1969, November 3, 1974, June 28, 1987.

"Stop playin' in your food and eat." (From *Daddy Is a Monster ... Sometimes* by John Steptoe. Illustrated by the author.)

Horn Book, December, 1969 (p. 667), October, 1971 (p. 477), August, 1972 (p. 382ff), August, 1984 (p. 462).

Times Literary Supplement, July 2, 1970.

Interracial Books for Children Bulletin, autumn, 1971 (p. 4), winter, 1972-73 (p. 7), Volume 5, number 6, 1974 (p. 7), Volume 6, number 1, 1975 (p. 4), Volume 6, numbers 3 and 4, 1975 (p. 8ff), Volume 6, numbers 5 and 6, 1975 (p. 10ff), Volume 12, numbers 7 and 8, 1981.

School Library Journal, February, 1972, October, 1974, May, 1976 (p. 73ff), February, 1981 (p. 60), September, 1983 (p. 112).

Washington Post Book World, November 5, 1972 (section 2, p. 2).

Ebony, November, 1972 (p. 60).

New York Age, August 17, 1974.

Negro History Bulletin, April/May, 1975 (p. 381).

Martha E. Ward and Dorothy A. Marquardt, *Illustrators of Books for Young People,* Scarecrow, 1975.

Barbara Bader, *American Picture Books from Noah's Ark to the Beast Within,* Macmillan, 1976.

Children's Literature Review, Gale, Volume 2, 1976, Volume 12, 1987.

Kirkus Reviews, April 15, 1976 (p. 484), April 1, 1980 (p. 437), May 1, 1983 (p. 521), March 1, 1984 (p. J10).

D. L. Kirkpatrick, *Twentieth-Century Children's Writers,* St. Martin's, 1978, 2nd edition, 1983.

Lee Kingman and others, compilers, *Illustrator of Children's Books: 1967-1976,* Horn Book, 1978.

Ellen Tremper, "Black English in Children's Literature," *Lion and the Unicorn,* winter, 1979-80.

Lynn Moody Igoe and James Igoe, *Two Hundred Fifty Years of Afro-American Art: An Annotated Bibliography,* Bowker, 1981.

Wilson Library Bulletin, September, 1984.

Language Arts, October, 1984.

Los Angeles Times Book Review, May 17, 1987.

Globe and Mail (Toronto), May 30, 1987.

Washington Post, December 18, 1987, May 13, 1990.

PEN Newsletter, December, 1989 (p. 7).

Linda Metzger, editor, *Black Writers,* Gale, 1989.

OBITUARIES

New York Times, September 1, 1989.

Times (London), September 2, 1989.

Chicago Tribune, September 3, 1989.

Then my daddy come pick us up and we go to my house. (From *My Special Best Words* by John Steptoe. Illustrated by the author.)

Washington Post, September 13, 1989.
School Library Journal, October, 1989 (p. 24).
Horn Book, November/December, 1989.

STERLING, Philip 1907-1989

OBITUARY NOTICE—See sketch in *SATA* Volume 8: Surname originally Shatz; legally changed, 1937; born July 12, 1907, in New Rochelle, N.Y.; died of lung cancer, September 11, 1989, in Wellfleet, Mass. Print and broadcast journalist, social agency employee, editor, and author. Sterling worked for the *Cleveland Press*, the *Omaha World Herald*, and for suburban New York newspapers before joining the New York Emergency Home Relief Bureau in 1933, serving first as a clerk and later as a caseworker. Between 1936 and 1939 he was associate editor of *Film Index* under the Federal Writers Project. Sterling became a television and radio writer for Columbia Broadcasting System (CBS) in 1945, and was made assistant director of CBS radio press information in 1959. His young-adult biography, *Sea and Earth: The Life of Rachel Carson*, won a 1971 Christopher Book Award. He collaborated on a number of other books for young readers, including *Polio Pioneers, Four Took Freedom: The Lives of Harriet Tubman, Frederick Douglass, Robert Smalls, and Blanche K. Bruce*, and *The Quiet Rebels: Four Puerto Rican Leaders*. Sterling also edited *Laughing on the Outside*, an anthology of African-American humor, and

wrote *The Real Teachers: Conversations after the Bell*, both for adults.

FOR MORE INFORMATION SEE:

Contemporary Authors, Volume 49-52, Gale, 1975.

OBITUARIES

New York Times, September 13, 1989.
Contemporary Authors, Volume 129, Gale, 1990.

STIDWORTHY, John 1943-
(John Howard)

PERSONAL: Born February 12, 1943, in London, England; son of Leonard (a local government officer) and Gladys (Moughton) Stidworthy; married Susan Elizabeth Cowell (an information scientist), January 1, 1966; children: Mark, Richard. *Education:* Pembroke College, Cambridge, B.A., 1964. *Home:* Ashdene, Beacons Bottom, High Wycombe, Buckinghamshire HP14 3XF, England.

CAREER: Zoological Society of London, England, lecturer, 1964-73; British Museum of Natural History, London, England, lecturer, 1973-78, exhibition development, 1978-83; free-lance writer, 1983—. *Member:* Zoological Society of London.

WRITINGS:

(With Gavin Maxwell and Avid Williams) *Seals of the World*, Constable, 1967.
Snakes of the World (illustrated by Dougal MacDougal), Hamlyn, 1969, revised edition, Putnam, 1975.
Reptiles and Amphibians, Macdonald Educational, 1980, Facts on File, 1989.
Black-Headed Gull (illustrated by John Thompson-Steinkrauss), Heinemann, 1981.
(Under pseudonym John Howard) *Prehistoric Life*, Macdonald Educational, 1981.
Birds: Spotting and Studying (illustrated by Alan Harris), Macdonald, 1983.
Birds, Newnes, 1985.
Life Begins (illustrated by Chris Forsey), Silver Burdett, 1986.
The Day of the Dinosaurs (illustrated by C. Forsey), Silver Burdett, 1986.
Mighty Mammals of the Past (illustrated by C. Forsey), Macdonald, 1986, Silver Burdett, 1987.
When Humans Began (illustrated by Chris Forsey), Silver Burdett, 1986 (published in England as *The Human Ape?*, Macdonald, 1986).
Creatures from the Past (contains *Life Begins, The Day of the Dinosaurs, Mighty Mammals of the Past*, and *When Humans Began;* illustrated by C. Forsey), Silver Burdett, 1987.
Mammals: The Large Plant-Eaters, Facts on File, 1988.
(With Christopher O'Toole) *Mammals: The Hunters*, Facts on File, 1988.
Fossils, Templar, 1989.
Insects, F. Watts, 1989.
Plants and Seeds, F. Watts, 1989.
Ponds and Streams (juvenile), Troll Associates, 1990.
Simple Animals, Facts on File, 1990.

JOHN STIDWORTHY

"A YEAR IN THE LIFE" SERIES

A Year in the Life of a Badger (illustrated by Priscilla Barratt and Rosalind Hewitt), Macdonald, 1987.
A Year in the Life of an Elephant (illustrated by R. Hewitt), Silver Burdett, 1987.
A Year in the Life of a Tiger (illustrated by P. Barratt), Silver Burdett, 1987.
A Year in the Life of a Whale (illustrated by Jeane Coville), Silver Burdett, 1987.
A Year in the Life of an Owl (illustrated by A. Harris), Macdonald, 1987, Silver Burdett, 1988.
A Year in the Life of a Chimpanzee (illustrated by Gill Tomblin), Macdonald, 1987, Silver Burdett, 1988.

CONTRIBUTOR

Gerald Durrell, *The Complete Amateur Naturalist,* Hamish Hamilton, 1982.
The Great Illustrated Dictionary, Reader's Digest, 1983.
The Reader's Digest Book of Facts, Reader's Digest, 1984.
Pocket Encyclopedia, Century Hutchinson, 1987.
Twentieth Century Encyclopedia, Century Hutchinson, 1988.

Consultant, reviewer and contributor to various books and magazines. Editor and writer, *Zoo,* 1964-73; editor, translator, and writer, Safari Cards, published by Edito-Service (Geneva), 1977-80; editor and translator of "Longman Nature Guides" series, 1986.

WORK IN PROGRESS: Volume on behavior for the *Junior Encyclopedia of Animals,* for Facts on File.

SIDELIGHTS: "All my life I have been interested in animals, plants and the natural world. Most of my work has been an attempt to pass on this interest, and the enjoyment it brings, to others, especially the young. Unless people under-

stand something of how the natural world works, there is little hope for our own species, let alone the others with which we share this planet."

HOBBIES AND OTHER INTERESTS: Tennis, badminton, woodland warden.

STRIKER, Susan 1942-

PERSONAL: Born December 24, 1942, in Queens, N.Y.; daughter of Ben (a manufacturer) and Sylvia (an interior designer; maiden name, Mann) Glaser; married Michael Striker (an attorney), April 9, 1966 (marriage ended); children: Jason. *Education:* Hofstra University, B.A., 1965; Hunter College, M.A., 1968, School Administrator Certificate, 1978; graduate study, Metropolitan Museum of Art, Bank Street School, and New York School of Interior Design. *Politics:* Democrat. *Religion:* Jewish. *Home:* Westchester County, N.Y. *Agent:* Chris Tomasino, RLR Associates, 7 West 51st St., New York, N.Y. 10019.

CAREER: Valhalla, N.Y., art teacher, 1964-66; California Avenue School, Uniondale, N.Y., art teacher, 1966-79, 1988-90; Uniondale Public Schools, Uniondale, art department chairperson, 1970-77; Hofstra University, Hempstead, N.Y., art instructor, 1971; author, 1978—; Elizabeth Seton College, Yonkers, N.Y., art instructor, 1982; Walden School, New York, N.Y., instructor, 1982-84; Young at Art, New York, N.Y., founder and owner, 1984-88; Lakeland Schools,

SUSAN STRIKER

Shrub Oak, N.Y., chairperson of art department. *Exhibitions:* Design Center, New York, N.Y., 1964; Guild Gallery, 1965; Cisneros Gallery, New York, N.Y., 1965, 1966; Mary Chilton Gallery, Memphis, Tenn., 1966. *Member:* National Art Teachers Association, New York State Art Teachers Association.

WRITINGS:

(With Edward Kimmel) *The Anti-Coloring Book,* Holt, 1978.
(With E. Kimmel) *The Second Anti-Coloring Book,* Holt, 1979.
(With E. Kimmel) *The Third Anti-Coloring Book,* Holt, 1980.
The Anti-Coloring Book of Exploring Space on Earth, Holt, 1980.
The Fourth Anti-Coloring Book, Holt, 1981.
The Anti-Coloring Book of Red Letter Days, Holt, 1981.
The Anti-Coloring Book of Masterpieces, Holt, 1982.
The Anti-Coloring Calendar 1983, Holt, 1982.
The Fifth Anti-Coloring Book, Holt, 1982.
The Anti-Coloring Book for Adults Only, Holt, 1983.
Build a Better Mousetrap: An Anti-Coloring Book, Holt, 1983.
The Sixth Anti-Coloring Book, Holt, 1984.
The Superpowers Anti-Coloring Book, Grosset, 1984.
Young at Art: An Anti-Coloring Book for Pre-Schoolers, Simon & Schuster, 1985.
Please Touch: How to Stimulate Your Child's Creative Development, Fireside, 1986.

Contributor of articles to periodicals, including *School Arts, Parent Guide, Our Town,* and *Family.*

WORK IN PROGRESS: A new "Anti-Coloring Book" about mysteries.

SIDELIGHTS: "I have always been interested in art and was inspired by a family friend who went to art school when I was growing up. My mother was also artistic and was always interested in interior design and art. She was very firm about wanting me to get teaching certification along with my art education, because she had an idea that teaching would provide me with some security and would allow me to have summers off and be home with my children, just 'in case.' I got my teaching certification because of her, but just as soon as I started student teaching, I was 'hooked.' About two years after I started teaching, I decided to give up my own art work and concentrate on being a super teacher.

"I worked long and hard for several years, and in 1978 went back to school to get a degree in school administration. My teacher, Herb Perr, suggested that I was too experienced to do the regular assignments that the younger students in the class had to do. He suggested that my grade be based instead on a more 'interesting' project. I was intrigued, and agreed. As the semester proceeded, I kept asking him what my assignment would be and he kept saying 'We'll think of something.' It seemed that we wouldn't and I was getting worried. I was getting straight 'A's' for the first time in my life, and wanted to keep up my record. One day in class we were discussing how terrible coloring books are for children. I raised my hand and said 'We knew all about how bad coloring books are for children ten years ago when I was in school, and I never met an art teacher who didn't absolutely hate them, but it is young mothers who buy them for their children and don't know any better. Instead of talking about it forever in art education classes, why doesn't someone write a more creative alternative for parents to buy for children?'

How can the dog be walked on days when you feel like staying indoors?

(From *Build a Better Mousetrap: An Anti-Coloring Book* by Susan Striker.)

Professor Perr looked at me, pointed his finger at me, and said, 'That's your assignment.'

"I prepared a class presentation of some of my best art lessons in 'coloring book' format at the end of the term. When I was finished with my oral presentation, the whole class applauded. I was shocked, and Prof. Perr said, 'You really ought to see if you can get that published.' A friend had a book published by Holt, and took it to his editor who passed it along to the children's department and it was rejected. She thought they were making a mistake, so she took it on and published it as a 'trade' book. It was reviewed beautifully and sold very well. I have done most of my books within the 'Anti-Coloring Book' format with Holt.

"My marriage broke up after twenty years, when my only child was six. He is eleven now, and I am planning to remarry, move to Westchester, and begin my new job as chairperson of the art department at Lakeland Schools.

"My mother passed away this past summer, and in the years before she died she sadly witnessed the demise of my marriage and, when I went back to teach, she often reminded me of how sound her advice had been, that I get my teaching degree 'just in case.' In fact I have taught over twenty years! All of my books grew out of my experiences teaching art. I am glad that I listened to my mother.

"*Please Touch* is not about drawing or painting well. It is about encouraging your child to think independently and confidently. It is about helping your child to explore his or her surroundings in an adventurous manner, but with sensitivity. It is about helping your child maintain the level of curiosity all children are born with, but most lose by the time they are ready for school . . . . I believe that most people who have special, talented children really have normal children and a special talent for parenting."

SULLIVAN, Mary Ann 1954-

PERSONAL: Born December 1, 1954, in Springfield, Mass.; daughter of John Joseph (a shipping supervisor) and Clara (a seamstress; maiden name, D'Ammaral) Sullivan. *Education:* Framingham State College, B.A., 1978; Norwich University, M.F.A., 1986. *Politics:* Democrat. *Religion:* Roman Catholic. *Home and office:* Mount St. Mary's Abbey, Arnold St., Wrentham, Mass. 02093.

CAREER: Member of the Cistercian Community at Mount St. Mary's Abbey, took the religious name, Sister Rosemary. Author, 1979—; free-lance fiction editor, 1984—; Springfield Technical Community College, Springfield, Mass., instructor in English and journalism, 1986-88; Our Lady of the Elms College, Chicopee, Mass., lecturer in rhetoric, 1987. *Member:* International Women's Writing Guild, Society of Children's Book Writers, Associated Writing Program. *Awards, honors:* Notable Children's Book in the Field of Social Studies from the National Council for Social Studies and the Children's Book Council, 1985, for *Child of War.*

WRITINGS:

Child of War, Holiday House, 1984.

Contributor of short story "Abbandonato" to *Chariton Review,* 1986.

MARY ANN SULLIVAN

"Maeve, I want to go home," Brendan said. (Jacket illustration by Peter Catalanotto from *Child of War* by Mary Ann Sullivan.)

WORK IN PROGRESS: Poetry; a novel for adults set in Italy between 1287 and 1320 based on the life of the Blessed Margaret of Castello.

HOBBIES AND OTHER INTERESTS: Swimming, living in the woods.

FOR MORE INFORMATION SEE:

Daily News Tonight, August 2, 1983 (p. 21), May 29, 1984 (p. 21).
Springfield Newspaper, September 11, 1984 (p. 21).
Valley Advocate, October 31, 1984 (p. 28S).
Sunday Republican, February 3, 1985, March 15, 1987 (p. B1).
Catholic Observer, March 15, 1985 (p. 19).
Charlene Postell, "Cloister Joins Nuns, World," *Holyoke Transcript-Telegram,* July 26, 1985.
Ram-Springfield Technical Community College Newspaper, December 11, 1985 (p. 4A).
Boston Herald, August 31, 1986 (p. 29).

TAMMUZ, Benjamin 1919-1989

OBITUARY NOTICE: Born July 11, 1919, in Kharkov, Russia (now U.S.S.R.); immigrated to Israel, 1924; died of cancer, July 19, 1989, in Jerusalem, Israel. Sculptor, editor, and author. Tammuz was one of Israel's most prominent writers and the literary editor and art critic for the prestigious daily newspaper *Ha'aretz*. He was also a leader of the Canaanite Movement, a now-defunct group of left-wing poets and artists founded before Israel's creation as a state in 1948 and dedicated to promoting cooperation between Arabs and Jews. Tammuz won a literary prize from Israel's Ministry of Culture in 1968 for his children's books, which include *Rizi, the Dog, Night on the Western Bank, The King Sleeps Four Times a Day,* and *The Second Soul,* but Tammuz is probably best known for his book about Israel's pioneer generation, *Hayei Elyakum* ("The Life of Elyakum"), for which he won the 1966 Talpir Literary Prize. During the 1930s Tammuz was a sculptor; among his works is a monument to Israeli pilots in Tel Aviv's International Park.

FOR MORE INFORMATION SEE:

International Authors and Writers Who's Who, 9th edition, Melrose, 1982.
International Who's Who in Poetry, 6th edition, Melrose, 1982.

OBITUARIES

Chicago Tribune, July 21, 1989.
New York Times, July 21, 1989.
Washington Post, July 21, 1989.
Los Angeles Times, July 22, 1989.

THOMPSON, George Selden 1929-1989
(George Selden)

OBITUARY NOTICE—See sketch in *SATA* Volume 4: Born May 14, 1929, in Hartford, Conn.; died of complications from a gastrointestinal hemorrhage, December 5, 1989, in New York, N.Y. Thompson, who wrote under the name George Selden, was best known for *The Cricket in Times Square,* a tale of a rural cricket who is transported to New York City where he makes new friends and learns big city ways. The book won the Newbery Medal in 1961 and was made into an animated movie in 1973. Six subsequent stories featured the main character, Chester, including *Tucker's Countryside* and *The Old Meadow.* Several of these stories were dramatized and are on cassette. He also wrote *Heinrich Schliemann: Discoverer of Buried Treasure* and *Sir Arthur Evans: Discoverer of Knossos.*

FOR MORE INFORMATION SEE:

Martha E. Ward and Dorothy A. Marquardt, *Authors of Books for Young People,* 2nd edition, Scarecrow, 1971.
Lee Bennett Hopkins, *More Books by More People,* Citation Press, 1974.
Doris de Montreville and Elizabeth D. Crawford, *Fourth Book of Junior Authors and Illustrators,* H. W. Wilson, 1978.
D. L. Kirkpatrick, editor, *Twentieth-Century Children's Writers,* St. Martin's, 1978, 2nd edition, 1983.
Children's Literature Review, Volume VIII, Gale, 1985.
Dictionary of Literary Biography, Volume 52: *American Writers for Children since 1960: Fiction,* Gale, 1986.
Contemporary Authors New Revision Series, Volume 21, Gale, 1987.

OBITUARIES

New York Times, December 6, 1989.
Los Angeles Times, December 10, 1989.
School Library Journal, January, 1990 (p. 18).

THURMAN, Mark (Gordon Ian) 1948-

PERSONAL: Born September 27, 1948, in Toronto, Ontario, Canada; son of Gordon Arthur (a salesman) and Catherine Jane (a homemaker; maiden name, Rennison) Thurman; married Gail Kitamura, October 6, 1973 (divorced, 1982); married Marianne Dworkin (an artist), February 23, 1987. *Education:* Central Technical School, diploma, 1966. *Home and office:* 14 Washington Ave., Toronto, Ontario, Canada M5S 1L2.

CAREER: Commercial artist in Toronto, Ontario, Canada, 1966-71; free-lance illustrator and artist, 1975—; *Owl* (magazine), Toronto, co-creator with Emily Hearn and Sylvia Funston of comic strip "Mighty Mites," 1976—; author, 1976—; Toronto School of Art, Ontario, Canada, life drawing and anatomy teacher, 1981— . Conducts writing and illustrating workshops in schools. Juror, Canada Council Writers Touring Program, 1988. *Exhibitions:* Masterpiece Gallery, Toronto, Ontario, Canada, 1969; Evans Gallery, Toronto, 1973, 1976 (one-man); Sir George Williams University, Montreal, Canada, 1973; "Drawings and Paintings of Animals," Gallery O, Toronto, 1975; "Just Imagine," Sarnia Art Gallery, Canada, 1981. *Member:* Writers Union of Canada, Canadian Society of Children's Authors, Illustrators and Performers (illustrator's representative, 1987-89),

MARK THURMAN

Alliance of Canadian Cinema, Television and Radio Artists. *Awards, honors:* Canadian Children's Book Centre Award, 1984, for *City Scrapes,* and 1985, for *You Bug Me; You Bug Me* was named an Our Choice/Your Choice Canadian Children's Book, 1985-86.

WRITINGS:

SELF-ILLUSTRATED JUVENILES

The Elephant's Cold, NC Press (Toronto), 1979, revised edition, 1985.
The Elephant's New Bicycle, NC Press, 1980, revised edition, 1985.
The Lie That Grew and Grew, NC Press, 1981, revised edition, 1985.
The Birthday Party, NC Press, 1981, revised edition, 1985.
Who Needs Me?, NC Press, 1981.
(With Emily Hearn), *The Mighty Mites in Dinosaur Land,* Greey de Pencier, 1981.
Two Pals on an Adventure, NC Press, 1982, revised edition published as *Two Pals,* 1985.
City Scrapes, NC Press, 1983, revised edition, 1985.
You Bug Me, NC Press, 1984, 2nd edition, 1985.
Old Friends New Friends, NC Press, 1985.
Two Stupid Dummies, NC Press, 1986.
Cabbage Town Gang (novel), NC Press, 1987.
Douglas the Elephant and Albert Alligator: Some Sumo, NC Press, 1988.
Draw and Write Your Own Picture Book, Pembroke, 1990.
Helping Kids Draw and Write Picture Books, Pembroke, 1990.
Illustration Ideas for Creating Picture Books, Pembroke, 1990.

ILLUSTRATOR

Joan Bodger, *Belinda's Ball,* Atheneum, 1981.
E. Hearn, *Good Morning Franny, Good Night Franny,* Women's Educational Press (Toronto), 1984.
E. Hearn, *Race You Franny,* Women's Educational Press, 1986.
E. Hearn, *Franny and the Music Girl,* Second Story Press (Toronto), 1989.

Also illustrator of cartoon features with E. Hearn for "Starship," *Toronto Star,* and of "ZAP" series published by Fitzhenry & Whiteside. Contributor of illustrations to anthologies for Nelson, McGraw-Hill Ryerson, TV Ontario, Ontario Educational Communications Authority, and *Discover Together,* for the Department of the Secretary of State of Canada.

WORK IN PROGRESS: Translations of "Doug and Albert" series; *One Two Many,* about a boy who wakes up with his clone and has to live with himself for a while with humorous consequences.

SIDELIGHTS: Mark Thurman worked as a commercial artist after receiving his diploma from Central Technical School. "That's when I learned what a deadline is. If you don't have the job ready on time, boy, *you're* dead. No money either. I learned how to juggle precious time so that I could still do work that came from myself while I earned my keep. And I learned the need for time out. I strum my guitar or go to the movies, good or bad—you often get more out of a bad one than a slick one. And I play tennis. That and jogging counteract those long hours hunched over a drawing table."[1]

Thurman's juvenile novel, *Cabbage Town Gang,* is a semi-autobiographical account of his childhood in Toronto's Regent Park. "It was a very caring, loving home. We were in a low economic bracket, but I had a good family to come home to. My father sold suits for Simpsons—which he still does—and my mother took in everyone.

"At the age of ten I was an artist. I was signing all my drawings 'Mark Thurman, Artist.' I never questioned it—though of course I did later, when I was in my twenties. In high school I was the top student in my class. In public school, when the rest of the kids were cooperating on a mural, I was doing one all by myself. I was drawing all the time.

"I enjoyed being read to in the public school library. My grade seven teacher would make up stories. I remember those as magical times, and I enjoyed making up stories myself. But I found my lack of grammatical skills very frustrating. So I often drew my stories as comic strip ideas. I drew students, teachers, everyone in all sorts of different visual situations."

"I work seven days and nights a week. When I started, I decided I probably would have to spend five years paying my dues. But now I'm so busy I almost can't stand it, and I'm having to pull back.

"[In 1984] I started doing a bit of TV work. I draw and cartoon and show how I make characters and how children can make characters. Television is fascinating; at the same time, I'm very wary of it and very aware that you can get locked into what other people want you to do. You can find yourself talking about something that you really think is junk.

"It's very nice to have a talent, but I want to be able to do things that I think are worth doing. I don't want to do a show-and-tell kind of thing. When I'm working with kids, I'm trying to open up their minds and extend their imaginations. By grade three, kids are starting to lock up already, starting to seize up. Sometimes they'll sit staring at a page, afraid to draw what's in their minds. I try to open them up.

"I now spend about fifty percent of my time in schools. I talk about myself, about children's books, about printing, about some of the problems of getting books done and working with other people, and about what I have to do as an illustrator. We make up a story and I draw it for them; some of the groups write and illustrate their own picture-books."[2]

"What I like best about these workshops is . . . helping them make up *their* own books . . . . I grew up with five sisters and brothers and I know how individual each kid is. I love it when someone wants to draw a book about 'Plutotrons that invade earth but can be melted in water' or another person invents 'a bear that suddenly loses all her fur because she eats salty food.' Their ideas are full of imagination and they keep you on your toes. If they don't like something they tell you directly. I appreciate that and try to keep their responses in mind when I write a new book."[1]

"I didn't set out to do children's books. When I graduated from Toronto's Central Technical School at seventeen, I wanted to be an illustrator, a designer, and a painter. The change-over came when Emily Hearn and I started doing the 'Mighty Mites' for *Owl.*"[2]

"We choose the topics . . . and Emily and I do research—at museums, in books, at the zoo. Most of the people we talk to are very creative and they actually give us story lines. When

(Jacket illustration by the author from *Douglas the Elephant and Albert Alligator: Some Sumo* by Mark Thurman.)

we've finished the research, we sit down and talk through how the story will go . . . . By the end of that, I have a set of thumbnails—small quick sketches of the whole comic.

"We take them to *Owl* and meet with Sylvia [Funston, the editor]. She's very important at this stage—she may change a whole page of the story. Next, I . . . do the master roughs. I trace the roughs on to the illustration board and ink in the basic details. These are what are called the final art boards. I then erase the pencil, and ink in more detail. I use three different thicknesses of rapidograph pen and Lettra-tone for the shading."

"I originally did my first book, *The Elephant's Cold,* for my nieces, who had very bad colds. That was [in 1973]. It took

another six years before I found a Canadian publisher. The book was so successful, NC Press asked me to turn it into a series—'Douglas the Elephant.' I had no intention of doing a series, but series have turned out well for me. I have done more than 100 'Mighty Mites' now and . . . four 'Douglas' books and four 'Two Pals on an Adventure'; the craft in keeping them looking the same but making each one fresh is something that works for me. It's part of my personality.

"I . . . revised the text in the 'Douglas' books. My training wasn't as a writer, and after reading the stories with children of all ages over the years, I found that some of the lines didn't work. All the books in the 'Douglas' series have little morals, and in some of the earlier ones, the morals come at you like a sledge-hammer. Some people didn't like the books because of that; they thought they were too preachy. But I'm a very moral person, and that was important to me.

"When I do a book, I'm consciously keeping in mind how it can be used. Emily and I became very careful with plots after a three year old imitated the 'Mighty Mites' and tried to climb a Christmas tree. But I don't think just about parents reading the books to their kids; I see how teachers use these books. They have the kids draw and paint, do collages and write poetry. They use them as a jumping-off point to discuss the differences between African and Indian elephants, or to talk about alligators or ostriches. So, keeping that in mind, I do the books on many levels."[2]

Thurman feels he is still learning to write and puts a great deal of thought into the kinds of stories he wants to write for children. "I simply couldn't turn out just decorative picture books. I wanted to do something that had a practical side as well. I wanted to do books dealing with what kids went through emotionally. I want to give kids things they will deal with, topics like sharing, disappointment and lying. I want to have them think about what kind of world they want to live in. And my ideas come when I'm trying to resolve something in my own personal life."

Two Pals on an Adventure began with a trip Thurman and a friend took to the Grand Canyon. *The Birthday Party* arose out of a desire to show children that some expectations cannot be met. "I wanted to show that it's okay to be disappointed. Hopefully the story allows a child to go through that process. I suppose I'm a moralist because without trying a message appears in my stories. I was surprised to find that children like *The Lie That Grew and Grew* the best so far."

"The stories themselves are very integrated with my life, though I didn't realize it until after the first four 'Douglas' books. Often the idea will be something that kids have suggested to me, but I start writing the story and suddenly realize it's me. *City Scrapes* was written after coming back to the city after a holiday and feeling very different about many things. When I did *Old Friends New Friends*, a lot of my own friends were changing partners. It's funny how things coincide, but it happens spontaneously.

"I used to begin a book by doing the pictures first, but now I half write and half draw, in a back-and-forth process. I might see the whole story in a giant visual flash—like a three-minute video. I may be walking or driving, or sometimes in a workshop a child says something that sparks me. I play with the composition a bit to try to get the right emotional effect. I might do ten or twenty thumbnails to try to hone it.

"I've never sold any originals from the series books because of the nature of the pigments I use. They're watercolour-based pigments that actually dye the board. Printers hate them because they have a very high degree of fluorescence, but I love them because the colours are so intense. Unfortunately, they fade away very quickly in the sunlight. Some of my other work is more permanent. *Good Morning Franny* was all paper cut-outs, and the 'Mighty Mites' are pen and ink.

"I rent two floors of a house on the University of Toronto campus but I do minimal writing at home. I do a lot of it in coffee shops . . . . I might sit in one for three hours and even do the rough drawings there. When you work alone, you want to get out sometimes. When I was doing fine art, I sometimes wouldn't get out for three days, and when I did I felt like a zombie. I was never anti-social, but I was non-social

for a while. When I started working with children, I found a whole other part of myself."[2]

"During the school year I visit at least two schools every week. I talk about writing and illustrating. I do some drawing. I read my stories. I especially like questions. One day in 1982 a student said, 'Why don't you do a book where Douglas and Albert have a fight?' During 1982-83 I heard the same thing about six times.

"I knew there was something there. A fight, eh! Everyone disagrees with something, sometime. Even your best friend can bug you.

"I grew up with five brothers and sisters, so I remembered the times we bugged each other and got into fights. The fight always happened over the simplest thing—like if someone was looking at you when you didn't want them to. I used the 'What are you looking at' idea in *You Bug Me*.

"When I was small and it was raining, people said, 'It's pouring buckets,' or 'It's coming down like cats and dogs.' All I saw was rain. This idea got me thinking. Rain is wet so it would probably rain wet things like fish and frogs instead of cats and dogs. Fish and frogs, I liked that.

"The name calling in the story came when I remembered as a child if I called someone a jungle mouth I saw a jungle growing out of their mouth.

"My stories come from a mixture of my early memories, my thoughts for today and listening to children and other adults."[3]

FOOTNOTE SOURCES:

[1]Emily Hearn, "Introducing: Mark Thurman," *CANSCAIP News,* December, 1982.
[2]"Mark Thurman," *Quill & Quire,* October, 1985.
[3]"Mark Thurman: *You Bug Me,*" *Our Choice/Your Choice,* 1985-86.

FOR MORE INFORMATION SEE:

Expositor, May 2, 1986.

COLLECTIONS

De Grummond Collection at the University of Southern Mississippi.

VANDER-ELS, Betty 1936-

PERSONAL: Born October 3, 1936, in Chengtu, Szechwan, China; daughter of Samuel Rhodes (a missionary) and Signe (a missionary; maiden name, Lundberg) Jeffery; married Barth Vander Els (a pathologist), August 27, 1960; children: Jonathan, Nathanael, Anne Maria, Alexis. *Education:* University of Toronto, B.S., 1958. *Politics:* Democrat. *Religion:* Christian. *Home and office:* P.O. Box 437, Shaftsbury, Vt. 05262.

CAREER: DuPage County Hospital and Health Department, Chicago, Ill., staff nurse, 1958-60; writer, 1982—; Southwestern Vermont Medical Center, Bennington, Vt., staff nurse, 1985-86; Bennington Association of Internal Medicine, Bennington, nurse-educator, 1987—. *Member:* Authors Guild, Society of Children's Bookwriters. *Awards,*

BETTY VANDER-ELS

honors: Parents' Choice Award from the Parents' Choice Foundation, 1986, for *Bombers' Moon;* Notable Book from the National Council for Social Studies and the Children's Book Council, 1987, and Award from the Artis-Zagone Reviewing Service, 1988, both for *Leaving Point.*

WRITINGS:

The Bombers' Moon (juvenile), Farrar, Straus, 1985.
Leaving Point (young adult), Farrar, Straus, 1987.

WORK IN PROGRESS: A contemporary story set in Vermont where the tragic and the comic meet and resolve in a surprising way.

SIDELIGHTS: "I've always thought that without stories, life would be dull indeed. I've listened to them, read them, told them, but until my own children were half-grown, I had not thought of writing for publication. When two of my children were in junior high school, they groaned and moaned about writing assignments. I was suddenly shocked to realize that I had done very little careful writing since college, so I could hardly get after them without trying my own hand at it.

"I continued to pursue my other interests: reading, gardening, spinning, and knitting, but writing became increasingly absorbing. Because I was unsure whether or not children would be interested in my stories, I tried out the first draft of *Bombers' Moon* on a group of sixth graders. Their response was so constructive that I've continued that practice.

"I think my main interest is in children facing difficult circumstances and growing through them, not necessarily succeeding, but being able to understand more fully the complexity, the possibilities, and the awe of life."

HOBBIES AND OTHER INTERESTS: Reading, gardening, spinning, knitting, gardening with a group of children (the Vermont branch of the Green Guerrillas; "We make surprise plant attacks to beautify Shaftsbury, and we grow vegetables, fruits, and lots of weeds!").

VARLEY, Susan 1961-

PERSONAL: Born July 26, 1961, in Blackpool, England; daughter of Kenneth (an executive officer) and Audrey (Clegg) Varley. *Education:* Attended Blackpool and Fylde College, 1979-80; Manchester Polytechnic, B.A. (with honors), 1983.

CAREER: Free-lance illustrator, 1983—. *Awards, honors:* Mother Goose Award, Prix de la Foundation of France, Prix des Treizes, and Wilhelm-Hauff Award (Germany), all 1985, and Kentucky Bluegrass Award, 1986, all for *Badger's Parting Gifts;* Children's Picture Book Award from *Redbook,* 1987, for *The Monster Bed.*

WRITINGS:

Badger's Parting Gifts (self-illustrated), Lothrop, 1984.

ILLUSTRATOR

Robert J. Taylor, *The Dewin,* Andersen, 1983.
Louis Baum, *After Dark,* Andersen, 1984, Overlook Press, 1990.
Kevin Crossley-Holland, reteller, *The Fox and the Cat: Animal Tales from Grimm,* Andersen, 1985, Lothrop, 1986.
Ursula Moray Williams, *Grandma and the Growlies,* Andersen, 1986.
Nigel Hinton, *Run to Beaver Towers,* Andersen, 1986.
Jeanne Willis, *The Monster Bed,* Lothrop, 1986.
J. Willis, *The Long, Blue Blazer,* Andersen, 1987, Dutton, 1988.
Richard Graham, *Jack and the Monster,* Andersen, 1988, Houghton, 1989.
Louis Baum, *Joey's Coming Home Today,* Andersen, 1989.

WORK IN PROGRESS: A picture book.

SIDELIGHTS: Susan Varley was born on July 26, 1961, in Blackpool, England, where she still lives. "Strangely, I can't remember any particular picture books that I had as a child, although I did read to myself later on. I was taught to read by I.T.A. which is a slightly different method than most, but was never a great reader as a child—nor was I ever good at sports. I had friends but I was always happy to be on my own drawing. Still, I had no idea what it meant to be an artist and can't even remember going into a gallery until age seventeen.

"As a child, drawing was the one thing I enjoyed doing more than anything else, so it seemed natural to carry on with it when I left school. I undertook a pre-B.A. Foundation course

But somehow he didn't feel sleepy. (Illustration by Susan Varley from *The Monster Bed* by Jeanne Willis.)

(From *The Long, Blue Blazer* by Jeanne Willis. Illustrated by Susan Varley.)

(1979-80) and then a course in illustration at Manchester Polytechnic (1980-83)." While there, Varley studied under the noted picture book artist Tony Ross. She also credits the work of E. H. Shepard, Edward Ardizzone and Beatrix Potter as decisive influences.

"The four years I spent at art college were very happy and important in my development; just being around others who were committed to art was of great benefit. It was whilst there I discovered that children's-book illustration was the area my work seemed to 'fit-in,' and it was also the area in which I felt happiest. At the age of 20, I read Kenneth Grahame's *Wind in the Willows*, which was a big influence on me. Although I've thought of it subsequently, I wasn't consciously aware that I was using three animals [in my first book] which also occured in it."

Varley completed her first picture book, *Badger's Parting Gifts* (1984), while still in college. This touching, poetic work presents the death of a loved one to young children by depicting an old badger who has "gone down the Long Tunnel." The badger's death saddens his animal friends, but each character learns to accept the loss by acknowledging the skills the badger taught him. "I tried to keep religion out of the book, although I think there's a suggestion of it, and I haven't any strong religious feelings myself. I've had letters from adults, mostly Americans, saying how much the book has helped them with children who are having to face up to the death of someone they knew."

This debut was an outstanding success, earning for the artist not only the 1985 Mother Goose Award for best book by a newcomer, but also the Prix de la Fondation de France, the Prix des Treize and the Wilhelm-Hauff Award. "The idea for the book came from my tutor. He didn't want to use it himself and I had to do a project so he said I could have it. He gave me the bare bones of the story and I did the drawings first and the text later.

"I found the drawings easier to do. I don't enjoy writing and never had any ambition to, which is why I haven't done another text since. Maybe I would find it easier if someone gave me a skeleton idea again. I get helpful criticism from my publisher and sometimes from critics. Friends also give an opinion, which can help. I received a great deal of encouragement from my tutors at college, and .... I have been lucky enough to continue illustrating children's books ever since."

Since her first success, most of Varley's work has been done in collaboration with other children's writers, yet like *Badger's Parting Gifts*, many of these books also explore childhood anxieties such as separation from parents, sibling rivalry and the acceptance of strangers. "The publisher sends me manuscripts and I choose what I want to do. I reject quite a few and haven't done a book for a while because we haven't found a suitable one.

"The project is always in the air; I never know what I will find attractive. I may have an idea of the kind of story I'm looking for and then get drawn in quite another direction. I work independently, but will show the author a rough and if there's anything missing we discuss it then and also at the end when changes can be made. I don't feel that there's only one way of approaching the drawings and am quite open to discussing them. I've enjoyed working with all the authors so far and don't have a particularly close relationship with one more than another."

In addition to her contemporary picture books, the artist has also illustrated traditional folk and fairy tales in *The Fox and the Cat: Animal Tales from Grimm.* Her award-winning illustrations for Jeanne Willis' *The Monster Bed*, a verse story about a baby monster afraid of humans, uses characters from Maurice Sendak's *Where the Wild Things Are.* Though the artist works mainly in water color, she has also produced black-and-white line drawings for Robert Taylor's *The Dewin*, Ursula Moray Williams' *Grandma and the Ghowlies,* and *Run to Beaver Towers*, by Nigel Hinton. Toward the end of the eighties, Varley also concentrated increasingly on commercial art.

"I don't know why I draw for children's books as I am not married, have no children and know next to nothing about them. I suppose I really just draw to please myself. I don't think children's books are taken seriously enough in this country on the whole. The world of children's books is exciting. I suppose on the day I start to find it dreary I will stop working in it."[1]

FOOTNOTE SOURCES

[1]Based on an interview by Cathy Courtney for *Something about the Author.*

VIVELO, Jacqueline J. 1943-
(Jackie Vivelo)

PERSONAL: Accent on first syllable, "*Viv*-uh-low"; born January 23, 1943, in Lumberton, Miss.; daughter of Jack (a mechanical engineer) and Virginia (an English teacher; maiden name, Bond) Jones; married Frank Robert Vivelo (an anthropologist and writer), June 19, 1965; children: Alexandra. *Education:* University of Tennessee, B.A., 1965, M.A., 1970. *Address:* c/o Putnam & Grosset Group, 200 Madison Ave., New York, N.Y. 10016. *Agent:* Sidney Kramer, Mews Books, Ltd., 20 Bluewater Hill, Westport, Conn. 06880. *Office:* Lebanon Valley College, 112 College Ave., Annville, Pa. 17003.

CAREER: Writer, 1968—; Middlesex Community College, Edison, N.J., English professor, 1970-72, 1978-80; University of Missouri, Rolla, Mo., English professor, 1975-77; Lebanon Valley College, Annville, Pa., English professor, 1981—. *Member:* Pennsylvania Children's Literature Council (member of executive board), Society of Children's Book Writers; Sigma Tau Delta. *Awards, honors: Super Sleuth* was named Book of the Year by the Child Study Association of America, 1985.

WRITINGS:

Handbook for College Reading Teachers, Southern Association of Colleges and Schools, 1969.
(Editor with Gloria Levitas and husband, Frank Robert Vivelo) *American Indian Prose and Poetry: We Wait in the Darkness,* Putnam, 1974.
Super Sleuth: Twelve Solve-It-Yourself Mysteries, Putnam, 1985.
Beagle in Trouble: Super Sleuth II, Putnam, 1986.
A Trick of the Light: Stories to Read at Dusk, Putnam, 1987.
Super Sleuth and the Bare Bones: Super Sleuth III, Putnam, 1988.

Contributor of articles and short stories to periodicals, including *Journal of the PA Children's Literature Council, Pennywhistle Press,* and *Learning and Media.*

JACQUELINE J. VIVELO

ADAPTATIONS:

"Super Sleuth" (weekly television series), featured on "The Read-Around Gang," PBS-TV, 1986.
"The Dirty Dog" (videocassette; based on *Super Sleuth*), Education Systems, 1988.
"Clues in the Diary" (videocassette; based on *Super Sleuth*), Education Systems, 1988.

WORK IN PROGRESS: Creature in the Doorway, a collection of ghost stories; *Giggle Soup.*

SIDELIGHTS: "One summer evening when I was very young I sat on a porch swing with two even younger cousins, the son of one aunt and the daughter of another. Because they'd asked for a story, I began the adventures of a creature that was both ogre and ghost. As darkness closed in, I described the monster as moving nearer to us—down the street, up the walk, at the gate. I never had to end the story because as the creature passed the gate my cousins shrieked in terror and raced into the house to find their mothers. Having felt the power of storytelling on this and similar occasions, I decided I wanted to be a creator of stories.

"My childhood was spent among wonderful storytellers. One of my aunts could hold us spellbound recounting the plots of suspense novels she'd read. Another, secretary to a U.S. Senator, told tales of her world of work. My youngest aunt, the harried wife of an underpaid college professor, made her own life the subject matter of an ongoing comedy series. My favorite aunt had only the events in our small town to draw on, but she told the best stories of all, turning gossip into drama. I learned from each of them, but probably I learned most from my mother who retold for my sister and me the

literature she taught. Asking her for a story might mean hearing Beowulf or a tale from Saki.

"Once she told us about a poor boy who was taken to an orphanage where he saw more food at dinner that first night than he had believed possible. He'd never in his life had enough biscuits; so each time the heaping platter passed him, he'd take one and hide it in his shirt. Years later when I read Richard Wright's *Black Boy* and found the biscuit incident, I felt that the author was an old friend.

"Characters from the books I read were the best friends of my youth. I roamed Alaska with Buck, though I was eleven before I saw my first snowfall. By turns I was rich or I was poor. Through the gaslit streets of London, I chased criminals and worked toward the downfall of Moriarty. I took the characters out of the books and lived with them, never climbing a tree without Robin Hood by my side.

"When I had exhausted other reading material, my father's matched set of Agatha Christie novels caught my eye, and I tried one. I'd never met anyone named 'Agatha' and assumed Christie was a man, a mistake that persisted for several years. I was amazed by the books and read all that my father had.

"I enjoyed stories of any kind, but my favorites were ghost stories, mysteries, and animal stories. The author of *Lad, a Dog,* Albert Payson Terhune, was one of my heroes. On the other hand, though I eagerly read his books, I've never quite forgiven Jack London for letting a dog named 'Billee' die. I soon came to see story*teller* as story *master,* lord of the world he creates, responsible for the events within it. I badly wanted to create worlds and to rule in realms of my own.

"Although I've written for adults, my most personally satisfying stories are those for young people. I loved creating Ellen and Beagle in *Super Sleuth* and setting them the task of solving mysteries. I like my characters, and I would have liked facing the challenges they encounter in their neighborhood. I want all the stories to be possible, to be the kinds of problems really happening in everyday life. Few of us can find mysteries as readily as Beagle does, but through him and Ellen readers get to share the mysteries.

"Beagle, though fictional, has much in common with a friend I first met in sixth grade, not always an admirable person but loyal and one of the best friends of my school years. *Beagle in Trouble,* second in the 'Super Sleuth' series, includes some actual incidents from those school days.

"My short story collection, *A Trick of the Light,* drew from my own life: a favorite, though dilapidated, book of ghost stories; a group of students who 'plagued' my mother when I was young (yes, they really did kill our cat); a comment my daughter once made about painting; a day when my dog was almost shot because he was mistakenly identified as rabid.

"As storyteller, I become master of the events I describe, even the ones I borrow from real life. In fact, my mother's horrid students all grew into decent adults. One by one they apologized to her and *she* forgave them. But she was not the only one affected by their malice. In fiction, I took great pleasure in devising the revenge exacted in 'A Plague of Crowders.'

Only one thing could ever have persuaded me to become Charles Beaghley's partner—boredom. (Jacket illustration by Leslie Morrill from *Super Sleuth: Twelve Solve-It-Yourself Mysteries* by Jackie Vivelo.)

"Throughout my life books and storytelling have helped to shape my world, giving it stability and peopling it with interesting characters."

FOR MORE INFORMATION SEE:

"On Becoming a Children's Author," *Journal of the PA Children's Literature Council,* 1989.

WARD, Jay 1920-1989

OBITUARY NOTICE: Born in 1920; died of cancer, October 12, 1989, at his home in Los Angeles, Calif. Cartoonist and television producer. Ward is most famous for creating, with partners Alex Anderson, and later, Bill Scott, the first cartoon show expressly developed for television, "Crusader Rabbit," in 1949. He and Scott created "Rocky and His Friends," which became "The Bullwinkle Show" and ran from 1959 to 1964. The stars of these shows, Rocky the Flying Squirrel and Bullwinkle Moose, his sidekick, were favorites of children and adults alike. Ward's last cartoon series, "George of the Jungle" ran from 1967 to 1970.

FOR MORE INFORMATION SEE:

OBITUARIES

New York Times, October 14, 1989.
Washington Post, October 14, 1989.

WARREN, Robert Penn 1905-1989

OBITUARY NOTICE—See sketch in *SATA* Volume 46: Born April 24, 1905, in Guthrie, Ky.; died of cancer, September 15, 1989, in Stratton, Vt. Educator, literary critic, editor, essayist, novelist, poet, and playwright. Warren will be remembered as one of twentieth-century America's most prolific and influential writers. A three-time Pulitzer Prize winner (once for fiction and twice for poetry) and first official United States poet laureate, Warren achieved widespread fame for his 1946 book *All the King's Men,* the fictionalized account of the political career of former Louisiana populist governor Huey Long. Originally drafted as a play titled "Proud Flesh," the book sold three million copies and has been translated into twenty languages. The screen adaptation of the story won an Academy Award in 1948.

Warren taught at many universities. While at Louisiana State, he joined colleague and writer Cleanth Brooks to found the *Southern Review* and served as its co-editor from 1935 to 1942. Also during this time Warren and Brooks wrote two influential college textbooks, *Understanding Poetry* and *Understanding Fiction,* both of which advanced the theories of New Criticism, developed by the authors as a means of analyzing literary texts not in terms of their social, biographical, or political contexts, but as works of art wholly independent of outside influences. He also wrote several children's books for Random House, among them *The Gods of Mt. Olympus,* an adaptation of Greek myths for young readers.

The recipient of numerous awards, including a National Book Award, a Copernicus Award, the Bollingen Prize for Poetry, the National Medal for Literature, and the National Medal of Arts, Warren was also elected to the Academy and

Institute of Arts and Letters, earning that organization's Gold Medal for Poetry in 1985. He was named poet laureate in 1986. Among Warren's best known works are the long narrative poems "The Ballad of Billy Potts" and "Brother to Dragons," the novels *World Enough and Time, Bands of Angels,* and *A Place to Come To,* and his early nonfiction books *Segregation: The Inner Conflict in the South* and *Who Speaks for the Negro?*

FOR MORE INFORMATION SEE:

Current Biography 1970, H. W. Wilson, 1971.
Contemporary Authors New Revision Series, Volume 10, Gale, 1983.
Contemporary Literary Criticism, Volume 39, Gale, 1986.
Dictionary of Literary Biography, Volume 48: *American Poets, 1880-1945,* Gale, 1986.
Current Biography, November, 1989.

OBITUARIES

Chicago Tribune, September 16, 1989, September 17, 1989.
Globe and Mail (Toronto), September 16, 1989.
Los Angeles Times, September 16, 1989.
New York Times, September 16, 1989.
Washington Post, September 16, 1989.

WASHBURN, Jan(ice) 1926-

PERSONAL: Born October 13, 1926, in Brockton, Mass.; daughter of Thomas W. (an attorney) and Louise (a legal secretary; maiden name, Attwood) Prince; married Roy Butrum, March 8, 1950 (divorced May 21, 1953); married John Washburn (a teacher), August 28, 1954; children: Linda Butrum Washburn Becker, Heather J. Washburn Tarpley, John D. *Education:* Bates College, A.B., 1947; also attended George Washington University, 1950-51, Barry College, 1963-64, and University of Miami, 1964. *Politics:* Republican. *Religion:* Congregational. *Home:* 4693 Southwest 19th St., Fort Lauderdale, Fla. 33317.

CAREER: Teacher of Latin, English, and physical education at girls' school in Alexandria, Va., 1948-49; U.S. Immigration Service, Washington, D.C., training clerk, 1945-52; Broward County Public Schools, Fla., teacher of English and German, 1957-73; Southeast Bank, Miami, Fla., personnel officer, 1973-89. *Member:* Broadview Park Civic Association. *Awards, honors:* Community Service Award from *Broward Times,* 1971.

WRITINGS:

The Family Name (young adult novel), Western, 1971.
The Secret of the Spanish Treasure (young adult novel), David C. Cook, 1979.

Work represented in anthologies, including *The Special Type and Other Stories.* Author of "Silver Beach," a column in *Brockton Enterprise,* 1942. Contributor of stories, poems, and articles to periodicals, including *Young World, Catholic Miss, Retirement Living, Reader's Digest, Swimming World,* and *Ladies' Home Journal.* Editor of newspapers of Broadview Park Civic Association, 1956-63, and Fort Lauderdale Swimming Association, 1968.

JAN WASHBURN

WORK IN PROGRESS: The Clue to the Secret Place, a teen mystery/romance set in New England; *The Sky Is Falling,* a romance set on a Caribbean cruise ship.

SIDELIGHTS: "I can't remember a time in my life when I didn't want to be a writer. I think I was still a preschooler when I made up a poem about 'A Cow Named Mormom Who Lived on Boston Common.' ('Mormom' and 'Common' rhyme if you're from New England.) I wrote my first novel in high school during study periods. An artistic friend who sat at the next desk did the illustrations. The story was almost totally plagiarized from Louisa May Alcott.

"My stories seem to develop a life of their own from some old incident or situation that has caught my interest. Although I do not consciously think about that incident, it seems to rattle around in the back of my brain until a whole story has formed around it.

"When I was raising my family, my husband was a swim coach and my children were all competitive swimmers. I timed and scored swim meets and also taught little children to swim. At some of the meets we attended, there was a boy who could not stand on the blocks to start the race. He had to sit on the edge of the pool until the starter fired the gun. Then he would plunge into the water and swim like crazy.

"The thought of this boy stayed in my head and led to my novel, *The Family Name,* about Ryndy Drews, who thought she had conquered the world when she was chosen for the cheerleading squad. When Ryndy broke both her legs in a water-skiing accident, her cheerleading days were over, but she found a new world to conquer in competitive swimming. My family doctor came through when I told her I needed a medical condition that would allow my heroine to swim, but not walk.

"We were returning from a trip to California and were passing through the state of Mississippi the day after Hurricane Camille devastated the Gulf Coast. Public service announcements were being broadcast on the radio, and one of the bulletins explained how to use a belt and the rear wheel of a car to pump gasoline from a tank when there was no electricity.

"That idea bounced around in my head and became the nucleus of my story *The Secret of the Spanish Treasure.* Stormy had been accused of stealing some salvaged treasure. A hurricane was approaching, but he and Lark did not evacuate the island with the others. They found the lost treasure just as the hurricane hit, but the truck, which was their only means of escape, was out of gas.

"When I worked in Washington, D.C., I lived in a very old house. There was a sign on the building which said, 'In 1814 this building was the home of James and Dolly Madison after the British burned the White House.' That intrigued me, but the idea didn't grow until many years later when I came across a book entitled, *The Day They Burned the White House.* This led to 'Fire in the Palace,' my story of Anne, a

"He's my friend," Jan proclaimed proudly. "I've named him Zorro." (Cover illustration by Joe VanSeveren from *The Secret of the Spanish Treasure* by Jan Washburn.)

young servant in the president's palace, who was inspired to bravery by the courage of her mistress, Dolly Madison. This story was published as a serial in *Young World.*

"Through my many years of teaching junior and senior high school and working with young people in sports and scouting, I relate well to teenagers. My favorite field of writing is fiction for young teens. I have found my personal experiences (family, jobs) to be a never-ending source of material. My primary purpose is always to tell an entertaining story, but if I can simultaneously teach a lesson or pass on some useful or unusual information, I feel I have truly succeeded as a writer."

HOBBIES AND OTHER INTERESTS: Golf, bowling, swimming, camping, travel.

FOR MORE INFORMATION SEE:

Fort Lauderdale News, February 28, 1960.
Hollywood Sun Tattler, November 22, 1963.
Bank Account, May, 1976.
Fort Lauderdale, November, 1976.

WEST, Bruce 1951-

PERSONAL: Born November 10, 1951, in London, England; son of Kenneth (an engineer) and Elda (a housewife; maiden name, Wespi) West. *Education:* Attended Southgate Technical College, O.N.D. Engineering, 1969. *Politics:* Dormant anarchist. *Religion:* Anglican. *Home and office:* 2 Bloor St. W., Suite 100-311, Toronto, Ontario, Canada M4W 3E2.

CAREER: Race car driver, 1971—; writer, 1984—. Also works in construction. *Member:* British Auto Racing Club. *Awards, honors:* Has received various trophies for race car driving.

WRITINGS:

Outrageously Yours: The Explosive West Letters, General & Stoddart, 1986, Putnam, 1987.
Retaliate. Write!, General & Stoddart, 1990.

SIDELIGHTS: "Both books published were inspired by the unconsciously amusing people who 'run' the world.

"My racing experiences include Formula Three, Formula Super Vee, Formula 2000, Formula 4, and long distance endurance racing."

HOBBIES AND OTHER INTERESTS: Chess, skiing.

FOR MORE INFORMATION SEE:

Toronto Star, December 20, 1986 (p. F1).
Globe, September 13, 1988 (p. 42).

WESTMORELAND, William C(hilds) 1914-

PERSONAL: Born March 26, 1914, in Spartanburg County, S.C.; son of James Ripley (a textile plant manager) and

Eugenia (a housewife; maiden name, Childs) Westmoreland; married Katherine Stevens Van Deusen, May 3, 1947; children: Katherine Stevens, James Ripley, Margaret Childs. *Education:* U.S. Military Academy, West Point, B.S., 1936; attended Advanced Management Program, Harvard University, 1954. *Politics:* Republican. *Religion:* Protestant. *Home address:* P.O. Box 1059, Charleston, S.C. 29402.

CAREER: U.S. Army, career officer, 1936-72; retired as general. During World War II was commanding officer of the Thirty-fourth Field Artillery Battalion in North Africa and Sicily; landed in Normandy offensive with Ninth Infantry Division, and became chief of staff of the division in 1944; commander, 504 Parachute Infantry Regiment, and chief of staff, both Eighty-second Airborne Division, 1947-50; instructor, Command and General Staff College, Fort Leavenworth, Kan., 1950, and Army War College, Fort Leavenworth, and Carlisle Barracks, Pa., 1951-52; commander of 187th Airborne Regimental Combat Team in Korea, 1952-53; secretary of Army General Staff, Washington, D.C., 1955-58; became major general, 1956; commander of 101st Airborne Division "Screaming Eagles," 1958-60; superintendent of U.S. Military Academy, West Point, N.Y., 1960-63; commander, 18th Airborne Corps, Fort Bragg, N.C., 1963; became general, 1964; commander of U.S. Military Assistance Command, Vietnam, 1964-68; Chief of Staff of the U.S. Army, 1968-72. Chairman of Governor's Task Force for Economic gorwth for the State of South Carolina,

The Westmoreland wedding, 1947.

1972-74. Author; lecturer; member of board of directors of several corporations and foundations.

AWARDS, HONORS—Military: Received more than thirty national and international awards, including: Distinguished Service Medal with Three Oak Leaf Clusters; Legion of Merit with Two Oak Leaf Clusters; Bronze Star with Oak Leaf Cluster; Air Medal with Nine Oak Leaf Clusters; Order of Military Merit (Brazil); Order of Guerrileros Lanza (Bolivia); Order of the Rising Sun, First Class (Japan); Order of Military Merit Taeguk (Korea); Legion of Honor (France); Order of Sikatuna (Philippines); Chuong My Medal, National Order of Vietnam. Civilian: More than twenty awards for service, including: Franklin Award from the Printing Industries of Metropolitan New York; Gold Medal for Distinguished Achievement from the Holland Society of New York; named "Man of the Year" by *Time,* 1965; Silver Buffalo Award from the Boy Scouts of America, 1967; and Patron of the Year Award from the University of Notre Dame. Doctor of Law from Temple University, 1963, University of South Carolina, 1967, and Howard Payne College; Doctor of Military Science from the Citadel, 1960, and Norwich University, 1970; South Carolina Hall of Fame, 1987.

WRITINGS:

A Soldier Reports (memoirs), Doubleday, 1976.
(With others) *Vietnam: Four American Perspectives,* Purdue University Press, 1990.

Contributor to reports on operations in Vietnam, 1969. Also contributor of articles to periodicals, including *New York Times.*

SIDELIGHTS: William C. Westmoreland born in 1914, developed an interest in the military at an early age. "My father, James Ripley Westmoreland, was indirectly responsible for my attending the Military Academy. The local manager of a textile operation, Pacolet Mills, near Spartanburg, South Carolina, a man of strong character, industrious, thrifty, scrupulously honest, intolerant of unreliability and immorality, he more than anyone tried to instill in me respect for those virtues for which I later learned West Point stands. Informed and well read, he encouraged me in a broad range of activities, from my high school studies to boxing and playing the flute. By enabling me at the age of fifteen to attend a world Boy Scout jamboree in England, he triggered in me a love of travel that in due time turned me toward West Point.

"[My father called 'Wana' by my sister and me] had no military experience, but since he was a graduate of The Citadel, the military college of South Carolina, I was almost foreordained to go there, although not with a view toward a military career. Having been thwarted in his own desire to become a lawyer, my father aspired for me, an only son, to achieve what he had missed. Expecting to obtain a liberal arts degree as a preliminary to the study of law, I entered The Citadel in 1931.

"I soon grew restless. Memories of my exciting trip to Europe kept coming back, including recollection of a meeting during the trip with a group of midshipmen from the United States Naval Academy at Annapolis. What better way, I deduced, to see the world than to go to a service academy? Receiving no encouragement from my father, I nevertheless outlined my plan.

"As I entered the Military Academy in July 1932, I had already learned from my experience as a Boy Scout and as a cadet at The Citadel that I enjoyed challenge and discipline, so much a part of military life. My days at West Point were long and often difficult, ranging from early struggles with English grammar and composition to later responsibilities in the post of First Captain. Yet they were rewarding days, replete with lasting friendships and with gainful associations with competent and moral officers, some of whom later joined the ranks of America's most distinguished soldiers."[1]

Westmoreland graduated with second Lieutenant's bars in place in 1936. "Having failed to qualify for service in the Army Air Corps because of minor sight impediment, I chose the Field Artillery, which brought me a first assignment in the fall of 1936 at the home of the Field Artillery School at Fort Sill, Oklahoma. I joined the 18th Field Artillery, a regiment that served as demonstration troops for the school. Our guns in that era of penury were horse-drawn Model 1897 French 75s with steel-rimmed wooden wheels.

"[At Fort Sill] aside from formal dinners and dances at the officers' club and amateur theater, much of the social activity centered around the horse: shows, hunter trials, polo, and colorful Sunday morning hunts with riders attired in traditional pink coats. The hunts were usually followed by lengthy hunt breakfasts where plentiful beer sparked the singing of colorful hunt songs and ballads.

"On one of my first hunts I spotted a nine-year-old girl at the head of the field, pigtails flying, riding as if the horse was a part of her. I learned later that she was Katherine Van Deusen, daughter of the post executive officer, Lieutenant Colonel Edwin R. Van Deusen, who clearly had passed along his own renowned prowess on horseback to his daughter. Known as 'Kitsy,' she was a precocious child, witty, always quick with a saucy remark. Since 'Van' and 'Kay' Van Deusen—one of the most popular couples on the post—lived only a few doors from my BOQ (bachelor officers' quarters), I observed Kitsy often, an active child with sparkling personality.

"Just over two years later, as I prepared for reassignment to Hawaii, the girl on the post whom I had been dating married another officer, which brought me considerable sympathy from the ladies of the post. Shortly before my departure, as I sat in the officers' club, apparently looking dejected, an eleven-year-old Kitsy perched on the arm of my chair. 'Cheer up, Westy,' she said. 'Don't worry. I'll be a big girl soon. I'll wait for you.'

"In the fall of 1946, my personal life underwent a marked change that had its origins in a Sunday morning hunt ten years earlier at Fort Sill.

"My telephone rang.

"'This is Kitsy,' a female voice said. 'Remember me?'

"Hesitating briefly, I said I did and asked, 'Are you a big girl now?'

"'Why don't you come,' she answered, 'and see for yourself?'

"I was scheduled for dinner that evening at [friends]. Aware that the ladies of the post had just about despaired of my ever marrying (I was all of thirty-two), I thought [my hostess] might welcome my bringing a date. When I called her, she was delighted.

"When I again set eyes on Kitsy, I found the pigtails gone, the little girl who had led the chase changed into a beautiful young woman.

"Seven months later, on May 3, 1947, in St. John's Episcopal Church in Fayetteville, outside Fort Bragg, we were married."[1]

Westmoreland's career with the United States Army spanned World War II, and the Korean War, and later he served as Commanding General of the Army's 101st Airborne Division. Following this he served his country as superintendent of the U.S. Military Academy at West Point, N.Y., and in the most unpopular war in the history of the United States, the Vietnam War. "The old soldier spoke with carefully measured words. 'Westmoreland,' he said, 'I know you realize that your new assignment is filled with opportunities but fraught with hazards.'

"With that he firmly shook my hand. It was to be my last meeting with a man whom I admired tremendously, General Douglas MacArthur. He was referring to my assignment to join the United States Military Assistance Command in Vietnam.

"Flying into Tan Son Nhut airport on the fringe of Saigon in a commercial airliner in late January 1964 was a strange experience, a swift plunge from a comfortable, peaceful world into an alien environment, neither peace nor war but with the trappings of war. Because enemy fire had hit a commercial plane a week or so earlier, pilots of Pan American Airways DC-707s had taken to making incredibly steep, stomach-churning descents to the runways. As the plane taxied to a stop, the accoutrements of war were conspicuous.

"Already struck with the beauty of Vietnam from the air, I was impressed as we rode into Saigon with the charm of the capital and the aura of Paris that the French had imparted to it. Spreading shade trees alleviated shimmering heat in the streets and wide boulevards. Delicate bougainvillea grew on walls surrounding pastel-colored villas and here and there clumps of colorful hibiscus. Slender, black-haired women riding bicycles displayed an impressive dignity, their *ao dai* (a kind of skirt split at both sides and worn over pajama-like slacks) flowing in the breeze. Yet the incongruity of fortifications intruded upon me in the city as it had at the airport. Atop many of the walls were concertinas of barbed wire. Chicken wire protected some sidewalk cafes against grenades. At bridges and the entrances to some buildings armed soldiers stood guard in concrete sentry boxes reinforced with sand bags.

"Neither Kitsy nor the children had special security arrangements at first. Kitsy drove herself around Saigon in my private car, a Ford Falcon shipped from the United States, but after I became COMUSMACV in June 1964, the Vietnamese furnished an armed guard to accompany her. A guard also went with the children when they left the house. American military policemen and a nurse rode the bus that carried the children to the American Community School near Tan Son Nhut. Wire mesh covered the windows as protection against grenades, and military police maintained a twenty-four-hour guard at the school, rifles at the ready. Kitsy said years later that the experience must have made an indelible impression on Margaret because it has taken a figurative gun at her back ever since to make her go to school.

"One of Rip's first essays at school told, with some exaggeration, of his impressions. 'We ride on a bus with wire on the

After a training parachute jump in Korea, 1952. (Photograph courtesy of the U.S. Army.)

windows so grenades won't get us and soldiers with real guns so the VC won't get us. When the bus stops, we march in front of two lines of soldiers. Guards are all around us and a big one on the roof with a machine gun to shoot down the VC planes.'

"At noon on a Sunday shortly before Christmas [in 1964], I received word that my eighty-six-year-old father, who had meant so much to me, had died. As Kitsy held my hand, for the first time since I was a child I cried.

"My family left Saigon in February 1965 . . . . After Kitsy moved to the Philippines in August 1966, she would join me on the occasion of special functions, usually at the Embassy, flying over on an empty medical evacuation plane, flying back on a plane loaded with wounded which she would help to attend. Having my wife and family relatively close was a real solace over the years, a benefit that I persuaded Secretary McNamara to extend to other officers whom I asked to serve extended tours in order to provide continuity in key positions. It is often the soldier's lot to be separated from his family, yet I was grateful that the long separation could be ameliorated to some degree during my children's formative years.

"The lady whom I first spied as a child with flying pigtails has contributed much to my career, including my service in Vietnam. She has been more than a wife, a companion, a sweetheart; as have so many service wives, she has been a colleague, sometimes performing unglamorous but neces-

sary tasks, helping me to execute my duties, easing my cares and concerns. Some idea of the dislocation she has experienced through the years can be realized from the fact that between our marriage in 1947 and 1975, we had lived in 36 different houses an average of more than one a year.

"As any television viewer or newspaper reader could discern, the end in South Vietnam, in April 1975, came with incredible suddenness, amid scenes of unmitigated misery and shame. Utter defeat, panic, and rout have produced similar demoralizing tableux through the centuries; yet to those of us who had worked so long and hard to try to keep it from ending that way, who had been so markedly conscious of the deaths and wounds of thousands of Americans and the soldiers of other countries, who had so long stood in awe of the stamina of the South Vietnamese soldier and civilian under the mantle of hardship, it was depressingly sad that so much misery and shame should be a part of it. So immense had been the sacrifices made through so many long years that the South Vietnamese deserved an end—if it had to come to that—with more dignity to it.

"No bells rang, no bands paraded, few turned out to cheer. Perhaps there could be no rejoicing after such a long, costly struggle, one that for all the sacrifice of American fighting men and for all their obvious dominance on the battlefield came to no conclusive end but kind of petered out. Yet the nation appeared to breathe a collective sigh of relief that the American role was essentially over, and there were a few

60 Tran Quy Cap, Westmoreland's home while in Saigon. (Photograph courtesy of the U.S. Army.)

heart-warming moments that did produce a kind of exultancy and seemed to pull the nation together: those touching times when at airports around the country the prisoners of war [from Hanoi] at last returned.

"For one looking back on thirty-six years of service in the United States Army, that is a rewarding thought. So, too, I am struck, upon reflection, by the unprecedented changes that occurred during those thirty-six years. From the World War I Stokes mortar and the Model 1897 French 75 artillery piece to sophisticated guided missiles; from the model 1902 rifle to the M-16; from carrier pigeons and Morse code telegraphy to walkie-talkies, computers, and sensors ... through three wars and a number of police actions; from volunteer army back to volunteer army; and from isolationism to multiple international commitments. As one in the middle of the changes at various levels of command responsibility, I have always been impressed by the loyalty, flexibility, durability, and over-all effectiveness of the United States Army. The traumatic experience of Vietnam was no exception."[1]

Westmoreland's book, *A Soldier Reports,* was published in 1976. "I wrote it because I appreciated that I had been involved in an important episode of history and that the public deserved a first-hand account of that experience and knowledge of the character of the man carring a major share of the responsibility."

In a 1982 "CBS Reports" documentary entitled "The Uncounted Enemy: A Vietnam Deception," Westmoreland among other American Military officials was accused of underreporting enemy troop strength during a crucial period of the Vietnam War, therefore deceiving the government and the public.

Westmoreland claimed that "The statements ... were false, unfair, inaccurate and defamatory" and were made "with actual malice; with knowledge that they were false, unfair, inaccurate and defamatory,"[2] and asked for an apology. "When CBS refused, I filed a libel suit."

After two-and-a-half years and many dollars spent on legal fees, Westmoreland settled for a statement that affirmed his honor. The statement said, in part, "CBS respects General Westmoreland's long and faithful service to his country and never intended to assert, and does not believe that General Westmoreland was unpatriotic or disloyal in performing his duties as he saw fit." Said Westmoreland, "It was in essence an apology. I'm going to try to fade away."[3]

"As I look back on my life, I thank God for the opportunity that was given to me to be a soldier. If given that opportunity again, I would with the same pride and even greater humility raise my hand and take once again the soldier's oath."[1]

FOOTNOTE SOURCES

[1]William C. Westmoreland, *A Soldier Reports,* Doubleday, 1976. Amended by W. C. Westmoreland.
[2]William J. Rust, "Westmoreland Vs. CBS: Story behind the Battle," *U.S. News & World Report,* October 1, 1984.
[3]William A. Henry III, "It Was the Best I Could Get," *Time,* March 4, 1985.

FOR MORE INFORMATION SEE:

New York Times, May 14, 1960, July 6, 1960.
Current Biography 1961, H. W. Wilson, 1962.
Time, May 8, 1964 (p. 26), February 19, 1965, January 7, 1966, May 5, 1967, February 16, 1968, March 29, 1968

Addressing the 4th Infantry Division, March, 1967. (From *A Soldier Reports* by William C. Westmoreland.)

The Westmorelands flank General and Mrs. Douglas MacArthur at MacArthur's farewell address, West Point, 1962. (From *A Soldier Reports* by William C. Westmoreland.)

(p. 21), May 10, 1968, June 14, 1968 (p. 25), December 12, 1969, January 18, 1971, January 21, 1974, May 9, 1983 (p. 63), May 23, 1983 (p. 52), May 21, 1984 (p. 86), October 15, 1984 (p. 79), October 29, 1984 (p. 72), November 26, 1984, December 17, 1984, January 21, 1985 (p. 60), February 18, 1985 (p. 75).

U.S. News & World Report, May 11, 1964, February 26, 1968 (p. 19), April 1, 1968 (p. 8), September 29, 1969, June 19, 1972, September 27, 1982 (p. 12), October 15, 1984 (p. 19), October 22, 1984 (p. 10), November 26, 1984 (p. 13), December 3, 1984 (p. 49ff), March 4, 1985 (p. 38ff).

New York Times Magazine, November 15, 1964 (pg. 27ff).

Reader's Digest, January, 1966 (p. 55ff).

Newsweek, April 18, 1966 (p. 32), May 8, 1967 (p. 31ff), February 19, 1968 (p. 33ff), April 1, 1968 (p. 45), June 24, 1968 (p. 52ff), April 21, 1969, January 11, 1971, April 12, 1971, February 8, 1982 (p. 93ff), October 15, 1984 (p. 96), October 22, 1984 (p. 60ff), December 3, 1984 (p. 93), December 17, 1984 (p. 49), November 10, 1986 (p. 77).

Ernest B. Furgurson, *Westmoreland: The Inevitable General,* Little, Brown, 1968.

Harper's, November, 1970 (p. 96ff), April, 1985 (p. 20ff).

Christian Century, June 9, 1971.

Biography News, February, 1974.

New York Times Book Review, February 1, 1976.

New York Review of Books, May 13, 1976, January 17, 1985 (p. 52ff), February 26, 1987 (p. 27ff).

Broadcasting, February 1, 1982 (p. 66ff), January 2, 1984 (p. 36ff).

TV Guide, May 29, 1982 (p. 2ff).

Esquire, October, 1984.

MacLeans, October 22, 1984, October 29, 1984, March 4, 1985.

People Weekly, October 22, 1984.

New York Times Biographical Service, November, 1984 (p. 1561).

New Leader, February 11-25, 1985 (p. 21ff).

Nation, March 2, 1985 (p. 227ff), March 30, 1985 (p. 367ff), July 5-12, 1986 (p. 6ff), August 30, 1986 (p. 134ff), November 8, 1986.

New Republic, March 18, 1985 (p. 7ff), April 6, 1987 (p. 21ff).

Columbia Journalism Review, May-June, 1985 (p. 25ff).

USA Today, September, 1985 (p. 85ff).

Pacific Affairs, Winter, 1985-86 (p. 663ff).

New Yorker, June 16, 1986 (p. 42ff), June 23, 1986 (p. 34ff).

Internal Auditor, April, 1987 (p. 53ff).

WEYN, SUZANNE 1955-

PERSONAL: Surname sounds like "wayne"; born July 6, 1955, in Flushing, N.Y.; daughter of Theodore (a pharmacist) and Jacqueline (a watercolorist; maiden name, Traub) Weyn; married William Gonzalez (in sheet metal construction), May 15, 1986; children: Diana. *Education:* Nassau Community College, A.A., 1975; State University of New York Harpur College, B.A., 1977. *Politics:* Democrat. *Agent:* Andrea Brown, Literary Agent, 301 West 53rd St., Suite 13B, New York, N.Y. 10019.

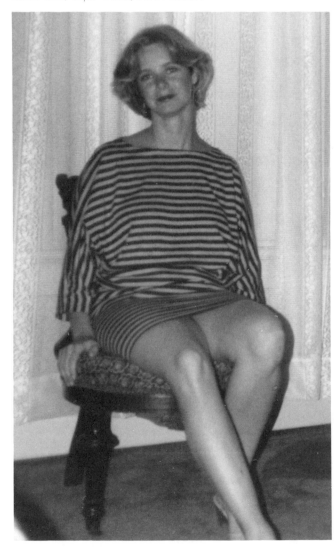

SUZANNE WEYN

CAREER: Ideals Publishing, New York, N.Y., editor, 1977-79; Starlog Press, New York, N.Y., editor, 1979-81; Scholastic, Inc., New York, N.Y., staff writer, associate editor, 1981-84; Parachute Press, New York, N.Y., senior editor, 1984-87; New York University, New York, N.Y., part time teacher of children's and business writing, 1987-89.

WRITINGS:

JUVENILE, EXCEPT AS NOTED

The Littles Sticker Book (illustrated by Manny Champana), Scholastic, 1984.
(With Grace Maccarone) *The Littles Help Out* (illustrated by Bob Clarke), Scholastic, 1984.
My Sticker Memory Book, Parachute Press, 1984.
(With G. Maccarone) *The Little Winner* (illustrated by B. Clarke), Scholastic, 1984.
The Makeover Club (young adult), Avon, 1986.
My Camp Diary (illustrated by Ann Iosa), Bradbury, 1986.
(With Ellen Steiber) *From Chuck Norris to the Karate Kid: Martial Arts in the Movies,* Parachute Press, 1986.
Snow White and the Seven Dwarfs (novelization of the Disney film), Scholastic, 1987.
The Makeover Summer (young adult), Avon, 1988.
Love Song, Ballantine, 1988.
Little Women Diary, Scholastic, 1988.
The Day the Frogs Came to Lunch (illustrated by John Speirs), Marvel Books, 1988.
Chip 'n' Dale's Rescue Rangers: The Missing Eggs Caper (illustrated by Paul Edwards), Golden Books, 1989.
Stepping Out (illustrated by Joel Iskowitz), Troll, 1989.
A Twist of Fate (illustrated by J. Iskowitz), Troll, 1989.
Emma's Turn (illustrated by J. Iskowitz), Troll, 1989.
Three for the Show (illustrated by J. Iskowitz), Troll, 1989.
Pointing toward Trouble (illustrated by J. Iskowitz), Troll, 1989.
Stage Fright (illustrated by J. Iskowitz), Troll, 1989.
Into the Dream (young adult fantasy), Fawcett, 1989.
The Makeover Campaign (young adult), Avon, 1990.
Sitting Pretty (six-book series; young adult), Troll, 1990.

WORK IN PROGRESS: A six-book series for mid-grade readers, for Scholastic.

SIDELIGHTS: "Stories and especially stories about people have always been the most interesting to me. I've always written, ever since grade school. I'd write stories and poems. I always kept a journal.

"My two other great loves while growing up were art and drama. I pursued them both all the way through college. Even though I decided to concentrate on writing, art and drama continue to help me. Drama has helped me with dialogue and art helps me visualize what I'm writing about.

"I enjoy telling stories that deal with growth. That's why writing for and about girls from ages ten to fifteen is so much fun. It's an exciting time. Old perceptions are melting, new potentials are emerging.

"When I worked at Parachute Press, I created a series called 'The Secret of the Unicorn Queen.' That idea came to me because I wanted to explore the ways in which a teenage girl might develop in a fantasy world without the expectations and pressures of our society influencing her. Other writers were hired to write the stories I outlined. They added their

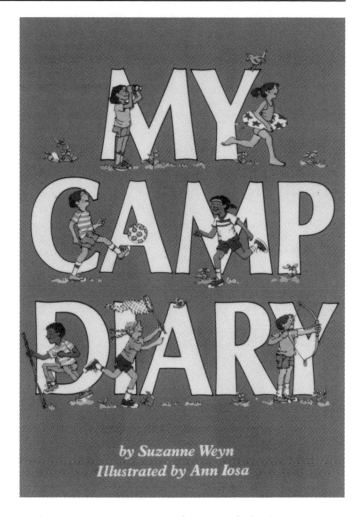

A summer at camp can be one of the best, most exciting times you'll ever have. (Illustration by Ann Iosa from *My Camp Diary* by Suzanne Weyn.)

own creativity to the outlines. It was an interesting way to work.

"Now I work full time as a writer. This is a dream come true for me. Up until now I've had to write late at night and on the weekends. I can't think of a more enjoyable way to spend my time—telling stories full time."

HOBBIES AND OTHER INTERESTS: Swimming, traveling, reading novels and history, learning about ancient religions.

WHARMBY, Margot (Alison Winn)

PERSONAL: Born in England; married Ewart Wharmby; children: David, Martin, Alison, Philip. *Home:* Cherry Burton, 3 Powys Ave., Leicester, England.

CAREER: Writer.

WRITINGS:

JUVENILE; UNDER PSEUDONYM ALISON WINN

Roundabout, Hodder & Stoughton, 1961.

Swings and Things (illustrated by Jennie Corbett and Peggie Fortnum), Hodder & Stoughton, 1963, Rand McNally, 1965.

Helter Skelter (illustrated by Janina Ede), Hodder & Stoughton, 1966.

A First Cinderella, Hodder & Stoughton, 1966.

Aunt Isabella's Umbrella (illustrated by Gladys Ambrus), Hodder & Stoughton, 1976, Children's Press, 1977.

Charlie's Iron Horse (illustrated by Val Biro), Hodder & Stoughton, 1979.

Patchwork Pieces, Hodder & Stoughton, 1980.

"Hello God," Word Books, 1984, Warner, 1985.

INTERPRETER OF ENGLISH TEXTS FROM SWEDISH; ALL JUVENILE

Gunilla Wolde, "The Thomas Books" series, ten volumes, Hodder & Stoughton, 1971-75.

Ulf Loefgren, *Who Holds Up the Traffic?,* Hodder & Stoughton, 1973.

U. Loefgren, *One, Two, Three, Four,* Hodder & Stoughton, 1973.

U. Loefgren, *The Flying Orchestra,* Hodder & Stoughton, 1973.

U. Loefgren, *The Magic Kite,* Hodder & Stoughton, 1973.

U. Loefgren, *The Colour Trumpet,* Hodder & Stoughton, 1973.

G. Wolde, "The Emma Books" series, ten volumes, Hodder & Stoughton, 1975-77.

U. Loefgren, *Harlequin,* Hodder & Stoughton, 1978.

Babro Lindgren, *The Wild Baby* (illustrated by Eve Eriksson), Hodder & Stoughton, 1981.

B. Lindgren, *The Wild Baby's Boat Trip* (illustrated by E. Eriksson), Hodder & Stoughton, 1983.

AUTHOR OF ENGLISH TEXT

U. Loefgren, *The Tale of Two Magic Hands,* Hodder & Stoughton, 1986.

B. Lindgren, *The Wild Baby's Dog* (illustrated by E. Eriksson), Hodder & Stoughton, 1986.

WHITNEY, Sharon 1937-

PERSONAL: Born May 14, 1937, in Portland, Ore.; daughter of Charles O. (a sign painter) and Helen (a waitress; maiden name, Foster) Boylan; married Morris Whitney (a sailor), 1957 (divorced, 1970); married Philip Shapiro (a psychiatrist), 1973; children: (first marriage) David, Jon. *Education:* Attended Mills College, 1955-57; University of Southern Maine, B.S., 1972; Columbia University, M.A., 1979. *Politics:* Democrat. *Religion:* Protestant. *Home:* 2712 Southwest Patton Rd., Portland, Ore. 97201.

CAREER: Juneau Empire, Juneau, Alas., part-time reporter, 1965-69; United States Forest Service, Juneau, Alas., film director, 1967-68; Gannett Newspapers, Portland, Me., reporter, 1970-73; WCBB-TV, Lewiston, Me., television host, 1970-71; Guidance Associates, New York, N.Y., filmstrip and video producer, 1975-77; Raynor-Whitney Associates, New York, N.Y., filmstrip and video producer, 1977-82; free-lance writer, 1980—; Alaska Radio Network, Anchorage, Alas., radio newscaster, 1982-84; KB00-FM, Portland, Ore., radio producer, host, and theatre critic, 1986—. Playwright-in-residence, Choate Rosemary Hall, Conn. President, Juneau-Douglas Little Theatre, 1967-68; board member, League of Women's Voters, 1966-68, and Women's Resource Center, Juneau, 1983-84. *Member:* Northwest Playwrights Guild (board of directors, 1987—), Dramatists Guild, Oregon Women's Political Caucus, Portland Drama Critics Circle.

AWARDS, HONORS: Eleanor Roosevelt was selected one of the National Council for Social Studies Best Nonfiction Trade Books, 1982; New Plays-in-Progress Winner from Portland State University, 1986, for "The Star-Crossed Musher" and "Anna's Latitude"; First Place in Playwriting from the Pacific Northwest Writers Conference, 1988, for "A Cowboy's Sweetheart"; New Play Competition Winner from Terra Nova Theatre, 1988, for "Totty"; winner of San Francisco Playwrights Center competition, Columbia Theatre Company (Portland, Ore.) competition, and Northwest Regional One-Act competition, all 1990; Grant for Experimental Theater from the Portland Metro Performing Arts, 1990.

WRITINGS:

(Contributor) *What to Do with the Rest of Your Life,* Simon & Schuster, 1980.

Eleanor Roosevelt (young adult), F. Watts, 1982.

The Equal Rights Amendment: The History and the Movement (young adult), F. Watts., 1984.

(With Tom Raynor) *Women in Politics* (young adult), F. Watts, 1986.

The Star-Crossed Musher (play), Alaska Department of Education, 1989.

A Talk from Brother Bob (play), Portland Review, 1989.

UNPUBLISHED PLAYS

"Anna's Latitude," 1986.

"Totty," 1986, revised edition "Totty: Young Eleanor Roosevelt," 1989.

"A Cowboy's Sweetheart," 1987.

"Five Minute Wars," 1988.

SHARON WHITNEY

Geraldine Ferraro, the first woman candidate for vice-president, salutes delegates at the Democratic National Convention in 1984. (Photograph courtesy of UPI/Bettmann Newsphotos from *Women in Politics* by Sharon Whitney and Tom Raynor.)

Theatre columnist, *InUnison* magazine, 1988-89, and *ProWoman,* 1990—.

WORK IN PROGRESS: A one-woman play based on the life of Margaret Mead.

SIDELIGHTS: "As soon as I began to read, I smuggled 'Dick and Jane' under the covers and stayed up late at night revising it. When I was in elementary school I lived with a foster family—good people who kept me clean, but never asked how I was or what I was thinking. With no one paying attention, I learned to watch and to form my own opinions. A lonely childhood isn't the worst fate. It provides time to wonder about the riddles of life. Why, for instance, would a fifteen-year-old girl, like my foster sister, get married? How can a city seize a house from an old lady, like my grandma, just to build a bigger street? If you press a special spot on your wrist like the leading character in *Harriet Hart, Detective,* can you become invisible? These were some of the situations I pondered, rocking by myself in the garden swing.

"Throughout school I enjoyed writing reports and debating subjects of interest, like the proof of right and wrong. I used my ready skills to scoot through subjects I didn't care about, though I probably should have paid more attention. I wrote breezy articles for my school tabloid, while at home I tried to write deep essays in the style of my favorite authors. I spent my sixteenth year influenced by T. S. Eliot and Kahlil Gibran, trying to articulate the conditions of sainthood. I was an ornery tomboy, so it didn't come easy.

"In high school I ran with a fast pack, but moonlighted with a more literate circle. We ate Chinese food, read the *Atlantic* and the *New Yorker,* and talked about Holden Caulfield. When my peers graduated to universities, I chose instead to go to a 'girls school,' Mills College in California. There I met young women from all over the world, girls who knew poetry, film, theatre, music, dance, and literature. For months I was too excited to sleep. Influenced by conversations that raged to 4 a.m., I declared myself a philosophy major.

"I studied fiction, but as a college girl I didn't take writing seriously as a vocation. Nevertheless, I improved because the competition was sharp and the standards were high. (Every class, even physical science, graded work on both content and language skills.) Girls were told repeatedly that they could be whatever they wished, but the only career mentioned by my advisor was teaching elementary school. I had no interest in the field, so it was suggested that maybe I could be a society editor for a newspaper like a Mills girl who was a philosophy major before me.

"I left school in frustration, having no clear goals. It was years before I finished my undergraduate degree and finally, graduate school. Instead I married young and had two children. My sons were preschoolers when I was recruited by a small town newspaper to write and edit copy. My first job was doing obituaries. The ink wasn't dry on the *Juneau Empire* when I seized the first professional story I had written: 'Mrs. Etta Jones Died Unexpectedly in Her Sleep at 95.' I howled with pleasure, noting that no one dies unexpectedly at ninety-five. The wonderful thing about reporting is, the next day you have a chance to do it better. So I improved. Soon I advanced to features, then hard news. I learned to write and rewrite, and to welcome the editor's pencil.

"In my subsequent career, which included newspapers, books, television, radio, and educational media, I was never attracted to the kinds of writing that make big money. When I was offered jobs in public relations and advertising, I was flattered but I also got an instant migraine. I've never had a moment's desire to sell a product or a personality, although I know very well that my work as a journalist has always been informed with a *point of view.* Like any writer, I sell ideas, whether the work is documentary or fiction.

"A few years ago I left New York City to return to the Northwest, where I grew up. I haven't lived here since I went away to college. In returning, I had two objectives: to find my roots, and to write fiction. Specifically, I wanted to become a playwright. I wasn't choosing this field out of the blue. I knew something about theater from various interludes as an actor, director, and critic. I gave myself two years to get my first play 'up,' and I made it. I believe my background as a journalist helped move me quickly into playwriting. Being a trained writer with self-discipline and editing skills is very helpful.

"'Totty,' my first play, grew from one of my books for young adults, *Eleanor Roosevelt.* It's the story of Eleanor's coming-of-age at Allenswood, a boarding school in England. In my book, I couldn't take the time to explore this important period in Eleanor's life. The play lets me imagine more fully the relationships and conflicts that prompted Eleanor's first

awakening as a woman of conscience. This play—like all of my plays—has won several awards. I plan to submit it for publication.

"I have twice been playwright-in-residence at Choate Rosemary Hall in Connecticut. This is where I work on my plays for young actors, like 'Totty' and 'Five Minute Wars.' Because of the Choate program, I'm committed to continue writing for teen-agers, and to not let my 'adult' plays claim all my attention. Practically speaking, I don't think there's a more important audience than youth."

HOBBIES AND OTHER INTERESTS: Film, travel.

WHYTE, Ron 1942(?)-1989

OBITUARY NOTICE: Born about 1942 in Black Eagle, Mont.; died of a cerebral hemorrhage, September 13, 1989, in New Haven, Conn. Editor and writer. A quadriplegic due to birth defects, Whyte was known for his plays concerning the physically handicapped. He earned an M.F.A. from Yale University's school of drama in 1967 and went on to write such plays as "Welcome to Andromeda," which won three Drama-Logue awards, and "Amerikan Shrapnel." Whyte's 1978 play about a quadriplegic, "Disability: A Comedy," was nominated for a Pulitzer Prize in 1983, and his "Funeral March for a One-Man Band" earned four Joseph Jefferson awards in 1979. Whyte also wrote a children's book, *The Flower That Finally Grew,* and screenplays, including "The Happiness Cage." In addition, he served as arts and book review editor for the *Soho Weekly News* and theater and film editor for the *American Book Review.*

FOR MORE INFORMATION SEE:

National Playwrights Director, 2nd edition, Eugene O'Neill Theatre Center, 1981.
Contemporary Theatre, Film, and Television, Volume 1, Gale, 1984.

OBITUARIES

Washington Post, September 17, 1989.
New York Times, September 19, 1989.
Contemporary Authors, Volume 129, Gale, 1990.

WIRTH, Beverly 1938-

PERSONAL: Born July 20, 1938, in Cleveland, Ohio; daughter of Howard Richard (a surgical/medical supplier) and Dorothy (Williamson) Schuemann; married Bradford P. Wirth (a pharmacist), August 26, 1960; children: Bradford P. II, Peter E. *Education:* Attended Sweet Briar College, 1956-58, and Rhode Island School of Design, 1958-60, Syracuse University, B.F.A., 1961, M.F.A., 1978. *Religion:* Protestant. *Home and office:* 2175 Patterson Rd., Marietta, N.Y. 13110. *Agent:* Maria Piscopo, 2038 Calvert, Costa Mesa, Calif. 92626.

CAREER: Artist, designer, and illustrator, with work exhibited at colleges and museums and commissioned by churches; author and illustrator, 1975—; Onondaga Community College, Syracuse, N.Y., instructor in illustration, 1976; Hartwick College, Oneonta, N.Y., assistant to Uri Shulevitz, 1981; Skidmore College, Saratoga Springs, N.Y., instructor

BEVERLY WIRTH

in children's book illustration, 1982. Judge, "Showcase of Children's Books," Everson Museum, Syracuse, 1983, 1984. *Exhibitions*—Group shows: Munson-Williams-Proctor Institute, Utica, N.Y., 1970; Everson Museum of Art, Syracuse, N.Y., 1975; Memorial Art Gallery, Rochester, N.Y., 1978; Maria Regina College, 1979; St. David's Celebration of the Arts, Fayetteville, N.Y., 1979; Schick Gallery, Skidmore College, Saratoga, N.Y., 1982; International Society of Interior Designers House, Los Angeles, Calif., 1985; Royal Ontario Museum, Toronto, Ontario, Canada, 1985; Sixty-eighth General Convention of the Episcopal Church, Anaheim, Calif., 1985; Dioceses of Kansas, Central New York, New Jersey, and Pennsylvania, 1985-88; Washington National Cathedral, Washington, D.C., 1986; Fortress Church Supply Stores, Philadelphia, Pa., 1987; United Church of Christ, Ft. Worth, Tex., 1989.

MEMBER: Stained Glass Association of America (associate member), Graphic Artists Guild of New York, Junior League of Syracuse, Glass Art Society, Interfaith Forum on Religion, Art and Architecture, Association Uniting Religion and Art. *Awards, honors:* Art and Poetry Contest First Honorable Mention from the National League of American Penwomen, 1983, for "The Wizard of Oz" collage; Graphic Achievement Award from the Fox River Paper Company, 1977.

WRITINGS:

Margie and Me (juvenile; illustrated by Karen A. Weinhaus), Four Winds, 1982.

ILLUSTRATOR

(Contributor of photographs) *All about Bulbs,* Ortho Books, 1981.
"Creation and Recreation" (filmstrip and educational packet), United Church Press, 1984.
Bible Discovery, United Church Press, 1988.
Health, Death, and Resurrection, United Church Press, 1989.

Contributor to periodicals, including *American Artist, Herald-Journal,* and *American* (Syracuse).

WORK IN PROGRESS: Writing and illustrating ten children's books on spiritual themes; audio visuals as slide presentations on Christian themes.

SIDELIGHTS: "I first started writing at the age of thirteen when influenced by a spiritual experience. My mother sent my meditations to Norman Vincent Peale who wrote me back a personal letter saying, 'You have the gift of spiritual insight and understanding.'

"In my schooling I pursued art in many media and forms, finally attaining degrees in advertising and then illustration. Since 1983 my professional efforts have been directed specifically to Christian art. The use of paper collage and glass mosaics are my favorite media. I enjoy writing my own spiritual journeys and illustrating them so that others can share in my trials and victories.

"*Margie and Me* is an elementary translation of my own personal experience with my dog, Margie. I meant to convey the sharing and love that a child may experience with its own pet.

"I am titled 'Artist for Christ,' as I feel my talents in art and religious gifts are best used and directed to the glory of God, in the many avenues of publishing. I have traveled widely in the United States and Europe photographing religious art and images of spiritual interest. I am compiling these slides into audio-visual presentations, such as 'Three Spiritual Journeys.'"

FOR MORE INFORMATION SEE:

The World Who's Who of Women, ninth edition, International Biographical Centre, 1987.

WOLFF, Alexander 1957-

PERSONAL: Born February 3, 1957, in Wilmington, Del.; son of Nikolaus (a chemist) and Mary (a musician; maiden name, Neave) Wolff. *Education:* Princeton University, B.A. (cum laude), 1980. *Home:* New York City; Portsmouth, N.H. *Office: Sports Illustrated,* Time and Life Bldg., New York, N.Y. 10020.

CAREER: Sports Illustrated, New York, N.Y., reporter, 1980-81, writer/reporter, 1981-82, staff writer, 1982-85, senior writer, 1985—. *Member:* Professional Basketball Writers Association of America, United States Basketball Writers Association, National Sportscasters and Sportswriters Association, Association Internationale de la Presse Sportive. *Awards, honors:* Four writing awards from the United States Basketball Writers Association.

WRITINGS:

(With Chuck Wielgus) *The In-Your-Face Basketball Book,* Everest House, 1980, reissued, Wynwood Press, 1989.

(With C. Wielgus) *The Back-In-Your Face Guide to Pick-Up Basketball,* Dodd, 1986.

(With C. Wielgus and Steve Rushin), *From A-Train to Yogi: The Fan's Book of Sports Nicknames,* Harper, 1987.

(With Armen Keteyian) *Raw Recruits,* Pocket Books, 1990.

(Contributor) Dave Sloan, editor, *1990 Best Sports Stories,* Sporting News, 1990.

WORK IN PROGRESS: One Hundred Years of Hoops, a celebration of basketball's centennial, to be published by Oxmoor House.

SIDELIGHTS: "I played basketball in high school and for one season, 1977-78, overseas for a club team in Lucerne, Switzerland. Sports have always fascinated me, but as I got older, I followed sports more and more for the opportunities they presented a writer—insights into people and how they go about pursuing the goals they set. Yet I consider myself a writer first and sportswriter second, and in my magazine pieces for *Sports Illustrated* I look particularly for subjects that transcend the arena. No matter how much you love sports, you will be a better sportswriter if you bring to your writing about the games a well-rounded sensibility.

"I am asked more often than anything else how I came to do what I do, and how someone hoping to become a sportswriter should go about it. Always I answer: I did it by writing, and you should do the same thing. Write at every opportunity; show your work to others for feedback; don't be discouraged by criticism. There are a few blessed geniuses for whom writing comes easily, but for most of us it's a painstaking undertaking, rife with trial, error, and discouragement. What makes it worthwhile is a finished product that somehow works.

"I have collaborated on all four of my books thus far, and enjoy the give-and-take of working with co-authors. Basketball, my area of speciality, is a very social game."

WOODHOUSE, Barbara (Blackburn) 1910-1988

PERSONAL: Born May 9, 1910, in Rathfarnham, County Dublin, Ireland; died July 9, 1988; daughter of William (a clergyman headmaster) and Leilah (Masterman) Blackburn; married Michael Woodhouse (a physician), August 7, 1940; children: Pamela, Judith, Patrick. *Education:* Harper Adams Agricultural College, Certificate in Agriculture, 1930. *Politics:* Conservative. *Religion:* Protestant. *Residence:* Hertfordshire, England.

CAREER: Dog and horse trainer; television personality; writer. Researcher for Ministry of Agriculture, 1931-33; affiliated with Liebigs Co., Argentina, 1934-37. Director, Barbara Woodhouse & Junia Ltd. (film company): produced and directed films, including "Trouble for Juno," "Juno Makes Friends," "Juno the Home Help," "A Star Is Made," "Sinner to Saint," "School for Problem Dogs," "Career with Dogs," "Sing a Song of Sixpence," "Trouble with Junia," "Love Me, Love My Dog," and "Along the Way." Star of British Broadcasting Corp. television series, "Training Dogs the Woodhouse Way" and a series on horses and ponies; star

of television special programs; guest personality on numerous television and radio programs and at public appearances throughout the world. *Awards, honors:* Numerous awards for work on television, including Pye Colour Television Award as the French television "Personality of the Year," 1980; Multi-Coloured Swapshop Star Award, 1980-81; and BBC Children's Television recognition as viewers' "Favourite Lady."

WRITINGS:

Talking to Animals (autobiography), Faber, 1954, Norton, 1955, new edition, Faber, 1970, Stein & Day, 1972.

Dog Training My Way, Faber, 1954, new edition, 1970, Stein & Day, 1972.

Chica: The Story of a Very Little Dog, Faber, 1955.

The A-Z of Dogs and Puppies, Parrish, 1956, Stein & Day, 1972.

Difficult Dogs, Faber, 1957.

The Book of Show Dogs, Parrish, 1957.

The Girl Book of Ponies, Longacre, 1957, published as *The Book of Ponies,* Parrish, 1965, Stein & Day, 1972.

The Barbara Woodhouse Book of Dogs, Longacre, 1957.

The A-Z of Dogs, Parrish, 1958.

Wendy: The Story of a Horse, Parrish, 1959.

(Author of introduction) *Dogs in Colour,* Viking, 1960.

Know Your Dog: Psychiatry or Sense?, Parrish, 1961.

The A-Z of Puppies, Parrish, 1962.

Almost Human (autobiography), Woodhouse, 1976, Penguin, 1981.

The World of Dogs, Cartwell Books, 1976.

(Author of foreword) *All about Dogs,* Octopus, 1976.

No Bad Dogs [and] *Know Your Dog,* Woodhouse, 1978.

Encyclopedia of Dogs and Puppies, Stein & Day, 1978.

My Story: Just Barbara, M. Joseph, 1981, Summit Books, 1986.

BARBARA WOODHOUSE

(Cover photograph by Peter Riding from *No Bad Dogs: The Woodhouse Way* by Barbara Woodhouse.)

No Bad Dogs: The Woodhouse Way, Summit Books, 1982, published as *No Bad Dogs: Training Dogs the Woodhouse Way,* 1984.
The Arco Color Book of Dogs, Arco, 1983.
Walkies: Dog Care the Woodhouse Way (illustrated by A. Scott), Benn, 1982, Summit Books, 1983.
Barbara's World of Horses and Ponies, Summit Books, 1984.

Also author of privately printed books, *Jyntee, the Tale of a Dog with a Broken Tail,* 1950; *Juno, Daughter of Jyntee,* 1953; and *Talking in Spanish, Talking in German, Talking in French,* and *Talking in Italian,* all 1961.

SIDELIGHTS: "Dogs may be man's best friend, but they worship and adore Barbara Woodhouse," declares Gerald Clarke in *Time.* "Given half a chance, the entire canine species doubtless would slobber and slurp all over her, tails wagging fast enough to cause gale warnings throughout the British Isles." The English dog trainer and author, however, "is not a slobbery, slurpy sort of lady," Clarke cautions. Barking orders to the human and canine students in her obedience classes, she "could be taken for a British school mistress or perhaps a well-heeled drill sergeant," puns the *Christian Science Monitor*'s Diane Casselberry Manuel. While Woodhouse's dog training career dates back to early childhood, she first gained worldwide acclaim at age seventy as star of the British Broadcasting Corp. (BBC) television

series, "Training Dogs the Woodhouse Way." Viewed throughout the world, the shows presented her practical, often ascerbic advice on how to turn unruly pets into pleasant companions. Comments Clarke: "The dogs appear to be enjoying themselves; the owners, a dozen or so terror-stricken men and women, do not. That, of course, is where all the fun lies for the viewer, in the comic reversal of the customary roles of man and beast."

Maintaining that "there is no such thing as a difficult dog, only an inexperienced owner," Woodhouse claims it takes most dogs only five or ten minutes to learn basic obedience—to sit, down, stay, heel, and come. Their owners, on the other hand, present a greater challenge. Week after week, the bumbling humans make mistakes—holding leashes improperly, getting the commands wrong—only to meet with sharp reprimands from their instructor. Accused of tongue-lashing the hapless handlers on the air, Woodhouse explained to Caroline Thompson in the *Los Angeles Times:* "It's a fun scold. My tongue is in my cheek. I couldn't stand it otherwise because, you see, the people do so many stupid things so many times that unless you have a joke about it, you'd be tearing your hair out, wouldn't you? Even if the people look like they're hanging their heads, they're not really. They know perfectly well it's all a joke. And the dogs love it. There's nothing a dog likes better than a good laugh."

Laughter, some critics claim, forms the basis of Woodhouse's appeal. Labeled "the most original—and unintentionally funny—female personality since Julia Child" by Clarke and, according to Manuel, "the first genuine hoot of the eighties" by a London *Daily Mail* writer, Woodhouse presents her subject earnestly while tolerating—even cultivating—an eccentric image that attracts followers wherever she goes. During interviews and guest appearances her comments can be "a little arrogant, a little batty, eminently practical, unswervingly frank and, at moments, totally absurd," Thompson contends.

Always ready with unusual or amusing anecdotes, the animal expert possesses a talent for recognizing and meeting her audience's expectations. She related in a *People Weekly* interview, for instance: "I love spiders. For years we had a pet spider. He had a hole in the fireplace and used to come out at night and sit on my lap and watch the telly." And, disliking the standard obedience command "heel," the trainer promotes an exuberant, sing-song "walkies!" The word has become a Woodhouse trademark, the title of her comic-strip picture book for young readers, and the target of much satire. "But as long as it makes people laugh, I don't mind," Woodhouse tells Thompson. "You see, this is the joy of the word 'walkies.' Everybody says it and then shrieks with laughter. I don't have to amuse them, they amuse themselves."

While her approach may seem light-hearted, Woodhouse makes it clear that her best-selling books, television programs, and personal appearances comprise a serious campaign to make every dog "a decent member of society and a joy to own." At a time when increasing numbers of people charge high fees as dog psychologists, the trainer states that "a lot of rubbish has been spoken about the psychoanalyzing of dogs in the modern world, and having now trained over 17,000 dogs in twenty years, I feel I am qualified to express an opinion on the subject of dog behavior." In the introduction to *No Bad Dogs: The Woodhouse Way,* she goes on to emphasize that "psychoanalysis is impossible . . . since [dogs] cannot answer questions and the concepts of their minds cannot be recalled and probed and changed, cast out or anything else." Instead, the author relies on common sense and ESP to assess difficult dogs. She approaches recalcitrant canines by tuning in on their mental wavelength; then, she expounds, it's simply a matter of training with firmness, fairness, and fun. "Telepathy, on the part of dog and owner, plays a vast part in the happy companionship between dog and mankind," she writes. Woodhouse summarized for the *Los Angeles Times's* Ursula Vils: "It doesn't matter what the words are. One day I ran a whole lesson in vegetables; I said 'potatoes' and 'carrots' instead of 'sit' and 'heel.' It's the tone of your voice, your touch. I use three things: touch, tone and telepathy."

Much of the star's reputation as a miracle-worker stems from impromptu demonstrations of "the Woodhouse way." As an awestruck owner stands aside, the trainer commandeers the leash and reforms the four-footed delinquent in less time than it takes to say "*What* a clever dog" (her favorite words of praise). The magic is worked by getting "simpatico," giving a few jerks on a large-link chain choke collar, and using firm commands and hand gestures. Anyone with "a working knowledge of dogs," Woodhouse admits in *No Bad Dogs*, could do the same: "A human personality can be so powerful that it can make a dog do and think things almost by hypnotism, just as a good actress can carry the audience to the height of happiness or despair with the part she is playing. But when the curtain drops, the atmosphere fades and the audience returns to its mundane affairs. That is why I have refused and shall continue to refuse to take dogs to train without their owners. I know I can make a dog do almost exactly as I wish when alone with it . . . . But will a dog that carries out orders with army-like precision for me, with evident joy on its face, do the same for an owner who may be out of tune with the dog, either from lack of experience or sympathy, or from being just plain stupid, conceited or pigheaded? I know it won't."

In addition to ignorance, selfishness, and stubborness, Woodhouse identifies sentimentality and lack of imagination as the human foibles owners must overcome to succeed in dog training. "Love is one thing; sentimentality is another," she writes. "Dogs like firm commands and loving praise . . . . Owners fail to realize that if they use firm, confident, kind jerks and a happy tone of voice, most dogs can be cured . . . in a few hours." A good jerk on the large-link chain collar makes a distinct "click" but doesn't hurt the dog, Woodhouse tells her students. Disagreeing with many animal behaviorists, she also maintains that the "sky's the limit" when training the household pet. Convinced that dogs can attain the vocabulary of a five-year-old child, she urges people to teach their canine family members as many tasks as possible. Assign a new chore each day, she suggests, pointing out that dogs, like humans, get bored. Left by themselves, they will find their own—often destructive—activities.

Although "the dog lady" (as she's known in Britain) enjoyed an "obscure" history before fame claimed her at age seventy, according to Roy Fuller in the *Listener*, her youth and early adulthood were not uneventful. "Born . . . into the comfortably-off middle-class . . . the death of her father when she was nine made her early life more unconventional than it would otherwise have been (though convention could never have ruled her)," Fuller writes. One of Woodhouse's earliest memories, not surprisingly, is of her first dog. At the age of two she was bitten on the nose by the pup—a mongrel bought from a gypsy. The unpropitious start, she tells interviewers, was her own fault. She simply hugged the dog too tightly. Several years later she rescued a pit bull from the Battersea

dog pound, smuggled it home on a bus, trained it to be a proper pet, and found it a good home. She's been training animals ever since.

A love of horses likewise began in childhood, when army mounts grazed at the Irish college where her father was headmaster. Woodhouse's interest in training horses eventually took her to Argentina, where she learned the Indians' trick of breathing into a wild pony's nose to tame it. Once you "speak" to a horse in this native language, he'll follow you anywhere, Woodhouse proclaims. Not content to limit the application of her "God-given gift," as she calls it in *People Weekly,* Woodhouse also has trained a pig on a live television program and a praying mantis during a tour of Africa.

Woodhouse's husband, Michael, comments on how she began writing her books: "Barbara never thought of writing until a friend introduced her to a BBC radio producer. She was a guest on his program and he suggested that she write a letter to a leading newspaper about her experiences. After this publishers wrote or called her asking her to publish a book—that was the start of her public career."

Woodhouse's autobiography *Talking to Animals,* first published in 1954, documents her pre-personality days. In addition to relating childhood experiences, it tells behind-the-scenes tales of her career as a motion picture animal trainer. Most famous of her animal proteges were Juno and Junia, Great Danes owned and trained by Woodhouse. They starred in innumerable television and movie productions, including feature films made by the trainer's own cinema company. Commenting on *Talking to Animals,* Fuller notes that "there are a good few useful hints about life . . . besides such general social information as how to . . . in a simple way increase milk-yield in cattle." He concludes: "The force of her narrative is such that one's opinion of Douglas Fairbanks Jr. goes up when one learns that her cow, Snow Queen, fell in love with him, and he is commended for his 'gentle behaviour with her.'"

FOR MORE INFORMATION SEE:

Kirkus Reviews, November 1, 1972, December 15, 1972, February 1, 1974.
Time, March 12, 1973, December 7, 1981.
Library Journal, March 15, 1973, June 1, 1974, April 15, 1982.
Publishers Weekly, January 28, 1974, February 19, 1982.
Listener, September 25, 1980.
Times Educational Supplement, September 4, 1981, October 1, 1982.
Booklist, February 1, 1982.
Washington Post, February 8, 1982.
People Weekly, February 15, 1982.
Los Angeles Times, March 14, 1982, February 9, 1984.
Christian Science Monitor, May 13, 1982.
Observer, December 5, 1982.
Minnesota Daily, January 17, 1983.
New York Times Book Review, January 30, 1983.
Chicago Sun Times, October 19, 1983.

WRIGHT, Betty Ren 1927-
(Revena)

PERSONAL: Born June 15, 1927, in Wakefield, Mich.; daughter of William (a teacher) and Revena (a teacher;

maiden name, Trezise) Wright; married George Frederiksen (a commercial art director), October 9, 1976; stepchildren: Judith, John, Deborah. *Education:* Milwaukee-Downer College (now Lawrence University), B.A., 1949; additional study, University of Wisconsin, and Breadloaf Writers' Conference at Middlebury College. *Politics:* Independent. *Religion:* Methodist. *Home:* 611 47th Ave., Kenosha, Wis. 53144. *Agent:* Larry Sternig, Larry Sternig Literary Agency, 742 Robertson St., Milwaukee, Wis. 53213.

CAREER: Western Publishing, Racine, Wis., editorial assistant, 1949-67, managing editor of editorial department, 1967-78; full-time writer, 1978—. Lectures, teaches workshops. *Member:* Allied Authors, Society of Children's Book Writers, Phi Beta Kappa.

AWARDS, HONORS: Alumni Service Award from Lawrence University, 1973, for contributions to children's literature; Children's Choice from the International Reading Association and the Children's Book Council, 1981, for *Why Do I Daydream?*, 1984, for *Ghosts beneath Our Feet,* and 1985, for *Christina's Ghost;* Notable Children's Trade Book in Social Studies from the National Council for Social Studies and the Children's Book Council, 1982, for *My Sister Is Different; Booklist*'s Reviewer's Choice, 1983, Edgar Allan Poe Award Runner-up for Best Juvenile from the Mystery Writers of America, 1984, Texas Bluebonnet Award from the Texas Library Association, Mark Twain Award from the Missouri Association of School Librarians, and Young

Reader's Choice Award from the Pacific Northwest Library Association, all 1986, California Young Reader Medal from the California Reading Association, 1987, Iowa Children's Choice Award, and Wyoming Indian Paintbrush Award, both 1988, and New Mexico Children's Choice Award, and Rebecca Caudill Young Readers Book Award from the Illinois Association for Media in Education, both 1989, all for *The Dollhouse Murders.*

Juvenile Book Award from the Council for Wisconsin Writers, 1985, Kansas City Children's Choice Award, Texas Bluebonnet Award, Sequoyah Children's Book Award from the Oklahoma Library Association, South Carolina Children's Book Award from the South Carolina Association of School Librarians, and Georgia Children's Book Award from the College of Education, University of Georgia, all 1988, Young Hoosier Book Award from the Association for Indiana Media Educators, 1989, and Virginia Young Readers Program from the State Reading Association 1990, all for *Christina's Ghost; The Summer of Mrs. MacGregor* was selected one of *Redbook*'s Ten Top Books for Teens, 1987.

WRITINGS:

Willy Woo-oo-oo (illustrated by Florence Sarah Winship), Whitman, 1951.

Snowball (illustrated by F. S. Winship), Whitman, 1952.

The Yellow Cat (illustrated by Sari), Whitman, 1952.

Jim Jump (illustrated by Sharon Banigan), Whitman, 1954.

Poppyseed (illustrated by F. S. Winship), Whitman, 1954.

(Under pseudonym Revena) *Mr. Mogg's Dogs* (illustrated by Si Frankcl), Whitman, 1954.

My Big Book (illustrated by Louise Myers and Jack Myers), Whitman, 1954.

Train Coming! (illustrated by Florian), Whitman, 1954.

(Adapter) *Bear Country* (based on the Walt Disney movie; illustrated by Edward Godwin and Stephani Godwin), Whitman, 1954.

(Adapter) *Beaver Valley* (based on the Walt Disney movie; illustrated by Marjorie Hartwell), Whitman, 1954.

(Adapter with Alice Hanson) *Water Birds* (based on the Walt Disney movie; illustrated by M. Hartwell), Whitman, 1955.

(Reteller) *American Folkore* (illustrated by Walt Disney Studio), Whitman, 1956.

Roundabout Train (illustrated by Charles Clement), Whitman, 1958.

Good Morning, Farm (illustrated by Fred Weinman), Whitman, 1964.

Histoire d'un Lapin Gris, Editions des deux coqs d'or, 1965.

I Want to Read (illustrated by Aliki), Whitman, 1965.

This Room Is Mine (illustrated by Judy Stang), Whitman, 1966.

Teddy Bear's Book of 1-2-3 (illustrated with photographs by Gerry Swart), Golden Press, 1969.

(With Joanne Wylie) *Elephant's Birthday Party: A Story about Shapes* (illustrated by Les Gray), Golden Press, 1971.

Bunny Button, Whitman, 1953, published under pseudonym Revena as *El conejo rabito* (illustrated by Bernice Myers), Organizaction Editorial Novaro, 1971.

The Cat Who Stamped His Feet (illustrated by Tom O'Sullivan), Golden Press, 1975.

The Rabbit's Adventure (illustrated by Maggie Swanson), Golden Press, 1977.

Roger's Upside-Down Day (illustrated by Jared D. Lee), Western, 1979.

BETTY REN WRIGHT

The Day Our TV Broke Down (illustrated by Barbara Bejna and Shirlee Jensen), Raintree, 1980.

Why Do I Daydream? (illustrated by Tom Redman), Raintree, 1981.

(Adapter) H. G. Wells, *The Time Machine* (illustrated by Ivan Powell), Raintree, 1981.

(Adapter) Stephen Crane, *The Red Badge of Courage* (illustrated by Charles Shaw), Raintree, 1981.

I Like Being Alone (illustrated by Krystyna Stasiak), Raintree, 1981.

My New Mom and Me (illustrated by Betsy Day), Raintree, 1981.

My Sister Is Different (illustrated by Helen Cogancherry), Raintree, 1981.

Getting Rid of Marjorie, Holiday House, 1981.

The Secret Window (Junior Literary Guild selection), Holiday House, 1982.

(Adapter), Emily Bronte, *Wuthering Heights* (illustrated by H. Cogancherry), Raintree, 1982.

The Dollhouse Murders (Junior Literary Guild selection), Holiday House, 1983 (published in England as *The Ghosts in the Attic,* Hippo Books, 1983).

Ghosts beneath Our Feet, Holiday House, 1984.

Christina's Ghost (Junior Literary Guild selection), Holiday House, 1985.

The Summer of Mrs. MacGregor (Junior Literary Guild selection), Holiday House, 1986.

A Ghost in the Window (Junior Literary Guild selection), Holiday House, 1987.

Chris's eyes flew open. (Jacket illustration by Stephen Mancusi from *Christina's Ghost* by Betty Ren Wright.)

The Pike River Phantom (Junior Literary Guild selection), Holiday House, 1988.

Rosie and the Dance of the Dinosaurs, Holiday House, 1989.

The Ghost of Ernie P., Holiday House, 1990.

Some Day You'll Be Sorry, Scholastic, in press.

The Cat Next Door, Holiday House, in press.

Wright's works have been published in Swedish and Spanish. Contributor of short stories to periodicals, including *Redbook, Ladies' Home Journal, Woman's Day, Woman's World, Cosmopolitan, Colorado Quarterly, Yankee, Mike Shane, Saint, Ingenue, Seventeen, Alfred Hitchcock's Mystery Magazine, Saturday Evening Post,* and *Young Miss.*

WORK IN PROGRESS: A novel, for Holiday House.

SIDELIGHTS: "My first book was a collection of poems begun when I was seven. My mother bought a black loose-leaf notebook, had my name lettered on it, and there it was—a book with my name on the cover. That was a dream come true, a dream that I wanted to repeat!

"I was blessed with teachers in grade school, high school, and college who encouraged me a great deal, always with the warning that I'd better plan on another job besides writing. With that warning in mind, I went to work as an editorial assistant; it was as close as I could get to writing and still be sure of a steady income. Editing turned out to be a wonderful occupation, and I enjoyed it for many years, while continuing to write, mostly adult short fiction, in my free time.

"When I left editing to free-lance in 1978, I intended to concentrate on adult fiction. First, though, I decided to try one novel for boys and girls—and since I'd recently married and become a step-grandmother that seemed like a good subject for a story. I'd married into a warm, welcoming family, but it was easy to imagine what life might have been like if there had been one grandchild who was totally hostile to the idea of a new grandmother. That was how *Getting Rid of Marjorie* was born.

"Writing that book was fun! I decided to try one more—and one more—and then another. Now I'm at work on number twelve, and I'm still loving it.

"Each of my books has sizeable chunks of my own life in it—people or events or feelings, or all three. The ideas sometimes grow out of a very small incident, but making that small incident grow seems to me to be the most exciting part of writing."

Betty Ren Wright is a life-long fan of ghost tales and mysteries, although she enjoys reading—and writing—other kinds of stories as well. She weaves the supernatural with the real in her mysteries. A friend gave her the idea of the haunted dollhouse in *The Dollhouse Murders.* "She shared with me the satisfaction and real pain that comes with recreating, in miniature, a beloved home remembered from childhood. She uncovered disturbing feelings when she began looking backward so intently, and it seemed to me that a dollhouse so laden with memory might well be haunted.

"I love being scared!

"The question I've heard most often is, 'Have you ever *seen* a ghost?' I'm sorry the answer has to be No—I do keep

(Jacket art by Stephen Mancusi from *The Dollhouse Murders* by Betty Ren Wright.)

looking, and hoping!—but since I haven't actually met one the next best thing has to be to make up my own.

"Like most stories, *The Pike River Phantom* had several starting points. The ghost herself—a peculiar creature who grows younger with each sighting—has been drifting around in my brain for a long time. Charlie Hocking, the person who discovers her, came about because so many boys had asked why all my books have been about girls. There is no *good* answer to that question—and so I began to think about Charlie.

"I've always been intrigued, too, by the special kind of problem Charlie has in getting to know and understand his father. When we are very young, our parents are simply our parents, perfect because they are who they are. As we get older, we begin to see them as individuals, and sometimes we must get to know them all over again. Since Charlie's father has spent five years in prison, they have missed a long period of getting to understand and appreciate each other, and they have a lot of catching up to do.

"Finally, I like to write about small towns, even though I've lived in fairly large cities most of my life. When I was a little girl, we spent summer vacations in a town much like Pike River; I remember it as a wonderful place in which to grow up. The town recently celebrated its centennial, and the parade in *The Pike River Phantom* is based on the parade that marked the climax of the centennial activities."

"In my mysteries, I like to explore relationships. Partial inspiration for *The Dollhouse Murders* arose from my interest in the problems and adjustments of life with a retarded sibling. One summer years ago, I saw two brothers in a restaurant, the younger one retarded. Their obviously loving relationship made me marvel at all the work necessary to reach that point."

The Summer of Mrs. MacGregor is about growing pains and the fact that sometimes the best medicine comes from unlikely sources. "Mrs. MacGregor is an unlikely source—an eccentric, wildly unreliable young lady who lives in a world of her own imagining, but who is, nevertheless, just what Caroline needs during a very painful time in her life.

"I suspect we each have a Mrs. MacGregor at some time or other—a person who could have hurt us but instead provided strength and inspiration.

"The book began as a short story, 'The Afternoon of Mrs. MacGregor,' published in *Woman's Day* magazine in October, 1974. As the title suggests, the story brought Mrs. MacGregor and Caroline together for just a few hours. I always felt, however, that there was more to tell about the two girls and how they affected each other, and writing the book gave me a chance to know them much better.

"The book also gave me an opportunity to write about some of the problems that come with failing health and old age, as seen in Mr. Jameson. It's a subject close to my heart, since my mother was in a nursing home for six years."

HOBBIES AND OTHER INTERESTS: Reading, travel, pets.

FOR MORE INFORMATION SEE:

Sharon McElmeel, *Bookpeople: A Second Album,* Libraries Unlimited, 1990.

Cumulative Indexes

Illustrations Index

(In the following index, the number of the volume in which an illustrator's work appears is given *before* the colon, and the page number on which it appears is given *after* the colon. For example, a drawing by Adams, Adrienne appears in Volume 2 on page 6, another drawing by her appears in Volume 3 on page 80, another drawing in Volume 8 on page 1, and another drawing in Volume 15 on page 107.)

YABC

Index citations including this abbreviation refer to listings appearing in *Yesterday's Authors of Books for Children,* also published by Gale Research Inc., which covers authors who died prior to 1960.

Author Index

The following index gives the number of the volume in which an author's biographical sketch, Brief Entry, or Obituary appears.

This index includes references to all entries in the following series, which are also published by Gale Research Inc.

YABC—*Yesterday's Authors of Books for Children: Facts and Pictures about Authors and Illustrators of Books for Young People from Early Times to 1960*, Volumes 1-2
CLR—*Children's Literature Review: Excerpts from Reviews, Criticism, and Commentary on Books for Children*, Volumes 1-19
SAAS—*Something about the Author Autobiography Series*, Volumes 1-9

G